T0335939

MEASUREMENT FOR
SOFTWARE CONTROL AND ASSURANCE

Proceedings of the Centre for Software Reliability Conference entitled

Measurement for Software Control and Assurance
held at the Watershed Media Centre, Bristol, UK,
14–18 September 1987.

Members of the CSR

Mr B. G. ANDERSON, British Aerospace Dynamics Group, Stevenage, UK
PROFESSOR T. ANDERSON, Centre for Software Reliability, Newcastle Upon Tyne, UK
Mrs J. ATKINSON, Centre for Software Reliability, Newcastle Upon Tyne, UK
Mr R. E. BLOOMFIELD, Adelard, London, UK
Mr C. J. DALE, National Centre of Systems Reliability, Warrington, UK
Mr J. E. DOBSON, University of Newcastle Upon Tyne, Newcastle Upon Tyne, UK
Ms G. D. FREWIN, Standard Telecom. Laboratories, Harlow, UK
Mr C. H. GRIBBLE, Ferranti Computer Systems Limited, Gwent, UK
Mr L. N. HARRIS, British Aerospace Dynamics Group, Stevenage, UK
PROFESSOR M. A. HENNELL, University of Liverpool, Liverpool, UK
DR B. A. KITCHENHAM, NCC, Manchester, UK
PROFESSOR B. LITTLEWOOD, Centre for Software Reliability, London, UK
PROFESSOR B. DE NEUMANN, Centre for Software Reliability, London, UK
Mr A. A. WINGROVE, Farnborough, UK

MEASUREMENT FOR SOFTWARE CONTROL AND ASSURANCE

Edited by

B. A. KITCHENHAM

and

B. LITTLEWOOD

Centre for Software Reliability, City University, London, UK

ELSEVIER APPLIED SCIENCE
LONDON and NEW YORK

ELSEVIER SCIENCE PUBLISHERS LTD
Crown House, Linton Road, Barking, Essex IG11 8JU, England

Sole Distributor in the USA and Canada
ELSEVIER SCIENCE PUBLISHING CO., INC.
655 Avenue of the Americas, New York, NY 10010, USA

WITH 27 TABLES AND 91 ILLUSTRATIONS

© 1989 ELSEVIER SCIENCE PUBLISHERS LTD
© 1989 SPRINGER-VERLAG – Chapter 14

British Library Cataloguing in Publication Data
Measurement for Software Control and Assurance
(Conference: 1987: Watershed Media Centre).
Measurement for Software Control and Assurance:
proceedings of the Centre for Software Control
Conference entitled Measurement for Software Control
and Assurance held at the Watershed Media Centre,
Bristol, 14–18 September 1987].
1. Computer programs. Quality control
I. Title II. Kitchenham, B. A. III. Littlewood, B.
005'.14

ISBN 1-85166-246-4

Library of Congress Cataloging-in-Publication Data
City University (London, England). Centre for Software Reliability.
Conference (1987: Bristol, Avon)
Measurement for software control and assurance/edited by B. A.
Kitchenham and B. Littlewood.
    p.   cm.
Proceedings of the Centre for Software Reliability Conference held
at the Watershed Media Centre, Bristol, 14–18, Sept., 1987.
Bibliography: p.
Includes index.
ISBN 1-85166-246-4
    1. Computer software—Quality control—Congresses. 2. Computer
software—Reliability—Congresses. I. Kitchenham, B. A.
II. Littlewood, B. (Beverley) III. Title.
QA76.76.Q35C57   1987
005—dc19   88-16553
                                                             CIP

Special regulations for readers in the USA

This publication has been registered with the Copyright Clearance Center Inc. (CCC), Salem, Massachusetts. Information can be obtained from the CCC about conditions under which photocopies of parts of this publication may be made in the USA. All other copyright questions, including photocopying outside the USA, should be referred to the publisher.

Typeset and printed in Northern Ireland by The Universities Press (Belfast) Ltd.

To the memory of Grace Palmer

Preface

For many years software engineers and managers have paid lip service to the need for quantitative methods for software product and process control. However, in practice industry has been slow to adopt such methods. This reluctance to use measurement methods has been excused, with some justification, on the grounds that many proposed metrics and models were of dubious relevance and/or inadequately validated, and methods of data collection were expensive and unreliable.

Many research workers and practitioners believe that quantitative approaches are now mature enough to be more widely used. In addition, the emergence of integrated project support environments (IPSEs) provide the framework in which many of the practical difficulties of data collection, storage and analysis can be avoided.

The aim of the CSR Conference on Measurement for Software Assurance and Control—and this record of the proceedings—are to:

—provide an overview of metrics and models which are suitable for industrial use immediately;
—indicate how such metrics and models are used in practice;
—indicate where current research ideas concerning software measurement and modelling are leading.

To this end the proceedings starts with two tutorials about measurement issues. Mike Dyer discusses the IBM Clean Room experiment which blends formal approaches to software development with statistical testing aimed at establishing final product reliability. Professor Darrel Ince discusses software metrics in general concentrating on research aimed at defining and validating product metrics and cost estimation models. These tutorials establish the setting for a number of themes that run through the remaining papers:

—practical examples of industrial use of metrics and models (Frewin, Sroka *et al.*, Ross);
—reliability modelling and prediction for product assessment (Brocklehurst *et al.*, Mellor, Littlewood and Miller, Bloomfield);
—development, validation and use of software metrics (Cowderoy and Jenkins, Fenton and Kaposi, Pickard, Ross);
—quality and productivity modelling and prediction (Cowderoy and Jenkins, Walker and Kitchenham, Hausen, Fenton and Kaposi).

The majority of the papers are presented in three sections which indicate the way in which metrics and models fit into the three generic phases of software engineering. The *definition* phase is supported by metrics and models which assist *project initiation and planning,* the *development* phase is supported by metrics and models which assist *project monitoring,* and the *maintenance* phase is supported by metrics and models which assist *product assessment* and *product support.*

The final few papers in the proceedings consider new ideas in metrics and modelling. They describe some of the approaches to measurement and modelling which are necessary to cope with novel software architectures and new software development methods.

We are grateful to the Alvey Directorate at the DTI (now the Information Engineering Directorate) for some financial assistance in running this conference.

Our job in editing this volume has been helped by many others, and we would like to take this opportunity to thank them all. Firstly, of course, our appreciation goes to our contributors—not least for the speed with which they produced final manuscripts. We depended on members of CSR for the success of this our fourth annual conference. In particular, as in previous years, the role of Grace Palmer was vital in ensuring the smooth running of the conference. Grace died on 15 November 1987 after a long struggle with cancer. She will be greatly missed by all of us.

B. A. KITCHENHAM
B. LITTLEWOOD

Contents

Preface vii

List of Contributors xi

SECTION 1: TUTORIALS

1 The Cleanroom Software Development Process
   M. Dyer 1

2 Software Metrics
   D. Ince 27

SECTION 2: PROJECT INITIATION AND PLANNING

3 New Trends in Cost-Estimation
   A. J. C. Cowderoy and J. O. Jenkins 63

4 Metrics in Procurement—a discussion paper
   G. D. Frewin 89

5 Quality Requirements Specification and Evaluation
   J. G. Walker and B. A. Kitchenham 103

SECTION 3: PROJECT MONITORING

6 The Collection and Use of Data for Monitoring Software
   Projects
   N. Ross 125

7 Analysis of Software Metrics
   L. M. Pickard 155

8 Using Quantitative Activity Models in Project Management:
   a Case Study
   J. V. Sroka and C. A. Gosling 181

9 Generic Modelling of Software Quality
   H.-L. Hausen 201

SECTION 4: PRODUCT ASSESSMENT

10 Aspects of the Licensing and Assessment of Highly
    Dependable Computer Systems
    R. E. Bloomfield and P. K. D. Froome 243

11 Adaptive Software Reliability Modelling
    S. Brocklehurst, P. Y. Chan, B. Littlewood and J. Snell . . 263

12 Modelling the Support Process
    P. Mellor 279

SECTION 5: NEW IDEAS FOR METRICS AND MODELLING

13 An Engineering Theory of Structure and Measurement
    N. E. Fenton and A. A. Kaposi 289

14 A Conceptual Model of the Effect of Diverse Methodologies
    on Coincident Failures in Multi-version Software
    B. Littlewood and D. R. Miller 321

15 The Relationship between Specification and Implementation
    Metrics
    W. B. Samson, P. I. Dugard, D. G. Nevill, P. E. Oldfield,
    A. W. Smith and G. Titterington 335

Index. 385

List of Contributors

R. E. Bloomfield
Adelard, 28 Rhondda Grove, London E3 5AP, UK

S. Brocklehurst
Centre for Software Reliability, The City University, Northampton Square, London EC1V 0HB, UK

P. Y. Chan
Centre for Software Reliability, The City University, Northampton Square, London EC1V 0HB, UK

A. J. C. Cowderoy
Imperial College of Science and Technology, School of Management, Exhibition Road, London SW7 2BX, UK

M. Dyer
IBM Corporation, Federal Systems Division, Bethesda, Maryland 20817, USA

P. I. Dugard
Dundee College of Technology, Bell Street, Dundee DD1 1HG, UK

N. E. Fenton
Centre for Software and Systems Engineering, South Bank Polytechnic, Borough Road, London SE1 0AA, UK

G. D. Frewin
Centre for Software Reliability, The City University, Northampton Square, London EC1 0HB, UK

P. K. D. Froome
Adelard, 28 Rhondda Grove, London E3 5AP, UK

C. A. GOSLING
Intermetrics Inc, 733 Concord Avenue, Cambridge, Massachusetts 02138, USA

H.-L. HAUSEN
GMD, Schloss Birlinghoven, D–5205 St Augustin 1, Federal Republic of Germany

D. INCE
Department of Computing, Faculty of Mathematics, Open University, Milton Keynes, MK7 6AA, UK

J. O. JENKINS
Imperial College of Science and Technology, School of Management, Exhibition Road, London SW7 2BX, UK

A. A. KAPOSI
Centre for Software and Systems Engineering, South Bank Polytechnic, Borough Road, London SE1 0AA, UK

B. A. KITCHENHAM
Centre for Software Reliability, The City University, Northampton Square, London EC1V 0HB, UK

B. LITTLEWOOD
Centre for Software Reliability, The City University, Northampton Square, London EC1V 0HB, UK

P. MELLOR
Centre for Software Reliability, The City University, Northampton Square, London EC1V 0HB, UK

D. R. MILLER
Department of Operational Research, SEAS, George Washington University, Washington, DC 20052, USA

D. G. NEVILL
Dundee College of Technology, Bell Street, Dundee DD1 1HG, UK

P. E. OLDFIELD
Dundee College of Technology, Bell Street, Dundee DD1 1HG, UK

L. M. PICKARD
STC Technology Ltd, Copthall House, Nelson Place, Newcastle-under-Lyme, Staffordshire ST5 1EZ, UK

N. Ross
STC Technology Ltd, Copthall House, Nelson Place, Newcastle-under-Lyme, Staffordshire ST5 1EZ, UK

W. B. Samson
Dundee College of Technology, Bell Street, Dundee DD1 1HG, UK

A. W. Smith
Dundee College of Technology, Bell Street, Dundee DD1 1HG, UK

J. Snell
Centre for Software Reliability, The City University, Northampton Square, London EC1V 0HB, UK

J. V. Sroka
Intermetrics Inc, 733 Concord Avenue, Cambridge, Massachusetts 02138, USA

G. Titterington
STC Technology Ltd, Copthall House, Nelson Place, Newcastle-under-Lyme, Staffordshire ST5 1EZ, UK

J. G. Walker
ICL, Kings House, 33 Kings Road, Reading, Berkshire RG1 3PX, UK

1

The Cleanroom Software Development Process

M. Dyer

IBM Corporation, Bethesda, Maryland, USA

ABSTRACT

The Cleanroom software development process provides a first practical approach for developing software under statistical quality control. In contrast to current methods the Cleanroom process embodies development and test within a formal system design where the focus is on software defect prevention and not defect removal. Mathematics based design techniques with an emphasis on correctness verification support the routine creation of software with significantly improved quality. Statistically-based testing methods support certification of reliability projections for delivered software, which should forecast operational experience.

A design methodology based on structured programming theory is introduced which identifies a limited set of primitives for capturing software logic, organizing product structure and supporting data structuring. These design building blocks can be used in a systematic stepwise process to refine any set of software requirements into provably correct designs. In this context correctness is the correspondence between stated requirements and the software designs which allege to satisfy those requirements.

Software quality is generally defined in terms of the number of defects in a product and normalized across products as defects per thousand lines of code. Industry averages of 50 to 60 defects per thousand lines of code are typical. Improved software design methodology is important since the majority of software defects (40–60%) are introduced in the design step, whereas the cost of removing design defects can be 100 times more expensive than that for other classes of defects. Use of the Cleanroom process results in software with fewer total defects (in the 0–20 range), which can also be detected and removed earlier in the development (90% prior to code execution).

Software testing is performed for two reasons, either to show that the software implementation matches its design or to confirm that the software product meets its requirements. In the Cleanroom process, correctness verification handles the first requirement and statistical testing the second. These statistical methods use input probability distributions and random sampling to form the basis for software reliability prediction. Reliability is a measure of software failure-free execution and quantified in terms of the software's MTTF (mean time to failure). Software MTTF is the statistic used for controlling the development process as well as providing a visible record of the product reliability.

Experience with the Cleanroom process for building software in the 50 000 lines of code range indicates that quality can be significantly improved, with operating characteristics of one error per thousand lines of code for the delivered software.

1. INTRODUCTION

The Cleanroom software development process[1] represents a first practical attempt at placing software development under statistical quality control. In contrast with current software practice, the Cleanroom process embeds development and testing within a formal statistical design where the focus is on software defect prevention rather than defect removal. Mathematics-based software engineering with an emphasis on functional verification supports the creation of software designs of requisite quality. Statistically representative usage testing supports the preparation of certified reliability projections for the delivered software.

Current experience with the Cleanroom process includes experiments with a COBOL language processor, the flight software in an avionics application and a database package for a space application. These were mid-sized software applications, in the range of 40 000 lines of code. The major findings from these experiments were that human verification could replace code debugging as a development activity, that statistical testing could be effectively performed for problems of reasonable complexity and that software reliability could be effectively measured during development. Staff productivity in all cases was equal to or better than what would have been realized if more conventional methods had been used. Product quality, as measured during development and as experienced during field use, was also better than in current experience. The results tended to confirm earlier findings from a University of Maryland[2] study which indicated both better productivity and quality from Cleanroom methods, even when introduced as the first experience in an academic environment.

Continued experimentation is required to insure the scale-up and applicability of these methods to large-scale complex problems. Work is also required on solidifying the techniques and procedures used in the Cleanroom process.

2. CLEANROOM SOFTWARE DEVELOPMENT

The ingredients for the Cleanroom process are a redefined software lifecycle and an insistence on independent quality assessment from statistical testing. The development lifecycle starts with a new form of structured software specification which organizes the development as a build-up of executable product increments. In the specification, software function and performance requirements are still critical but are identified as a nested sequence of function/performance subsets to be developed and tested as incremental releases. The inclusion of operational probability distributions for the product functions and function subsets is the second new feature in the specification. The structured specification bridges the separation between the test and development groups and at the same time supports software test as an independent check of product quality from a user perspective.

The quality control process for software is similar to counterparts found in modern manufacturing control—where outputs are sampled, measurements are computed and corrections, as needed, are fed back into the process. In the software case, reliability in terms of mean time to failure (MTTF) can be measured and process changes (e.g. added verification rigor, tighter specifications etc.) can be introduced to achieve higher product quality levels. The process is graphically

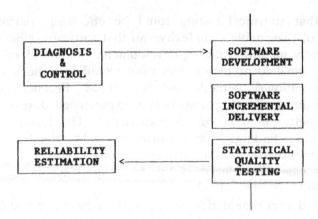

Fig. 1. Software statistical quality control.

illustrated in Fig. 1 which helps point out the importance of the incremental release strategy to quality control.

To implement the software process, a statistical basis for evaluating the software product has to be established. Unlike the manufacturing case, the basis cannot be the large number of similar products that are produced, since software is a logical one-of-a-kind product. The basis for software lies in the variation in its usage, which can be captured as probability distributions on the product inputs and give direction to the testing process. The statistical test approach used in the Clean-room process creates randomly selected test samples that reflect these probabilities and, in turn, the expected product usage.

The measure of software quality is taken as its mean time to failure (MTTF) in executing representative input samples, whether in real operating environments or in statistically generated test environments. Statistical models are used to predict software MTTF, which account for reliability growth in the software as it is developed. The growth results from the repairs that are made as software errors are found during test execution. More conventional software measures, such as errors per lines of code, were not selected since they have less relevance to user operations, where software failures and not errors are what the user experiences.

Two underlying principles for developing software come out of this approach to statistical quality control; product development should be performed without unit debugging, and product test should be done independently with representative usage scenarios. Trial and error software development, which relies on unit debugging to get quality, leads to idiosyncratic designs from which meaningful statistics cannot be gathered because of unpredictable execution characteristics and typically high error content. A software development process is required which relies on rigorous error prevention rather than unit debugging to obtain quality software and deliver code to independent test without any prior execution. On the second point, selective test, no matter how thoughtful and thorough, can provide only anecdotal evidence on software quality and can make no judgments on operating reliability. Statistically based testing must be introduced since it can offer both execution in simulated user environments and a basis for making inferences or extrapolations from test observations.

The Cleanroom combination of rigorous software engineering and statistically based functional testing offers a meaningful procedure for software development under statistical quality control.

3. SPECIFYING THE SOFTWARE PRODUCT

To develop software under statistical quality control there is an implied requirement for stability in the software specification. In general, software requirements are typically neither fully known nor verified during early product development and it might appear that the process has limited or no application. On the contrary, the idea of forcing requirement deficiencies into the open and of instigating management control of the requirements process, as espoused in the Cleanroom process, should be mandatory across all development.

As long as the development of software is treated as a trial and error process, incomplete requirements can be accommodated as just another source of trial and error. The result is a dilution in the accountability between specifiers and developers. A different and preferred method to trial and error would be to develop software to the early statements of requirements but to iterate on stabilizing those requirements which drive each incremental release. This would force stricter accountability between the specifiers and developers and insure management control of the requirements process.

In conventional practice, requirements are typically documented in natural language and attempt to provide a total perspective on software function and performance. As the development starting point, the structured specification attempts to define the packaging of the software requirements as executable product releases. It establishes the flow of incremental releases which contain subsets of executable software function over the development lifecycle. This perspective, and the introduction of more precise notation, are the real benefits offered by the structured specification.

The existing Cleanroom experiments did not address the specification question to any significant extent but rather relied on available forms of requirements description. Separately generated build plans and product usage analyses were combined with available requirements statements to simulate development with structured specifications. If poorly formulated requirements were delivered to the software developers, there tended to be an extended period of interaction to establish a starting development baseline on which specifiers and developers could agree. This is exactly the situation that the structured specification was designed to remedy, by forcing the bulk of the specifier/developer interaction to take place prior to specification delivery.

4. DESIGN PROCESS OVERVIEW

Structured programming theory provides a framework for generating software designs with conviction on their correctness and confidence in their solution to stated requirements. Software design is itself a creative process which requires subject matter proficiency and intuition about solution strategies. Design methods cannot become a substitute for the designer experience but can provide a control mechanism that gets the maximum payoff from the designer's innate knowledge. The design method described by Linger, Mills and Witt[3] is based on structured programming principles and gives software engineers new techniques for organizing and documenting designs that are verifiably correct. This basic method has been incorporated into the Cleanroom software development process.

To get started with a major software design, the software engineer must sort out the total set of requirements and collect them into some manageable number of subdivisions—the 'divide and conquer' principle at work. Problem experience and familiarity with the customer's application needs are most helpful in this analysis. Before formulating a solution, all development requirements, not necessarily limited to functional/performance requirements, must be considered. In this regard, software packaging is an opportunity for the software engineer to evaluate different product forms, their interplay with control and support software, and their compatibility with planned releases for product function. A second consideration is the systems environment in which the software will operate—the characteristics of operating hardware, the nature of hardware/software interfaces and the budgeting of performance, reliability, availability and other requirements to the software. As an aside, both are key ideas that should be folded into standard methods for preparing structured software specifications.

When the total set of requirements is organized to a point where their individual importance and priority with regard to a solution can be appreciated, design can proceed. At that point the design method plays a major role by providing the models and mechanisms for design elaboration. The design practice[4] adopted for Cleanroom development defines a stepwise refinement of requirements into successive levels of design until all requirements are addressed. The design strategy is one of divide, connect and verify to insure that the evolving design correctness, and the integrity of the software requirements, are continuously assessed.

5. STEPWISE REFINEMENT PRACTICE

A systematic refinement of design obviously cannot be started until a reasonable outline for the overall design is available and basic details of data representations and processing algorithms have been considered. When considering a design many control, data and flow alternatives rumble about in one's mind. The point is to sift through all these ideas, record the significant ones first and pick up the less important ones in subsequent refinement steps. The goal should be a coherent logical description that runs from product summaries at a top level to implementation details at the bottom.

Refinement starts from the product level software requirements expressed as a set of intended functions. These functions are then reexpressed in an equivalent structure of connected subfunctions, each solving some part of the problem, and each simpler than the original functions. The subfunctions are themselves subdivided and reexpressed as lower level subfunctions with the process repeated until all requirements have been resolved. Throughout this process, the software engineer looks only far enough ahead to be comfortable with the requirements decomposition. If a function is familiar, say sorting a small table, further thought and elaboration may not be necessary. If a function is not familiar, it should be refined to the point where an obvious solution is apparent.

This systematic design approach provides a natural development plan for allocating effort to those parts of a problem most in need of thought and elaboration. Each refinement offers a working hypothesis for further investigation, which is accepted as sound or modified as details of the evolving solution become clearer. The design becomes organized as a tree structure of named segments, each of which should be self-contained without any side effects on control logic outside its particular segment. This structure supports several designers in concurrently developing different parts of the design, where each designer can work independently and let the segment hierarchy worry about the interface between designers. The structure also provides a vehicle for monitoring the status and content of the total design as evidenced from the completed segment designs. Figure 2 illustrates a typical refinement for the top level design of a software product.

An important part of successful refinement is to continually rethink and rework a design, since one's first attempt seldom embodies the clarity required for the final design. Alternative designs should be considered and evaluated at each refinement step, with no reluctance

ACTIVITY	RECORDING	LEVEL
Specify	pkg a spec	1
Design Specify	body uses b,c end a proc b pkg c [fcn] spec	2
Design Specify	body uses d end c pkg d spec	3
Design	body end d	4

Fig. 2. Stepwise refinement example.

to rework large or small parts of a design at any point. Probably the best debugging technique available to the software engineer is to redesign his designs into simpler and simpler forms before they are finalized, let alone executed.

A second important aspect of successful refinement is to verify the correctness of each refinement step, from highest to lowest, as it is originated. If verifying design correctness is to become practical, refinements must be rigorously expressed and done in manageable steps. Rigor at all levels of expression, whether with formalized design languages or natural languages, is critical to completeness and thoroughness. Confidence in a total design can be obtained only by checking and being confident about a few lines of the design at a time. This is true whether the few lines summarize the product level functions or the lowest level details of its implementation.

The emphasis should be on developing a design in concert with its correctness proof, either a simple mental conviction or an extended analysis. Software designs that are easily verified should be favored and sought, whereas any designs that are difficult to verify should be considered suspect and be redone for simplicity. A reasonable rule of thumb should be that whenever rereading a design becomes difficult and its correctness arguments become obscure, then it is probably time to think harder and come up with a simpler and more valuable design.

6. ELEMENTS OF STRUCTURED DESIGN

The early work of Mills[5] and Dijkstra[6] indicated that a small number of primitives (the structured primes) would suffice for formulating designs of any size and/or complexity. Specifically, this minimum set includes two forms of software packaging—module and program—and three forms for handling software logic—sequence, selection and iteration. With only two subforms of the sequence and iteration cases and three subforms of the selection case, a total of nine primitives is all that is needed to formulate designs for any application problem. Only single predicate primitives are considered since Mills showed[7] that designs expressed in multiple predicate form were reducible to equivalent single predicate form.

For software designs, the designer must be capable of separately packaging the major components of an application (modules) and the procedural logic within each component (programs). Modules are useful for the design of software components whose input processing depends on the component status as defined by retained or history data. In this case, processing for a given input value can result in various output values, depending on the current history, and is not a simple one-to-one mapping of inputs to outputs. The account withdrawal part of a banking system would be a good example where the output from a simple withdrawal request varies depending on whether there is an account, there is a positive balance and similar considerations.

Programs on the other hand are good models for organizing component logic when an exact mapping of inputs to outputs is needed. For this case, a deterministic algorithm is described that uses values from a well defined input collection to create values for an equally well defined output collection. In a banking application the computing of a mortgage schedule would be a program example, with the fixed inputs mapped to the outputs according to a prescribed algorithm.

The use of these design constructs has been well documented in the professional literature, but generally for relatively small problems. However, there is reported evidence[8] of their effective use and scale-up to software solutions requiring millions of lines of code.

7. STRUCTURED DATA DESIGN

As discussed in Linger and Mills,[9] a systematic approach to data design is as necessary as it is for logic design. Three ideas are particularly useful in defining a data design method—data typing, data encapsulation and data abstraction. The combined use of these ideas simplify the data aspects of a design, reduce overall design complexity and make designs more amenable to verification.

Data typing is an old idea that has recently taken on importance in software engineering. It refers to assigning characteristics to each data variable, which identify allowable value domains and processing operations for the variable. All programming languages make use of the concept but have also been very forgiving about its misuse. In particular, default definitions, mixed mode operations, conversions etc. are generally supported in most languages. This disregard for enforcing typing rules is now recognized as a cause for correctness and design problems, which modern programming languages are avoiding by mandatory and explicit definitions for all variables.

Data encapsulation is another vintage programming term that has taken on new correctness significance. With correctness the emphasis is on restricting visibility about data variables to the smallest audience, for two reasons. Specifically the design for data operations can be localized into one design component (or a small number) and subsequent implementation changes to those operations can also be localized to the fewest number of components. The module and program primitives support this idea, with the module particularly useful in isolating retained data in a single component with which the rest of a design interacts.

Data abstraction is a newer correctness-driven idea that elevates the consideration of data from the bit implementation (machine) level to the appropriate problem level. Programming languages generally offer some relief in this area by providing data structures such as files, arrays and records for collecting problem data as meaningful units. The software engineering initiative is directed at relaxing current restrictions and providing an open-ended capability. Modern design and programming languages support the open-ended definition for data and associated processing modules. Particularly useful abstract data forms are the set, stack, queue, list and tree. These expand the horizons available to the software designer in considering his data, with the only kicker that he must eventually define the mapping from the abstract form (data and operations) to an acceptable programming language (implementation) form.

8. SOFTWARE VERIFICATION OVERVIEW

Software correctness is defined as the correspondence between a software design and its specified requirement(s). As the software design is elaborated, the requirements at each refinement step are stated as the intended function for that step. Design primitives are invented which, the designer hypothesizes, will satisfy that intended function. Verification validates the hypothesis.

In the refinement of a design, the choice of design primitives and the method for verifying refinement correctness must both be based on a formal model so that the process has a rigorous underpinning. Two models have been proposed: an axiomatic model as defined by Hoare[10] and a functional model as defined by Mills,[5] both of which were examined by Basili and Noonan.[11] The combination of being variable-free and requiring only local reasoning make the functional approach more universally acceptable for designs of any size and complexity.

Verification is therefore concerned with one of two questions, namely: is the intended function identical to the design (complete correctness) or is it equivalent to some subset of the design (sufficient correctness)? For complete correctness, a design should produce results only for the input values identified by the intended function. With sufficient correctness a design might also correctly produce results for input values not identified by the intended function. Complete correctness is generally the rule, but reusability considerations might dictate the need for sufficient correctness in a given application.

Verification of complex software, like its design, can be reduced to checking the correctness of the constituent design components which are described by design primitives. Correctness theorems are in fact defined in terms of the set-theoretic relations inherent in design primitives, so that the problem of software verification may exceed a designer's time and patience but not his knowledge.

9. FUNCTIONAL VERIFICATION PROCEDURE

The correctness arguments for functional verification are defined in terms of the design primitives and are identical regardless of what levels of design are described by the primitives. This independence from the content and application details offers some relief to the software engineer as far as application expertise and experience are concerned. For software verification it is more important to be conversant in the correctness rules than expert in the application content. The correctness considerations that need to be addressed with each design primitive are identified in Table 1.

When the structured programming principles are applied with care and concentration, correct software designs can be consistently defined. The same holds for carrying out correctness proofs, both during and after the construction of software designs.[12] A proof should be viewed as a repeatable experiment in which the intended result is a subjective conviction by another party that the logical hypothesis leads to a given conclusion. A convincing proof must attract the interest of

Table 1
Functional Verification Considerations

Primitive	Number	Correctness topics
Module	2	Equivalence between mapped and unmapped cases
		State data initialization
Procedure	1	Match of allocated function and input domain
Sequence	1	Sum of function parts equal whole
Ifthenelse	2	Function equals thenpart when predicate true
(Ifthen)		Function equals elsepart when predicate false
Case	N	Function equals casepart of selected choice
Whileloop	3	Termination of any loop argument
		Function equals looppart when argument true
		Function equals identity when argument false
Loopexit	3	Termination for any loop argument
		Function equals looppart when argument true
		Function equals looppart followed by next
		argument test when argument false

the listener since many different conclusions can be drawn from the same hypothesis. If the proof has too few steps, the jump in intuition may be too large; whereas if there are too many, then distraction or exhaustion may result. A balanced approach is needed that generally comes with experience and judgement.

The proof can be carried out in conversation or in writing. In any proof mathematics should play an indirect role, offering notation to facilitate human communication. It should permit rapid agreement on a succession of claims by helping a person extend his memory for details and by allowing him to cover more ground with less effort.

10. VERIFICATION EXPERIENCE

Verification proofs are packaged as sets of questions to be asked about the correctness considerations for a given design primitive. Formal verification uses the same proofs but introduces symbolic notation with algebra and/or set theoretic ideas to document a proof for later review or study. Formal verification is required in very few cases and probably accounts for less than 5% of the verification in software developments of any significance.

In the Cleanroom experiments mentioned earlier, this combination of formal design methods and functional verification had many positive impacts on the software development. First, there was a reduction in the total defect rate (measured in errors per line of code) by as much as half what would be expected for comparable products. Second, better than 90% of the total product defects were typically found prior to first execution, which is a marked improvement over the 60% typically experienced with the best conventional methods. Both facts highlight the Cleanroom focus on error prevention as opposed to error removal and its economic importance when dealing with industry averages in the range of 50–60 errors per 1000 lines of code.

The net effect was that the generated code was sufficiently robust that it could be moved directly to statistical test without any need for conventional unit debugging. With the sizes of the experimental projects this meant that software increments of as much as 10 000 lines of unexecuted code could be introduced into test and at least cycle within the execution environment. Subsequent failures might occur during statistical testing, but the increment was basically able to execute.

11. STATISTICAL TESTING OVERVIEW

In the Cleanroom process software (design and code) is released to an independent tester prior to its first execution. This requires that the software be placed under strict configuration control at the point of its transfer from development to test. Visible records are maintained for all failures uncovered during test and all fixes to the software to correct the causes of failures. This very public record is the basis for subsequent reliability certification since there is assurance that the total execution history is recorded.

In the typical Cleanroom experiment, software was released to test in predefined increments where each increment contained some subset of the total product function. The developer's responsibility was to deliver software which had been rigorously verified and inspected but never executed. While possibly counterintuitive, the software from many contributors to an increment could be integrated together and would cycle. Since this typically involved in the order of 10 000 lines of code, the mere fact that the code would cycle is another testament to the benefits of formal development methods. Subsequent independent testing might uncover defects, as was usually the case, but the defects were not of the severity that would prohibit initial cycling or force reversion to unit debugging.

Software is generally tested for two reasons, first, to verify that the software implementation matches its design (structural testing) and second, to verify that the implementation and design match the given requirements (functional testing). Debugging and unit tests are forms of structural testing, whereas system and acceptance tests are forms of functional testing.

Statistically based software testing has been identified as a valid approach to functional testing,[13] even though test literature tends to negate its role. The principal concerns that have been voiced on the use on random or statistical techniques for testing are the lack of adequate requirements coverage, the need for extraordinarily large test samples and an overall inefficiency in test case and data value selection. In the Cleanroom experimentation these concerns did not materialize and in fact test samples of reasonable size and with meaningful application data content were generated which typically satisfied some 90–95% of the total application requirements. These results were realized because sampling was driven by the operational input distributions for the application and not based on theoretical uniform distributions.

12. STATISTICAL TESTING APPROACH

This statistical approach to software testing requires a different characterization of software inputs, demanding a knowledge of the input usage probabilities as well as the more standard definitional parameters. These probabilities control the random selection such that the test samples reflect typical operational product usage and provide a formal basis for software reliability prediction.

The testing strategy is organized so that the chance of finding a software defect is ordered precisely according to the rate at which the defect will trigger a software failure. This feature might be unique to the statistical approach but is definitely a desirable property of any testing method.

Identifying all product inputs and their distributions guarantees a level of completeness and objectivity in the software testing that is not available with current test methods. Traditional methods rely on the tester defining scenarios to address the maximum number of product requirements, from his own experience and insight. The statistical approach uses considerable upfront analysis to define the software usage, and this attention seems to benefit the design and specification effort as well as testing.

Descriptions of product inputs and their distributions are organized into a database from which test samples can be selected. Standalone test sequences are defined for each input, and these are structured to contain appropriate input and initialization values of the software. Initialization is included to provide known starting conditions for the software against which to consider pass/fail criteria. Trying to determine processing correctness, when the starting state of software is not precisely known, is not possible with software of any size or complexity. In this context, standalone should not be interpreted as batch but rather self-contained since the test method has been used in realtime and online software applications.

Software tools are available to provide on-line support for database creation and sample generation.[14] The generator formats test cases for the specific application in terms of command sequences and input strings appropriate to the application. Skeletons for these sequences are included in a test database and define the discrete steps for a test case as well the application data needed at each step. When the skeletons are selected for inclusion in a test sample, they are filled out to give a representative user input. A sample will contain test cases in the same proportion as the probabilities defined for the application inputs. Data values are randomly selected and are assigned to the variable fields in the skeleton, again based on the predefined data domains and distributions. Domains can include both legal and illegal values as appropriate for the testing.

The actual software testing is conducted as done for conventional functional testing. The tester must make the pass/fail determination to insure that the software satisfies the intended requirement (i.e., the functional test goal). Aside from recording test case execution times (subsequently used in reliability measurement), the tester works in a conventional manner. The real change is that test samples are automatically generated with representative data rather than hand-crafted by the tester.

13. STATISTICAL TEST EXPERIENCE

While there had been some published evidence[15] that test methods based on randomized selection were useful in structural testing, it was not obvious whether they would scale up to functional testing of complex systems. The ideas have been successfully applied to the functional testing of commercial, scientific, interactive, realtime and similar complex software. Determining probability distributions for software inputs may be challenging in these cases but are generally obtainable from predecessor systems (even manual), mission analyses or some combination of the two. The added time spent in this new test tends to be balanced by the subsequent savings in test preparation.

As predicted, the statistical test samples did tend to find defects according to the rate that they would force software failures. In fact the defects in any given software release were usually found by the first handful of test cases that were run in a sample. When these defects were repaired, the remaining cases in the sample were typically run without incident. Another surprising result, which probably points up a synergism between verification and statistical testing, was the ease with which discovered defects could be diagnosed and repaired. The deep-rooted problems tended to be handled by verification, and the developers were able (99% of the time) to fix defects without machine debugging.

14. SOFTWARE RELIABILITY OVERVIEW

After software has been released to the field (user), estimating its reliability (MTTF) is reasonably straightforward and involves the simple averaging of the number of failures over an execution period. This simplicity results from the assumption that repairs were not made, which is the typical case with centrally maintained software. Performing the same estimate for software that is under development is not so straightforward, because of the changing reliability as the product moves through test. During test, as failures are uncovered, changes are introduced to correct the failures, which essentially creates a new product, similar to its predecessor but with different reliability. The intent is to always improve the reliability, but this may not necessarily be possible (reliability drops with a particular incorrect change).

A further complication arises from the building and testing of many incremental product forms as the software is evolved. Each of these intermediate forms receives some limited amount of testing before it is superseded by its successor which can include both added function and corrections to previously delivered function. The confidence in the reliability estimate for any given intermediate form is directly proportional to the adequacy of its testing. Since the total product reliability is aggregated across these successive intermediate forms, the levels of confidence also carry over to the product estimate.

15. PREDICTING RELIABILITY

Predicting reliability with analytical models is a common technique where the model parameters are estimated from the recorded failure data, obtained during test. To reflect the change activity as the software is developed, the model formulation has to take the general form:

$$MTTF = MTTF_0 * R^c$$

where $MTTF_0$ is an estimate of the initial reliability (MTTF), R is an estimate of the effectiveness of change introduction, and c is the number of changes being considered at a given point.

Reference 1 provides a derivation and technical rationale for models of this form, many of which are currently used to predict software reliability. Since there will be statistical variations in the model predictions, statistical estimators for parameters $MTTF_0$ and R are generally defined in terms of the test data being analyzed. These estimators are essentially sophisticated techniques for averaging inter-fail times, while, at the same time, accounting for the changes introduced during the software testing.

Current experience with software reliability prediction suggests the use of more than one statistical model to accommodate variations in the timing data recorded during test. Different models make different decisions from their assumptions on input data, their computational approaches and their methods for estimating parameters. Using more than one model can improve the reliability predictions for a given set of test data since there is more opportunity to better match the specific characteristics of the particular data. The other benefit of using multiple models is that a universal model is not required to satisfy all software development situations.

The set of models with their relevant features which are currently used in Cleanroom developments are as shown in Table 2.

Table 2
Current Models used in Cleanroom Developments

	Certification (1)	Littlewood (16)	Littlewood/ Verall (17)	Shanthikumar (18)
Interfail distributions	Exp	Gamma	Pareto	Exp
Prediction form	Mean	Mean	Median	Mean
—Number of defects		×		×
—Test time	×	×	×	×
—Repair effects	×	×	×	×
Inference method	Log LS	ML	ML	ML

LS—least squares; ML—maximum likelihood.

16. SOFTWARE RELIABILITY MEASUREMENT

To implement statistical quality control for software development, measurements of the software product and of the product quality must be regularly taken. In the Cleanroom strategy, these measurements are MTTF reliability predictions based on timing data recorded during the independent testing of the software. As the software increments are released and tested, predictions of the incremental and product MTTF are made and used as the control for process correction and/or product release to the field.

In tracking incremental timing data, it is typical to experience a buildup of short execution times (resulting from failures) at the start of each incremental release. The introduction of new but untested functions in the increment and of corrections to previously released functions is the reason for the buildup in failures. Trying to work with the interfail data as a single distribution of data is not practical, because of the sawtooth shape in the distribution that reflects the failure spikes at each release point.

On the other hand, the timing data for a given increment as it moves through successive software releases tends to exhibit a more regular shape. When the increment is first released, there will be significant testing of the increment functions and the bulk of the failures, specifically those caused by the high failure rate defects, should be encountered. With subsequent releases of the software, the testing of functions in earlier released increments will be more of the order of regression testing. Fewer failures will be seen, and the reliability prediction for the functions in the increments will tend to show fairly regular growth.

The timing data from software testing is appropriate input for the prediction models, which can compute reliabilities (MTTFs) for each increment. A separate summing of these increment reliabilities will then be necessary to arrive at a total product reliability. This calculation of the product MTTF after any release point is shown in terms of failure rates (MTTF reciprocals) as:

$$\text{MTTF}_i = 1/R_i$$

where the product failure rate (R_i) is computed after each release as follows:

$$R_1 = C_{11}R_{11} \qquad \qquad \text{after the 1st release}$$
$$R_2 = C_{12}R_{12} + C_{22}R_{22} \qquad \text{after the 2nd release}$$
$$\vdots$$
$$R_n = C_{1n}R_{1n} + C_{2n}R_{2n} \cdots + C_{nn}R_{nn} \qquad \text{after the } n\text{th release.}$$

The discrete failure rates $(R_{ij}\text{s})$ for the jth increment at the ith release are the predicted outputs from the statistical models, using the timing data from the testing at the ith release. The weighting coefficients $(C_{ij}\text{s})$ account for the jth increment's portion of the total product functionality, available with the ith release, and for the scaling of test (fast) time units to operating time units.

17. RELIABILITY MEASUREMENT ILLUSTRATION

To illustrate the application of the measurement technique, data for one increment of Cleanroom developed software are listed in Table 3. The interfail times (seconds of execution time) were computed from the execution times recorded during testing. Five sets of data are given which summarize the interfail history over five successive software releases, in which testing of the increment occurred. Most testing was performed with the first release, but regression tests of the increment functions were also run during subsequent releases.

For any given release, the last interfail time may correspond to an actual software failure or may be an estimate when the last-run test

Table 3
Failure Data and Reliability Predictions for a Software Example

	Release 1	Release 2	Release 3	Release 4	Release 5
Interfail times (s)	405 150 6144 3064 2319 6127 6077 994 28212 1350	405 28212 14956 3516	405 28212 14956 1971 5308	405 28212 14956 1971 17392	405 28212 14956 1971 25108
MTTFs Certification Littlewood	11405 18529	18869 25041	18291 19258	22930 27061	24591 33087

case executed successfully. In this more likely case, the accumulated execution time from the last real failure is arbitrarily doubled and used as the interfail time for the end point. When testing starts up with the next release, times are added to the running accumulation from the testing in the last release and a new interfail will be developed, based on encountering a failure or completing the testing for the release. This is the reason why the 10th value in column 1 is different from that value in subsequent columns, and similarly for the 11th and 12th values.

At each release, the interfail history data for the functions in the particular increment are collected and input into the prediction models. The model output is an updated MTTF value for that increment at the particular release level of the software. MTTF reciprocals or failure rates (the previously discussed R_{ij}s) would be used in computing product reliability. Predictions from the Certification and Littlewood models at each release point are listed, and the MTTF plot for the increment after the first release is shown in Fig. 3.

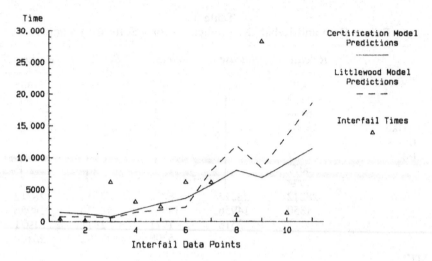

Fig. 3. MTTF predictions for example increment at first release.

18. EVALUATING MODEL PREDICTIONS

As model predictions are made, they are continuously analyzed to assess their reasonableness on the basis of the particular set of data that was recorded during the software test. A statistical technique (the Quantile–Quantile plot)[19] is used to examine the correlation between predictions and subsequently reported interfail data.

If predictions were perfect, a normalized plot of predicted times against actual failure times should give a line of unit slope. The Q–Q plot technique uses this idea to examine goodness of fit against a line of unit slope, and a statistical measure of goodness can be based on distance from the line. Goodness is measured in the 0–1 range, where zero would correspond to perfect correlation.

The technique is used to evaluate two aspects of a model's MTTF predictions, their accuracy and their tracking of trends. The first checks for bias (optimism/pessimism) in the model predictions. The second checks whether the predictions are capturing the reliability trend in the test data (growth and/or decay).

In Fig. 3, reliability growth for the increment is predicted by both models but there are apparent differences in the predictions, particularly when large jumps in interfail times are encountered. To decide

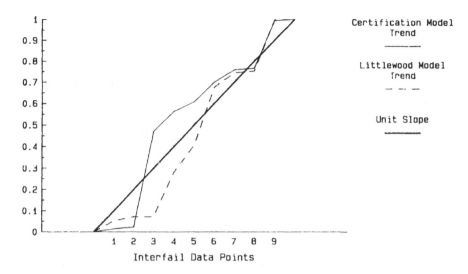

Fig. 4. Trend plot for example increment at first release.

which (if either) model is providing realistic projections, the Q–Q plot analysis can be run (Figs 4 and 5) and an assessment made. The first Q–Q plot (Fig. 4) tracks how well the two models are capturing the trend in the recorded timing data (i.e. the ups and downs in interfail times). The Certification model seems to be better at capturing the

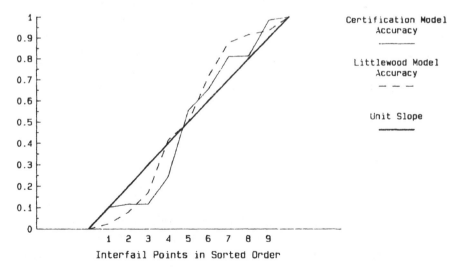

Fig. 5. Accuracy plot for example increment at first release.

trend in the these data (i.e., smaller value for maximum distance off the line of unit slope). The second Q–Q plot (Fig. 5) is a check on the accuracy of MTTF prediction (i.e., matching predictions against the subsequent interfail times). Again, the Certification model tends to give better results, though the measures of maximum distance are less pronounced.

From this analysis, one would conclude that the Certification model would be preferred for predicting reliabilities from this particular set of interfail data. For different software with different timing data from the test process, a different model might be selected.

19. SOFTWARE RELIABILITY EXPERIENCE

The Cleanroom experiments have shown the feasibility of predicting software reliability as part of the development process, using a statistical approach to software testing. The analytical models used for MTTF prediction were validated against published data as well as the statistical techniques used for checking predicted results. The procedures for factoring prediction into development were defined as part of the experimentation.

Only in one case were predictions correlated with actual field data to assess how realistic the earlier predictions had been. A simple averaging of error reports over the field usage period was performed, and this MTTF estimate was within 20% of the predictions which had been made as much as two years earlier. Not much can be made of this comparison, other than that the approach seems workable. More experiments which stress follow-up with field results and use reliability as the control on development should be conducted to check these two aspects of the overall approach.

20. CLEANROOM TECHNOLOGY TRANSFER

To establish a statistical control process for software development, changes are required in the organizational and educational plans for the development organization. From an organizational perspective, a split in responsibility between the software developers and the software testers is required. The developers should be knowledgeable in the latest software engineering methods and expected to design, code and document software which can be delivered to software test prior to any execution. They should feel comfortable with using verification methods to obtain product correctness and having their products put under configuration control upon delivery to test. The developer is responsible for delivering correct products and will be expected to correct product defects uncovered during independent testing.

The software tester, on the other hand, is responsible for delivering a product for which a statement concerning its reliability can be made and certified. This requires knowledge of statistical methods, specifically sampling theory, software reliability, modeling and statistical analysis. All testing will be functional (blackbox) and based on statistically representative usage samples. The tester is responsible for delivering a product with a certified reliability and is expected to generate the plans, procedures and samples needed to insure proper product testing and reliability measurement.

Education and training in the formal techniques used by both the developers and the testers is critical to the successful introduction of software statistical control into a business enterprise. Developers require mathematics-based software engineering training, similar to what is offered at IBM's Software Engineering Institute for internal consumption. Formal design methods and data-structured design are bolstered by functional verification methods to provide a baseline for developing high quality software. Testers require statistics and operational analysis training to effectively implement and use user-representative testing strategies and reliability measurements. Tool support and consultation on applying the ideas to specific problems is the other part of effective technology transfer into standard business practice.

REFERENCES

1. Curritt, P. A., Dyer, M. and Mills, H. D., Certifying the reliability of software, *IEEE TSE*, Vol. SE–12, Jan. 1986.
2. Selby, R. W., Basili, V. R. and Baker, F. T., *Cleanroom software development: an empirical evaluation,* University of Maryland, TR–1415, Feb. 1985.
3. Linger, R. C., Mills, H. D. and Witt, B. I., *Structured programming: theory and practice,* Addison–Wesley, 1979.

4. Dyer, M. *et al.*, The management of software engineering, *IBM Systems J.*, Vol. 19, 1980.
5. Mills, H. D. The new math of computer programming, *CACM*, Vol. 18, Jan. 1975.
6. Dijkstra, E. W., *A discipline of programming*, Prentice–Hall, 1976.
7. Mills, H. D, *Mathematical foundations for structured programming*, FSC Technical Report 72–6012, 1972.
8. Jordano, A. J., DSM software architecture and development, *IBM Technical Directions*, Vol. 10, No. 3, 1984.
9. Linger, R. C. and Mills, H. D., Data structured programming: program design without arrays and pointers, *IEEE TSE*, Vol. SE–12, Feb. 1986.
10. Hoare, C. A. R., An axiomatic basis for computer programing, *CACM*, Vol. 12, Oct 1969.
11. Basili, V. R. and Noonan, R. E., A comparison of the axiomatic and functional models of structured programming, *IEEE TSE*, Vol. SE–6, Sept. 1980.
12. Dyer, M, Inspection data analysis section, *State of the art report on software reliability*, Pergamon Infotech Ltd, 1986.
13. Dyer, M, A formal approach to software error removal, *J. Systems and Software*, July 1987.
14. Gerber, J. F., *Cleanroom test case generator*, IBM Technical Report 86.0008, June 1986.
15. Duran, J. W. and Ntafos, S. C., An evaluation of random testing, *IEEE TSE*, Vol. SE–10, July 1984.
16. Littlewood, B., Stochastic reliability growth: a model for fault renovation of computer programs and hardware designs, *IEEE Trans. Reliability*, Vol. R–30, Oct. 1981.
17. Littlewood, B. and Verrall, J. L., Bayesian reliability growth model for computer software, *Applied Statistics*, Vol. 22, 1973.
18. Shanthikumar, J. G., A statistical time dependent error occurrence rate software reliability model with imperfect debugging, *Proc. 1981 National Computer Conf.*, June 1981.
19. Iannino, A., Littlewood, B., Musa, J. D. and Okumoto, K, Criteria for software reliability model comparisons, *IEEE TSE*, Vol. SE–10, Nov. 1984.

2
Software Metrics*

D. INCE

Open University, Milton Keynes, U.K.

ABSTRACT

Software metrics are numerical measures extracted from the products and processes of a software project. This paper describes research work that has been carried out in this area over the last fifteen years. In particular it describes work carried out in defining and validating product metrics and cost estimation models. The paper concludes with an agenda for future research in the metrics area.

1. INTRODUCTION

The software project manager has to carry out a number of functions; these are: monitoring, controlling, planning, representing, predicting and innovating. Of these the most important function is predicting. Typical questions that a project manager has to ask during the course of a software project, and which involve prediction, are:

- Given a particular system specification, how much resource will be needed to carry out a project to build the software corresponding to the specification?
- Given a particular design, how much resource should I allow for maintenance?

* This work is partly based on research carried out on project MUSE, funded by the EEC as part of the ESPRIT programme.

– Given a particular detailed design, how much resource will be required to unit-test the module corresponding to the design?

Metrics are a means whereby such questions might be answered in the future. It is fair to point out at this stage that software metrics research is still in its early days, and we have not reached the point where such questions can be answered accurately.

1.1   Software metrics

A software metric is a numerical value extracted from a software project. There are two types of metric: *product metrics* and *process metrics*. The former is a numerical value extracted from some document, or a piece of program code: the latter is a numerical value which describes a software process, for example, the time taken to debug a module, or the amount of errors that remain in a system after final testing.

Metrics can also be categorised as *result metrics* or *predictor metrics*. A predictor metric is normally a product metric which can be used to predict the value of another metric. The metric which is predicted, normally a process metric, is known as a result metric. Thus, using a system specification to predict the amount of resource that will be expended on a software project is an example of a product metric (the system specification) being used to predict a result metric (project resource).

The discussion in the previous paragraphs has been somewhat abstract. In order to describe how metrics are used, and what can be done with them, four examples of work in the area will be described. They each address different aspects of the project life-cycle.

1.2   Function point analysis

Function point analysis is a technique whereby a specification for a commercial data processing system can be used to predict the cost of the project which implements the system. Another use is to calculate project productivity.

The conventional way of estimating the cost of a project involves a number of simple but time-consuming stages. First, the manager carries out an outline requirements analysis followed by an outline system design. From the outline system design he defines a number of tasks that need to be carried out. For example: prepare a test data file, design a module or write some documentation. The manager then looks up standard tables of cost for each of these activities and calculates the total cost for all the activities.

Unfortunately, such a technique is a poor predictor for medium to large projects. The reason for this is that calculations are carried out with the assumption that the only activities on a software project are developmental. For small projects this is a valid assumption. However, on other projects there is a large amount of resource put into communication between staff which is not taken into account.

Function point analysis is a technique which attempts to overcome this problem. It was developed in IBM during the late 1970s by Allen Albrecht who, at the time, was manager of the application and maintenance measurement programme for that company. The idea of function point analysis is that one can measure the size of a system, in terms of the functions it delivers, by counting the number of inputs, outputs, enquiries, master files and interfaces that make up the system. This information can be easily gathered during requirements analysis. The counts are then weighted by numbers designed to reflect the function value to the customer. The weights that are employed were determined by Albrecht, after a long process of trial and error. They are:

– Number of inputs* 4
– Number of outputs* 5
– Number of enquiries* 4
– Number of master files* 10
– Number of interfaces* 7

These weights are then adjusted for other factors. For example, if the inputs, outputs or files are especially complicated, 5% is added. Complex internal processing can add another 5%. On-line functions and performance considerations also affect the weighting. Once the weightings have been adjusted, the figure so formed is the number of function points delivered by the system which has been measured.

Originally, Albrecht used function points to measure productivity throughout IBM over a five year period.[1] He found that a productivity improvement of about three-to-one took place due to the more disciplined organisation of programming teams, the use of PL/1 rather than COBOL, the use of interactive computing and the adoption of structured programming techniques and better documentation standards.

Function points are useful for two reasons: first, they can be

D. Ince

collected at an early stage of a project and, second, it does not take much time to carry out a function point calculation. For a large data processing system it would take two to three days at most. Compared with the large amount of work that has to be carried out with conventional project sizing techniques, this is a small figure indeed.

There are a number of uses for function points: they can be used as a check against more conventional estimating methods; they can be used to judge the effect of new developmental methods, new software tools and novel ways of organising a project; or they can be just used to judge project productivity. In order to use function points in calculating project productivity, the following steps need to be taken.

For each project that you have completed, calculate the number of function points delivered. This figure can be extracted from the system specification for each project. Then, look up the cost, in staff hours, of each project from your historical records. Plot the cost against the number of function points, and fit a curve to the graph that you have constructed. A typical graph is shown in Fig. 1.

The next stage is to plot a graph of the number of hours per function point against the number of function points. The number of hours per function point is a productivity index: it shows how much effort has been expended in delivering one function point. An example of this second type of graph is shown in Fig. 2.

It is a rising line which shows that as projects get bigger their productivity decreases. This is just common sense: the larger a project,

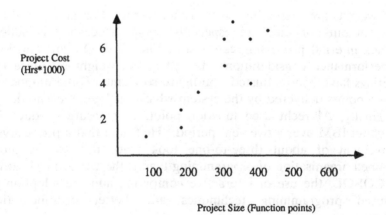

Fig. 1. The effect of function point values on project cost.

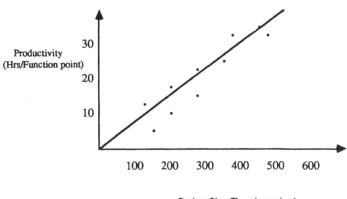

Project Size (Function points)

Fig. 2. The relationship between productivity and project size expressed in function points.

the more communication has to take place between project staff and, consequently, less useful developmental work is carried out. If you want to find out how productive a project is, the next stage is to calculate a productivity index. A good one is to calculate the ratio of the number of hours per function point actually expended on a project, by the expected number of hours per function point. This second figure can be taken from Fig. 2. If this ratio is greater than 1 then, for some reason, the project is less productive than it should be.

For example, assume that your staff have just finished a project which delivered about 300 function points and their productivity was 29 hours per function point. From Fig. 2 you would have expected them to deliver about 22 hours per function point; the productivity index would then be $29/22 = 1\cdot3$, which means they are being less productive than you expect them to be.

The function point method is still in the experimental stage. However, a number of major software developers in this country are beginning to use it as a resource estimate check against more conventional methods of project sizing. These users include: British Rail, Prudential Assurance, Lloyds of London and Logica.

1.3 A design metric
Software maintenance is now a significant activity for many companies. It has been estimated that as much as 60% of project resource

is currently committed to this activity. A useful metric would be one which was able to predict the extent of this activity as early in the software project as possible.

Staff carrying out maintenance have to study the design and program code of the system being maintained and apply changes to that system. A good measure of the difficulty of this process is the degree of independence that each module in a system has with respect to other modules. If a module can be understood in isolation, and modified in isolation, then it is clear that the effort required to modify that module will be considerably less than that expended on modifying a module which is connected to a large number of other modules. The reason for this is that the programmer has to carry less information in his head, and there is a lower probability that changes to a module will necessitate changes to other modules.

For many years software engineers have believed that the degree of connectivity of a software system is an indicator of the quality of the system.[2] We now believe that a well-structured system is one in which the components of the system exist in relative isolation, resulting in fewer errors and consuming less resources during maintenance.

Two researchers, Sally Henry and Dennis Kafura,[3] decided to test the hypothesis that maintenance was easier when a system consisted of loosely connected components. They examined the structure of the UNIX operating system and drew diagrams such as the one shown in Fig. 3. Circles represent modules and squares represent data structures. A thin line joining two program modules represents a call by one module on another module. For example, the thin line joining C to D indicates that a module C calls a module D. A thick line indicates a flow of data from a module to another module, or from a module to a data structure. For example, module D passes data to module E via a parameter, and module F writes data to the data structure DS.

From such diagrams they derived metric values which measured the degree to which each module was isolated from other modules. What their metric measured was the amount of information passing through a module. A module where there was a high information flow required more maintenance effort, or encouraged errors to be made during maintenance.

After calculating metric values for parts of the UNIX system, Henry and Kafura examined programming statistics which had been generated during maintenance of the system. In particular, they examined the incidence of change to modules in the system. This product metric

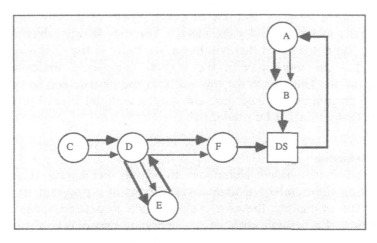

Fig. 3. Information flow diagrams used by Kafura and Henry.

is in fact a good indicator of the number of errors in a module. Their results are shown in Table 1.

The first column shows values of their metric. The second column shows the number of program units with that degree of complexity. The third column represents the number of program units which contained changes. Finally, the fourth column contains the percentage of those program units that were changed.

Table 1
Experimental Results from the Kafura and Henry Study

Information flow complexity	Number of procedures	Number of procedures with changes	Percentage
10^0	17	2	12
10^1	38	12	32
10^2	41	19	46
10^3	27	19	70
10^4	26	15	58
10^5	12	11	92
10^6	3	2	67
10^7	1	0	0

The figures show an increase of development effort with increasing complexity as measured by the metric. The only figures which, on the surface, do not support the hypothesis are those in the final line which show that the module with the highest complexity underwent no change at all. The reason for this was that the module was so complex that no programmer would dare change the code for fear of producing effects that could not be predicted!

1.4 Bebugging

A useful metric-based technique known as bebugging is used in estimating the number of undiscovered bugs in a program. It is also useful for evaluating the efficiency of code inspection teams. Code inspection is a formalisation of the everyday experience of programmers who might have worked for hours trying to detect an error, only for a colleague who has just come in from lunch to lean over their shoulders and detect the error extremely quickly.

The technique was originally pioneered at IBM,[4] and involves a team of participants unconnected with a project, examining completed program units in order to discover errors. An important concern of a project manager who utilises code inspection is the efficiency of the inspection process, i.e. how many errors are slipping through the inspection process.

In order to predict the number of undiscovered errors a technique known as bebugging has been devised.[5] It is based on the following technique used to discover the number of fish in a pond.

> I own a pond which contains only white-coloured fish. Once I needed to estimate how many fish were contained in this pond. What I did was to visit my neighbour Jack and buy 100 of the fish in his pond. These fish are red. I dumped the fish in my pond and, over the next few days, I did some fishing. After I had completed the fishing I counted the number of red fish and the number of white fish. I caught 20 white fish and 10 red fish. This must mean that there are approximately 200 white fish in my pond.

If we substitutes 'bugs' for 'fish' we get a description of what bebugging is all about:

> I have a system which contains bugs. Once I needed to estimate how many bugs were contained in this system What I did was to insert 100 artificial bugs into the system. Over the next few days, my inspection teams processed the modules in the system and sent their results to me. They had discovered 20 real bugs and 10 of the artificially inserted ones. This must mean that there are approximately 200 bugs in the system.

This example is a little unrealistic: the inspection team were rather inefficient, and should have discovered a lot more errors. Nevertheless, it does give a flavour of what bebugging is. Bebugging is thus used in two ways. First, as an estimator of residual bugs and, secondly, as a measure of staff effectiveness.

A further use for bebugging is in estimating when system testing is ready to be terminated. Normally, there is a fine dividing line between carrying on system testing until there are no errors left, and starting acceptance testing. A manager does not want to delay the acceptance testing process until the last few trivial errors are discovered: neither does he want to pass a system containing a fair number of errors as ready for acceptance testing. Bebugging enables the manager to gain an estimate of the number of residual errors in a system and enables him to make an informed decision about terminating the system testing phase.

1.5 Mutation testing

System testing is probably the most nerve-wracking activity in the software project. At the end of the system testing process, staff usually feel fairly confident that the data that they have produced have adequately tested the system under development. However, they often require some final confirmation that the testing has progressed well. One technique which can be used to provide a degree of confidence and produce a metric is mutation testing.[6]

At the end of system testing the testers will have produced a suite of test data which has given the correct answers during the testing process. In order to ensure full coverage has occurred, the tester creates a number of mutants from the code of the original system. A mutant is created by applying one change to the system. Typical changes include replacing a multiplication operator by an addition operator or replacing one variable by a similar variable.

These mutants are then executed with the system test data and their output is monitored. If the output differs from that obtained from the original system, then the mutant is assumed to have died. However, if the mutant gives the same result then it is regarded as living. If, at the end of the mutation testing process, some of the mutants are still alive, then the test team should be worried: what has happened is that their test data have been unable to distinguish between the original system and the original system with an artificial error added.

The tester is then set a target of deriving more test data which will kill off all the remaining mutants. The metric used in this unusual

method of testing is the number of living mutants, a high number
indicating a poor set of test data. The major advantage of this method
of testing is that it sets the tester a numerical target, and the use of the
living mutant metric always provides feedback on the quality of the
testing process.

2. METRICS AND THE SOFTWARE PROJECT

There are currently a number of uses for metrics on the software
project. First, as a predictor of resource requirements for later parts of
a software project. This is one of the major areas of weakness in
current project management. For example, software costing using
current techniques is still rather a hit-and-miss affair. One of the aims
of metrics workers is to enable accurate and quick estimates of project
resources to be calculated. This is not only important during the
planning stage, but is also useful during execution of a project: many
software projects are impacted by changes in requirements during
their execution; it can be an extremely time-consuming business to
re-calculate the effect of these changes using conventional techniques.
Current work on metrics is aimed at producing automated software
tools which are able to calculate new values of project cost very
quickly.

Secondly, metrics can be used as a quality assurance enforcement
mechanism. If a project manager is confident that there is a direct
relationship between a predictor metric for a software product and an
important result metric, then he can ensure that values of the product
metric are kept within the numerical bounds which lead to acceptable
values for the result metric.

Metrics can also be used as a mechanism for evaluating the
performance of staff on a software project. Project managers usually
have a gut feeling about who is performing well and who is performing
badly on a project. Normally, they do not get sufficient evidence about
performance until a late stage of the project, when little corrective
action can be taken. For example, the effect of poor design is usually
felt during the integration, acceptance test and system testing phases.
By using metrics the project manager is able to monitor work
produced by staff and enable them to reach higher standards.

A fourth use for metrics is in evaluating competing development
methods, organisational structures and individual ways of working.

The boom in software engineering has led to the promotion of a number of competing development methodologies being promoted. The proponents of these methodologies claim that, by adopting them, the developer will benefit by a reduction of testing time, more easily maintainable software and lower programming costs. Metrics can be used as a basis for examining these claims dispassionately—although, to be fair, it is worth pointing out that there is very limited experience in using metrics in this way.

Metrics can also be used to help development staff gain a quantitative estimate of the quality of their work. The vast majority of staff employed on software projects are professionals: they care about the quality of the product that they produce. Metrics are able to give more than just a gut feeling about how well they are performing.

Finally, metrics can be used as the basis for intelligent and semi-intelligent software development tools. A burgeoning area of research is aimed at developing tools which, at worst, provide major assistance to specifiers and designers and, at best, totally automate their jobs. One area of research involves using metrics to evaluate designs which are automatically synthesised by artificial intelligence-based tools.

3. SOFTWARE PRODUCT METRICS

3.1 Token Metrics

Token metrics are calculated by counting tokens in the source code of a system, program or program unit. A token is a single entity which makes up a program; for example, PERFORM, BY and NEW_ ACCOUNT are examples of tokens in COBOL: the first two are keywords while the third is a variable identifier.

Probably, the most well known example of token-based metrics work is that of the late M. H. Halstead[7] who was a professor at Purdue University. Halstead categorised the tokens in the source code of a system as being either *operands* or *operators*. The former are tokens such as operations, delimiters, arithmetic symbols, punctuation and key words that control the execution of a program. Examples of operators are: $+$, $-$, $*$, IF THEN, GOTO followed by a label and REPEAT UNTIL. Operands are objects that operators act on. For example, variables and constants are examples of operands. In counting operators, keywords which go together, for example IF and THEN, are counted as one operator.

From counting the number of operands and operators in a program a number of metrics can be calculated. An important metric is E, the amount of effort required to understand a program. Halstead metrics are probably the ones most cited in the literature since, compared to say design metrics, automatic extraction is easy: all that is required is a program which processes programs, and extracts their operand and operator count. The typical Halstead experiment cited in the research literature of the 1970s would time some aspect of a task performance, for example, debugging time, and compare such performance against a Halstead metric.

There have been a number of criticisms of Halstead's work. First, there is the difficulty of estimating whether a token is to be interpreted as an operator or an operand. The most quoted example of this is a function which may serve the purpose of an operator and an operand at the same time.

The second criticism is that Halstead's derived formulae depend on assumptions which are theoretically dubious. For example, in deriving measures related to programming effort, Halstead made the assumption that humans are capable of making a constant number of discriminations per second. Cognitive psychologists now tend to dismiss this assumption through lack of experimental evidence.

The third criticism is that the experimental design of the studies used to confirm or reject Halstead's work are flawed. There are a number of reasons for this. Firstly, the sample sizes used were small. To get meaningful statistics out of the experiments that were performed requires a substantial increase in the number of samples used. Second, the programs used in the studies were small. Very few experiments were carried out using industrial-size systems. If Halstead's work is to have any significance for the industrial developer, a large number of experiments will need to be carried out within real contexts. Third, many of the experiments involved single subjects who were in a sense untypical: they were normally university students.

The fourth criticism, and probably the most serious, is that to measure the properties of a system during programming is too late. If the project manager wants to affect a large number of subsequent activities, it is much better to carry out monitoring of metric values earlier in the software project, say during system design. Measuring metrics during coding, after almost all the strategic decisions about system structure have been made, is rather too late. The major advantage of Halstead's work is that it is exceptionally easy to extract metric values: the program that carries out the extraction process is not very long (a Pascal version is given in Ref. 8), and the values can be extracted automatically from the code of a project, which is always kept in a machine-readable form. Other metrics, which will be discussed later, require that designs be processed; unfortunately, there are few developers who have automated sufficiently for these designs to be kept in a machine-readable form.

3.2 Control flow metrics

During detailed design, each program unit in a software system is expanded and the flow of control determined. The flow is expressed in terms of some detailed design notation such as a program design language. An example of such a notation is shown below. It represents the detailed design of a procedure to calculate the average of a series of temperature readings.

```
PROCEDURE average_readings (av)
Set a sum to zero
Set a count to zero
WHILE there is still a reading to process DO
    Obtain a reading
    Add 1 to the count
    Add the reading to sum
END_WHILE
Set av to sum/count
END_PROCEDURE
```

At the end of detailed design the whole of a system will be expressed in a detailed design notation such as that shown above. A project manager, at this stage of a project, would like to know how much effort and time might be spent in performing the next phases: unit coding and unit testing.

The answer to this problem was first supplied by Thomas McCabe in the mid-1970s.[9] In order to understand McCabe's work it is first necessary to digress and describe a simplified way of representing detailed design notations graphically. The graphical notation is known as a *directed graph*. It consists of a series of *nodes* and lines joining these nodes known as *edges*. A node represents a decision, or the end of some processing in a design or program, while the edges represent some processing that occurs. The directed graph for the design fragment

> IF the temperature is out of bounds
> THEN
>   Activate alarm
> ELSE
>   Output temperature
> END_IF

is shown in Fig. 4. The nodes are labelled with lower-case letters and the arcs are labelled with numbers. The arrow attached to an arc shows the direction of processing. Figure 4 shows that the fragment can be represented by two nodes: *a* and *b*. Node *a* represents the decision in the IF statement and node *b* represents the point where the processing in the two branches of the IF statement joins up. If one assumes that a left-most arc represents the true branch of an IF statement and the right-most arc represents the false branch, then arc 1 represents the processing *activate alarm* and arc 2 represents the processing *output temperature*. A directed graph of the design fragment

> WHILE there is data DO
>   Read a data point
>   IF the data point is invalid
>   THEN
>   Print an error message
>   ELSE
>   Add the data point to sum
>   END_IF
> END_WHILE
> IF there was an error in the data THEN
>   Check monitors
> ELSE
>   Calculate average
> END_IF

is shown in Fig. 5. It consists of five nodes and seven arcs. Node *a* represents the decision in the WHILE statement, node *b* represents the decision in the first IF statement, node *c* represents the destination of both parts of the processing associated with the IF statement, and

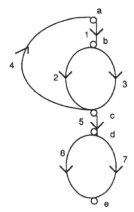

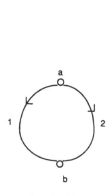

Fig. 4. A simple directed graph.

Fig. 5. Directed graph with a cyclo-matic complexity of 4.

nodes *d* and *e* are associated with the second IF statement. Arc 1 is associated with the processing *read a data point,* arc 2 with the processing *print an error message.* Arc 3 is associated with the processing *add the data point to sum.* Arc 4 represents the loop back to node 1 in order to re-execute the WHILE loop. Arc 5 represents the transfer of control from the WHILE statement to the second IF statement. Finally, arcs 6 and 7 represent the two processing actions *check monitors* and *calculate average.*

Directed graphs have been known to researchers for some time and have been used in applications such as the design of pipelines, the calculation of currents and voltages in electrical systems and the design of optimal one-way traffic systems in a city. Mathematicians have developed a number of measures of the complexity of a graph in terms of the number of its nodes and arcs. Probably, the most important of these is the *cyclomatic complexity* of a graph. It is defined as:

number of arcs − number of nodes +2

Using this definition, the cyclomatic complexity of the graph shown in Fig. 5 will be:

$$7 - 5 + 2 = 4$$

McCabe in his research postulated that the higher the cyclomatic complexity of a directed graph representing a program unit, the more difficult it is to read, program and test that unit.

In the paper describing the work McCabe suggested that a cyclomatic complexity of greater than 10 was intolerable in a program unit. He related his experiences in applying the measure to a group of programs from a software project that he was not involved in. In the extract that follows the reference to FLOW is a reference to a software tool that McCabe used to monitor and calculate the cyclomatic complexity of FORTRAN subroutines:

> It has been interesting to note how individual programmers' style relates to the complexity measure. The author has been delighted to find several programmers who never had formal training in structured programming but consistently write code in the 3 to 7 complexity range which is quite well structured. On the other hand FLOW has found several programmers who frequently wrote code in the 40 to 50 complexity range (and who claimed there was no other way to do it). On one occasion the author was given a DEC tape of 24 FORTRAN subroutines that were part of a large real-time graphics system. It was rather disquieting to find, in a system where reliability is critical, subroutines of the following complexity: 16, 17, 24, 24, 32, 34, 41, 54, 56 and 64. After confronting the project members with these results the author was told that the subroutines on the DEC tape were chosen because they were troublesome and indeed a close correlation was found between the ranking of subroutines by complexity and a ranking by reliability (performed by project members).[9]

There have been a number of modifications, improvements and refinements made to McCabe's original work. For example, Myers[10] has pointed out that the complexity of the conditions in program code are a determinant of how complex that code is. For example, the fragments of Pascal below differ because the second fragment contains a much more complicated predicate in its IF statement

```
(*First fragment*)
IF (x > 0) AND (j = 10) OR (l = 4) THEN
      count := count + 1
ELSE
      count := count - 1;
```

```
(*Second fragment*)
IF x > 0 THEN
      count := count + 1
ELSE
      count := count - 1;
```

Unfortunately, McCabe's cyclomatic complexity measure will give the same metric value for both. Clearly this is wrong: a maintenance programmer trying to understand the first fragment will take longer than if he was trying to understand the second fragment. What Myers suggested as a measure was one which consisted of an interval: the lower bound of the interval represents the number of decision

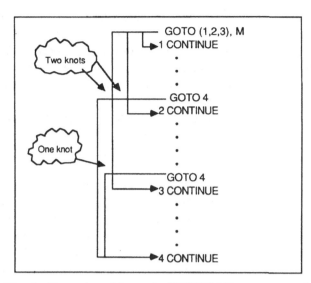

Fig. 6. Examples of knots in FORTRAN program code.

statements in a program plus 1. This corresponds in essence to McCabe's cyclomatic complexity metric. The second element of the interval is the number of *individual* conditions plus 1. Thus, the first fragment of code shown above would have a value of [2, 4] while the second would have a value of [2, 2].

Gilb[11] has also proposed another metric based on control complexity known as the *logical complexity metric*. This is relatively easy to calculate: the number of binary decisions in a program or program unit are counted and are divided by the total number of statements.

Woodward, Hennel and Hedley[12] have also suggested a metric known as a *knot*. A knot measures the overlap of control jumps in a program. An example of three knots in a fragment of FORTRAN code is shown in Fig. 6. Here the flow of control of a computed GOTO to statements 1, 2 and 3 intersect the flow of control from two GOTO statements at three points. These points are the knots and the fragment shown above therefore has a knot complexity of three.

3.3 Composite metrics
A number of researchers have pointed out that metrics solely based on control structure complexity are inadequate, that although control structure complexity has an obvious effect on process metrics such as

time to debug, other factors are important. For example, the distribution of data references in a program unit can be a major factor: a programmer trying to understand and debug a program unit is faced with a greater task if that program unit contains a wide distribution of variables. In debugging the unit he has to remember the location and the function of a set of variables at differing parts of the unit. Because of this multi-dimensional aspect to complexity, hybrid metrics have been proposed which attempt to overcome the weaknesses of single metrics.

Probably the most well-known hybrid metrics are those due to Hansen[13] and Oviedo.[14] Hansen's metric attempts to combine the cyclomatic complexity metric and one of Halstead's metrics. It consists of a pair (contr, op), where *contr* is a count of condition constructs such as IF statements and CASE statements, and *op* is the count of arithmetic operators such as +, − and *; assignments; subroutine and function calls; subscripts in an array; and input/output statements. Hansen's motivation in developing such a hybrid metric was to measure both the complexity of the processing *contr,* and the amount of function delivered by a program or program unit *op.* Hansen argued that *op* was a good measure of the size of what was going on in a program and hence measured its functionality.

Oviedo's metric measures both control complexity and data complexity. It is a single figure formed from the sum of two metrics. The first is simply a count of the number of edges in the graph of a program or program unit. The second is calculated by counting the number of times a variable takes part in statements such as output statements and assignment statements, and by counting the number of times a variable gains a value, say by being referenced on the left hand side of an assignment statement or in an input statement. The full calculation of Oviedo's metric is rather complicated. It is described fully in Ref. 14.

3.4. System metrics

The previous categories of metric, token-based and graph-based, concentrate on measuring the properties of program code; although it is fair to say that if a developer had a sufficiently precise detailed design notation, then graph-based metrics could be extracted during detailed design. System metrics measure large-scale properties of a system, usually the quality of a system design. Potentially, they are the most useful because they can be extracted during an early phase of a project, system design, and hence are capable of predicting more. The major disadvantage of token-based and graph-based measures is that they can usually be extracted only after coding has taken place and, hence, can only predict the extent of activities which take up a relatively small part of project resource.

In order to examine the basis of system design metrics, it is first worth examining some of the activities that occur after system design. First, consider *unit programming and testing*. In this activity the programmer takes a detailed design, produces the code for that design, and tests the unit in isolation. This testing involves selecting data which execute a percentage of branches or statements which are specified in the quality assurance standards of the project, and rectifying any errors found. *Rectification* involves studying the program code, checking the function of units that are called by the unit under test, and checking that the global variables used by the program unit have the correct values before and after unit testing.

Second, consider *maintenance*. This involves the programmer modifying a system in response to a change, or set of changes, and either the programmer or a quality assurance organisation checking that the change is properly implemented. Further checks are also required in order to ensure that a change has not affected the existing functions of the system. In applying change to a module the programmer has to keep in his head the details of any other unit called, and the potential values of any global variables which are updated by these called units.

Similar descriptions to those above also hold for activities such as integration testing and system testing. From the descriptions above, one can see that the programmer involved in these activities is concerned not only with what happens inside an individual unit, but also with the relationship between a unit and other units in a system. For example, Fig. 7 shows part of a software system. The square boxes are program units, while the rounded box is a database. If a programmer applies a maintenance change to program unit C, then that programmer has, while designing the change, to worry about what the functions of units E and F are. Furthermore, he has to worry about the effect of the call on unit B upon the database D1. For example, he may have assumed that a data value is unchanged in D1, but there is the possibility that the call to B will have changed that data value.

It is clear, then, that a major worry of a programmer is the relationship of a unit with the other units and databases that surround it, that a unit which is isolated from other units, and from databases,

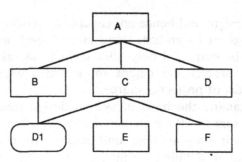

Fig. 7. A structure chart representing the system design of part of a system.

can be read in isolation, understood in isolation and modified in isolation, with little effect on other units.

This proposition, which, as software engineers, we now take for granted, was first stated by the architect and designer Christopher Alexander. In his book *Notes on the synthesis of form*[15] he demonstrated that the quality of a design of an object, be it a refrigerator, building, electronic circuit or bridge, was intimately related to the degree of interconnection that occurred in the object; it is this degree of interconnection that system metrics are intended to measure.

One of the best pieces of experimental work which backs up Alexander's proposition was carried out by Troy and Zweben.[16] These two researchers isolated a large number of features of program design, and correlated them against errors discovered in 73 separate designs. These designs were expressed using a design notation known as a structure chart, similar to that shown in Fig. 7. The result of this experiment was that features of a design which indicated one program unit to be coupled to another program unit were highly correlated with errors. Typical features that come under this coupling category include: the average number of interconnections per box, the unique number of common interconnections and the number of boxes accessing control interconnections (items of data which determine the flow of control within a program unit).

Much of the work that has been carried out on system metrics has been inspired by Alexander's work. A typical piece of research, which is based on this idea, is described in Ref. 17. In this research, a number of metrics were defined which measured the complexity of a system design and were validated against error data monitored from the project which employed the designs. One metric which the authors

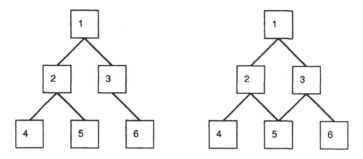

Fig. 8. A tree structure and a graph structure.

employed is called *graph impurity*. In order to describe what is meant by this, examine the system designs shown in Fig. 8. The system on the left is an example of a *tree*: an arrangement of units where each one is only called by one other unit. The system on the right is known as a *graph*: an arrangement of program units where at least one unit is called by more than one other unit. The system on the right is a graph by virtue of the fact that program unit 5 is called by both program units 2 and 3.

The more a system tends towards a graph, with large numbers of program units being called by other units, the worse the quality of the system. Yin and Winchester[17] attempted to measure how much a system deviated from the ideal tree structure. In order to do this they calculated the metric C_i which measured graph complexity for one level of a design i. C_i is calculated from the formula

$$C_i = A_i - N_i + 1$$

where A_i is the number of arcs to the level i and where N_i is the number of nodes to level i. For the system on the left, the value of C_i for $i = 3$ is $5 - 6 + 1 = 0$ since there are six program units and five arcs to the third level of the design. For the system on the right, the value of C_i is $6 - 6 + 1 = 1$. The higher the graph complexity, the higher the value of C_i. Almost all systems will be graph-like. Normally they will resemble trees at the top of a design but, as one progresses towards the bottom of the design, there will be multiple calls on service routines which carry out tasks needed by many units. Because of this it is not advisable to use C_i as an absolute value of system quality. Where it is useful is in examining trends in a system design.

The graph shown as Fig. 9 plots C_i against level for a large system.

D. Ince

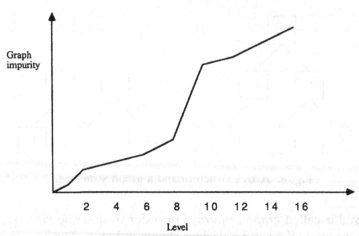

Fig. 9. The growth in C_i in a software system.

There is a large increase in C_i between levels 8 and 10. This should indicate to the designer that there will be major problems in this part of the design during later stages of the software project. A similar approach to this is described in Ref. 18, where the shape of the calling tree was used to characterise a large system which evolved during software maintenance.

A refinement of the approach described above is based on measuring the effect of a change to one program unit on another program unit in a system. This was initially described in Ref. 19. The effect of change on program unit is characterised by a probability matrix P, whose elements represent the probability that a change to a program unit will give rise to a change in another program unit. As an example, consider a system containing five program units whose probability matrix is shown below. The element in row i and column j represents the probability that a change to program unit i will result in a change to program unit j. The highest probability is 1 (certainty) and the lowest probability is 0 (no probability at all). The diagonal of the matrix will always contain ones since if a change occurred to a module it is certain it occurred to the module!

$$\begin{bmatrix} 1 & 0{\cdot}1 & 0 & 0{\cdot}2 & 0 \\ 0 & 1 & 0{\cdot}1 & 0{\cdot}1 & 0 \\ 0 & 0{\cdot}3 & 1 & 0 & 0 \\ 0{\cdot}1 & 0 & 0 & 1 & 0 \\ 0 & 0 & 0 & 0 & 1 \end{bmatrix}$$

From the matrix above, it can be seen that the probability that a change in program unit 1 will result in change to module 4 is 0·2 and that there is no chance of a change to module 5 affecting modules 1, 2, 3 and 4.

From a probability matrix it is possible to estimate how many changes are required to a system. As well as a change to one program unit having a probable effect on another program unit, there will also be a second-order effect. As an example, consider the effect of a change to program unit 1 in the system described by the probability matrix above. There is a probability of 0.1 that it will affect program unit 2 and a probability of 0·2 that it will affect program unit 4. However, by examining row 2 you can see that there is a probability of 0·1 that a change in program unit 2 will affect both program unit 3 and program unit 4. Hence a change to program unit 1 will, by virtue of the fact that it affects program unit 2, have a probability of 0·1* 0·1 of affecting program unit 3 and program unit 4.

As well as a second-order effect there will be a third-order effect which arises from the fact that if a change occurs to a program unit, it may give rise to changes in other program units which, in turn, give rise to further changes in other program units that again give rise to changes in further program units.

By considering second, third, fourth, up to nth-order effect changes Haney[19] demonstrated by simple matrix algebra that the total effect of change can be characterised by the matrix

$$(I - P)^{-1}$$

where I is the identity matrix: a matrix with its leading diagonal containing 1, but with the remainder of its elements containing zero. Initially, Haney used the idea of a probability matrix to estimate the resources required to implement changes to a software system, given the number of changes required to each program unit.

There are some criticisms that can be made about Haney's work. First, it assumes that all changes require the same amount of resource. Second, it is time-consuming and difficult to estimate the elements of the probability matrix. Consequently, there is little evidence that it has been used extensively on software projects. However, it is an epoch-making piece of work, as it was one of the first attempts to articulate the relevance of Christopher Alexander's work to software project management and quality assurance.

Probably the best exposition of the research which logically continues Haney's research is contained in Ref. 20. Here, the authors approach the question of the quality of a system design from the same direction: that of the ripple effect that occurs when maintenance changes are applied. They attempt to characterise the quality of a system by examining the assumptions made by each program unit in a system about other program units.

In order to understand this work it is probably worth explaining what is meant by the word *assumption*. As an example consider two program units A and B in an order processing system; both of these program units access a global variable which is a string, and carry out manipulations on that global variable. Program unit A may compare the global variable with a series of string constants, and carry out processing that depends on the result of the comparisons, and program B may convert the global variable to a character and place it in a record in a database. Both these program units assume that the variable is a string and carry out processing based on this assumption.

Now, assume that during maintenance the system in which A and B are embedded is required to be made faster, and program unit A is modified to carry out a fast table-lookup. Assume also that the consequence of that table-lookup modification was that the global variable was changed to become an integer. This being so, there is not only a need for a change to program unit A, but also a change to program unit B and any other program unit which makes assumptions about the global variable. Clearly, the greater the number of assumptions that a system design has, the greater the amount of effort that will be expended on maintaining that system.

The work described in Ref. 20 attempts to quantify the assumptions made. It describes how the interface to a program unit can be examined and the assumptions identified. The simple algorithm which is described involves examining parameters, global variables and files, identifying parameters and global variables passed between program units, and forming a series of counts. The process is relatively straightforward; it only requires a system design which shows the hierarchy of the program units in a system, and the inputs and outputs to the program unit. Hence, the metrics calculation process can be carried out during an early stage of the development process.

Another piece of work inspired by the idea that the quality of a system is dependent on the isolation of the various program units in the system has been described in Section 1.3 of this paper. Here the flow of information through program units in a system is used to characterise the quality of that system. On the surface, this work seems to be quite different to that described above. However, the differences are only superficial: the amount of information flowing through a program unit is almost totally dependent on the size and complexity of the interface of a program unit with other program units.

In general, system metrics tend to be more useful than graph complexity metrics and code metrics because they are capable of being used earlier in a software project. If a suitable notation is available, they can be used during system design. Unfortunately, a large amount of validation has not been carried out on such metrics as compared, say, with software science metrics. However, many of the measures proposed as the basis for system metrics have the advantage that, intuitively, they seem right: convincing arguments can be given that a good system is one where program units are in relative isolation, and modern programming methods and languages are based on this proposition. In this respect system metrics are superior to graph-based metrics and certainly more superior to code-based metrics such as those derived from software science.

The comparative lack of validation can be blamed on two factors. First, because system metrics are intuitively appealing, researchers may not have felt that there was much point in deploying effort in this area. Second, it is quite difficult to extract system metrics automatically as compared, say, with software science metrics, where all that is required is a simple extraction program. However, this state of affairs may change quite drastically. A new breed of designer and analyst workbenches is now emerging from commercial developers. Typically, these workbenches are implemented on IBM PCs and are able to offer the user the facility to draw, format, query and store design notations. The very fact that such notations are stored internally means that automatic calculation of metrics really requires small changes to such software tools.

3.5 Specification metrics
As one progresses backwards in the software project towards activities such as system design and specification, the major observation that can be made is that the amount of work on the definition and validation of metrics decreases quite appreciably. The major reason for this is that it is only comparatively recently that we have regarded front-end activities as important. A subsidiary reason is that metrics validation is easiest when the product whose metric is to be validated exists in a

machine-processable form. Until recently the only viable machine-processable form was the program code of a system. Consequently, a large amount of research has been carried out on code metrics and much less on front-end metrics. Nowhere is this more noticeable than in the area of specification, where the smallest amount of work has been carried out. This is a major deficiency: functional specification is probably the earliest phase of the software project where metrics can be extracted and where the predictive effect of metrics can be utilised to maximum effect.

The major work carried out on specification metrics is based on that carried out by Allen Albrecht; this was described in Section 1.2 of this paper. Another treatment of specification metrics can be found in Ref. 8. In this treatment De Marco hypothesised that the size of a system, in terms of functionality, can be measured by the counts of various functions and objects which can be defined during the specification phase. Typical of these are the number of functional primitives, the count of all data objects which exist at the man-machine interface, and the count of output data elements.

However, De Marco's approach differs from Albrecht's in that, instead of taking a weighted average or total of the various counts, he states that the weights should differ depending on the software to be computerised: if the developer was building a software project which was dominated by the functions that it had to carry out, for example, a robotics application, then the total metric count for specification would be weighted so that functional factors would dominate; however, if, say, the product was data dominated, for example an enquiry program, then those elements which measured the amount of data in the program would dominate the metrics collection process.

De Marco suggests that a developer should divide his projects up into a number of domains, with each domain corresponding to some dominant characteristic such as its functionality. Each domain would be associated with a particular weighting of its counts, and a total based on these weightings could be used to compare the functionality of projects within that domain.

De Marco's work and Albrecht's work are the only major examples of metrics that can be used very early in the software project. They can be used in two ways. First, as an indicator of cost: function points and De Marco's metric are the independent variables that drive cost. A second use for the metrics is in calculating project effectiveness. A good measure of project productivity is the amount of function delivered per dollar or pound. Since both these measures can be obtained relatively easily, the effectiveness of a project can be gauged. This enables the manager to carry out exercises such as measuring the effectiveness of new tools, development techniques and organisational structures.

4. MACRO ESTIMATORS

Macro estimators are those metrics which can be used to predict large-scale quantities such as the amount of resource to be expended on a project. One type of estimator is based on fitting a curve to the resource/time data for projects. Probably the best known model that falls into this category is Putnam's resource allocation model.[21] The basic assumption behind this model is that manpower utilisation during program development follows a Rayleigh curve defined by the differential equation

$$y' = 2 \, Kat \exp^{-at^2}$$

where t is elapsed time, y' is the manpower utilisation rate, a is a parameter which affects the shape of the curve and K is the area under the curve. Relatively simple mathematics applied to the equation above gives:

$$S_s = CK^{1/3}T^{4/3}$$

where C is a constant called a technology factor, T is the time when manpower rate is at its highest, and K is the total life-cycle effort from the start of the project to its finish. C, which can be extracted from historical data, is a reflection of the technological environment in which the project takes place. For example, it is a measure of such factors as application constraints, tool support and staff experience. S_s is the number of source lines of code produced. Putnam's ideas are used in a tool called SLIM which is used for project sizing.

There are a number of criticisms of Putnam's work. First, it only seems to work well on projects that are very large. Secondly, it is a poor estimator for a project which consumes resources past release time. When a project releases a software system, everybody gives a sigh of relief and staff leave the project for other projects. This leads to a discontinuity in the resource curve which cannot be described by Putnam's smooth Rayleigh curve. Thirdly, it is quite difficult to estimate C. Fourthly, the model gives poor results when used in calculating the effect of project compression. It certainly tells the user that more staff would be required but, unfortunately, overestimates the number. An improvement over this model is described in Ref. 22.

Probably, the best known technique for project estimation is COCOMO. This is an example of a composite model: one which consists of a combination of equations, statistical data fitting and human judgement. In COCOMO the amount of effort expended in a project can be described by the equation

$$E = a_i S^{b_i} m(X)$$

where S is the source lines of code in thousands of lines. a_i and b_i are constants which depend on the project and $m(X)$ is a composite multiplier which depends on 15 cost drivers. COCOMO can be used in three modes: basic, intermediate and detailed, depending on the level of sophistication required. It is applied to three types of project mode. Where a project corresponds to an *organic mode,* it is small and relatively easy to implement. When a project corresponds to an *embedded mode,* it contains factors such as stringent real-time requirements which make it difficult to implement. A third mode, *semi-detached mode* lies between these two. a_i depends on both the mode and the level of COCOMO: b_i depends solely on the COCOMO mode.

To use COCOMO a developer first calculates the expression $a_i S^{b_i}$ by looking up a table of values which relate the level of COCOMO used, and the mode of the project which is to be estimated, to a_i and b_i. Next, the number of source lines is estimated. From the statement of requirements, and a knowledge of the development environment, each of the cost drivers associated with $m(X)$ can be given a rating on a five- or six-point scale varying from very low to extra high. The values of the cost drivers are then looked up in a set of tables. These are then combined to give $m(X)$, and hence E can be calculated.

COCOMO is undoubtedly the most complete cost model in existence. It is extremely well documented in Ref. 23. However, there are some problems with it. First, it requires the estimation of too many parameters. There is, as yet, no evidence that such a large number of parameters is needed when an approximate cost is required. Second, the parameters for the effort estimation were all obtained by tuning a metrics database against effort for one company (TRW). There is still little evidence that the parameters used in the COCOMO model are optimal for other developer databases.

5. FUTURE RESEARCH AND DEVELOPMENT IN METRICS

There is still a large amount of research and development work required in the metrics area.

5.1 Empirical validation of metrics

There seems to have been a large number of metrics defined in the literature. However, very little empirical validation of these metrics has occurred. What validation has been reported has been deficient in a number of respects. A major criticism is that the experimental design of metrics projects has been flawed. This is usually manifested in a sample size which is too small. Typically, the results from two or three programmers working on a few programs have been analysed and dubious claims made from inadequate data.

Another criticism is that the sample of programmers or designers used has been artificial. Usually the subjects have been university students and not staff involved in serious software development. A further criticism is that much of the research carried out on metrics has ignored the large variation in ability that occurs in the subjects who have been studied.

Finally, there is the criticism that reporting procedures can distort the validity of any experiment. A typical metrics experiment in the last decade would involve a metric such as the cyclomatic complexity of modules being monitored, and the effort expended on the programming and testing of these modules being measured. The latter stage of such an experiment would then attempt to correlate the predictor metric (cyclomatic complexity) against the result metric (effort expended). Unfortunately, programmers are often inaccurate or sloppy in reporting results such as effort expended in testing. This tends to distort, and hence invalidate, any results from a metrics experiment.

The optimistic side to all these criticisms is that there is now sufficient evidence to back up the conjecture that many product metrics are good indicators of result metrics such as readability, ease of programming and maintenance effort. While we cannot precisely predict result metrics, we now feel confident enough about current predictor metrics that they can be used as quality assurance standards on today's software projects.

Research and development in metrics in the next decade should concentrate on a number of areas. A major activity over the next few years will be the empirical validation of metrics on *real* projects, with *real* staff, and in experiments which have been *properly* designed. The main reason for inadequate validation of metrics over the past two decades has been the immaturity of software engineering. In order for thorough, statistically valid experiments to be carried out there is a need for a large and widely-differing sample of products and processes.

In the past, adequate sample sizes have not been achieved for a number of reasons. First, until comparatively recently, most software engineering notations—specifications, system designs and detailed designs—have not been stored on computers. Calculating metrics values from notations which are not held in computer-processable form is a tedious and time-consuming process; it is quite understandable for a company with a full order book to concentrate on fulfilling these orders, rather than expending a large amount of resource on the manual collation and calculation of metrics.

Secondly, until recently, the notations used for products such as specifications and system designs have not been exact. Typically, such notations included a fairly heavy dose of natural language together with a little graphics. Again, extracting metrics from such notations is a manual process. Artificial intelligence technology has not yet reached the point where natural language can be processed to automatically extract metric features. This is the reason why a very large amount of metric work has been carried out in the area of code metrics: no matter what development techniques, specification notations, design notations or tool support a developer uses, he will always have to employ a programming language which is exact, and which is stored on a computer. However, the growing maturity of software engineering has meant that more exact notations are being used for specification and design. At present the majority of these notations are based on graphics, although notations involving mathematics are now emerging from research laboratories and universities.

A third reason for small sample size has been the difficulty in collecting values of process metrics. For example, in an experiment which measures the effect of a control flow metric on the number of errors in a program, the determination and collection of data describing the errors is a manual, error-prone and tedious process; in an experiment which evaluates how good a product metric was as a predictor of resource expenditure, the major difficulty is to determine how much a project has consumed in resources. In the past the only mechanism available for the experimenter was the manual collection of data in documents such as time-sheets. Two developments over the last few years should ensure that this collection process will be easier.

The first is the realisation that the analysis of change on a software project is a good estimate of factors such as errors. For example, by instructing editors to monitor various types of change it should be possible to automatically collect a wide variety of figures which are closely related to process metrics such as the number of errors discovered during coding. The second development is the emergence of project support-environments. Such environments enable the collection of cost data to be a much smoother process than previous paper-related methods.

5.2 The integration of metrics
Another area where more work needs to be carried out is in integrating metrics together. Some metrics measure one aspect of a system, while others measure a completely different aspect. For example, McCabe's metric measures the complexity of individual modules in a system, while the Kafura and Henry metric measures the complexity of a whole system. A maintenance programmer is involved in handling various levels of complexity: he has to cope with the complexity of the control structures of individual modules, the complexity of data referencing in a module and the interface complexity between modules.

Clearly, no single metric can measure *all* the characteristics of a product. This issue has already been addressed by researchers who have attempted to define the hybrid metrics described in Section 3. Unfortunately, the amount of research carried out on hybrid metrics has been small and has solely concentrated on metrics which contain data and control complexity measures, or metrics which embody control and functionality measures. Much more work is required in this area.

5.3 Managing the metrics project
We need to establish management structures which ensure that metrics collection is a painless process which has a high integrity factor. A project can have the most up-to-date tools for monitoring a software project, yet any gains from this can be completely nullified by insufficient management controls to ensure process metric data are adequate and that staff hostility does not distort the metrics collection process.

One typical problem that occurs in this context is: how do you reconcile the fact that the calculation of a metric should be hidden from staff yet, at the same time, ensure that when metrics are being used to evaluate performance, some convincing explanation is given to staff to back up your opinion of their poor performance?

5.4 The automation of the metrics process

We need to establish how metrics should be used in the coming generation of programming support environments and programmer workbenches. Metrics research over the last two decades has been held back by a lack of automation. New developments in the tools and environments areas now provide us with an opportunity for the automatic extraction of many metrics. Research is needed into how such metrics are extracted and the structure of the metrics database.

This is probably not high-level research but is still quite challenging. All that is required is a full data analysis of project structures: the identification of entities, their attributes and the relationships between the entities. The actual process of developing a tool for extracing a metric, say for extracting cyclomatic complexity, is not difficult. However, the difficult part is deciding what to do with the metrics and designing a metrics database which reflects this.

5.5 Metrics and artificial intelligence

There has recently been a massive expansion in interest in artificial intelligence. This has occurred because of the Japanese government's fifth-generation computing plans which lay stress on novel computer

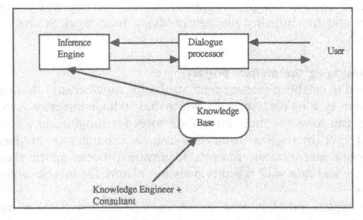

Fig. 10. The architecture of an expert system.

architectures, logic programming and the use of expert systems. An expert system is an artificial intelligence program which attempts to replicate the skills of an expert consultant. Its architecture is shown in Fig. 10. It consists of a knowledge base which contains the rules that a consultant uses. This knowledge base is constructed by means of a human consultant interacting with a knowledge engineer. The knowledge engineer is usually an artificial intelligence expert who uses structured interviewing techniques, together with interview protocols, to extract the essence of the consultant's knowledge.

The knowledge base usually consists of a series of 'IF . . . THEN' rules which are an encoding of the consultant's expertise. A typical rule which might be included in a software design system is shown below:

IF there are more than two global variables AND less than three
   parameters AND the module size is less than 50 lines
THEN
   make one of the global variables a parameter.

The part of the expert system that processes these rules is known as the *inference engine*. Typically, a user is prompted for data about the problem domain over which the expert system works, and the inference engine calculates which rules to select and interpret. For example, an expert system for diagnosing computer hardware faults would ask an engineer what error messages occurred on the operator's VDU, what hardware configuration was currently used and the settings on the engineer's monitoring console.

Expert systems have had a mixed success. They are at their best when dealing with exact numerical quantities. For example, one application area where they have been successful is in medicine. Here they are able to process numerical inputs such as: temperatures, numerical values of lab tests, pulmonary rates and respiratory rates, and infer possible patient malfunctions. If expert system technology is to be used extensively in software engineering and experience in other fields is to be repeated, then it is certain that metrics will form a major component of such systems.

One area where there is a need for intelligent or semi-intelligent tools is system design. There are three categories of tools which can assist the designer in the tasks that are required during system design. First, there are dumb tools. These are usually graphical: they allow the designer to input a design, usually using a pointing device such as a mouse, to modify the design, to focus in on parts of a design and to develop a data dictionary which contains details of program unit names, parameters etc. More and more of these tools are emerging on the market in the form of programmer's workbenches for current design methods.

Secondly, there are semi-intelligent tools. These act as a medium for decision support. Such tools do not take the design process away from the designer, but act as an intelligent assistant. These tools would continually monitor what the designer was doing, check the complexity of an evolving design, and suggest changes as soon as it was discovered that the complexity of units was exceeding a limit, or that the overall complexity of the system was becoming too high. The suggestions that the tool would make would be constructed from rules held in a knowledge base.

Thirdly, there are inteligent tools which would take a system designer's first attempt at a design, and try to improve it with little assistance from the designer. To do this the tool would use a series of heuristics which would have been culled from the human designer.

At the Open University we have developed a tool which lies half-way between the dumb tool described above and a semi-intelligent tool. What the tool does is to process a representation of a design which contains the choices made by the designer during the design process. The particular representation used is known as ·an AND/OR graph. Such a graph is shown in Fig. 11. It shows a system design consisting of seven program units. When an arc is drawn between the program units, the designer has indicated that the design

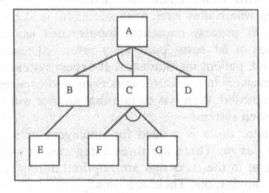

Fig. 11. An AND/OR graph.

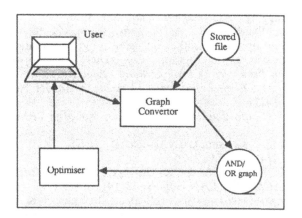

User

Stored
file

Graph
Convertor

AND/
OR graph

Optimiser

5. Gilb, T. Bebugging, *IAG Communications*, **1**, 1975.
6. Budd T. A., DeMillo, R. A., Lipton, R. A. & Sayward, F. G., Theoretical and empirical studies on using program mutation to test the functional correctness of programs, *Conference Record of the 7th ACM Symposium on Principles of Programming Languages*, 220–2, 1980.
7. Halstead, M. H., *Elements of software science*, Elsevier North-Holland, Amsterdam, 1977.
8. De Marco, T, *Controlling software projects*, Yourdon Press, New York, USA, 1978.
9. McCabe, T. J., A complexity measure, *IEEE Trans. on Software Engineering*, **2**(4), 308–20, 1976.
10. Myers, G. J., An extension to the cyclomatic measure of program complexity, *ACM SIGPLAN Notices*, **12**(10), 61–4, 1977.
11. Gilb, T., *Software metrics*, Chartwell–Bratt, Bromley, UK, 1976.
12. Woodward, M. R., Hennell, M. A. & Hedley, D., A measure of control flow complexity in program text, *IEEE Trans. on Software Engineering*, **5**(1), 45–50, 1979.
13. Hansen, W., Measurement of program complexity by the pair (cyclomatic number, operator count), *ACM SIGPLAN Notices*, **13**(3), 29–33, 1978.
14. Oviedo, E. I., Control flow, data flow and program complexity, *Proc. COMPSAC 80*, 146–52, 1980.
15. Alexander, C., *Notes on the synthesis of form*, Harvard University Press, Cambridge, MA, USA, 1964.
16. Troy, D. A. & Zweben, S. H., Measuring the quality of structured designs, *J. Systems and Software*, **2**, 113–20, 1981.
17. Yin, B. H. & Winchester, J. W., The establishment and use of measures to evaluate the quality of software designs, *Proc. ACM Quality Assurance Workshop*, **3**(5), 45–52, 1978.
18. Benyon-Tinker, G., Complexity measures in an evolving large system, *Proc. Workshop on Quantitative Software Models*, 117–27, 1979.
19. Haney, F. M., Module connection analysis—a tool for scheduling software debugging activities, *Proc. AFIP Fall Joint Computer Conference*, 173–79, 1972.
20. Yau, S. S. & Collofello, J. S., Design stability measures for software maintenance, *IEEE Trans. on Software Engineering*. **11**(9), 849–56, 1985.
21. Putnam, L. H., A general empirical solution to the macro sizing and estimating problem, *IEEE Trans. on Software Engineering*. **4**(4), 345–61, 1978.
22. Jensen, R. W., An improved macro level software development resource estimation model, *Proc. 5th IPSA Conference*, 88–92, 1983.
23. Boehm, B. W., *Software Engineering Economics*, Prentice-Hall, Englewood Cliffs, NJ, USA, 1981.

3

New Trends in Cost-Estimation

A. J. C. Cowderoy and J. O. Jenkins

Imperial College School of Management, London, UK

ABSTRACT

It is expected that the discipline of estimating the costs, staff levels and timescales for software development projects will progress in several different areas during the next 5–10 years:

(1) improved parametric models of the development process and understanding of the circumstances under which they can be used;

(2) greater use of code-size estimates based on the functionality to be provided, rather than measures such as lines-of-code or complexity; automatic measurement of these values from design and coding tools; and improved techniques for their estimation prior to the availability of a detailed product description;

(3) improved monitoring of project progress so that trends can be detected and deviations from the plans analysed; and research into estimation techniques suited to projects where a design-to-cost or incremental approach to development is being used;

(4) provision of estimation tools that allow great flexibility in the expression of parametric models and other calculations by the use of an Estimation Modelling Language Interpreter, EML–I (which allows such models to be expressed as a simple high-level language);

(5) development of knowledge-based techniques for supporting estimations of cost by (a) analogy with sections of previous projects (a top-down product-oriented approach), and (b) analogy with previous tasks (a bottom-up project-oriented approach).

This paper summarises the progress being made in metrics and parametric models, but concentrates on the last two of the above five issues and the implementation of future estimation tools, using the experience gained from the Integrated Management Process Workbench project—a project partially funded by the Commission of the European Communities ESPRIT Programme, as project number 938.

1. BACKGROUND

When reviewing the role of cost-estimation within the management of software projects it is important to recognise that the ability to estimate accurately is an acquired skill. A good estimator has at his or her hands a variety of techniques, some of which are based on statistics and others on behavioural studies and still others which are based on intuition. There is no simple technique or tool that can be learnt in a classroom and then applied with a high level of accuracy to fulfil all managers' needs in all situations.

The last decade has seen an increasing use of parametric models to help with the estimation of costs,[5,6] but these have generally been used to supplement, rather than replace, the traditional analogy-based methods of estimation. The approach to estimation we will describe in this paper combines parametric models and analogy estimates. These techniques can be extended to make effective use of a project histories database, a modelling interpreter, an expert system, and an icon-driven user interface.

Such a new generation of estimation tool differs from the current generation in two fundamental aspects:

—it aims to support and enhance the current working practices of each development centre and the project managers within them;
—it is closely integrated with other tools to provide support for a wide range of the managers' needs.

This paper covers future trends under three headings:

—discussion of improved metrics and parametric modelling techniques;
—description of an interpreter suited for performing the calculations needed within parametric cost-estimation, and possibly also performing simple logic statements for more general use within estimation;

—outline of how estimation, by analogy with previous experience, can receive support by both conventional techniques and expert systems.

1.1 The use of cost-estimation

Cost-estimation within the software development process enables us to identify:

—how much a project is likely to cost (both in terms of staff—months and money);
—both how long and how many people it will need to develop;
—the relative proportions of effort spent on each activity (types of work, such as coding or quality assurance) and phase (period of work in the life-cycle, such as coding and then integration);
—an indication of the potential risk: 'this project might cost as much as three times the forecast value'.

The term 'cost-estimation' is used to describe the set of procedures that produce this information.

Cost-estimation is not a single task performed once by the managers of software development, but a continuing process whose nature changes throughout the development process:

—providing initial estimates of cost and risk for the project proposal;
—monitoring the progress of development, so that the impact of milestone slips can be evaluated;
—analysing the completed project, both to evaluate apparent changes in productivity and to provide information for other software development projects.

1.2 Description of estimating methods

For convenience, the cost-estimation techniques can be grouped into 2 types

—top-down estimation: where the effort is estimated for the entire product development and then proportioned between the separate development activities;
—bottom-up estimation: where the effort for each task within the project is estimated, and then summed to derive a total estimate of effort.

Within this grouping there are two main approaches to estimation:

(1) Analogy: For top-down estimation this involves comparing each major module or the entire product with previous similar developments and considering the differences in order to guesstimate the cost and risk; for bottom-up analogy, performed during the planning phase, the project is broken down into a number of discrete tasks, and the effort and risk for each of these is guesstimated by comparison with previous similar tasks.

(2) Parametric forecasts: If it is possible to guesstimate the final size of the modules (either as lines-of-code or in terms of program functionality such as function points,[1,9] together with such characteristics as its complexity, then it may be possible to use 'models' like COCOMO,[3] SLIM,[16] or COPMO,[5] to forecast the project cost and timescales; once the size of the programs in the system can be measured (such as during the design stage for function-point metrics) the effective predictive accuracy improves significantly; a top-down parametric forecast involves estimating the total cost of a product development and then subdividing it between activities, while a bottom-up estimation involves using a separate parametric calculation for each project task to be performed.

Each of these is independent of the others, so it is possible to use two or more methods and compare the results—if such estimates are not similar then it is necessary to work out why this is the case.

The monitoring of progress during the development will often reveal a difference between the actual and original estimates. Often the project details (and especially the amount of functionality required) will have changed since the original estimate; only after re-estimating the cost and timescales will it be possible to see whether the difference between real and observed cost is significantly outside the statistically likely range. There is then the question of whether *either* there has been a change in productivity (which might be used to adjust the estimates for the remaining work), *or* there are special circumstances that may have a different effect on the remaining development (such as an improved design which could increase development costs but potentially decrease testing, integration and maintenance costs).

1.3 Using knowledge-based techniques in estimation

Handling milestone slips and gains provides an example of how knowledge-based techniques can be used for cost-estimation purposes.

Firstly, consider the information that the estimation tool can use:

—initial data provided during the project proposal and planning phases, but which may no longer be accurate;
—recorded progress data;
—information held in other parts of a manager's workbench, such as records of quality metrics.

If necessary, these can be supplemented with requests for further information from the project manager.

Secondly, consider an estimation tool provided with a set of rules so that, when considering estimation errors, it uses this knowledge to deduce one of several different reasons that may have caused the slip and thus recommend (or perform) a particular calculation to improve the estimate. Ideally, the development centre could amend the rules supplied with the estimation tool so that specific local aspects can be considered.

Example 'rule':

> Assuming that if the design documents were thoroughly inspected, then design costs could have increased by 10% but testing and validation costs would drop by 20%.

2. CHARACTERISTICS OF PARAMETRIC MODELS

This section outlines the background of parametric models of software development cost, and briefly considers possible future trends.

2.1 Single-variable models

A number of simple cost-models were produced in the 1960s, 1970s and early 1980s which relied on a single variable (typically code-size) and which would adjust their initial estimate up or down to compensate for special factors, such as complexity, quality constraints, computer facilities available and staff ability.

Sometimes these models would add in these compensatory factors (such as in the Nelson[13] model which adds up to 9·15 staff-months for lack of requirements) and sometimes they would adjust the cost by a proportion (such as in the Walston–Felix[19] model which adds 29% for an unstable interface complexity). Likewise, sometimes the code-size would be assumed to be proportional to the effort, while at other times it would be assumed to change exponentially. It is thus possible to express most of these models in a general form such as:

$$\text{Effort} = \text{BrcryOverheads} + \\ \text{GlobalFactors} + \\ (\text{BiasFactors} \times \text{ProductivityFactor} \times \text{CodeSize}^{\text{ExpFactor}})$$

where

BiasFactors = Factor-1 × Factor-2 × etc.
GlobalFactors = Factor-A + Factor-B + Factor-C + etc
BrcryOverheads, ProductivityFactor and ExpFactor are
　　constants for a given development environment

2.2　The COCOMO model

The most well known of these is the COCOMO model, which is covered in considerable detail in Boehm,[3] and has since been tried by numerous organisations—although not always with complete success (e.g. Ref. 12). Like most models, it needs recalibrating for each new development centre, and is often adjusted to use a different set of attributes.

The COCOMO model exists in different forms, according to its context. For the intermediate model used in an 'organic' (or free-standing) environment and a product of about 32 000 lines of code, the basic equations would be:

$$\text{TotalEffort} = 3 \cdot 2\ \text{CostDrivers} \times (\text{Newness} \times \text{EffectiveCodeSize})^{1 \cdot 05}$$
$$\text{TotalTime} = 2 \cdot 5\ \text{TotalEffort}^{0 \cdot 38}$$

where the size of code is measured in lines of source-
　　code, excluding blank and comment-only lines; and
　　time and effort are measured in months.

Although this is combined with other calculations:

$$\text{Newness} = (0 \cdot 4\ \text{PercentNewDesign} \\ + 0 \cdot 3\ \text{PercentNewCode} \\ + 0 \cdot 3\ \text{PercentNeedingIntegration})/100$$

$$\text{CostDrivers} = \text{RELY} \times \text{DATA} \times \text{CMPLX} \\ \times \text{TIME} \times \text{STOR} \times \text{VIRT} \times \text{TURN} \\ \times \text{ACAP} \times \text{AEXP} \times \text{PCAP} \times \text{VEXP} \times \text{LEXP} \\ \times \text{MODP} \times \text{TOOL} \times \text{SCHED}$$

(Each of which are cost-driver factors, given by a set of standard values according to well defined criteria).

StaffLevels = TotalEffort/TotalTime

ProductDesignEffort   = 0·16 TotalEffort
DetailedDesignEffort = 0·25 TotalEffort
Code&TestEffort   = 0·40 TotalEffort
IntegrationEffort   = 0·19 TotalEffort

ProductDesignTime   = 0·11 TotalTime
DetDesign&Code&TestTime = 0·59 TotalTime
IntegrationTime   = 0·22 TotalTime

2.3 SLIM
The SLIM cost model precedes COCOMO.[15,16] Precise details of SLIM are proprietary, existing within a software estimation tool, but it appears to be based on the equation:

$$CodeSize = TechConst \times ProductLifeCycle^{1/3} \times DevTime^{4/3}$$

where the TechConst is a 'technology constant'
that depends on a variety of attributes
of the development

The SLIM model is based on the assumption that project staffing levels fit a predefined pattern (the Rayleigh curve). It is obviously important to determine whether this assumption is justified for a particular environment before spending significant amounts of money on the SLIM tool.

A variation on this type of model was used by Jeffery[11] in studying productivity within commercial environments, using both third and fourth generation languages. He found that within these environments it was possible to simplify the SLIM type of model.

2.4 The Bailey and Basili Meta Model
A variation on models such as COCOMO and SLIM was proposed by Bailey and Basili.[2] Their 'Meta Model' is a set of techniques that can be used for constructing new models to suit a particular development environment.

The approach is to first identify the main equation, such as

$$TotalEffort = constA \times CodeSize^{constB}$$

This can be done by trying a variety of such equations to see which gives the best results.

The second stage is to identify collected attribute factors that might effect costs. These are included one at a time into the equation and calibrated to give the best results, such as:

$$\text{TotalEffort} = \text{ComplexityFactor} \times \text{ProductivityConstant}$$
$$\times \text{CodeSize}^{\text{ExpConst}}$$

In some cases it will be found that a proposed attribute does not improve the accuracy of the model, and in these cases the attributes can be ignored. For a development environment that has limited product history records it may only be possible to calibrate a few such attributes.

A particular advantage of this approach is that it can make use of data that is already available, or can be collected easily.

The Meta Model approach tends to call into question the universal validity of a model such as COCOMO which uses 15 general attributes and three further attributes to describe code porting.

2.5 The COPMO model

The more recent COPMO Model[5] changes the basic equations for effort and development time to the general form of:

$$\text{TotalEffort} = \text{constA} \times \text{CodeSize} + \text{constB} \times \text{StaffLevels}^{1.5}$$

The model provides methods of estimating values of *constA* and *constB* based on attributes taken from models such as COCOMO.

There are aspects of COPMO of particular interest:

(1) It regards costs as increasing exponentially with staff levels, rather than code-size
(2) This form of equation is particularly useful when the number of staff available for a project is known.
(3) There is some evidence, offered by Conte *et al.*,[5] that it may offer a significant improvement in accuracy compared with models such as COCOMO, and apply to a wider range of environments.

Work in this area of improving cost models is continuing, and in the next few years other forms of cost-model may occur—the increasing availability of recorded project data making it easier to experiment with new ideas.

2.6 Function metrics

An area of major interest within the estimation field has been the use of metrics of program functionality, rather than lines-of-code, for use in models to estimate effort.

The advantage of function-based metrics is that they can be counted during the design stage and can potentially be estimated reasonably accurately from a specification or detailed requirements document. They can potentially even be collected by semi-automated design aids.[18]

Function metrics help to avoid possibly the biggest problem with parametric cost-estimation: not the accuracy of the models themselves, but the accuracy of the data that they use.

The most widely known metrics of functionality are:

—the function-points of Albrecht;[1]
—the System Bang of DeMarco;[8]
—natural measures of functionality, such as the number of classes and methods that are defined and reused within object-orientated programming.[7]

Discussions with industrial contacts and management consultants suggest that the use of function points is becoming widespread in some types of application; however, extremely little is being published giving the results of this type of metric.

2.7 Incremental development

Another area of potential interest is the production of software in small increments, such as the design-to-cost approach of Quinnan.[17] This can supposedly lead to improved usability of designs and lower development costs resulting from smaller products.[4]

When a product is developed in relatively small increments, there is the potential for monitoring progress in the earlier increments and using this to forecast progress in the future increments. Such a forecast could be produced by recalibrating an existing cost model based in part on the observed results. Modelling for this type of forecasting is likely to receive a lot more attention in future years.

2.8 Quality monitoring and forecasting

Closer links are likely to occur between quality monitoring and cost-estimation. For instance, there is an increased use of matching fault-detection rates to an expected pattern for that type of development to see whether an unexpectedly high level is accounted (possibly due to low quality), or a low level (possibly due to insufficient testing).

Potentially, there may also be increasingly close links between forecasts of reliability and the cost of maintaining the product.

2.9 Improved estimation of attributes

Many of the attributes used in cost-estimation could be better defined so there is less room for ambiguity. Progress in this area, and especially in the areas of defining code complexity and quality attributes, is expected to be made in future years.

How to define the experience and abilities of staff with reference to a given project will become a more contentious issue with the development of workbenches that provide staff allocation; many of these will have information about individuals which could potentially be converted into numerical values corresponding to observed experience and ability. but how accurately can this be achieved? Is it politically acceptable in an organisation? And how do you handle the 'I can't work with *him*' syndrome?

Finally, there is the problem of the moving goal-posts: for many developments the requirements definition is not stable. The number of functions required tends to increase during the development project, and often quality objectives and other resources may change from those originally expected. A simple estimating approach to this problem has been to make statements like 'add $nn \cdot nn\%$ for unstable requirements' but this may not be sufficiently accurate in some situations. This is particularly important with estimates of functionality, such as function-points, where the initial designs may be found to exclude a variety of functions that will be defined later. Work should be done in modelling these changing levels of attributes, even if such models need to make extensive use of production rules rather than statistical techniques.

3. ESTIMATION MODELLING LANGUAGE

In performing parametric cost-estimation, the models have tended to be manipulated *either* by using a spreadsheet, such as with the Pena-1985 LOCOMO implementation of COCOMO using Lotus-123; this type of approach allows easy adjustment of models but provides little support (such as help) and enforces little control of data-collection and estimation methods between projects; *or* with a cost-estimation tool, such as SLIM,[15,16] using one or more fixed models with a variety of supporting information and control mechanisms, and occasionally with limited access to a database of previous projects.

It is proposed that there is now a need for a new type of estimation tool that combines the merits of the traditional algorithmic tool (controllability, supporting information and records of previous projects) with the flexibility of the spreadsheet. Within the IMP Workbench this is being achieved by producing an Estimation Modelling Language which can be read by an interpreter (EML–I, pronounced 'emmil eye') that has access to the workbench database. It is thus possible to state calculations such as:

TOT_EFFORT = 2·5 * CODE_SIZE * * 1·05;
@ where " * * " means raise to the power
TOT_TIME = 2·4 * TOT_EFFORT * * 0·34;
AV_STAFF = TOT_EFFORT/TOT_TIME;

These calculations can be easily changed using editing facilities, to tailor them to local and changing needs. It helps if the EML–I uses a simple syntax for names and commands, and allows blank lines and comments (such as following the '@' in the above example).

The EML–I used within the IMP Workbench is unusual in that it is a portable module which can also be built into other systems that provide access to project data; EML-I makes calls to the database to retrieve project data, and then requests changes following completion of its calculations. All that is needed is a small amount of code to interface the database and user-interface to a set of potentially standard and simple calls for the EML–I.

3.1 EML–I user-interface

No user-interface need be provided by an EML–I: it could merely perform calculations on specified files or data-strings upon request, and then return a response indicating the success or otherwise of the database access and command validity. However, messages can be embedded within the file, such as with:

IF (TOT_EFFORT < 4) @ 4 staff-months
    WARN(" * * The calculation will be inaccurate",
        "for such a small product.");

Depending on the EML–I implementation, these messages would either be sent straight to the screen or concatenated and returned to the caller as a string in a format ready for display on the screen. If run-time errors occur, then standard error messages are returned. This allows the calling system considerable control.

In simplified form, a call to run an EML–I calculation would be in the form:

```
EML_INTERPRET_FLOAT
    filename          @ gives name of file containing commands
    trace             @ = YES if tracing required
    update            @ = YES if updates to data-store permitted
  * return_float      @ returns floating number from calculation
  * return_msg        @ returns message (and error) string
  * response          @ returns result-code, or zero for success
```

The command sequences themselves can exist as files (which could be amended by anyone) or as large data-strings supplied by the caller. Likewise methods might be included for returning strings or integers instead of the floating-point numbers in the above example.

Within the EML–I a variety of features can be provided, including trace-files (to show what calculations have been performed, or what changes have been made to the database), and self-test routines (to ensure that it has been properly configured).

3.2 EML–I interface with data store

The EML–I would present a view of the data store schema that can be, as in the case of IMPW, a simplification to ensure that only information relevant to cost-estimation is available. It could also allow different names to be assigned to the database entities, so that they are more understandable to project managers and technical staff and so that production of foreign language variants is easier.

The facilities for defining the scheme with which the EML–I sees the data store can allow easy alterations and additions, although this is a facility that would be used only by the system builder and not by the project manager who might use the estimation package.

Facilities available within the modelling language include a variety of data types (floating-point numbers, integers, strings, and freely definable enumerated ranges) and of data collections (freestanding variables, lists and hierarchic trees). All values that are calculated by the EML–I could be validated before being returned to the data store to ensure that they are within the range permitted for that variable (defined within the EML–I subschema). The EML–I can also provide a wide range of manipulation facilities (such as to sum all values in a list), standard arithmetic functions (such as logarithms and statistical actions), and sequence control functions (such as IF and GOTO).

The EML–I must provide a method of defining temporary data variables used within the calculations and lost as soon as the calculation is complete. For instance:

```
NEW_DATA($my_temp_int,    @ name of temporary variable
        int,              @ variable type is integer
        0-10000,          @ range of permitted values
        4);               @ exists as a list of 4 integers
```

It is helpful to differentiate between the names of temporary variables and database variables, such as by using the $-sign prefix in the above example.

The call to an EML–I can even specify that no database updates be performed, so that only the values of temporary variables are changed and all results must be output as messages. Thus it is possible to define a system where the EML–I is included within a system, both to perform predefined calculations and to allow a manager or technical person to perform statistical analysis.

3.3 Other domains

An Estimation Modelling Language need not, despite its name, be confined to the role of cost-estimation. It can be extended to provide an easy-to-use language for handling risk analysis, financial modelling and statistical analysis.

There is potentially another use for the EML–I; any tool using it can perform all database accesses via the EML–I; rather than directly. A restriction is that the EML–I must have facilities for returning one or more values to its caller, such as the instruction 'RETURN' in the example below. A tool using this approach is easier to port to new environments.

```
@ (1) Retrieve value TOT_EFFORT from data-store,
@      achieved by a 1-line command-string
@      passed to the interpreter
RETURN(TOT_EFFORT);
```

@ (2) Pass string to EML–I to update data-store
@   with new value of 2·35 for TOT_EFFORT;
@   achieved by 1-line string
@   passed to the interpreter
TOT_EFFORT = 2·35;

3.4 Multiple simple calculations

A system using an EML–I need not use it with merely a single command-file containing the complete cost-estimation calculation of effort, costs, timescales, staff levels and risk. It can adopt the approach of the IMP Workbench of using many small calculations. This allows a modular approach to be used, for instance switching the main *effort = funct(code_size)* formula to a simpler format when certain conditions arise. It is also much easier to maintain small command-files, with the implications of change being easier to understand and document.

A good EML-I provides efficient calculations to perform on command sequences that often consist of a single simple instruction:

MONEY_COST = TOT_EFFORT * 4000;
@ pounds sterling per month

A further EML–I facility is to allow calls to other EML–I command-files, and allow them to return a value, such as with a 'Perform' command:

@ For calculation held as a disc-file
TOT_EFFORT = PERFORM_FILE (/usr2/mylib/emli/SmallOne);

@ For calculation held as a data-string "SmallProdPtr"
TOT_EFFORT = PERFORM_STR (SmallProdPtr);

It is obviously important for there to be a method of stopping the EML-I when a calculation is taking so long that it appears to be permanently recurring, or looping.

3.5 Help text

It is possible to supplement EML–I command-files with a standard display of help information—for instance, following the end of the calculation, as for:

MONEY_COST = TOT_EFFORT * 4000;
@ where TOT_EFFORT is in staff-months
STOP;

This calculation converts the predicted total
effort for the project into an equivalent financial
forecast. It assumes that a typical development
person costs £48,000 per year, including a
proportion of corporate overheads and use of
computer resources.

In this example a special call to the EML–I could, instead of
performing the calculation, retrieve the above help text and either
display it or return it as a string ready for further processing.

3.6 The implication of changes

EML–I command-files can be easily changed, and new calculations
can be easily defined—it is now important to be sure that the full
implications of making changes to the command-files is apparent.

To this end, recommended procedures for describing each
command-file, and the data it uses, must be available. If the final user
can amend the values, then the information must be available to him
or her, together with instructions of how to maintain the records.

There may come a future generation of EML–Is that provide
computer-based help in the definition and amendment of command-
files—in particular, help-texts and possibly expert-system support, so
that project managers or their technical assistants can set up and
modify cost-models without the need for expensive support from
management consultants.

3.7 Use of knowledge

An EML–I can be used in conjunction with an expert system. For
example, the tool can store knowledge concerning cost-estimation,
such as:

— knowledge about which EML–I calculation can perform in which
  context;
— advice on incompatibilities, such as when two data values used in
  an EML–I calculation appear to contradict each other;
— advice on risk, where a comment is made when the available data
  and observed project details are likely to be relatively risk-free or
  risk-prone;
— representation of local standard methods of working as help-
  screens coupled with rules governing which standard applies in
  which situation;

—knowledge about attribute values used in cost-models, such as the inter-dependence of attributes with known project details;

—information on how much more information to acquire from the manager, and how much more effort it is worth the manager expending on the cost-estimation process (the increase in accuracy gained for an hour's work generally dropping as the various estimation processes continue).

A potential extension to the EML–I concept would be to include facilities to make it a simple expert-system shell, suited to the needs of cost-estimation. This would allow easy access to the database and intermixing of the deductions with calculations and messaging.

A first step in this direction would be to allow handling of complicated conditionals; there is then no need to use reasoning for knowledge which can be expressed as a large, easily amended conditional within an EML–I command-file. A second step would be to allow definition of knowledge in an easily edited form of production rule, which could be stored separately and accessed when required by an inference engine (such as that provided by Prolog or LISP interpreters).

4. ANALOGY

Estimation by analogy involves comparing what is being proposed with what happened on a previous occasion.

Comparison by analogy ranges from (at one extreme) a systematic point-by-point comparison with one or more specific developments, to (at the other extreme) a 'gut feeling' condensed from an individual's experience and understanding of the work involved. Both extremes, and all points between them, need to be supported by the cost-estimation tool.

There are two general types of analogy-based estimation: a top-down view of the total effort needed to produce each major module of the product, and a bottom-up view of the effort needed for each of the many tasks within the development project. Thus top-down estimation takes a product-view and bottom-up estimation takes a project-view. The top-down estimate can usually be done fairly early in the development cycle, but the bottom-up will only be possible following task decomposition (work breakdown). Comparison of the two estimates is often performed by the project manager; if the results are significantly different, then *both* estimates should be examined to see which assumptions may be invalid.

An immediately apparent advantage of estimation by analogy is that it allows a rough cost-estimate to be obtained when all that is available is a list of 'desirements' rather than a specific set of requirements. Naturally, estimates produced under such circumstances may produce results that are completely misleading.

A more subtle advantage of such analogies is in planning contingency for a development—the project manager typically being required to specify when the task is expected to finish, both if all things go as planned and also if an unexpected number of things go wrong. The difficulty of knowing how much contingency to allow is considerable: typically a project manager can answer a question such as 'what is the probability of the task effort being 50% more than expected?' even less accurately than he or she estimated the original value of the effort. However, if two or more estimates are made using analogy with previous projects, then it is possible to set a cost contingency based on *both* the recorded cases of problems that happened in previous situations *and* the preferences of the project manager of how to consider contingency (thus letting him express risk in a manner that seems natural to him).

4.1 Top-down (global) view of each module
To carry out this process we need to:

—understand the proposed product and hence carry out an initial decomposition;
—perform initial estimates by a combination of systematic comparisons and intuitive guesstimates;
—compare estimates from different people, and estimates representing different scenarios (such as best-case, most-likely and worse-possible estimate), and allow these to be revised;
—be able to rearrange project characteristics so as to meet constraints and achieve objectives as closely as possible.

Each of these is discussed below, together with the potential for support from future generations of estimation tools.

The best time to perform this first estimate of costs is early in the project, and preferably during the feasibility study and before undue external or self-imposed pressure is applied to reduce costs. It will need to be performed after the initial study has identified the major product components. Once estimates have been made and effort has been expended, it is difficult not to introduce bias into further estimates in an attempt to reach objectives and maintain constraints.

In many cases these estimates of effort will be for development time, including detailed design, coding, unit testing and initial testing; they will exclude global designs, integration, validation, user-manual production, quality assurance and management activities, all of which may add substantially to costs.

4.1.1 Understanding of proposed product

As part of the tendering or project-proposal phase of development, work may be needed to form initial ideas of the kind of functionality that the product must provide, and the general nature of how it would work. This activity is conducted by some combination of the customer (or his representative) and the producer. For the development environment, part of this task would involve breaking the product down into a number of modules; normally each module would have characteristics similar to the ones produced for previous projects.

This is an important preliminary to the estimation of costs, since it is easier to estimate costs for a well-defined product. A new-generation cost-estimation tool would expect the workbench in which it is built to provide support in a number of areas:

—recording a short description of each proposed module;
—validating information about each module to identify possible inconsistencies;
—recording any dependencies on people or projects;
—recording any known aspects of risk;
—recording assumptions;
—providing a facility for viewing a list of all sections of the product, arranged in an order that suits the nature of the development, and then inspecting details of any specific section and comparing it visually with any information currently displayed on the screen or on printed output.

4.1.2 Systematic estimation

Systematic top-down analogy identifies the major modules of the product and then looks for previous product developments that seem similar. These will often be projects about which the manager and the development staff have personal experience. The important things to try and achieve are:

— that the overall size and purpose of the previous product are roughly similar to those of the proposed new one;
— that the overall method of working (and the corporate style of management) in the previous project is roughly similar to that of the new project;
— that there are either very detailed records about the work, or people available who remember it accurately.

Automated support for finding similar previous developments can be produced in a number of ways:

— a browsing facility, allowing the manager to look through a project database;
— a filter mechanisn, where the manager specifies a permitted range of size and attribute values;
— a best-match mechanism, where the manager makes a rough estimate of the attributes of the new product, and a search mechanism listing those projects whose attributes are closest to those chosen by the manager according to some pre-defined algorithm; the manager then selects the more suitable projects from this list;
— a knowledge-based best-match mechanism, where the best match is performed by a combination of statistical algorithms (that can be changed by the manager) and specific rules (some of which may be common to all developments while others constitute local standards or customs).

There will be times when there appear to be no similar projects with which to compare. In such cases it could be worth asking:

— can the product description be broken down into smaller modules with which there are analogies? (For instance, a module in the new product might consist of a file-server interlinked with an archiving routine—in this case, a record from previous projects may exist for the effort of producing a file-server, and a separate record may exist for a utility similar to an archiver);
— are the comparisons being made too rigidly; trying only to find previous products that were almost identical? Have colleagues

been consulted in other development areas to see whether they
have tried similar projects?
—should there be plans to develop something in which there
appears to be limited local experience? (The conventional rule-of-
thumb is to push forward on only one major technological or
experience front at a time.)

4.1.3 Intuitive estimation

For the smaller and more routine projects it is inevitable that many of
the cost-estimates will be based on intuition (experience) rather than
the result of a systematic analysis. It is the role of the estimation tool
to support this so as to ensure the estimate is as accurate as possible. It
will later be necessary for the estimation tool to provide assistance
with optimisation, and for this certain numerical information to be
elicited during the current stage of the estimation process.

The recording of assumptions and verbal statements of dependencies and risk should be supported by the workbench that includes
the estimation tool. The nature of such information will often be
unsuitable for further processing.

The techniques used in systematic estimation could also be used at
this stage. For instance, help-texts could be made available on request,
being chosen according to:

—characteristics of the module, and other background information;
—precedent: giving preference to those aspects that appear to be of
the greatest concern;
—special knowledge represented as expert-system rules about local
needs and the characteristics of this project.

The estimates for some modules might benefit from a more
systematic analysis, despite individual preferences for using intuition.
Sections where the cost is relatively high, or the risks appear great,
would be such cases. If an EML–I is in use, then command-files can be
easily written to recognise these and give a suitably worded warning.
Use of simple conditions in an EML–I could be used, but greater
versatility could be offered if production rules could be defined and
handled by an inference engine. .

A specific problem is how to handle cost overheads (such as for
management and quality control) and general factors excluded from
the estimate. These are likely to be done differently in each environment. One approach is to write a simple algorithm for the calculation

and allow the EML–I to perform the calculation. A much bigger problem is how to ensure that the numbers used within such a calculation are valid: to say that design, coding and testing cost 65% of total costs could cause a significant estimation error if that value was inaccurate.

4.1.4 *Examination of assumptions*
Initial estimates of the cost of a module will have been made using a number of assumptions. There would seem to be several ways in which computer-based support could be offered:

—helping people to record their assumptions and then keep track of them; highlight the greatest assumptions, and provide lists of those assumptions that remain;

—ensuring that any information available from other sources that may be relevant to the assumptions can be accessed;

—provision of a query session to help people explore assumptions, using a checklist of queries that can be modified by expert-system rules.

At this stage of the development, there is, typically, little numerical data available.

4.1.5 *Comparison of estimates from different people*
There may be a large number of different estimates for each section of work. These may come from different people, or as a result of altered assumptions. There must be facilities for adding, editing, checking and removing such estimates. The underlying assumptions should be recorded.

Whether or not it is sensible to record more than a small number of estimates within an estimation tool would depend on the potential value of such information. The various facilities for examining estimates are a major advantage, yet may achieve little since almost the same thing could be done on a spread-sheet. The potential advantages of a computer-assisted comparison come with such features as:

—very easy access to information relating to each estimate;

—improved accuracy of that information, compared with paper records;

—availability of psychology-based techniques for helping the project manager select between the estimates;

—statistical (and potentially rule-based) advice on the differences: (a) between any two estimates, and (b) between any one estimate and the overall average;

—facilities for a controlled Delphi-technique approach to estimation (where estimators work independently and are informed of their error compared to the mean, and asked to revise their own estimate) despite the apparent problems with the technique expressed by Eilon.[10]

4.1.6 Optimisation of estimations

Certain types of optimisation could potentially be automated within an estimation tool, provided sufficient data is held about each task. For instance, if the total calendar time for the development is too great, the operation of increasing staff levels for tasks could be partly performed automatically, provided information was available for each task about how increasing staff levels would affect its cost.

Such changes could be performed by a combination of statistical methods and standard rules: this potentially allows a range of different types of change to be made. Combining an EML and an expert-system shell could achieve this, and would make it relatively easy to add new types of optimisation and change existing ones.

Should this operation be automated, various (other) practical aspects might be considered, such as:

—improved monitoring of the objectives and constraints for the project, and rationalising them with the above processes;

—listing of items that might still be considered;

—warnings of the effect of making certain changes (potentially using an expert system).

4.2 Bottom-up estimation by analogy

As part of the planning exercise it is normal to breakdown the project development into a number of separate tasks. Within the IMPW workbench this will be done by a work-breakdown and network-editor tool.

Bottom-up cost-estimating involves assigning an estimate of effort to each of these tasks, and then summing them to produce a total.

Where analogy methods are used, these estimates are arrived at in the following way:

—how much effort did it take for an identical task last time according to project records?

—how long do the people concerned think it will take?

The opportunities for providing computer-based support for this activity are:

—providing an 'electronic black book', in the form of a list of tasks that take a known amount of time; the details relevant to each such standard task would include a description, a value for the typical amount of effort involved, an indication of the optimum number of people and the effect of increasing that level, and an indication of the variability (risk) of that task. The records in this 'electronic black book' would need to be arranged in a fashion that allows easy perusing;
—providing easy access to records of tasks from previous projects. As with top-down analogy, a variety of strategies could be applied, including browsing, filtering, best-fit and knowledge-based techniques;
—ability to input an estimate based on intuition or informed experience;
—facilities for indicating the validity of a task estimate; unfortunately, the information available at the task level is usually so little that such checking would merely be reimplementing the above facilities of comparing the task with other records; however, it may be possible to express some general and local knowledge as a set of adjustable rules that prompt the end-user with advice.

5. THE WAY AHEAD

There have been a large number of possible changes outlined in this document, and it is doubtful that the research resources have been allocated to perform all this work. However, in certain areas it does seem reasonably certain that progress will be made:

—the metrics used within parametric models will be increasingly accurately defined, and some (like function points) will be available early in the development cycle; increasing use of data libraries will be made to record project records suitable for further analysis;
—new parametric models and methods will be developed, giving greater accuracy (measured retrospectively on a project);
—managers' workbenches will become available that will make

sophisticated use of estimation methods, incorporating Estimation Modelling Language Interpreters, expert-system support for analogy-based estimation methods, and improved use of progress monitoring.

It should become increasingly possible to monitor and control software projects with greater accuracy than is currently achieved. There should also be a growing number of development environments that can predict with sufficient accuracy the cost and necessary planning contingency they need. The greatest remaining problem could be the difficulty in predicting cost and risk for projects for which there is no previous similar experience, such as in some aspects of the aerospace industry; this should be improved by the techniques described in this paper, but it will not be resolved.

REFERENCES

1. Albrecht, A. J. (1979), Measuring application development productivity, *Proc. Joint SHARE/GUIDE/IBM Application Development Symposium*, Guide Int. Corp., Chicago, USA.
2. Bailey, J. W. and Basili, V. R. (1981), A Meta-Model for software development resource expenditures, *Proc. 5th Int. Conf. on Software Engineering*, IEEE/ACM/NBS, March, 107–16.
3. Boehm B. W. (1981), *Software engineering economics*, Prentice-Hall, New Jersey, USA.
4. Boehm B. W., Gray, T. E. and Seewaldt, T. (1984), Prototyping versus specifying: a multiproject experiment, *IEEE Trans. on Software Engineering*, May.
5. Conte, S. D., Dunsmore, D. E. and Shen, V. Y. (1986), *Software Engineering Metrics and Models*, Benjamin/Cummings Menlo Park, CA, USA, ISBN 0–8053–2162–4.
6. Cowderoy, A. J. C. and Jenkins, J. O. (1986), *State of the art survey for software cost-estimation*, Esprit P938 report W/P5 1a (Issue 3), Dept. of Management Science, Imperial College, London.
7. Cox, B. J. (1986), *Object orientated programming—an evolutionary approach*, Addison–Wesley, ISBN 0–201–10393–1.
8. DeMarco, T. (1982), *Controlling software projects: management measurement and estimation*, Yourdon, New York.
9. Drummond, S. (1985), Measuring applications development performance, *Datamation*, February.
10. Eilon, S. (1979), *Aspects of management*, 2nd edition, Pergamon, Oxford, U.K.
11. Jeffery, D. R. (1986), *A comparison of models describing third and fourth generation software development environments, with implications for*

effective management, PhD dissertion, Dept. of Information Systems, University of New South Wales, Australia.

12. Kitchenham, B. A. and Taylor, N. R. (1984), Software cost models, *ICL Tech. J.,* May.

13. Nelson, E. A. (1966), *Management handbook for the estimation of computer programming costs,* AD–A648750, Systems Development Corp., 31 October (reported in Boehm, 1981).

14. Pena, A. G., 1985 *MSc dissertion,* Imperial College School of Management, London.

15. Putnam, L. H. (1978), A general empirical solution to the macro software sizing and estimating problem, *IEEE Trans. Software Engineering,* July, 345–61.

16. Putnam, L. H. and Fitzsimmons, A. (1979), Estimating software costs, *Datamation,* September, 189–98, October, 171–8 and November 137–40.

17. Quinnan, R. E. (1980), The management of software engineering, Part V: Software engineering management practices, *IBM Systems J.* **19**(4), 466–77.

18. Verner, J. and Tate, G. (1986), A model for software sizing, *COCOMO/WICOMO Users' Group Meeting,* Wang Institute of Graduate Studies, Massachusetts, 29–30 May.

19. Walston, C. E. and Felix, C. P. (1977), A method of programming measurement and estimation, *IBM Systems J.,* **16**(1), 54–73.

APPENDIX: THE INTEGRATED MANAGEMENT PROCESS WORKBENCH

This workbench is being developed under a grant from the CEC's ESPRIT programme (Project P 938). It provides integrated planning of tasks, staff allocation, quality management and risk assessment, and also provides extensive monitoring facilities to enable the project manager to control a project. By using a database containing records of previous projects coupled to an inference engine, the workbench can provide decision support and expert system facilities to managers.

The workbench is unusual in that, instead of requiring the project manager's development environment to be changed to work in accordance with the workbench's own conceptions of the development process, IMPW allows for considerable adjustment of development models, quality standards, planning methods, resource estimation techniques, risk analysis methods and progress monitoring. It is aimed at projects that involve in the region of 15 staff-years of development effort.

Prime contractor: ICL, Westfields, West Avenue, Kidsgrove, Stoke-on-Trent, UK; tel: +44. 782–771000; telex: 22971. Contact person: Derek Creasy.

Partners: Imperial College School of Management, London, UK;
CETE Méditerranée, Aix-en-Provence, France;
Verilog SA, Toulouse, France;
National Institute for Higher Education, Dublin, Ireland.

4

Metrics in Procurement—a Discussion Paper

G. D. Frewin

Centre for Software Reliability, London, UK

ABSTRACT

This working paper is in response to the need to support software procurement in an area with a diversity of needs and environments. The approach taken has been to identify the stages of a generic software procurement cycle, and to explore the classes of metric appropriate to each stage. It is suggested that 'open metrics', customised by each user to reflect his specific procurement priorities, will provide the best possible assistance from a procurement support service.

1. INTRODUCTION

What is procurement? What are its particular problems? Where can metrication help—and if so, what kind of metrication should it be? These questions have been brought forward recently while considering the nature and procedures needed to enable planning and support for an extensive programme of evaluation and procurement of software support systems and support tools. Since there was an immediate need for a framework within which the activities and procedures could be planned, this discussion paper was prepared. This was not with the intention or expectation of being able to give authoritative answers, but as a contribution to the evolution of common understanding, and eventually to agreement on the main steps to be taken.

2. WHAT IS 'PROCUREMENT'?

Procurement is the obtaining of a desired item: since we are all concerned mainly with software and software-based systems, we shall think of our discussion as relating only to *software procurement*. There is no essential difference between obtaining software and obtaining anything else, but there are differences of degree, and of terminology, which might make the context important for ready and complete understanding.

Software can be loosely divided into that which is made in-house and that which is bought-in; and the 'bought-in' can be further divided into that which is bespoken from a supplier for a specific buyer and purpose and developed solely for that buyer, and that which has been made to be available for any buyer and, possibly, for a range of purposes. These divisions are neither precise nor comprehensive—and do not need to be: they serve to indicate that a procurer may need to be active in what are significantly different situations.

Complete items, ready for use, may be bought from various suppliers; bespoken items may be supplied by an external organisation or from within the procurer's own company. Also, the choice of supplier may be entirely open or closely constrained, and a received preference may not be a constraint but open to reasoned argument. An in-company supplier may be organisationally and/or geographically remote from the procurer or might even be the department in which the procurer and/or user is himself located. Similarly, there will be a range of possible relationships between the procurer and those who will use the item sought. For example, the 'procurement' of software may be:

—a separate and professional service for a whole organisation or for an identified area within an organisation;

—an independent consultancy or advisory service;

—associated with the Quality function (because of the testing and inspection of in-coming goods);

—an occasional function of the supplier of software services to users within a company;

—something which a software user does for himself, when he has a need.

For simplicity, we have recognised three divisions of procurement:

—bought-in, bespoken;
—bought-in, general purpose;
—in-house, bespoken.

These groupings are not enough to cover all the possibilities. There is, for example, the very interesting special case where the procuring body gives advice and trial facilities to an organisation which is preparing a new 'general-purpose' product, in exchange for influence on the nature of the product and the opportunity to obtain a highly desired product earlier and possibly cheaper than others in the market. There is also the case of picking up a partially developed product (or a product which is not a good fit with current requirements) and adjusting and completing it within the procuring body. However, the chosen divisions are sufficient to highlight similarities and differences in the processes and support required across most of the range of software procurement.

It is clear that there are frequently occurring factors in all procurement, no matter how large or small, if only because of common objectives—to *reduce* the risks of early failure or later regrets, and to *increase* the likelihood of ending up with:

—a suitable item,
—of appropriate qualities,
—of appropriate cost and value,
—at the required time.

Fortunately, there is sufficient commonality between all instances of procurement to make it possible that general approaches and means can be devised and recommended for local use, in the confidence that they will fit in with most particular needs, will be clearly helpful in most cases, and will not worsen any given case.

When there are common objectives, and recognisable common parts of processes, it is natural to begin to think in terms of a life-cycle as an 'organising principle'. Although a true lifecycle would always repeat exactly the same stages, in the same sequence, it seems to be the nature of all software-related activities that their 'lifecycles' actually repeat themselves in only a few aspects and with a degree of predictability which is short of complete certainty. Added to this, it is characteristic of procurement in general that much time is spent in recognising and overcoming unexpected deviations from the initially agreed process and requirements. However, although attempts to gain control over the software procurement process are necessarily complicated, they are not impossible: once a general model exists and has been validated, any elements apparently absent in a particular instance can be sought with some assurance that they are either there somewhere (though possibly obscured) or that their real absence is significant and signals the need for special care.

A general, high-level, procurement 'Life-cycle' is shown as Appendix A1 to the paper: its most interesting property is the way in which the three identified divisions of procurement can be seen to need their own patterns of support, while still following the same process. Appendix A2 shows the 'short form' of the wording of the life-cycle, and A3 lists some of the questions associated with each phase.

3. WHAT ARE THE BEST METRICS FOR PROCUREMENT AND EVALUATION?

The range of items which could need to be procured, and the tendency of every instance of procurement to throw up its own set of new and interesting problems, make this a difficult question to answer. Perhaps the most severe problem, and one which is being addressed by many people concerned with making and using software, is that of getting the best possible statement of requirements as a starting point for procurement or for development.

The procurer is often faced with deciding not what to do for the best, but what to do for the least risk or the least undesirable outcome. The situations on which he has to judge are rarely reliably predictable or closely constrained; therefore he cannot do anything other than make his decisions on whatever is the available mixture of quantitative (but possibly irrelevant or untrustworthy) 'facts' and the qualitative impressions of himself, the supplier, the user and other concerned parties. In this situation, he does not ask 'what can I measure?', but 'what are the key questions which both define the situation *and* whose answers indicate what I can best do about it?'.

Once the form of the questions is clear, then the range of answers and the necessary support for choosing between them also becomes clear: it is at this point that a 'good' scheme of metrics, or a single metric, can be sought. As every situation is highly specific (in its value and significance, if not in its elements) it is not unreasonable to expect that the supporting metrics will also tend to be specific, and that therefore the best person to define and apply them is the procurer/evaluator himself. Like personal computing, this may be the age of personal metrication!

Software metrication is still at the stage where its productions and processes are open to discussion—and need to be discussed, in order to clarify their implications and usefulness. A very simple split of types of metric is suggested here, principally to provide a compact means of reference within the discussion paper: if it is obviously unsuited to that purpose, or if it is likely to cause confusion beyond its context, then readers are asked to make this known and to help provide a more useful classification.

Classification of metrics

—*Simple*—Simple, or basic, measures. For example, counts of identified things such as LOC, reported faults or required functions.

—*Summary*—Summary decision support metrics. For example, a readability index, based on simple measures such as counts of syllables per word, words per sentence, sentences per paragraph, etc., all eventually combined into a single number intended to give a direct index of the degree of ease with which the text would be understood. A number of different summary metrics exist attached to the concept of complexity, and an example of an interlinked set of summary metrics is that proposed by the Software Science workers.

—*Open*—Open decision support metrics. For example, a list of contributory factors (which might be either or both of simple and summary in themselves) each with a measurement scale and a fixed criterion value, to be displayed with the measurements for the given case and its eventual weighted YES/NO result. (Note that this is effectively the 'design by objectives' format).

In Appendix A4, the short form of the procurement cycle is augmented with its relationship to the three modes of procurement, and with the forms of metric which seem best fitted to use in each of the combinations of phase and mode. Some surprise has been expressed at the comparatively low usage suggested for summary metrics, and for the almost universal use of open metrics. This is a result of a number of factors, which include the present state of availability of appropriate and reliable metrics of the simple and summary kinds, and the nature of the procurement process and its problems. The case for open metrics is argued further below for completeness sake, although for most practical purposes there does not seem to be any serious possibility of having adequate summary metrics available for some time to come.

Where a metrication scheme is meant for common use, it is perhaps best to concentrate on the simple and open metrics. Software has suffered for a long time from the lack of genuinely fundamental metrication, and software procurement shares the need for proven, accepted and genuine simple basic measures for the objects with which it is concerned. Unfortunately, for various reasons, there are far more summary than simple metrics reported, and too often these reports are without the contributory reasoning, analysis, experimentation, examples, scoping, etc., necessary to make them usable in practical situations.

With appropriate summary metrics hard to find, we are left with the open and simple types. Given the range of kinds of procurement, and different motivations and requirements for product evaluation, plus the shifting ground throughout most procurement exercises and the frequent need for rapid and largely intuitive decision making by the procurer, we need a range of metrics by which aspects can be described, and discriminated between, both quantitatively and qualitatively. Available simple metrics are rarely powerful enough to characterise the question areas adequately. Thus there appears to be a real need in procurement for the expressive and discriminatory power of open metrics, which are easily understood, are highly adaptable, and can be quickly constructed (and sufficiently validated) to meet the needs of a current and local situation.

Is there any reason why open custom-built metrics are not more often used or, indeed, why they should not be used? There are two major arguments against all custom-built metrics: one from those professionally concerned with metrics, and one from the (largely indifferent) public. The first group point out that there are problems of comparability and comprehension once away from the site of origin— and that there is a serious danger of losing the full information content of basic measures once one begins to combine them into a local second- or third-generation metric. There may also be some element, with these specialists, of trying to retain control over this interesting and expanding area. The second group, the software public at large, may be unaware of the potential strength and expressive power of a metric constructed for a specific purpose, or perhaps, while recognising the benefits, is either too shy or unwilling or unable to begin the process of constructing its own.

Leaving the experienced metricians to their own devices, and concentrating on the innocent potential user, there are counter-arguments to the specialists and points of support for the fearful, some of which are given below:

—Fear of loss of comparability. If available metrics meet the user's need (and are known to him) he will take them up with gratitude. If they do not meet his needs, they will not be used and the question of comparisons hardly arises.

—The possibility that the metrics will not be understood away from their point of origin. There are two main points here—if a metric is properly defined, there should be little problem in understanding it; and, if a local metric happens to spread, this will presumably be because it has the merit of being both useful and comprehensible.

—The actual difficulty in defining and proving local metrics—or fears that there will be such difficulties. A metric is a compact and precise form of communication: creating and using one is no more or less demanding than finding an appropriate form of words for a concept which needs to be used consistently. The fact that its creation and application is localised is greatly in its favour, since a certain degree of shared assumptions and experience will help others use it naturally and easily.

A simple generic format for a custom-built metric is given below in Appendix B, together with an example of a procurement question and a possible complementary open metric. Finally, in Appendix B3, there is a suggested kernel of the questions which should be asked when a metric (of whatever type, and from whatever source) is being considered for use. While these are not sufficient for a true beginner— or for the expert, who will recognise the format as being a cut-down version of more elaborate forms currently in use—they should give at least a flavour of the way in which custom-built metrics come about.

4. RECOMMENDATIONS

These are directed both to the author's local activities and to any prospective user of open metrics and the procurement cycle.

(a) Complete the list of questions/phase (Appendix A3).
(b) Recast the 'questions/phase' as phase review checklists.
(c) Propose metrics to support as many as possible of the checklist items.
(d) Extract the list of information required, and its sources.
(e) Propose, and (if approved) carry out, required proving exercises on the principal proposed metrics.
(f) Report on the cost and value of completing the exercise.
(g) Review the phase structure, checklists and metrics for their success in meeting local needs, documenting and implementing the outcomes as needed. In particular, assess whether the whole exercise has been worthwhile, whether it should be continued, and what changes and support are needed.

APPENDIX A: THE BASIC PROCUREMENT/EVALUATION CYCLE

A1

Within all procurement and product evaluation, a single high-level process/cycle can be observed which runs:

DEFINE REQUIREMENTS

Phase 1 Receive request (or discover need) for procurement/ evaluation to take place.

Phase 2 Collect, analyse, synthesise and prove detailed requirements on product. Create or cause to be created a detailed requirements document.

SELECT SUPPLIER OR EVALUATOR

Phase 3 Locate possible suppliers or evaluators.

Phase 4 Produce, or cause to be produced, a product specification, including details of all the required tests and test results whose outcomes will be used to characterise the item and to determine its acceptability.

Phase 5 Select supplier (or evaluation group).

Phase 6 Set up (or take part in) the making of the contract(s), including making and reviewing detailed process and control plans.

DEVELOP OR EVALUATE PRODUCT

Phase 7   Ensure (as far as possible) that the work is carried out expeditiously, visibly, in a suitable manner, and according to the spirit and letter of the contract.

Phase 8   Set up (or take part in) creation and management of release and acceptance (or evaluation and report) activities.

Phase 9   Handle (or help handle) any significant queries, changes, failures to perform as agreed (on both sides), and failures to meet requirements.

Phase 10   Ensure that customisation, hand-over, installation, training and support are performed as and when agreed, to the standards agreed.

Phase 11   Do, or have done, all that is needed to close the active part of the procurement or evaluation (for example, finalising financial matters, collecting and securing all relevant materials, changing smoothly from 'new installation' to regular support basis, finding suitable back-up facilities, setting up regular recording schemes by which quality and performance can be monitored in service use, etc.).

CONSIDER THE PROCESS JUST CONCLUDED

Phase 12   Characterise and consider the process so far: where has it worked well? where not as well as it could? where is there not enough evidence to show what was happening and what those unknown happenings could have caused, and been caused by?

Document the findings, and (if needed) set up new procedures and metrics for the next occasion.

PREPARE FOR THE NEXT INSTANCE

Phase 13   While waiting for the next trip round the cycle, continue to collect information and review metrics and procedures, in order to be ready to act when required.

A2: Short form of procurement cycle

Phase 1   Receive request.
Phase 2   Collect and analyse requirements.
Phase 3   Locate possible suppliers.
Phase 4   Product specification.

Phase 5   Select supplier.
Phase 6   Set up plans and contract(s).
Phase 7   Watch work closely.
Phase 8   Set up release and acceptance.
Phase 9   Handle queries, changes and failures.
Phase 10   Manage hand-over and installation.
Phase 11   Close active procurement.
Phase 12   Characterise and document.
Phase 13   Refine and review, till needed.

A3: The PROCUREMENT cycle (to Phase 5) plus implied questions

Phase 1   Receive request (or discover need) for procurement to take place.

Should this item be procured at all? Does it seem feasible? Is it really needed? Will the need still exist by the time the item can be procured? Is its procurement particularly liable to suffer from crises? Are the cost and value reasonably in line? Are there tight and important constraints? Are there foreseeable problems of finance, timing, interfacing, policy changes, requirement changes? Who supports it and who is against it? Might the political balance change and the procurement be cancelled or significantly altered?

Phase 2   Collect, analyse, synthesise and prove detailed requirements.

Are all the 'requirements' really needed? Can the 'need' be quantified and demonstrated? Are the requirements suitably expressed to allow their evaluation and communication? Are there too many for the size of the item, or its apparent value and/or assumed cost? Are the requirements mutually compatible? Are they feasible? What qualitites should the functions have? What qualities should the complete item have? Is the form and content of the requirements document suitable as the basis for a procurement exercise?

Phase 3   Locate possible suppliers.

What would make a supplier 'possible'? What 'impossible'? What would cast doubt, and how much? What information is available, and is it both appropriate and sufficiently accurate?

Phase 4   Select supplier.

On what grounds? What factors are most important? What factors are least important? What would make one suspect that there might be difficulties later on? How much weight should be put on suspicions? Are there additional safeguards which could protect against possible risks? Are there known risks, with predictable likelihood of happening? Where should the accept/not accept line be drawn? If you had to go back from the first choice to the list of possibles, how should they be re-assessed? Should the chosen supplier be made aware of any reservations? What should be done if the chosen supplier is unwilling? What should be done if no willing and able supplier is found?

Phase 5   Set up (or take part in) the making of the contract.

Is the plan and the price believable? Is it given in sufficient detail? If there is little detail, is there no detail to be given? What process has been used by the supplier in reaching his plan, and what development and control processes will he use? How much access to progress and quality records should be asked for? How should the response be interpreted? If the price is fixed, is it too high or too low? If it is too high, does this indicate avarice or incompetence? If it is too low, does it indicate desperation or incompetence? In either case, what should be done about it?

A4: Short form of procurement cycle

—in relation to the three modes of procurement (not including pure evaluation), and the three classes of metric.

Modes of procurement: Bought-in and bespoken (BB)
Bought-in, general purpose, (GP)
In-house and bespoken (IB)

Classes of metric: Simple/Basic (b)
Summary (s)
Open (o)

PROCUREMENT CYCLE PHASE		BB	GP	IB
Phase 1	Receive request	*	*	*
		(b, o)	(b, o)	(b, o)
Phase 2	Collect and analyse requirements	*	*	*
		(o)	(o)	(o)

		BB	GP	IB
Phase 3	Locate possible suppliers	* (o)	? (o)	0
Phase 4	Product specification	* (b, s, o)	* (b, s, o)	* (b, s, o)
Phase 5	Select supplier	* (o)	? (o)	0
Phase 6	Set up plans and contract(s)	* (b, o)	? (b, o)	X (b, o)
Phase 7	Watch work closely	* (b, s, o)	0	X (b, s, o)
Phase 8	Set up release and acceptance	* (o)	? (o)	X (o)
Phase 9	Handle queries, changes and failures	* (b, s, o)	? (b, s, o)	X (b, s, o)
Phase 10	Manage hand-over and installation	* (b, o)	? (b, o)	X (b, o)
Phase 11	Close active procurement	* (b, s, o)	* (b, s, o)	* (b, s, o)
Phase 12	Characterise and document	* (b, o)	* (b, o)	X (b, o)
Phase 13	Refine and review, till needed	* (b, s, o)	* (b, s, o)	* (b, s, o)

Legend   'X' indicates some phases which might need great tact to
implement when working with an in-house supplier.
'*' indicates that the phase is active.
'0' indicates that the phase is probably absent.
'?' indicates that the phase may or may not exist.

APPENDIX B

B1: A simple generic format for metrics definition

(a) METRIC IDENTIFIER	— (Name)
(b) APPLICABILITY	— (Kind of use envisaged, including specific forms of question and decision to which it might contribute)

(c) DESCRIPTION	— (Brief definition)
(d) EXPLOSION/IMPLOSION	— (Contributory attributes and measures, with details of how they are to be combined for the quality in question)
(e) MEASUREMENT DETAILS	— (Conditions, procedures, tools, etc.)
(f) UNITS, RANGE AND CRITERIA	— (Unit definition, plus its range of validity, and the meaning to be ascribed to significant values or ranges of values)

B2: An example of a question and its complementary open, customs-built metric

QUESTION: Is the supplier's proposed price acceptable?

(a) METRIC IDENTIFIER	— 'Accept price' (this is the name of the metric being defined)
(b) APPLICABILITY	— Used as basis for YES/NO to supplier's proposed price
(c) DESCRIPTION	— Weighted sum of plus and minus points on price
(d) EXPLOSION/IMPLOSION	(NOTE: THIS SECTION IS NOT COMPLETE)

— Calculate and add the factors.
— Factors are:
Is price within 10% of that expected?
Yes = 3   No = 0
Are the supplier's calculations shown?
Yes = 1   No = −2
Is the calculation in sufficient detail?
Yes = 2   No = −1

(e) MEASUREMENT DETAILS	— Do (d) ASAP: give procurer the opportunity to adjust if result is 3 or 4
(f) UNITS, RANGE AND CRITERIA	— At first cut, over 5 = YES 5 or less = NO

B3: METRICS review criteria

While any metric needs to be examined for its usefulness in a specific situation, there are some general questions which should always be asked:

(a) Was it necessary to define a new metric? Is there any equivalent with which users are already familiar? Is there a simpler form with equivalent information and/or discriminatory power?

(b) Is the new metric sufficiently informative, or discriminatory, for the intended purpose or range of purposes? Where deficiencies or constraints are recognised, are these clearly and firmly attached to the metric definition? Does the construction and/or calculation really add to the information content of the constituents? Do the constituent elements justify the interpretation and/or apparent accuracy of the resultant metric?

(c) Is the effort needed to understand the metric, collect contributory data and then make the defined decisions and calculations, matched by the value of the metric to the user?

(d) Is the metric intended for one-time use, or for use over a long period and for more than one purpose? Has the metric been validated against uses similar to that currently proposed? If not, can historical or simulated information be used to demonstrate that it has an acceptable chance of giving the support required? If lengthy and broad usage is expected, has it been demonstrated that the metric is sufficiently meaningful and robust to meet *all* the requirements likely to be laid on it?

(e) Has the metric definition been thoroughly reviewed against both the general criteria *and* the specific questions which it is intended to support? Have review results and applications been followed up and documented? Are the results encouraging?

5

Quality Requirements Specification And Evaluation

J. G. Walker*

ICL, Reading, UK

and

B. A. Kitchenham

Centre for Software Reliability, London, UK

ABSTRACT

This paper describes a method of specifying the non-functional requirements for a software product in unambiguous and measurable terms. This method has been implemented within a prototype Quality Management System, developed as part of the work of the Alvey Test Specification and Quality Management project. The paper also describes an experimental approach to evaluating such a requirements specification, based on the relationships between various quality factors and the software engineering techniques which may be used to support them.

1. INTRODUCTION

As part of the work of an Alvey-supported project concerned with test specification and quality management, a Quality Management System (QMS) is being developed. This system is intended to provide quality management assistance to the user at various stages in the life of a software product.

---

* J. G. Walker is employed by STC Technology Ltd, but is located at an ICL site.

103

The main functionality of the QMS is to be provided by three principal components, which reflect at a high level the stages in a product's life, and at a lower level the management tasks which are associated with each of these stages. These components are concerned with:

— project planning and initiation;
— project monitoring;
— project assessment.

This paper discusses the approach adopted to the specification of non-functional requirements, which is one aspect of the project planning and initiation component. It describes the underlying model of the relationship between quality factors that supports the evaluation of a quality requirements specification, and indicates the current status of the prototype Quality Requirements Specification Subsystem (QRSS) which is being produced to automate quality requirements specification and evaluation.

The QMS as a whole aims to assist software producers develop high quality software products, where 'quality' is meant to imply a degree of excellence. The QRSS addresses the overall goal by assisting the specification of the non-functional characteristics of a product, which are often referred to as 'qualities'. The sum of these 'qualities' is not equal to quality (i.e. degree of excellence), but failure to produce without the required non-functional characteristics will seriously compromise the quality of a product.

2. THE PROBLEM

The QRSS is intended to be a tool which helps product specifiers (whatever their actual titles may be) to specify the non-functional attributes of a product objectively, unambiguously and measurably. The solution to the problem of how this can be done has been pursued by a number of researchers, and our own approach blends the concept of quality factors, derived from McCall *et al.*[6] and Boehm *et al.*,[1] with the techniques of quality attribute specification described in Gilb.[2]

When faced with the task of specifying the requirements for a product, those concerned are usually well able to write down the functions that they expect the product to perform, and even the calendar date by which it must be available to the customer! It is when they are faced with the apparently less tangible aspects—the qualities—of the product, that they find the specification harder to pin down.

It is at this stage, when considering 'usability' or 'maintainability', or even 'performance', that emotive words, motherhood noises and arm-waving begin to creep in. Who has not seen a requirement specification which calls for the product to be 'easily maintainable', 'highly reliable', or 'extremely user friendly'? No-one could complain that the intentions behind such a specification were anything but honourable. The only problem is: how will anyone know if the end product has met its requirements? What is 'easily maintainable' to one person may be impossibly difficult to another. A system that is extremely user friendly, to someone who has come to know and love its little ways, may seem irritating, obtuse and downright unhelpful to someone else.

This, then, is the sort of problem that the QRSS, as part of the wider Quality Management System, is setting out to address. It aims to help not only in achieving a quantified and measurable specification of quality requirements, but also by providing an evaluation of what is specified. The user is offered advice on the feasibility of achieving the specification, and on the selection of software engineering techniques which are likely to help in this achievement. These several aspects are discussed in greater detail in what follows.

3. SPECIFYING THE REQUIREMENTS

The primary objective of the QRSS is to encourage and enable the user to set a quantified and measurable set of targets for product qualities. This task can seem impossibly difficult—we have heard people deny most emphatically that it can be done at all.

The only way we know to grapple successfully with this problem is to define a number of different quality factors, representing various important product characteristics. We have chosen nine of these for the present implementation of the QRSS, but one could probably defend a variety of different alternative selections. The nine are:

extendability	performance	security
integrity	reliability	survivability
maintainability	reusability	usability

For each factor, one or more definitions are proposed. It seems entirely reasonable, and a strength rather than a weakness, to permit more than one definition for a given quality factor. This flexible approach, it is felt, encourages the user to think constructively about how this particular aspect of quality should be harnessed to the specification of the product. A simple example of multiple definitions will serve to illustrate the approach: usability is defined as either 'the ease with which users can learn to use the system', or 'the extent to which users of the system are satisfied with its facilities'.

Has this advanced our cause? The perceptive reader will be swift to point out that we appear to be no nearer to applying objective criteria to the achievement of 'usability' than we were to start with. But please read on.

Each definition has to be broken down further into more and more specific detail, until it *is* possible to set a quantified target. Following the terminology of Gilb,[2] the word 'explosion' has been chosen for this level of description, and the QRSS currently contains some 30 specific explosions covering the nine quality factors.

To show how this works in a relatively simple case, consider the explosions that correspond respectively to the two definitions of usability given above:

—the average time for identified classes of user to achieve a specific level of competence with the system

and

—the percentage of users who express satisfaction with the system, in a survey of user opinion.

Perhaps this does not seem very wonderful. But remember how the good Dr Watson used to progress, under Sherlock Holmes' exposition, from a state of complete bafflement, to amazement at how simple the solution to the crime turned out to be after all! We do not set ourselves up in competition with the Great Detective, but it does seem that something useful can be achieved by quite simple means, applied with persistence.

In the case above, we have for the moment identified only one explosion for each of the two alternative definitions of usability. For other quality factors, however, there are up to four separate definitions, with up to three different explosions for a definition. To some extent this process can be carried on indefinitely, until one's imagination runs dry. Because of this, the user has been offered the chance to create new definitions. For each quality factor, the user may, if wished, make up fresh definitions, and incorporate therein appropriate explosions. The ultimate complexities of how to evaluate these open-ended specifications in detail remains a problem to be addressed in future research.

4. QUALITY FACTOR TEMPLATES

There is more to it, of course, than just concocting a suitable form of words. For one thing, it is not only important to have quality requirements which are measurable, but also to have the means to measure them. When the user is guided to set targets in numerical terms, the QRSS also requires specification of the measuring tool by which it will be subsequently verified that the target has been met. If there is no such tool available, then the user will need to plan to produce one: there is little point in setting a target if you can never find out whether you have met it!

Since the same kinds of information arise for each of the quality factors, the QRSS uses a 'template' of headings as the medium for communicating with the user about the quality requirements. The detailed contents differ from factor to factor, of course, but the template provides a consistent layout, with common headings, with which the user can speedily become familiar.

As well as a definition, or series of definitions, for each quality factor, the template contains one or more explosions for each definition, as described above. It also identifies possible synonyms for the name of the quality factor. The names that have been chosen happen to seem reasonable to the authors, but there are many similar names by which they may be known to others. The template includes a list of such synonyms simply to clear up any possible confusion on this point. For instance, 'user friendliness' is often found instead of usability.

As already observed, it would be possible to choose an alternative set of quality factors, individually different in substance, not just in name, from those adopted in the QRSS. Due to this, the template also shows a set of related quality concepts which are closely connected to the chosen quality factor. The notion of 'understandability', for example, is related to that of usability, without being identical to it.

The template is not only the vehicle for conveying information about the quality factor to the user; it is also the form on which (via a terminal) the user specifies the quality requirements. There are two main aspects to this: the target value(s) for each factor, and the importance of the factor for this product, as perceived by the user.

To establish a measurable target for each quality factor, the user selects one or more explosions—whatever seems most appropriate for the product—and specifies a numerical value for each explosion. Associated with each is an entry for the measuring unit (e.g. elapsed hours of use), a measurement tool (e.g. a log of user progress), and any relevant measurement conditions (e.g. how many users, and of what type, are to be involved in the measurements).

As well as a planned (target) value, the template permits the user to specify a worst case and a best case. There is some contention about this, on the grounds that if you admit the existence of a worst case, then human nature tends to shift its focus to that and away from the true target. The purpose of establishing a worst case, however, is to make it clear that if the product performs worse than this, then it is in principle totally unacceptable. The consequences of the product failing to achieve this level can also be specified, via the template, in simple terms, e.g. danger, cost, delay, dissatisfaction. For a product whose achievement falls somewhere between the planned value and the worst case, there is usually some room for negotiation. If the user is not prepared to allow the product to fall short of the target value in any way, then the worst case and the planned value can be specified to be identical.

The best case is quoted to show what can be done. It is a level of achievement that has been realised somewhere; it is the 'state of the art'. It helps to put the planned value in perspective. There is also a space for the user to state the current level of achievement for this explosion. This is the value that can be observed either in the user's present system (presumably the system that is to be replaced), or else in another similar system which exists and is known. This value provides a comparison between what is being asked for this time and something that is already familiar.

The QRSS, via the template, also requests the user to rate the significance of this quality factor as part of the total quality requirement for the product. It is assumed that in general this level of significance will be closely related to the intuitive way in which the user regards the planned value(s) specified for the factor. In other words, a high level of significance will tend to be associated with what the user feels is a 'high' value for the factor.

Possible values for the level of significance are very high, high, medium and low; 'low' simply means that this particular quality factor has no particular significance for this product. This field is used by the QRSS when it comes to evaluate the quality requirements specification, and when it offers advice to the user on the appropriate choice of software engineering techniques. This is explained in more detail in a later section.

When the user has specified the planned values, with their attendant units, tools and conditions, for as many aspects of the different quality factors as seems appropriate, the quality requirements specification may be deemed complete. The process of formulating it can, of course, be carried out in steps. The system preserves the partial specification in whatever state it is in, unless the user decides to delete it. The end result, which may well include certain aspects flagged as 'not applicable'—perhaps even whole quality factors—can be either printed out in hard copy form or simply retained for inspection from a terminal.

5. EVALUATING THE REQUIREMENTS

At this stage the user can leave well alone, content with what has already been achieved, or the QRSS can be invoked to offer some comment on the quality requirements as specified. We must here make it clear that this process, as currently embodied in the QRSS, is very experimental. The 'evaluation' which the ORSS undertakes, and the comments and suggestions which it may offer to the user, are based on the experience and opinions of the authors and certain other software engineers, but have not yet been evaluated in practice. The relationships between the techniques mentioned, and their likely impacts on particular quality factors, have emerged from studies done by others. There is also an underlying assumption that the quality requirements specification refers to a normal commercial software product development. If, therefore, the development is one with very specialised requirements, or needing extraordinary techniques, then the evaluation offered by the QRSS may not be appropriate.

The system assumes that the development will be based on standard techniques, and that the following will normally be in evidence: structured design; structured code; modularity; isolation of time/space critical modules; interface definition standards; naming standards; configuration control; the use of high level languages, with comments in the code and the use of 'pretty printing'; program documentation, including cross-reference lists; reviews; code walk-throughs; test strategies and plans; unit, integration, system and acceptance testing.

So what sort of comment can the QRSS offer? All that is currently devised is based on a coarse evaluation of the specification. The QRSS uses the 'level of significance' specified by the user for each quality factor, together with data on the relationships between the quality factors themselves, and between quality factors and software engineering techniques, to draw certain conclusions. On these are based the advice and ideas which it offers to the user.

The first type of comment that the QRSS can offer reflects the inherent overlap between related pairs of quality factors. In some cases this overlap is beneficial, as certain factors tend to pull together, so to speak. For example, many of the techniques that are used to achieve reusability are also relevant to extendability. Other factors, however, pull against each other, such as performance and usability. In fact, using conventional techniques, performance tends to be at odds with most of the other factors, as many of us have found out to our cost.

These overlaps between factors, both helpful and otherwise, are magnified if the significance of the factors is raised to high or very high levels. The conflict between performance and usability, alluded to already, becomes even more serious if the user attaches a high level of significance to both. In this case the user is saying, in effect, 'I regard performance and usability as equally and highly significant, and (by implication) I am setting what I think are stiff targets for both of them'. The QRSS is not able to resolve this problem, but it is able to draw attention to the situation, which may have arisen unthinkingly in the course of specifying the various factors individually.

If that is the bad news, there may also be good news for the user. Where two quality factors are both supported by similar techniques, it may be that the user is potentially getting 'something for nothing'. If maintainability has been rated as highly significant, then the chances are that the end product will also show a fair degree of extendability, and reliability should also be enhanced. These may be spin-offs that the user had not expected. Whether they will be regarded as a special

	ext	int	mai	per	rel	reu	sec	sur	usa
Very high									VVV
									VVV
High	HHH		HHH			HHH			VVV
	HHH		HHH			HHH			VVV
Medium	HHH		HHH	MMM	MMM	HHH			VVV
	HHH		HHH	MMM	MMM	HHH			VVV
Low	HHH	LLL	HHH	MMM	MMM	HHH	LLL	LLL	VVV
	HHH	LLL	HHH	MMM	MMM	HHH	LLL	LLL	VVV

Fig. 1. A quality profile.

bonus depends, of course, on the user's attitude to the factors concerned, but we should always try to avoid looking gift horses in the mouth!

Before offering these comments on the quality requirements specification, the QRSS displays to the user a simple 'quality profile'. This shows the level of significance that the user has attached to each of the quality factors (see Fig. 1).

It is against this profile that the evaluation is carried out, the first stage being to highlight the areas of potential conflict and those of potential gain. The technique by which the conflict and overlap between quality factors is assessed is described in more detail later in this paper. In addition, the QRSS draws attention to the difficulty of giving high, or very high, significance to more than a few quality factors simultaneously. As stated by Gilb,[2] you cannot arbitrarily determine the planned level of all attributes. In other words, it is no good saying 'I want the best of everything', because in the real world you are most unlikely to get it, or at least not within an acceptable cost or timescale.

6. THE SCALE OF THE TASK

The next stage of the evaluation process is really concerned with helping the user grasp the scale of the task which has just been set. How great that task is, in absolute terms, is not yet visible to the QRSS. What is known, however, is the extent to which the user has assembled major quality hurdles to be jumped.

Suppose that performance and maintainability have both been set at a high level of requirement, and usability has been set very high. This is clearly a much more difficult specification to implement than the case of a functionally identical product for which all the quality factors have been set at medium or low levels.

The intention of the QRSS is to encourage the user to set appropriate quality targets. It is nonetheless necessary to provide a warning of the likely burdens that these may incur. Armed with this information, it is hoped that the user will be better placed to plan the implementation realistically, ensuring that adequate resources and time are available and that the right techniques are in place. In this way users should be able to avoid the frustration of aiming for the moon without having the means of getting there.

The QRSS attempts to express the burden of a demanding quality requirements specification in terms of additional cost, expressed as a percentage of the basic cost of implementing the product at all. How this is done requires some explanation of the 'knowledge' that is held inside the QRSS.

The assumption is made that, for each quality factor, there are various software engineering techniques which could be brought into use during product development to help achieve that factor. To make the product more usable, for instance, self-explanatory dialogues might be included. It is further assumed that the higher the level of significance attached to the factor, the more techniques the user will be prepared to bring to bear during the implementation.

These techniques have been ranked in the QRSS's database to show that some of them are assumed necessary even for a nominal level of requirement for a given quality factor; others would be additionally invoked to support a medium level of significance; others again for a high level; and finally there are some which would only be brought into play if a very high level of significance were attached to that factor.

For example, to support a very high level of requirement for usability, it is suggested that psychological experimentation and also evolutionary delivery should be considered, on top of all the other techniques which are included in support of usability. The aggregate of the techniques shown against the nominal levels of requirement, across all the quality factors, defines the basic approach to implementation assumed by the QRSS, and has already been summarised in the previous section.

Before the information on techniques can be used by the QRSS in a particular evaluation, it needs to be adjusted in order to relate it to a user's current working practices. This is not a proper tailoring of the system, about which more is said later on, but a certain amount of local trimming for the purposes of this evaluation.

For example, the user will be asked to indicate whether a library of reusable components is available. If it is, the option of reuse is available as a technique for reliability, and there is no cost associated with providing such a library for reusability. Also, the maintenance and production procedures and tools currently available need to be identified. The cost associated with introducing tools which already exist can then be removed from the information held by the QRSS for this evaluation. (Existing tools might be known error logs, automatic dump analysers or a data description database, for example.)

Each technique that contributes to a higher level of significance for a quality factor (i.e. medium, high or very high) is assumed to incur an additional cost. Values for these costs have been assigned somewhat arbitrarily, and vary from technique to technique and factor to factor. It must be stressed, however, that these are not actual costs, since more data would need to be known about the product, the timescales required and the resources available, before these could be assessed in absolute terms. The value is shown as an 'overhead' cost, which is the notional additional cost incurred, as a result of using that particular technique, in order to have a better chance of achieving the planned values of the quality factor concerned.

The notional additional cost for evolutionary delivery, to support a very high level of requirement for usability, is assumed to be 20% of what it would cost to implement the product without giving priority to any particular quality factor. It is worth noting, however, that if evolutionary delivery is adopted as a technique on behalf of usability, it also—without extra cost—helps to enhance the extendability of the product (according to the model built into the QRSS).

Whether or not the detailed figures currently held in the QRSS are regarded as reasonable, we would maintain that they serve the purpose of helping the user to appreciate the consequences (at least to the right order of magnitude) of attempting to make the product to the specified quality requirements.

As a further means of highlighting the scale of the task implied by the quality requirements specification, the quality profile (described earlier) is extended to show the costs, as well as the level of significance, associated with each quality factor. This cost figure is expressed as a percentage, as before, and is the sum of the notional additional costs of all the techniques which, according to the QRSS, *might* be invoked to support that level of significance for that factor. A single synthetic figure is also displayed for the quality profile, which is calculated from the individual quality factor overhead costs. The calculation allows, crudely, for the degrees of conflict and overlap that occur between quality factors, as already discussed.

These figures will tend to exaggerate the likely overall additional costs, as it is improbable that all the relevant techniques will actually be employed, or will even need to be employed, in a given development. For the moment, however, they are a means of catching the user's attention.

At a later stage, once the user has chosen the techniques to be used during the implementation, the QRSS can offer a revised quality profile. This will show how the overhead figures have been reduced, in all probability, as a result of any changes made to the levels of significance of the quality factors, and as a result of the QRSS knowing which techniques the user has decided to adopt.

6.1 Assessment of the relationships among quality factors

The first stage of the quality profile evaluation discussed in Section 5 is also driven by the QRSS database. The original discussion of the relationships between quality factors by McCall *et al.*[6] only identified the existence of a relationship between the quality factors and indicated whether the relationship was one of conflict or synergy. This qualitative assessment was too crude to offer any information about the extent or degree of the relationship, and since the existence of the relationships was based on subjective assessment they were not able to be verified.

The technique used by the QRSS to assess the degree of *synergistic* relationships between quality factors is based on the number of supporting techniques which are common to pairs of quality factors. This implies a possibly asymmetrical influence of one factor on another as follows:

Percentage influence of factor 1 on factor $2 = [N_{12}/N_2] * 100$

Percentage influence of factor 2 on factor $1 = [N_{12}/N_1] * 100$

where $N_1 =$ number of techniques supporting factor 1, $N_2 =$ number of

	EXT	REU	MAIN	REL	SEC	SUR	INT	USA	PER
EXT		83	46	13	21	10	21	9	17
REU	38		14	9	14	10	21	0	0
MAIN	50	33		26	21	20	14	0	0
REL	12	17	21		50	80	43	27	17
SEC	12	17	11	30		50	21	0	17
SUR	3	8	7	35	36		43	0	17
INT	12	25	7	26	21	60		0	17
USA	3	0	0	13	0	0	0		0
PER	8	0	0	8	14	20	14	0	

Fig. 2(a). The percentage of techniques common to pairs of quality factors.

	EXT	REU	MAIN	REL	SEC	SUR	INT	USA	PER
EXT		4	2	0	1	0	1	0	0
REU	1		0	0	0	0	1	0	0
MAIN	2	1		1	1	0	0	0	0
REL	0	0	1		2	3	2	1	0
SEC	0	0	0	1		2	1	0	0
SUR	0	0	0	1	1		2	0	0
INT	0	1	0	1	1	2		0	0
USA	0	0	0	0	0	0	0		0
PER	0	0	0	0	0	0	0	0	

Fig. 2(b). Influence matrix for quality factors.

techniques supporting factor 2, and N_{12} = number of techniques which are in common.

This provides the initial assessment of the relationship between pairs of factors as shown in Fig. 2(a), and simplified in Fig. 2(b) (by converting the percentages to a 5-point scale where $0–20 = 0$; $21–40 = 1$; $41–60 = 2$; $61–80 = 3$; $81–100 = 4$). The figures are oriented so that the columns indicate the degree that the specified quality factor (named at the column head) is influenced by the remaining factors.

It can be seen, from Fig. 2(b), that the influence matrix indicates three major groups among the factors. Group 1 comprises extendability, maintainability and reusability, which appear to influence each other fairly strongly but which are mainly independent of the remaining factors. Group 2 comprises reliability, security, integrity and survivability, which appear to influence each other fairly strongly while remaining relatively independent of the remaining factors. Group 3 comprises usability and performance, which appear to be fairly independent of each other and of the other factors.

However, there do appear to be some specific cross-group relationships. Maintainability is related to reliability as a result of techniques which assist in the localisation and diagnosis of faults. Reusability and integrity are related as a result of common techniques which support module definition standards, which simultaneously reduce the chance of corrupting module interfaces and increase their visibility. Usability is influenced by reliability as a result of techniques which attempt to ensure the correctness of the requirements document. The influence that maintainability and extendability both exert on security exists as a result of techniques which control changes to system components. The influence of extendability on integrity is due to the same techniques which relate reusability and integrity, and can therefore be discounted as an independent effect.

A more detailed analysis of group 1 and group 2 was necessary to determine whether the influence among qualities within each group was a simple pair-wise effect or is more complex.

For group 1, a total of 19 techniques were identified which support at least two of the factors. Investigation of these factors indicated that the influence of maintainability on reusability was not independent of their relationships with extendability; on each of the four occasions that techniques supported both reusability and maintainability, they also supported extendability.

For group 2, a total of 14 techniques were identified which supported at least two of the four factors. Investigation into the relationships between techniques and factors showed that 43% of the techniques supported three or more of the quality factors.

This assessment method is itself fairly crude, and must be combined with a subjective assessment that the non-overlapping techniques are independent and not conflicting. In the case of performance, most of the techniques which were not common to other factors did conflict, whereas this was not the case for usability. However, it does provide some rationale for assessing the relationships between factors, and has led us to a somewhat different model of the relationships between quality factors to that proposed by McCall et al.[6] In particular, it seems that pairwise effects are not sufficient to describe the relationships between factors, and a number of the conflicts were not observed which McCall et al. suggested. Using our terms, they suggest conflicts between reusability and security (which they call integrity); security and extendability (which covers their use of flexibility and interoperability); and reliability and reusability; whereas we observed no such conflicts and, indeed, observed some synergy between security and extendability was seen.

The above investigation led to the development of a number of heuristic rules which tempered advice concerning the number of quality factors specified at high levels, with a recognition that it is easier to achieve a specification which has high requirements for a number of supporting qualities than one which has high requirements for independent or conflicting requirements. The analysis of the influences among the quality factors led to an overall assessment of the specification in terms of potential overhead based on the following formula:

$$\begin{aligned}
\text{Profile overhead} = OH_{OF} &- ADJ(REU) \\
&- 0{\cdot}50\,(\min[OH_{MAIN}, OH_{EXT}]) \\
&- 0{\cdot}25\,(\min[OH_{MAIN}, OH_{REL}]) \\
&- 0{\cdot}25\,(\min[OH_{REU}, OH_{INT}]) \\
&- 0{\cdot}25\,(\min[OH_{REL}, \max[OH_{INT}, OH_{SEC}]]) \\
&- ADJ(SUR) \\
&- ADJ(REL) \\
&- ADJ(SEC) \\
&+ W * OH_{PER}
\end{aligned}$$

where OH_X stands for the overhead at the specified quality level for factor X, and OH_{OF} stands for the sum of all factor overheads.

$$ADJ(REU) = (IF\ OH_{REU} > OH_{EXT}\ THEN\ 0{\cdot}25 * OH_{EXT}\ ELSE\ 0{\cdot}75 * OH_{REU})$$
$$ADJ(SUR) = (IF\ OH_{SUR} > OH_{REL}\ THEN\ 0{\cdot}25 * OH_{REL}\ ELSE\ 0{\cdot}75 * OH_{SUR})$$
$$ADJ(REL) = (IF\ OH_{REL} > OH_{USA}\ THEN\ 0{\cdot}25 * OH_{USA})$$
$$ADJ(SEC) = (IF\ OH_{SEC} < \min[OH_{EXT}, OH_{MAIN}]\ THEN\ 0{\cdot}25 * OH_{SEC})$$
$$W = 2 * (\text{no. of factors, excluding PER, at very high level})$$
$$+ (\text{no. of factors, excluding PER, at high level})$$

7. TECHNIQUE SELECTION

The coarse evaluation of the quality requirements specification can only be further refined if the QRSS is told which software engineering techniques are to be adopted during the development of the product. The next stage is, therefore, to take the user through the list of quality factors and offer a set of techniques for consideration.

For each factor, the techniques offered to the user are those which, according to the QRSS's database, are most likely to have a primary

Table 1
Techniques to Support Usability

Level required	Techniques	Overhead cost (%)	Contribution to achievement (%)
Very high			
	Evolutionary delivery[a]	20	70
	Psychological experimentation	25	50
High			
	Animation (unsophisticated)	5	50
	Fast prototyping	25	50
	Requirements language & analyser (e.g. SREM)	50	60
	Reuse (design, code, docn)[b]	5	25
	User interface standards	5	25
Medium			
	Inspection	7	50
	Modes of system use (training and normal)	10	50
	Self-explanatory dialogues	5	50
Low			
	Review (requirements only)		100
	Unit/integration/system/acceptance testing		
	Test strategies and plans		

[a] Evolutionary delivery may increase costs by extending the development cycle.
[b] This assumes that a library of reusable components is available, together with the techniques to identify and extract the relevant items.

influence on the achievement of that factor. As an example, Table 1 shows the techniques which would be offered for the user's selection to support usability.

As the user progressively selects techniques, factor by factor, a consolidated list of those already chosen will be built up. When the user moves on to consider the techniques for a further quality factor, those which are already on the consolidated list will be flagged accordingly, thus simplifying the selection process as it goes along.

When this selection is complete, the QRSS is in a position to provide the user with, firstly, the consolidated list of selected techniques, and then with a revised quality profile overhead cost. This revised figure now shows the notional overhead costs (still in percentage terms, as before) which are attributable to the user's chosen list of techniques rather than to the total list of techniques held in the QRSS.

8. TAILORING THE SYSTEM

What happens if the user wants to use a technique which the QRSS does not 'know about'? This can easily arise if this particular technique has not been included anywhere in the QRSS (we make no claims to omniscience).

The present state of the prototype system is unable to handle this situation, though it goes without saying that this should not inhibit the user from adopting that technique if it is right to do so! At a later date, however, it is intended to allow some degree of tailoring of the system over and above the limited trimming described earlier. This would enable the user to build in 'knowledge' of further techniques, as necessary, and remove data about particular techniques from the QRSS, if these were never likely to be adopted in the particular environment. By the same token, it will also be possible to modify the notional additional cost figures and other data currently fixed in the system.

By these means, the system will be able to remain responsive to new software engineering techniques, and to be progressively tuned to a particular development environment.

9. ASSESSING THE RISKS

The final piece of advice from the QRSS's coarse evaluation concerns the user's prospects of achieving the specified quality requirements. As with the suggested cost figures, this advice is based on somewhat arbitrary data, and must be regarded as extremely tentative and experimental for the present.

The data held in the QRSS on the various techniques includes a figure which represents the notional contribution of that technique, in percentage terms, to the likely achievement of the particular level of the quality factor with which it is associated. Thus the adoption of inspection, for example, is reckoned to contribute 50% towards the achievement of a medium level of usability (see Table 1).

The way in which the QRSS calculates the chances of success, for a given implementation, will probably be frowned on by mathematical readers. Indeed, no great claims are made for the accuracy of this particular crystal ball. As with the overhead cost information described earlier, the intention is to alert the user to the sort of picture that is emerging, even if the detail is a little imprecise.

For each factor, the QRSS totals the percentage 'contributions to achievement' for each technique selected, and then divides by a number from one to four, according to the level of significance specified for that factor. Thus, to score 100% for a factor with a high level of significance, the total contribution to achievement from all the techniques selected would need to sum to 300%! This likelihood of success may seem highly improbable, but it is felt that a low figure will at least alert the user to look again at the task in hand, and the plan for setting about it. The risks so indicated are intended to give the user some feel for the 'safety factors' which would be given for any hardware engineering project.

Where the chance of success falls below 100% for any factor, the system should comment on this and suggest that further techniques and/or other approaches to solving the problem need to be considered. Depending on the factors concerned, and the nature of the product, these might include, for example, hiring in specialist skills, adopting a new form of organisation, or arranging extended user trials.

This sort of problem is being tackled by the COQUAMO model described by Hamer *et al.*,[3] which is being developed by the ESPRIT REQUEST project.

10. THE IMPLEMENTATION

The QRSS is currently being developed as a prototype system, running under UNIX† on the ICL DRS300. The specification part of the QRSS has been implemented using a customised version of the STC Generic Toolset, itself the product of another Alvey project. Another application of the Toolset is described by Hook.[4]

---

† UNIX is a registered trademark of AT&T in the USA and other countries.

The Toolset is a structured editor generator, so the QRSS implementation is achieved via the construction of a grammar, which includes the text of the various quality factor templates. This is a mixture of narrative (e.g. a particular definition of a quality factor) and the framework of embedded fields for which the user will subsequently supply values.

Using the generated editor, the user is able to create and browse through a specification, starting with any one of the nine quality factors. By using the cursor movement keys, the user can either work through the text line by line; skip from one specifiable field to the next; or return to a higher level (to another quality factor, say) and move on from there. The user creates a specification step by step, inserting values into the quality factor templates.

As an example, the planned level for a particular 'explosion' appears on the screen as

planned level: ⟨value⟩

The user has the option of specifying the 'value'. In this particular implementation, 'value' has been defined so that the user has the choice of specifying it as an integer, or a real number, or as a form of approximation—which may be the most realistic value that can be specified at that stage in the project. Examples of the sort of approximation allowed are: 18 ± 2; 250?; 75–130.

Once the user has specified the 'value' for this particular field, that is what will appear—on screen or in a hard copy print-out—until the user either deletes it or alters it; e.g.

planned level: 60

The user may indicate that a factor does not apply.

The system allows a short help text to be displayed at each point, and extended help information can be provided where necessary (by accessing a separate text file).

The user can create a specification, save it when partially or totally completed, subsequently amend it, print it out, and eventually delete it.

11. CONCLUSION

The QRSS does not attempt to insist on any partisan approach to quality. It has been argued elsewhere, in Kitchenham and Walker,[5] that there are at least five approaches to quality: the transcendental, the product-based, the user-based, the manufacturing-based and the value-based; all of which have validity and must be reconciled. It is hoped that the QRSS assists with the reconciliation process, at least with respect to the last four approaches. The user-based approach is served by providing a standard format for quality specifications which allows a user's non-functional requirements to be stated unambiguously, and in a manner which permits 'fitness for purpose' to be objectively demonstrated. The manufacturing approach is supported by identifying a variety of possible production techniques which should assist the goal of 'conformance to specification'. The product-based approach, which is concerned with product grade and thus regards a product in terms of its quantifiable ingredients, and the value-based approach, which may be summarised as 'design to cost', are equally served by the concept of a quality profile which can be assessed in terms of overheads and risks, and which allows a quality manager to consider the trade-offs between cost, market position and quality.

That then, is the Quality Requirements Specification Subsystem. At the moment it contains much that is debatable, but it is believed that the approach embodied in the QRSS is one worth testing.

If the prototype system appears to be successful, the aim will be to develop a 'production' version. This will be capable of being tailored to accommodate local skills and procedures, as already described. It will also, it is hoped, contain increasingly realistic values of the 'overhead costs' and 'contributions to achievement' for the various software engineering techniques.

ACKNOWLEDGEMENT

This work was supported by the Alvey Directorate as part of the Test Specification and Quality Management project (reference ALV/PRJ/SE/031).

REFERENCES

1. Boehm, B. W., Brown, J. R., Kaspar, H., Lipow, M., Macleod, G. J. and Merrit, M. J. (1978), *Characteristics of software quality*, North-Holland, Amsterdam.

2. Gilb, T. (1985), *Design by objectives* (unpublished manuscript available on request from the author).
3. Hamer, P. G., Frewin, G. D., Anderson, O. and Davies, S. P. (1986), *The COnstructive QUAlity MOdelling system*, ESPRIT REQUEST project report number R1.8.0.
4. Hook, P. (1986), *VDM Toolset userguide* (725 07831, Ed 1).
5. Kitchenham, B. A. and Walker, J. G. (1986), *The meaning of quality*, Proc. BCS/IEE Conference on Software Engineering.
6. McCall, J. A., Richards, P. K. and Walters, G. F. (1977), *Factors in software quality, Vols I, II and III*, RADC reports NTIS AD/A–049 014, 015 and 055.

6

The Collection and Use of Data for Monitoring Software Projects

N. ROSS

STC Technology Ltd, Newcastle-under-Lyme, UK

ABSTRACT

Although collection of software data can be of great benefit to future software projects, the Software Data Library (SWDL) project believes that it will not occur unless the collecting project sees an immediate return on the effort of collection. Hence procedures for collecting data from a project, and procedures for making prompt use of it to control that project, must be integrated.

The introduction to the chapter expands on the above concept. The middle sections discuss SWDL's approach to using data during a collecting project's lifetime. They introduce simple techniques of data analysis (with a strong emphasis on graphical techniques) and demonstrate these in examples. The final section looks at the possibility of integrating procedures for data collection with those for its short-term use.

1. INTRODUCTION

Data collection is driven by data use. SWDL believes that unless those collecting data make more-or-less immediate use of it in progressing and controlling their software development work, data collection will not take place to a sufficient standard to allow meaningful subsequent analysis (and usually does not occur at all). Hence, in order to meet SWDL's objectives (which are to create widespread data collection

125

within the UK software community), it was not sufficient to produce definitions of the data required, forms for recording them and guidance to companies on procedures for data collection. Only in the context of a theory about how, and for what purpose, data could be immediately used by its collectors, could collection procedures be sensibly defined.

During a project's lifetime, data collection can support cost and quality management. The former topic is addressed in the papers by Frewin and Ross[3] and Cowderoy and Jenkins (Chapter 3). Macro cost models are created from data on completed projects; they use only a limited amount of data from projects to which they are applied. By contrast, synthetic cost estimation methods obtain an overall project estimate by summing estimates of the many low-level processes that make up the project. Hence, they rely on their estimates being continuously refined by the inclusion of actual cost data from the early phases of the project being estimated. This leads to increased precision and a rapid response to changing circumstances. SWDL therefore recommends these methods.

Conceptually, this use of project data to refine a synthetic estimate does not conflict with the initial estimating method itself. The product and task breakdowns devised at project startup form the basis for both the estimate and its subsequent monitoring. The metrics used in each case are the same (estimates being replaced by actuals) and it is reasonable to use resource measures to predict final resource expenditures.

The topic of quality management is more complicated. The use of data to *measure* quality is the subject of other work (see, for example, Chapter 5). The research described there aims to provide measures for the qualities (i.e. non-functional attributes), such as maintainability, usability, reusability, etc., that might be desired in a software product. (Of these, reliability is the most easily quantified. Hence it is, at present, the most easily measured and the best understood of the software qualities.) Such qualities can be specified in objective, measurable terms in a project's requirements document. As the project nears completion, data from the later testing phases can be used to calculate the current level of any given quality of the created product and so predict its value of that quality on release, just as actual cost data can be used to refine cost estimates.

The use of data to *achieve* quality is not so well understood at present. The precise specification of a quality such as reliability at project startup is useful, only to a limited degree, if the knowledge of whether the objective is likely to be met or not is revealed as a (pleasant or unpleasant) surprise only when the project is well into integration testing. If the project is to be controlled, then its management must recognise and correct trends and events that threaten to prevent it from meeting its quality requirements. If this is done early, then it can be done cheaply. However, managers who do not collect data during development may not even see such trends and events. Managers who have no theory of how to use such collected data may not realise that what they see threatens what they are trying to achieve.

One approach, recommended by McCall *et al.*,[6] Bowen *et al.*[1] and others is to look for metrics available during development that are good predictors of final product quality. A cost model uses the measures of size and complexity that can be collected at various points in the lifecycle to obtain progressively more accurate predictions of the final size and cost. Analogously, McCall *et al.*[6] suggest seeking metrics that can be collected during development and that are progressively more closely correlated with final quality. These will therefore warn of divergence of the project from its specified quality goals.

It is not believed that this approach can work. Whereas the refinement of synthetic cost estimates with actual cost data, or the prediction of reliability on release from reliability at integration test, involves extrapolating from the current values of data of a certain kind to future values of data of the same kind, the McCall approach intends to predict final quality values using data from a completely different domain. There is simply no reason to expect data available in earlier phases to be linearly (or even ordinally) related to quality metrics that are measurable only in late testing and in use. Section 2.3 below explains in detail (with examples) why this is so.

Other research[4] has advocated a three-stage procedure for creating quality products. In the requirements phase, target values for re-liability and other qualities should be specified and then assessed against the project plan (using data from past projects) to determine their feasibility. In the integration testing phase, achieved values should be measured and extrapolated to predict the values that will be attained in use. Between these two phases, software production processes applied to individual items should be monitored to detect whether they have diverged from the norm and, if so, to diagnose the cause of this divergence. This diagnosis will show if any quality is likely to be affected and can guide the choice of management response.

Monitoring a software project during its development in order to refine synthetic cost estimates, or to perform quality control activities, will require the rapid interpretation of collected data and its prompt feedback to those who collected it. This paper begins by examining how data can be used to monitor software development. Then it lists techniques (mostly graphical) for analysing data and looks at how these may be used and how their results may be interpreted, using a set of simple examples to clarify the discussion. The final chapter discusses the attributes that a data collection scheme must have to support, and be supported by, such use of data.

2. USING SOFTWARE DEVELOPMENT DATA

There are three ways of analysing data for software project control. These correspond to three stages in the gradual development and systematising of software engineering knowledge.

(a) *Simple examination*: at the beginning of data collection and use there will often be a lack of clear ideas on how to assign a meaning to the data. In such a situation a manager who feels that certain metrics are likely to indicate the state of the project may collect them and look at them. At this stage all interpretation proceeds from the manager, none from the analysis technique.

(b) *Modelling*: at the other extreme, well understood processes, on which a volume of past data is available, can be described by models. These largely de-skill the interpretation of data. The manager supplies the input variables and the model announces its prediction.

(c) *Trend and exception analysis*: between these two extremes, managers may acquire a knowledge base of what kinds of relationships they expect to see among their data, and what values indicate a departure from these. Certain graphical statistical analysis techniques can help in developing this knowledge base and in applying it.

Each of these will now be described in more detail.

2.1 Simple examination

A surprising amount can be learned about the progress of a project simply by collecting data about it and looking at the data, in default of any analysis method. The managers decide, using their experience of software engineering, what factors are likely to be interrelated, and put the relevant data into a table. All too often, undesirable trends do not need to be searched for but leap out as soon as the data is examined.

As an example, consider Fig. 1: It describes the testing of modules in a project, dividing them into small and large, tested for long or short periods and with or without errors subsequent to testing. The managers would expect to see the number of remaining errors varying directly with size and inversely with testing time. They might intend to look at a number of such tables, varying in the turning point value separating large from small modules, and short from long testing times, in order to decide what the optimal values for these should be.

What they might not expect to see is the high proportion of modules appearing in the diagonal boxes. The table is showing the effect of a common human tendency to perform easy tasks before turning to hard ones. In this case it was the coding phase, not testing, that was at fault. Small, easy modules were being coded first and so were available to testers for longer. By the time the larger modules were ready for

	Available testing time (days)	
Program size	<= 40	> 40
>200 lines Number of errors	11	11
Programs with subsequent errors	8	3
Number of errors	20	3
<= 200 lines Number of programs	9	27
Programs with subsequent errors	2	2
Number of errors	4	2

Fig. 1. Classification table: Size and testing time effects on errors.

testing, phase deadlines were looming and testing time could not be easily extended.

The table, originally intended to guide the management of future testing phases in assigning appropriate testing times to modules in given size groups, has revealed an effect of the management (or lack of management) of activities in the coding phase that will hinder this. It is impossible to say how much effect this practice will have on the final product quality, but clearly it will have some. This example has highlighted the two uses of simple examination of collected software data. Firstly, it enables managers to assign target values, which they can then enforce, to effects that they may previously have believed in but been unable to quantify. Secondly, it can reveal effects they had not noticed.

2.2 Modelling

Producing a model is the ideal solution to the problem of using data for the management of software engineering. Like most ideal solutions, it is not always feasible.

A model has two aspects. The first is that of a process model which identifies the objects involved in the situation of interest, the relevant attributes of each and the relationships between them. This demands a high level of understanding of the problem area. Failure to recognise the nature of the processes involved, failure to identify relevant data and confounding of objects that are separate in the area being modelled, may all lead to a model that is too poor a description of its subject area ever to be useful.

The second aspect is that of an algorithm (or set of algorithms) relating the values of the relevant datatypes. Choosing the functional form of such an algorithm needs conceptual insight into the problem area. Calibrating its parameter values needs much data, especially if cross-validation (calculating the algorithm on one set of data and checking its validity on another) is used.

As an example, consider Remus and Zilles' model for error detection and removal.[5] Figure 2 shows the process model. Figure 3 shows the model algorithm. As can be seen from Fig. 4, this model proved to be a poor predictor in at least one software engineering environment. The process model was too simple to capture the way of working in the environment, and the algorithm had evidently been calibrated using data too different from that of the environment of use for its predictions to be even approximately valid.

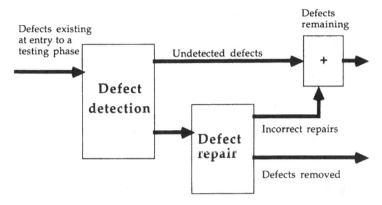

Fig. 2. Remus and Zilles defect removal model.

This example demonstrates the drawbacks of relying solely on models of this kind. Their demands for large volumes of past project data, and for clear understanding of the processes involved, mean that for the foreseeable future there will be many areas of software development that will be controllable by means of software data, but not sufficiently measured and understood to be wholly captured by models. Models are most trustworthy when they are locally produced and calibrated, and describe small-scale processes. Such models are discussed further in Chapter 8.

$$\text{let } \mu = MP/PTM$$

where $MP \equiv$ major defects found
during inspections
& reviews

$PTM \equiv$ number of defects
found during testing

then, $TD = MP^*\mu/(\mu - 1)$

where $TD \equiv$ total defects over life
of product

$$Q_2 = MP/\mu(\mu - 1)$$

where $Q_2 \equiv$ remaining errors over
life of product

Fig. 3. Predictions from Remus and Zilles model (theory).

	D1	D2
Predictions of errors remaining after testing (Q2)	34	175
Errors found during use in-house	30	39
Prediction of errors remaining at release (Q3)	13	6
Errors found after release (release time)	3 (6 months)	27 (7 months)
Product size (lines of code)	13334	39000

Fig. 4. Predictions from Remus and Zilles model (practice).

2.3 Exception and Trend Analysis
This denotes a collection of techniques intermediate to the two extremes discussed above. A manager needs to know:

  (a) what the normal outcome of a software production process is, so that they can predict future outcomes;
  (b) when a process has resulted in an unusual outcome, which may impact the quality of the final product;
  (c) how to diagnose the causes and consequences of such abnormal results.

Such knowledge can be obtained from combining the information contained in software data collected from the project with the manager's experience and knowledge of the work being done. Data from past projects enhances the effectiveness of this but is not necessary to it. SWDL's techniques aid this activity in the following ways.

  (i)   Effective graphical data presentation techniques allow the manager to concentrate more on understanding what the data is telling them and less on simply endeavouring to grasp the data values and their interrelationships.
  (ii) Statistical techniques can help the eye to recognise and calculate trends, and exceptions to trends, in the data.
  (iii) Expertise in managing software development consists in part of knowing what exceptions to look for, how to diagnose them and what factors to consider in choosing an appropriate response.

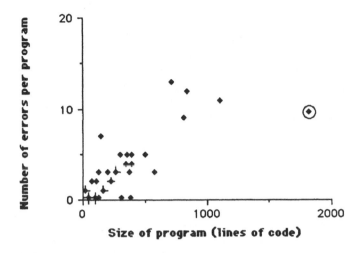

Fig. 5. Scatterplot: Program size versus number of errors.

By classifying and cross-relating kinds of exceptions, diagnoses and responses, it is possible to simplify the task of reaching a preliminary interpretation of the data, leaving the manager free to concentrate on modifying this interpretation in the light of his knowledge of the particular project concerned.

As a simple example of these ideas consider Fig. 5. It displays module size against the number of faults found during unit testing for a group of modules.

Figure 5 shows the expected trend for such a graph. Where the size is small, other factors outweigh it in determining how many faults a module has, producing the spread in the lower left quadrant of the graph. Larger modules show a strong relation between size and faults, and an exception to it is indicated by the circled point. Statistical techniques exist that can help the eye in calculating the exact relationship and measuring the degree to which exceptional points diverge from it (formal statistical analysis is especially useful in more than two dimensions).

Possible causes of a module being large but with few detected errors include good coding, poor testing, simple control flow structure, etc. By preparing tables cross-referencing each diagnosis to the results of other analyses that confirm or contradict it, a shortlist of plausible causes can be quickly obtained.

3. CHOICE OF GRAPHICAL DATA
PRESENTATION TECHNIQUES

This section discusses the criteria for selecting data analysis and presentation techniques for software data. It then looks at ways of dealing with common problems in data display. Lastly it briefly lists a number of techniques used by SWDL.

3.1 Credibility and usability in data analysis

If it is to be applied to software data, any analysis technique must possess certain attributes. One is trustworthiness of the result that the technique gives. This means that it must not be dangerously affected by a few erroneous or widely atypical values in the data, and that it must not make assumptions about the data distribution. Classical statistical methods tend to assume that whatever data set one is working with was drawn from some underlying distribution of data commonly found in nature (usually one assumes the Gaussian distribution, i.e. the famous bell-shaped curve of, for example, intelligence tests, or the log-normal distribution often observed in physical phenomena). Classical techniques are very efficient when this is true and dangerously misleading when it is not, as is usually the case for software data.

Figure 6 illustrates these points and another of equal importance: user-friendliness to software engineering managers and staff. Four datasets are shown in tabular form in Fig. 6(a). Each dataset has identical classical summary statistics. No clear pattern is discernible in the table. The adjacent classical statistics are no more informative. Software managers may not instantly recognise the meaning of such quantities as 't' or 'r', nor is the phrase "residual sum of squares" guaranteed to bring immediate enlightenment. Software engineers may not care to wade through some tome on statistics trying to find out its meaning. And they would be absolutely right.

Graphs of the data sets (in Fig. 6(b)) reveal that these statistics are more than uninformative. They are positively misleading. If one set represented the output from a model of software development, and the other was real data from an environment in which the model might be used, then analysing the data with any technique that could suggest an equivalence could be disastrous.

Communicability is another essential feature of analyses that are intended to inform those working in software production. The result of

2 Dimensions

A		B		C		D		
X	Y	X	Y	X	Y	X	Y	
10.0	8.04	10.0	9.14	10.0	7.46	8.0	6.58	N = 11
8.0	6.95	8.0	8.14	8.0	6.77	8.0	5.76	mean of X's = 9.0
13.0	7.58	13.0	8.74	13.0	12.74	8.0	7.71	mean of Y's = 7.5
9.0	8.81	9.0	8.77	9.0	7.11	8.0	8.84	regression line: Y = 3 + 0.5 X
11.0	8.33	11.0	9.26	11.0	7.81	8.0	8.47	st. error of est. of slope = 0.118
14.0	9.96	14.0	8.10	14.0	8.84	8.0	7.04	t = 4.24
6.0	7.24	6.0	6.13	6.0	6.08	8.0	5.25	sum of squares X - $\bar{X}$ = 110.0
4.0	4.26	4.0	3.10	4.0	5.39	19.0	12.50	regression sum of squares = 27.5
12.0	10.84	12.0	9.13	12.0	8.15	8.0	5.56	residual sum of sq. of Y = 13.75
7.0	4.82	7.0	7.26	7.0	6.42	8.0	7.91	correlation coefficient = 0.82
5.0	5.68	5.0	4.74	5.0	5.73	8.0	6.89	r^2 = 0.67

Fig. 6(a). Table: Anscome's quartet.

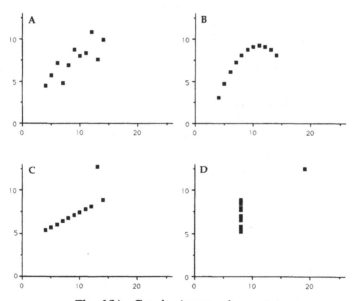

Fig. 6(b). Graph: Anscome's quartet.

a graphical analysis can be directly presented to people who would regard a table of numbers marked with intimidating statistical buzz-words either with uncomprehending acceptance or with distrust.

For these and other reasons SWDL is researching for its own use, and recommends for the use of software managers and engineers, a set of data analysis and presentation techniques that satisfy the following criteria:

—*Resilience*—the technique must not be dependent either for its validity or for its efficiency upon underlying assumptions about the data distribution.

—*Robustness*—the technique must recognise exceptional points in the data and protect summary statistics from being unduly affected by them.

—*Presentation*—the technique must allow the data to speak for itself so that anyone familiar with software engineering can understand the result.

—*Honesty*—the technique must indicate the true degree of uncertainty attached to its own results.

Pickard's paper (Chapter 7) discusses the degree to which these objectives are met by the currently available techniques.

3.2 Avoiding problems when using graphical techniques

SWDL's approach to graph production is based on the belief that preparing a graph of data is an iterative, experimental process and may result in displaying several different graphical representations of the same data set. With care, a large amount of quantitative information can be packed into a small region. (Note that the aim is to increase the information content of a given area, not to decrease the area in which a given amount of information is displayed.) Many useful graphs nevertheless require careful, detailed study.

SWDL has adapted various graphical approaches[2] and developed standards for the graphical presentation of data, as well as suggestions for avoiding common problems that may be encountered. Some of these are described below.

3.2.1 Avoiding overlap

A problem frequently met when plotting two variables is the overlapping of graphical symbols caused by two data values being identical or very close. This results in the symbols obscuring one another and so degrading the viewer's ability to grasp the distribution of the data or, in the cases of exact overlap, to grasp its density. This can be dealt with by:

(1) *Choice of symbol.* Circles intersect in shapes that are very unlike circles themselves. Overlapping circular plotting symbols can thus be distinguished more easily than overlapping squares or triangles or crosses, each of which intersect in very similar, and so confusable, shapes.

(2) *Sunflower.* Where exact overlap is the problem it is often best to put dots on the graph to represent single values and sunflower symbols (a dot with a number of radiating spokes) to represent multiple values at a point, with each spoke of the symbol denoting an additional overlapping point (see Fig. 5).

(3) *Moving and jittering.* Where the overlapping symbols occur in pairs or small groups surrounded by empty space, or where the overlap is due to all the data having to take one of a small number of discrete values (e.g. a group of modules all with zero or a small number of errors), then the graph can be improved by moving all overlapped data values a small amount in a given direction or by jittering the data (randomly displacing all the values by a small amount). A very small displacement can sometimes greatly improve the clarity of a graph without altering its basic message (for example, the zero-error values in Fig. 5 have been displaced upwards to avoid their cluttering the axis line).

(4) *Transforming the data scale.* Sometimes bunching of data points occurs at one end of a scale because the data set being plotted is heavily skewed (perhaps because a scale is being used to record data being produced by a process which is non-linear with respect to that scale). Applying a transformation can reveal the trends in the data more clearly. (N.B. Transformations can have side-effects and should only be done after considering these.)

(5) *Residuals.* Where the problem being examined involves comparing actual data with some predicted line, a plot of the difference between actual values and predictions (called a residual plot) is often useful. As a side effect, such a plot may make it possible to increase the scale and so resolve the most obstinate dataset, provided closeness, not exact overlap, is the problem (but note the warning after (4) above).

(6) If it is impossible to resolve the data clutter in a single graph, it may be permissible to split the dataset into two or more groups distinguished by their values of some third variable.

3.2.2 Choosing whether to juxtapose or superpose

Data analysis frequently involves the comparison of two datasets. For one-dimensional datasets the boxplot (described in Section 3.3.1) is ideal. Comparison of two-dimensional datasets, however, involves either superimposing them on the same graph or juxtaposing two graphs. Both methods have their advantages and disadvantages. Superposition allows easy comparisons between the datasets, but distinguishing which data values belong in which datasets, in the general clutter, may be a problem. Juxtaposed graphs keep the datasets distinct but it is harder to compare values and trends when one has to look across from one graph to another. SWDL's guidelines are:

(1) If the data sets will be distinguishable on the resulting graph, use superposition. Differentiate between data values belonging to differing data sets. Do this using colour or texture or shading if possible (but consider whether the result must be photocopiable). Otherwise, differentiate by using plotting symbols from the sets shown in Fig. 7 (use the top set if overlap is not a serious problem and the bottom set otherwise). For two categories of data use the first two symbols on the left, for four categories use the first four symbols, and so on (see Figs 8(a)(b) and (d)).

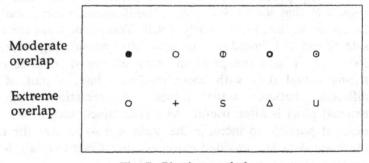

Fig. 7. Plotting symbols.

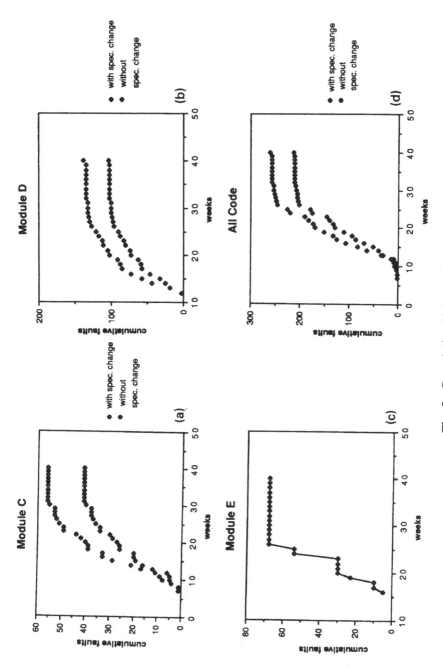

Fig. 8. Cumulative fault graphs.

(2) Where superposition does not give a distinct result, use jux-
    taposition. Comparison is greatly facilitated if one or more
    reference lines are drawn on the juxtaposed graphs, preferably
    parallel to the trend of the data in at least one of the graphs.
    Wherever possible the graphs should be placed so that they
    share an axis (see Fig. 8). It is important to ensure that the
    other scales do not distort the comparison.

3.2.3 Displaying time-varying data

A time-series chart resembles a scatterplot, but in this case the points
are the values of one item as these change over time rather than the
values of a group of items at a given time. There are five main
methods of displaying time-series charts, suitable to various situations:

(1) *Symbol charts.* Where the data is slowly varying (in relation to
    the chosen graph scales) a straightforward symbol plot is
    appropriate (see Figs 8a and 8b).
(2) *Connected symbol charts.* Where much variation in the data is
    crowded into a small time-period, it is advisable to connect the
    symbols with straight lines drawn on the graph (see Fig. 8c).
(3) *Vertical line charts and histograms.* Sometimes the vertical
    variable may be a sum of several quantities (for example, effort
    may be split into effort spent in coding, effort spent in review,
    etc.). Vertical lines drawn down from the symbol to the
    horizontal axis can be split by shading or colour-coding to show
    the contribution of each to the total value (Fig. 9 gives an
    example of this, though not in a time-varying context).
(4) *Area charts.* When a histogram has a time-varying trend, joining
    the separate bars together to create continuous lines which
    bound shaded areas may help to emphasise trends on the graph.
(5) *Double-axis charts.* A variable that always increases, or always
    decreases, with time can be shown on the opposing axis of the
    graph.

3.2.4 Choosing graphical elements to convey data

A series of psychological experiments[2] has revealed great variations in
the efficiency and accuracy with which data encoded in different
graphical forms can be decoded by the average human being. Seven
ways of encoding values on a data scale, given in order of their ease of

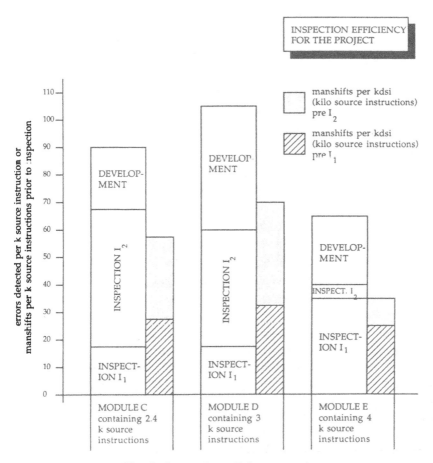

Fig. 9. Inspection efficiency graph.

visual decoding from easiest to hardest, are:

(1) position along a common scale;
(2) position along identical, non-aligned scales;
(3) length;
(4) angle or slope;
(5) area;
(6) volume;
(7) colour hue, colour saturation, density.

It is a basic principle of data display to encode data on a graph so that

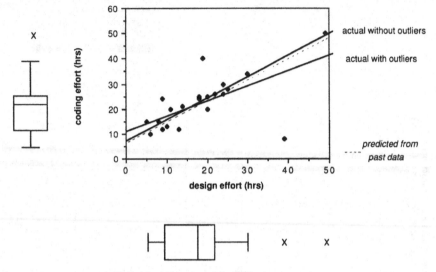

Fig. 10.   Scatterplot: Effort expansion.

the visual decoding involves tasks as high as possible in the ordering (see Fig. 10). Two qualifications must be made.

Firstly, the ease of detection of a data item (its size, prominence in relation to surrounding graph elements, etc.) and the distance between data items that are to be compared are factors affecting the ease of understanding of a graph. It can be worth departing from the order given above if detection is thereby simplified or distance minimised.

Secondly, the low rating of colour refers to the difficulty of decoding a data scale shown in terms of colour. For distinguishing a small number of categories, or showing qualitative as opposed to quantitative variations, colour is excellent and should always be preferred, as stated in Section 3.2.2 above.

3.3 Statistical techniques
The best explanation of a statistical technique is its demonstration in a context familiar to its audience. This is especially true of the techniques recommended in this document, whose suitability depends in part on their ability to communicate to, and be used by, software engineers and managers. Hence SWDL's techniques are briefly described here and a range of them are demonstrated in the next section.

3.3.1 Univariate techniques

(1) *Distribution plot* (or *frequency histogram*). This shows the values of a number of items (e.g. the sizes of a number of modules) plotted against an axis (see Fig. 11(a)).

(2) *Boxplot*. A boxplot is a diagram that displays the lower, lower middle, upper middle and upper quarters of a one-dimensional distribution of data values (see Fig. 11(b)). It summarises the data without distorting it by oversimplification. The small amount of effort needed to become familiar with it is outweighed by its usefulness.

(3) *Transformation*. Common transformations are: natural logarithm, square root, square of cube root, etc. There do not appear to be transformations which are optimal for all datasets, so the following strategy is cautiously suggested for selecting transformations:

—for duration, effort and cost data use the natural logarithm transformation which has been used extensively for software cost models and conforms to general econometrics practice:
—for counts based on incidents, failures and faults, two different

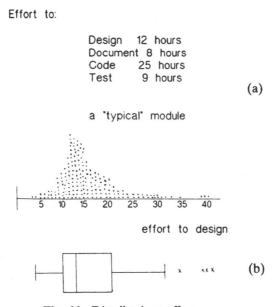

Fig. 11. Distribution: effort.

transformations are particularly appropriate:

(a) the square root to stabilise the variance and so permit the accurate identification of outliers,

(b) the square of the cube root to approximate normality and so permit (cautious) use of classical techniques.

No single transformation can achieve both objectives.

—for size metrics related to code or design, use the natural log transformation for metrics which do not take the value zero (or very rarely take the value), and the square root transformation otherwise.

(4) *Classification* (often shown as a *histogram*). Often the data is naturally divided into values relating to a small number of items or categories. Where this is not so, it may be convenient to impose a classification scheme on a dataset and count the number of items in each category. A bar histogram is an effective way of displaying such data (see Fig. 9).

3.3.2 Bivariate techniques

(1) *Scatterplot* or *Time-varying plot*. A scatterplot or time-varying plot is the most common way of displaying software data for monitoring purposes. It can help comprehension if the axes of a scatterplot also display the boxplot (or frequency histogram) showing the spread of data along that axis (see Fig. 10).

Visual examination of the plot will indicate whether techniques for investigating relationships, such as regression, curve fitting or smoothing, could be profitably applied. Alternatively, the data may be classified into groups with respect to one axis. The boxplot for each group (seen as a one-dimensional dataset along the other axis) can then be drawn above its interval on the first axis. The result can simplify a complex scatterplot.

(2) *Regression*. Many relationships can be usefully approximated by a linear equation. However, the need to protect analyses from being distorted by the presence of exceptional points means that it would be desirable, in the calculation of such equations, to use special 'robust' algorithms. These are still being researched. Once an equation has been obtained, the differences between it and the data values (called residuals) should be examined. Points which deviate grossly from it should be removed from the dataset and the equation recalculated.

Comparison of the first and second equations will reveal something of the effect of the exceptional points, and so indicate the trustworthiness of the equations. No regression should be relied on further than visual examination suggests is reasonable.

(3) *Curve fitting*. Non-linear equations may appropriately be fitted to some time-varying graphs, especially those involved in measuring reliability. Outside a limited range of software applications, lack of robustness makes it essential to use these techniques most cautiously.

(4) *Smoothing* (LOWESS). Some relationships do not resemble any easy mathematical function and are best described by an approximation technique.

(5) *Residual analysis*. If regression, curve fitting, smoothing or some other method of obtaining a predictive line has been applied to the data for a scatterplot or time-varying plot, then a scatterplot of the differences between the data and the predicted line (called a residual plot) is often useful.

(6) *Classification tables* (often shown as a *Three-dimensional histogram*). An ordinary two-dimensional histogram uses one dimension to show the classifications and one to show the histogram bars. Three-dimensional histograms use two dimensions to show the classification table categories and one dimension for the histogram bars.

Three-dimensional histograms are ideal for emphasising gross trends in two-way classification tables but, unlike ordinary histograms, cannot have values easily read from them. Hence a table showing the numerical values should always be shown beside it. It helps to show, for each axis of the base of a three-dimensional histogram, an associated pie chart showing the total number in the table in each of the classes of that axis as a proportion of the total number in the entire table. This serves the same function as displaying a boxplot against an axis of a scatterplot.

3.3.3 Multivariate techniques

(1) *Scatterplot matrix*. A group of scatterplots of three or more variables against one another can be arranged in a matrix format to show multi-dimensional effects (see Fig 12). The clarity with which such an effect is revealed can be enhanced by brushing (i.e. distin-

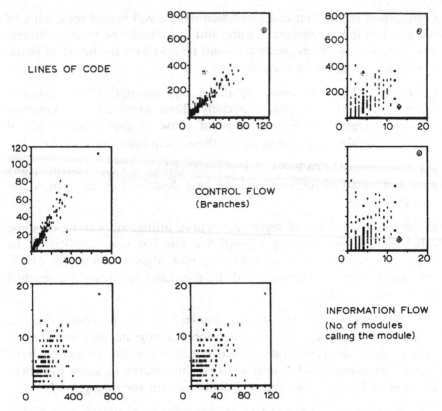

Fig. 12. Scatterplot matrix: Loc versus control flow versus information flow.

guishing by colouring or shading) a subset of the points on all the diagrams.

The clarity of the resulting matrix, and whether it shows any multivariate effect, will determine whether to plot a group of variables as a scatterplot matrix or simply as a succession of individual scatterplots. Often it will be best to combine the two styles of presentation by showing, first, a scatterplot matrix (reduced in size) and, second, the scatterplots of which it is made up (each shown at full size). The scatterplot matrix acts as a contents list for the succeeding plots and emphasises major effects.

(2) *Profiles.* When the form of the relationship between a number of variables is unclear, they may be plotted against a common axis, or on radial axes of a circular graph. Studying the shapes produced for a

number of cases may suggest patterns which can guide further analysis. In Fig. 9, detected faults and workshifts per kloc.† of delivered source lines are plotted against a common axis.

(3) *Multivariate regression*

(4) *Principal components.*

Techniques (3) and (4) are still being researched. Although they would appear to have potential, there are problems in their use. These are discussed in Chapter 7.

4. EXAMPLES OF IN-PROJECT DATA USE

The following examples are intended to demonstrate the kind of graphs that an organisation might choose to produce routinely at appropriate points in a product's development lifecycle. The interpretations provided in the text are intended to be examples of the possible results of selecting, from lists of exceptions and their possible causes, the ones that apply to the particular datasets being displayed.

All the data is real, but the relationships between different datasets have been altered to preserve confidentiality. The indicated interpretations of the data are legitimate but not necessarily those that actually applied in the projects which originally supplied the data.

4.1 Project inspection efficiency

Figure 9 shows the effort expended on and errors found in three programs (created as part of the same development) at three points in development (the inspections at the end of high-level and low-level design and at the end of integration testing). Because the upper elements of this graph describe data that becomes available later in development than the lower, it could be started early in development and completed at the appropriate phase crossings.

Our interpretation of this graph is that efficient early inspections reduce subsequent development costs. It is already suggested by the lowest blocks of the histogram bars. As the real-life project from which this data comes did not produce this graph, it went on to successively create the data for the middle and upper blocks of the bars, confirming the interpretation. A clearer demonstration of the

† kloc = 100 lines of delivered source code.

advantages of front-loading projects and devoting resources to early inspection would be hard to devise.

Much of the effectiveness of this graph is due to its intelligent use of graphical elements to encode the data. The same information in a table would contain the same meaning, and that meaning could be grasped by a concerned manager, but it would be much less effective in motivating subordinates to front-load their work or in persuading superiors to release the necessary resources.

4.2 Reliability growth

Figure 8 shows the reliability growth curves for each of the three programs of Fig. 9, and for the subsystem of which they were part. This time-varying data is slowly varying for modules C and D and so has been shown as unconnected points. The rapidly varying module E data is better shown using a line connecting the points. Modules C and D have two error lines, one for total errors and one showing only errors that did not result directly from an external interface change, and these two lines are shown superposed on the same graphs.

The graphs for modules C and D are similar in overall shape but their scaling is very different, an effect best seen by juxtaposing the two graphs with a common errors axis (note differing scales). Module E is shown with a common time axis to module C as it differs from the other two in the overall shape of its curve.

Module E was acting as a test harness for modules C and D and this explains the differing shape of its curve. The chief point of interpretation to note is that flat stretches of module E's curve correspond to changes in the slope of the curves on the other graph. It would be cause for anxiety if this were not so, as this would imply that fault detection and correction in the test harness was not affecting fault detection in its subjects.

Reliability growth, techniques for fitting curves to such graphs, etc., are the subjects of other papers. A project using graphs like these would need such techniques to predict their expected growth curves and to interpret any deviations of the actual curves from these.

4.3 Effort expansion ratios

In most software production environments there is a relationship between effort expended in one phase and effort expended in later phases. Figure 10 plots design effort against coding and testing effort for the modules of a subsystem. Three lines show the predicted line, the regression line and the regression line recalculated after removing the indicated exceptional points.

The recalculated regression line is close enough to the prediction (based on past projects) to suggest that no overall change in the environmnent's way of working has occurred on this project. The outlying point at the upper right of the diagram should have been recognised as exceptional in the design stage and examined then to see if the module needed splitting or redesign. If this was not possible, then extra pro-rata effort in coding may be expected.

The other two exceptional points have several interpretations. A high ratio of design to code effort can mean:

—good design;
—slapdash or incomplete coding;
—overdetailed design (i.e. coding done in design) or creeping elegance (design more elaborate than necessary);
—extremely elegant coding;
—a problem whose complexity resides in its interfaces.

A low design-to-code effort ratio can mean:

—poor design;
—creeping functionalism (coding more than the design);
—excessive design or requirements changes;
—high algorithmic complexity of the problem;
—designer familiarity with (or clear grasp of) the problem.

The project manager, or project staff, will be able immediately to discard some of these explanations as being inconsistent with facts they already know. Distinguishing between others can be helped by examining other graphs, such as those showing size ratios of the relevant modules.

4.4 Size and information flow ratios

Figure 12 shows a scatterplot matrix of lines of code, control flow complexity and information flows (number of modules calling the module) for modules of the system containing the subsystem of 4.3 above. The strong linear relationships on all the graphs are typical of those normally observed between these metrics.

Two of the exceptional points indicated are the modules shown as exceptions on Fig. 10. The module with a large effort is, unsurprisingly, large in all the size metrics also, while the module with a high design-to-code effort ratio has a high information-to-control flow ratio, possibly indicative of a module whose complexity is mainly in its interfaces.

The other outlying point indicated is high in lines of code but low in control flow and in information flow. This may indicate a module which, despite its codes size, is innately simple. If so, future graphs which plot codesize against faults or other factors may highlight this module unnecessarily.

Clearly, other points on this graph could be examined, and those that have been considered could be analysed in far greater detail. The discussion here, as in the sections above, is intended to indicate, rather than to exhaust, the information in this graph.

5. PROCEDURES FOR DATA COLLECTION AND USE

The sections above indicate how data collected from a project might be used to control that project. This section returns to the theme of the introduction, that data collection and short-term use should be integrated. It considers how to design procedures that will achieve that aim.

Very little of the data which SWDL recommends for collecting is new to project managers. Most of it is known during software development and briefly recorded, sometimes on the backs of envelopes and sometimes on forms designed so as to collect that data (but seldom so as to enable its comparison with data from outside its immediate environment). Because of this, setting up a data collection scheme usually involves recording standard data in a way that allows it to be stored and easily retrieved for later reuse, rather than discovering and recording novel data items. Hence data collection procedures are concerned with ensuring that data is retrievable and comparable, not with identifying new data types. (SWDL recognises that where data, such as vocabulary measures, is not automatically available, its widespread collection may have to await tools.)

5.1 Compulsory data collection to monitor stage completion
Some data values describe attributes of objects that are created and kept as a result of software development (for example, lines of code of modules). In principle such values can be measured at any time

(although their usefulness decreases with time). Other data, such as time to complete items, will be forgotten if not promptly recorded and cross-related. Hence the first need of a collection scheme is to ensure that data is captured as it occurs. This will not happen unless such capture is made part of the development process, and since software development proceeds as a series of stages this means creating checkpoints, as part of the structure of these stages, at which the recorded data is examined.

Data collection procedures associated with checkpoints are easy to create and enforce because they serve a number of useful management functions. Data usually becomes available at the end of some process (for example, the end of designing or coding or testing some item). The conclusion of such processes will (or should) involve some procedure of reporting completion, often with a review to ascertain that completion has been satisfactory. Data on items created by and resources used during a process, presented in a comprehensible manner, would be useful to such a review, or in such a report. The quality of a completed item, its relation to others, and the mere fact of completion itself, are all more reliably demonstrated by the use of such data.

Consequently, SWDL advises its data providers to establish criteria for phase and process completion that involve the handover, not only of the specified items, but also of data about these items and their construction in a format that permits easy analysis.

5.2 Support for data collection

It is axiomatic that the circumstances in which data collection is likely to prove most valuable (tight deadlines, demanding requirements) are precisely those in which spare time and effort to spend on collection will be least available. An ill-considered or unsupported collection scheme that involves staff in multiple recording of numbers, and in copying values that their machines calculate but do not keep, will not alleviate the problem. A database in which to keep software metrics is essential, as are tools to collect compiler-produced size metrics and spreadsheets to record timesheet and other resource data.

The creation of the data model from which the database is designed, and the appointment of a data collection supervisor to create and maintain collection tools and oversee collection procedures, are topics that have received much study by SWDL[7,8] but are beyond the scope of this paper.

5.3 Support for data analysis

Time to master statistical analysis techniques or to prepare informative data displays is likely to be no more abundant than time to collect data. A graphical statistics package should be interfaced with the database and programmed to extract routinely those basic graphs that have been made part of the stage completion procedures. This package should also enable the further investigation of exceptions, the exploration of hypotheses and the creation of simple local models.

Equally necessary is a facility for recording data interpretations. Ideas about what kinds of exceptions are significant and what they mean, and notes on what diagnoses of particular exceptions were made by review groups or managers, need to be recorded if an organisation is to acquire and reuse expertise about its own software development environment. The data collection supervisor has an important role in reviewing and systematising this material.

5.4 Feedback of results

Feedback is the best way of motivating the participants in any data collection scheme. Those who record, not just their managers, must be involved in the process of explaining trends observed in the results of data analysis and in diagnosing exceptions from these. No statistical technique, however subtle, can replace the interpretative skills of someone who understands the items that the data is describing. The role of statistics is to draw attention to dangers that might otherwise not be noticed until too late, and to speed the finding of a solution.

SWDL recommends that the results of data analyses be made visible to all involved in the relevant part of the project.

5.5 Graphical collection of data

The above sections require the data collection scheme to be part of the process completion criteria, to make collection and analysis easy and promptly to feedback the results of analysis to those who originally supplied the data. It is sometimes possible to meet all these requirements by the simple procedure of recording datapoints directly onto pre-prepared graphs.

As an example, consider Fig. 13 (cf. Fig. 10). As individual modules are designed, the effort used can be recorded by placing a symbol on the axis of a prepared chart (or a value into the data table of a programmed graphics package). During the coding and testing phases the symbols can be moved up to assume their final positions on the

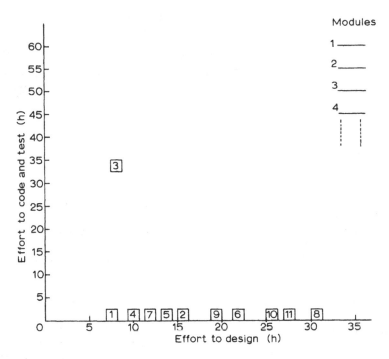

Fig. 13. Example data collection graph: Effort expansion.

graph. In this way a single action suffices to record and analyse the data. The overall trend of a graph, and any deviations from it, will quickly become visible.

6. CONCLUSION

In the past, data collection schemes have sometimes been started on the assumption that once data has been collected uses for it will materialise. Such activities have usually failed. It is true that, once a collection scheme is in operation for a given software environment, many additional ways of using the data will emerge. However, any collection activity that is not planned to support the immediate needs of those providing the data is unlikely to succeed well enough to meet any other objectives.

ACKNOWLEDGEMENT

Although this paper describes techniques used by the Alvey SWDL project, some of the research that developed these techniques was done in the Alvey TSQM and Esprit REQUEST projects by the author, Dr Barbara Kitchenham and others.

REFERENCES

1. Wigle, G. B., Tsai, J. and Bowen, T. B., *Specification of software quality attributes—Final technical report*, Boeing Aerospace Company Engineering Technology, 1985.
2. Cleveland, W. S., *The elements of graphing data*, Wadsworth Advanced Books and Software, Monterey, CA, 1985.
3. Frewin, G. and Ross, N., Synthetic estimation and control systems, SWDL Report SWDL/COLL/DA1, 1987.
4. Kitchenham, B. and Walker, J., *An information model for software quality management*, Alvey, deliverable from the TSQM project, report A24, 1986.
5. Kitchenham, B., *Management metrics Proc. 2nd CSR conf.*, 1985.
6. McCall, J. A., Richards, P. K. and Walters, G. F., Factors in software quality, Vols I, II and III, 1977, RADC Reports: NTIS AD/A–049 014, 049 015 and 049 055, 1977.
7. Ross, N. and Burgess, E., Initial contact presentation, SWDL Report SWDL/COLL/ICP, 1987.
8. Ross, N., A model to support the collection and analysis of S/W data, *Proc. SARSS87 Conf.*, 11–12 November 1987, Manchester, UK (in press).

7

Analysis of Software Metrics

L. M. PICKARD
STC Technology Ltd, Newcastle-under-Lyme, UK

ABSTRACT

This chapter gives a practical statistical analysis of two sets of software metrics data. The aim of the analysis is to identify relationships between the metrics and atypical values of the metrics which deviate from any identified relationships. The work is part of an ESPRIT project, REQUEST, but also has wider applicability.

During the analysis several problems were encountered with the application of the statistical techniques. These problems were mainly due to characteristics of the software metrics data which were causing violations of the underlying assumptions of the techniques. Such problems are typical of those found in software data and, as such, the method of identifying them (and in some cases overcoming them) has general applicability in practice.

This chapter gives the results of the analysis, and details where the problems occurred.

1. INTRODUCTION: THE USE OF STATISTICS IN ANALYSIS OF SOFTWARE DATA

Statistics is essentially a tool to help provide information. There are several ways that it can do this. For example:

—It provides techniques for collecting, analysing and drawing conclusions from data. This aspect of statistics is applicable to

investigators who attempt to draw general conclusions from samples or planned experiments.
—It provides a monitoring mechanism for quality control—e.g., in assembly line production.
—It is a succinct means of presenting information. Many news items present their information in terms of statistics, e.g. inflation increased by 3%.

Basic statistical concepts assist in promoting clear thinking about a problem, provide some guidance to the conditions that a problem solution must satisfy and enable valid conclusions to be drawn which could not be obtainable by any other way.

It can provide information in two main forms—numerical and graphical. Graphical representation is very useful for:

—summarising the data;
—providing a simple representation of the results from more detailed analysis;
—identifying trends or features in a preliminary analysis of the data prior to more formal analysis.

Numerical techniques serve as objective yardsticks against which the informal conclusions, based on visual assessment of the information contained in the graphical displays, can be evaluated. They also provide a more detailed analysis of the data by providing more information than can be gained from graphics.

In the software development area, the project manager often 'senses' whether the project is running well or not. He/she also, from experience, has some idea of what characteristics of the product are related and which are the most useful. However, little evidence exists of how to quantify the expert's intuition. Statistics should prove useful in the field of software engineering as a means of providing quantitative information about what is happening during development and identifying when something is going wrong.

Like data collection, statistics is likely to be more useful to the software manager if it can be automated and therefore save the manager time and effort in manual application. However, statistics cannot be used in an intellectual vacuum. The requirements of the investigation must be specified before any data analysis can be undertaken. In particular, the hypothesis under test or the relationship being investigated must be decided before any statistical analysis can confirm or reject it. For example, if a relationship between size and number of errors is investigated, the statistical technique of correlation might be used to confirm or reject the existence of the relationship, but it will not identify what the correct functional form of the relationship is.

The choice of which technique to use in which circumstance is well defined in certain fields of use. For example, in the agricultural area, the techniques are well known and have been used with success for many years. The underlying assumptions of techniques are known to be approximately valid.

In general, these techniques are called classical techniques and often assume that the data is drawn from a Gaussian or normal distribution, i.e. the data is symmetrical, possesses a constant variance, and contains a predeterminable number of outlying values.

In the software engineering area the appropriate techniques are not known; in particular, the validity of the classical assumptions of data distribution is not proven.

2. CONSTRUCTIVE QUALITY MODEL (COQUAMO)

This section aims to provide the context in which the statistical analysis was undertaken. The analysis of software data reported in this paper was performed as part of the work of an ESPRIT project called Reliability and Quality of European Software Technology (REQUEST). One of REQUEST's initial aims was to develop an algorithmic quality model. The development of this model, called COQUAMO, was inspired by COCOMO (Constructive Cost Model developed by Boehm[1]).

The aim of COQUAMO is to provide assistance to project managers in quality-related issues throughout the development of the project.[8] The basic underlying assumption is that quality is created during the project and that each decision taken during development may have some influence on the final quality.

Research has now caused COQUAMO to deviate from being just an algorithmic model. It has basically three parts (or modes)— planning, monitoring/steering, and extrapolation/assessment.

2.1 Planning mode
COQUAMO will have a planning mode which will be used primarily during the initial project planning, the subsequent replanning, and

when quality requirements are changed. It will attempt to predict the final product quality, using quality drivers based on the initial requirements of the product and the initial constraints under which the product will be developed (e.g. staff ability, support environment).

2.2 Monitoring/steering mode

This mode is intended to assist the project manager in monitoring and controlling the project development by quantitative measures. It falls into two interactive parts—statistical analysis and advice. The statistics will identify anomalies or atypical values which might be an indication of a potential problem. The advisory system will provide help in the interpretation of possible causes of the anomaly. This mode will be active in development from the end of requirements specification until the integration testing phase.

2.3 Extrapolation/assessment mode

This mode will be useful only as the development reaches completion. Essentially its aim is to estimate the qualities of the final product using data. Examples of such data are error reports, change reports, and effort measurements related to changes during the testing and early life periods. It will contain predictive models to indicate features such as the support costs of a product and/or the constraints for future development enhancements.

3. REQUIREMENTS AND SUGGESTED TECHNIQUES FOR ANALYSIS

It has been mentioned previously (in Section 2.2), that statistics will be required for part of the COQUAMO development. The statistical analysis detailed in the later sections has drawn its requirements from the development of COQUAMO.

In order to formulate COQUAMO, there are three requirements on the statistical analysis:

—to identify consistent or general relationships;
—to identify trends and atypical values;
—to construct stable, predictive models.

3.1 Consistent or general relationships

There are two types of general relationship that can be identified which require different kinds of statistical analysis—algorithmic relationships and group classifications of data.

Algorithm relationships are in the form of an equaiton. For example, number of errors = module size/100. To identify this type of relationship the usual statistical techniques are regression and correlations.

An example of a relationship which requires assigning ungrouped data to groups is:

Module group Expected errors per module	Assignment criteria Module size
0	<20
1	21–50
2	51–100
>2	>100

This type of procedure is likely to require classification or discriminant analysis to identify it.

3.2 Identification of trends and atypical values

The monitoring mode of COQUAMO will require statistical techniques to identify atypical values. It is possible to use metrics as anomaly detectors (that is, indicators of unusual or atypical events) to allow the software development process to be monitored.[2,4] There are two different areas which require anomaly identification: comparison between similar components within a project, and comparison of a single metric value with values obtained from other similar products.

The first area requires the establishment of a relationship or trend and highlighting of those components which do not follow the relationship. A regression technique could be used to establish a relationship, but a technique is required to detect when a component (or components) deviates from the general relationship. Analysis of the residuals obtained from the regression line may be used to identify anomalous components because the size of the residual identifies how much a particular component deviates from the identified relationship. For example, to detect particularly error-prone modules within a subsystem, the error rate per module for the modules within the subsystem must be compared with the average (or median) rate. This is achieved by establishing a relationship between number of errors and module size.

The second area requires identification of a metric value as outside the 'normal' range compared with the values obtained from other similar products. This can be achieved by using a measure of central location of a group plus a measure of the expected variability about the central location. For example, it may be useful to determine whether the testing effort used to produce a product of given size and application type is unusually large or small compared with other similar products. A measure of the central location of a group of testing productivity values from various similar products plus a measure of the expected variability about this central location is required to establish whether the testing effort for a new product is in any sense abnormal (for example, the median as the measure of location and ± 2 median absolute deviations[7] as the expected variability).

3.3 Stable, predictive models

To evaluate any identified predictive model, cross-verification studies are required. One method is to use a subset of the data to establish a relationship and validate this relationship against the remaining data. More detailed descriptions of cross-validation techniques are given by Mosteller and Tukey.[6]

4. THE DATA

The particular data sets were selected because they had previously been collected over a range of different metrics, many of which are likely to be used by COQUAMO, and none of which had missing values. The data set comprised all the modules from two subsystems of ICL's general purpose operating system, VME, which were implementations of the same functional requirements (implemented a few years apart).

The data used is shown in Tables 1 and 2, and the descriptions of the software metrics are as follows:

(i) *Machine code instructions* (MCI)—this is a count of the number of machine-level instructions in the compiled version of the module, in bytes (*code-based metric*).

Table 1
Software Metrics for Data set 1

Module	Machine code instructions	Lines of code	Modules called	Data Items	Parameters	n_1	n_2	N_1	N_2	McCabe's V	Changes
1	303	181	8	9	2	35	68	206	193	36	2
2	787	396	11	14	7	70	98	472	394	76	22
3	300	142	7	4	1	36	55	194	190	21	2
4	312	150	3	17	0	29	61	175	162	20	4
5	11	67	2	7	1	29	34	99	92	9	2
6	812	352	10	8	2	53	95	445	402	27	11
7	144	90	9	7	3	30	27	69	69	14	3
8	151	103	4	2	1	30	49	93	100	8	4
9	4	2	0	3	4	4	2	4	2	1	2
10	753	343	9	8	4	59	120	474	440	30	7
11	81	34	0	2	3	14	21	68	56	4	2
12	91	54	0	2	1	12	30	95	80	5	3
13	428	268	5	11	8	54	74	286	243	49	9
14	86	57	4	3	2	22	16	46	42	8	4
15	85	34	0	2	1	15	20	65	55	4	2
16	127	49	0	2	3	21	17	80	66	14	2
17	118	60	1	3	1	15	20	91	62	7	2
18	175	82	6	5	2	29	56	103	95	14	4
19	1435	409	5	4	7	52	134	705	661	57	18
20	174	108	8	8	2	36	41	106	101	9	12
21	333	191	7	11	3	46	58	236	217	18	4
22	1354	786	3	32	3	38	79	1469	1198	77	5
23	520	276	6	4	2	39	86	315	313	43	3
24	71	45	0	1	8	18	23	60	40	10	2
25	134	55	3	2	3	29	24	92	68	12	2
26	4	2	0	0	1	5	2	5	2	1	1
27	95	47	4	6	1	23	33	59	60	4	4

Table 2
Software Metrics for Data Set 2

Module	Machine code instructions	Lines of code	Modules called	Data items	Parameters	n_1	n_2	N_1	N_2	McCabe's V	Changes
1	32	20	1	2	0	7	13	10	17	2	2
2	186	161	8	4	2	43	47	120	125	12	2
3	73	54	5	2	2	19	20	42	43	3	2
4	3	3	0	0	0	4	2	4	2	1	1
5	3	3	0	0	5	4	2	4	2	1	1
6	3	3	0	0	5	4	2	4	2	1	1
7	583	383	8	8	10	60	114	367	370	28	4
8	480	337	6	4	2	48	92	361	338	32	2
9	95	61	1	2	4	28	29	106	103	9	1
10	34	23	1	2	2	15	13	20	16	5	1
11	558	386	5	5	7	46	84	344	332	55	4
12	136	37	1	4	9	23	38	123	114	17	3
13	994	809	11	9	7	61	103	682	711	86	5
14	696	399	2	5	5	44	93	501	508	51	7
15	219	115	1	2	5	30	50	147	130	17	1
16	755	516	5	3	5	60	124	502	493	42	8
17	434	298	3	4	4	41	86	293	267	47	4
18	425	330	3	3	4	37	73	313	289	38	5

19	99	81	1	2	5	27	19	68	48	16	4
20	455	378	13	6	2	58	104	287	282	36	8
21	205	174	6	4	6	34	47	133	126	22	4
22	110	82	1	4	6	22	37	76	67	16	1
23	168	113	7	3	2	28	28	76	84	9	4
24	222	138	3	2	4	31	47	146	143	12	5
25	583	446	14	6	2	61	95	399	379	38	5
26	292	199	10	4	4	43	49	200	191	22	4
27	386	177	5	1	4	28	55	185	207	22	7
28	570	446	8	4	9	47	110	441	404	55	9
29	152	96	4	2	2	21	32	204	196	7	2
30	112	86	6	2	2	32	22	72	58	11	3
31	78	62	3	1	8	22	27	44	52	5	1
32	112	81	4	2	3	25	26	56	61	8	2
33	106	97	3	2	2	31	37	96	85	7	1
34	89	77	5	2	7	27	28	64	59	7	1
35	60	25	2	1	2	16	21	33	31	2	1
36	277	182	7	4	7	33	56	195	182	20	1
37	80	47	3	3	2	19	26	41	39	13	1
38	346	283	5	2	6	38	53	180	197	20	1
39	168	146	4	2	5	31	38	104	102	8	2
40	192	225	7	4	4	31	39	159	156	10	1

(ii)   *Lines of code* (LOC)—this is a count of the number of lines of code in the module listing between the first BEGIN and the ENDMODULE lines. A line was included in this count if the first non-space character was not a comment character (i.e. not the start of a comment). Blank lines were not included (*code-based metric*).

(iii) *Number of modules called* (MC)—this is the number of other modules called by a module (*design-based metric*).

(iv)   *Data items* (DI)—the number of external global static (i.e. common) data items accessed by the module (*design-based metric*).

(v)   *Parameters* (PARMS)—the number of parameters on the interface of the given module (*design-based metric*).

(vi) n_1—the number of distinct operators appearing in a module. This and the next three metrics may be used in calculating Halstead's Software Science Metrics[3] (*code-based metric*).

(vii) n_2—number of distinct operands appearing in a module (*code-based metric*).

(viii) N_1—total number of operators appearing in a module (*code-based metric*).

(ix) N_2—total number of operands appearing in a module (*code-based metric*).

(x)   *McCabe's V* (VG)—McCabe's[5] cyclomatic number which defines the complexity of a module in terms of its control structure and is represented by the minimum number of linearly independent paths through the module (*code-based metric* because collected at coding stage, but could be derived from its design).

(xi)   *Changes* (CHNG)—this is the number of changes made to a module after it was put under formal configuration control (*code-based metric*).

(xii) *Halstead's E* (HE)—Halstead's Effort metric, the mental effort to produce a module (*code-based metric*).

Some combinations of the basic metrics are used in this chapter:

$$\text{ETA} = n_1 + n_2 \text{ (because (vi) and (vii) are very highly correlated);}$$

$$N = N_1 + N_2 \text{ (because (viii) and (ix) are very highly correlated);}$$

$$\text{HE} = n_1 N_2 \log(\text{ETA}/2n_2)\left(\text{Halstead's Effort metric.}[3]\right).$$

5. PRACTICAL ANALYSIS OF SOFTWARE DATA

This section deals with the initial exploratory analysis of the two data sets described in the previous section. The exploratory analysis is to investigate the nature of the data and also to allow a check of the underlying assumptions of the more detailed statistical techniques which follow.

The next sub-section attempts to establish the relationships between the metrics required for the monitoring part of COQUAMO, using the standard metrics available for the two developments. Using these relationships, the next step for the monitoring part of COQUAMO is to identify anomalous modules.

5.1 Initial exploratory analysis

One of the first steps in any analysis is to calculate a measure for the centre of location which is required to allow identification of abnormalities between projects; therefore it provided a good example for the general results found by the exploratory analysis.

The usual measure of the centre of location is the arithmetic mean. This is the numerical average of the metric values for the data set. One alternative to the mean is the median, which is the mid-point of the metric values for the data set. To emphasise the problems of using the mean, the mean and the median were compared.

Tables 3 and 4 show the comparison between the mean and the median as measures of the centre of location for data sets 1 and 2 respectively. In general, for these data sets, the mean value is far larger than the median because of the extreme values. Figure 1 shows an example of the plot of the mean and the median for machine code instructions. It is clear that the median is a more plausible measure of centre of location. The box plots in Fig. 2 provide some idea of the nature of the data and why there is a difference between the mean and the median values.

A boxplot provides a visual impression of the following features of the data:

centre of location (median);
spread;
range of data;
outlying atypical data points;
skewness.

Table 3
Comparison between mean and median measures of
central location—dataset 1

	Mean	Median
Machine code instructions	335	161
Lines of code	162	90
Modules called	4	4
Data items	7	4
Parameters	3	2
n_1	31	29
n_2	50	41
N_1	226	99
N_2	200	95
McCabe's V	21	14
Changes	5	4

This compact data display is also very useful for comparing several groups of data.

The fourth spread is shown by the length of the box, which is the range of the data defined by the difference between the upper and lower fourths, i.e. the middle 50% of the data. The median is shown by a crossbar. The outlier cut-offs are defined as

$$F_u + 3/2d_F$$

Table 4
Comparison between mean and median measures of
central location—dataset 2

	Mean	Median
Machine code instructions	263	177
Lines of code	189	126
Modules called	5	4
Data items	3	2
Parameters	4	4
n_1	32	32
n_2	49	38
N_1	180	128
N_2	175	125
McCabe's V	20	14
Changes	3	2

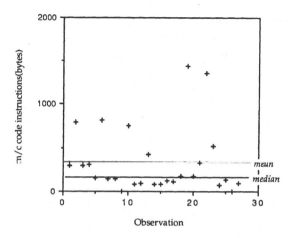

Fig. 1. Median against mean (dataset 1).

and

$$F_L - 3/2d_F$$

where F_u and F_L are the upper and lower fourths and d_F is the difference between the fourths, i.e. the fourth spread. Data values

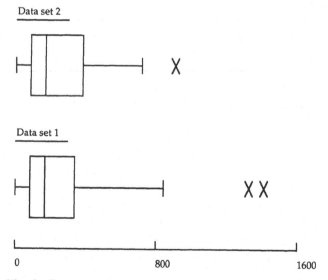

Fig. 2. Boxplots for machine-code instructions (bytes).

which lie outside the cut-off range are considered potential outliers. The lines from the edge of the box extend to the most remote data values in the data set which are not outliers.

For data set 1, in Fig. 2, the spread of data is from just under 100 to 380 bytes. The data is heavily positively skewed since the median (160 bytes) does not lie close to the centre of this range. The plot indicates the tail length starts just above 0 and extends to just over 800. The outliers are indicated by the crosses at around the 1350 and 1425 marks.

For data set 2 the spread of the data is similar to that of data set 1 and ranges from 92 to just under 430 bytes. As with subsystem 1 the data is positively skewed; in this case the median is 177 bytes. The anticipated range of the data lies between just above 0 and just over 750 bytes. As can be seen from the comparison of the two boxplots of the machine-code instructions, the nature of the data is markedly similar between the two data sets. The boxplots for the other metrics were also similar, which indicates that there seems to exist some consistency in the nature of software data in this environment.

Looking at all the box plots provides some idea of the nature of the data and the dangers in the use of the mean rather than the median. If the underlying distribution of the data is symmetrical about its mean, then the mean and the median coincide. However, if the distribution is highly skewed, as it is with the data under study, then the median appears to represent a more intuitively appealing measure than the mean. However, there is more danger in applying the mean when extreme outlying points are present in the data since they will distort the value of the sample mean and provide misleading results. The further away the outliers are from the rest of the data (shown by the area between the tail lengths), the more misleading the mean is.

Most of the data, as well as having some outliers, was also heavily positively skewed. This is not unexpected since programmers, as a matter of good programming practice, tend to keep the modules as small as possible. The result of this does not mean that every module will be small, because the optimum size depends on the underlying problem; if the problem is large, then the module representing the solution will probably be large. Also, the data is always positive. This trend can, therefore, be expected to be present in most software data. It is also probable that other software data will reveal a number of outliers.

A technique which is useful for investigating relationships between

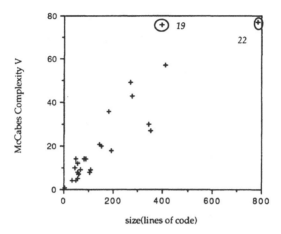

Fig. 3. Complexity against size (dataset 1).

two metrics is scatter plots. A scatter plot is a two-dimensional diagram in which one variable is plotted against another. Figure 3 shows the scatter plot of size against McCabe's Complexity V. Intuitively it was expected that as size increases, complexity increases. This plot shows a strong positive relationship but evidence of heavy, positive skewing. Skewing can be detected by a high density of modules in a particular range of values and, in this case, the skewing is positive because there is a tendency towards the smaller values. There also exists more outliers than would normally be expected from 27 data points. This is consistent with the results obtained from the single dimensional boxplots. It is also possible that the increased number of apparent outliers is caused by an increase in the variation of the data.

A common way of stabilising the variance is via a logarithmic transformation. Figure 4 shows the Fig. 3 plot after the metrics have undergone a natural logarithmic transformation. The relationship is clearer ($r = 0.94$ compared to $r = 0.91$ using unlogged data), with the effects of skewing and outliers greatly reduced. Therefore it appears that more confidence can be placed in detection of true underlying trend between the metric values of McCabe's Complexity V and the size of the module.

The transformation has reduced the problem of the increasing variance and the outliers. However, this transformation may not be as useful as it looks. If the relationship is being used to identify any abnormal values the transformation can cause misleading results with

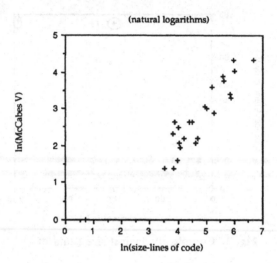

Fig. 4. Complexity against size (dataset 1) (natural logarithms).

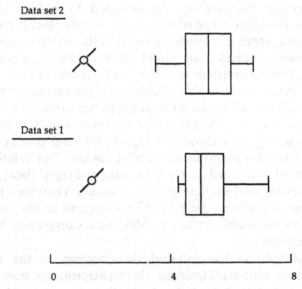

Fig. 5. Boxplots for machine-code instructions (natural logarithmic transform).

certain data characteristics. Figure 5 shows boxplots for the transformed data sets 1 and 2 respectively (natural logarithmic transformation). The smaller modules are now highlighted as being anomalous, whereas previously to the transform they were not. This implies that the transform itself is incorrectly introducing anomalous modules. This is an artifact of the logarithmic transformation and only happens if a relatively large gap exists in the data values between a few very small data points (less than 5) and the majority of the data.

When this occurs in a data set (or there are many zero value data points) another transformation should be applied, for example the square-root transformation. It is unlikely, however, that a single 'common' transformation is suitable for all types of software metric. This lack of a common transformation will cause problems when using multivariate techniques or when trying to automate single or bi-variate techniques.

5.2 Determination of relationships among software metrics
One statistical technique to enable the determination of relationships is regression.

The objective of regression is to determine if a relationship exists between the dependent variable and explanatory variables, and, if so, to predict the dependent variable from the explanatory variables for new datapoints. Although regression is being used to determine relationships between indicators in this document, it may be of use in the planning model to predict the quality factors in terms of their quality drivers.

5.2.1 Prediction of change-proneness
On the current data sets, regression was used in this section to determine if the design and code-based metrics can indicate whether a module is likely to require a large or a small number of changes.

Initially an ordinary least squares (OLS) regression was investigated to obtain some idea of both the nature of the relationship among all the metrics and the number of changes and the problems likely to exist with software data. The OLS regression is unlikely to be useful on its own for predicting change-proneness due to the non-Gaussian nature of software data, but the analysis will indicate whether the technique is robust with respect to deviations from its assumptions.

The significant regression obtained with data set 1 was

$$CHNG = 0 \cdot 042MCI - 0 \cdot 075N + 0 \cdot 00002HE \qquad (1)$$

with an adjusted R^2 of 0·57. There are some doubts as to the validity of this equation as a predictive equation of change-proneness because of the negative sign for N (the total number of operators and operands). The negative sign is saying that if N increases this reduces the number of changes the module will require. Therefore, from a predictive viewpoint, the above equation does not conform with our intuition. However, the high correlation between the explanatory metrics themselves might be causing this negative sign, which might indicate that not all of the explanatory variables, which the regression has shown as having a significant effect on change-proneness, are having a significant independent effect.

The residual plot (Fig. 6) showed five potential outliers. The removal of the outliers reduced the adjusted R^2, which indicates that the outliers were contributing to the significance of the equation; i.e., the regression was being noticeably altered by one or two data values. The metric 'lines of code' was now also significant in the equation and all the coefficients were marginally significant. Therefore the outliers are obviously affecting the detection of any relationship, and it is likely that the non-Gaussian nature of the data is causing untrustworthy results to be obtained from an OLS regression.

The results obtained from data set 2 were totally different from data set 1:

$$CHNG = 0.25MC - 0.53DI + 0.09\,VG \qquad (2)$$

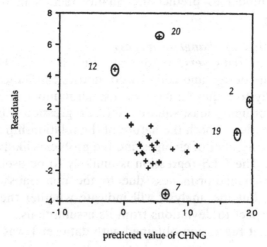

Fig. 6. OLS–residual plot (dataset 1).

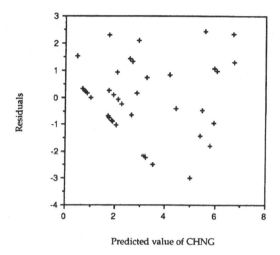

Fig. 7. OLS–residual plot (dataset 2).

with an adjusted R^2 of 0·57. Instead of being totally code metrics, the predictive equation is based predominantly on design metrics. Again, there is an unexpected negative sign in the equation. No major outliers were identified by the residual plot (Fig. 7).

One of the scatter plots (Fig. 3) shows evidence of an increasing variance and, since an increasing variance can cause insignificant coefficients to look significant, it was decided to apply a natural logarithmic transformation to the data. With both data sets, the taking of natural logarithms dramatically altered the results obtained. With data set 1 none of the previous metrics shown to be significant were now significant. The only significant metric shown now was the number of parameters. Again, no confidence can be put in this result because its correlation with change-proneness is low. With data set 2 the effect of the transformation was to show only McCabe's Complexity V to have a significant effect.

Taking natural logarithms has clearly not solved all the problems; therefore, a different technique was investigated. The technique is called robust regression. Instead of reducing the effect of the characteristics present in software data, it attempts to be less sensitive to them. This should mean that deviations from the Gaussian assumptions required by the OLS regression will not cause the regression technique to give invalid results.

Formally, the two robust regressions used were a 'least absolute residual' regression and a 'one-step Andrew's' robust regression.[7] The 'least absolute residual' regression minimises the sum of the absolute values of the residuals, and the residuals can be used as input into the 'one-step Andrew's'.

The raw, original data was used for the robust regression. Initially, with data set 1, the results looked encouraging. The significant regression equation was:

$$CHNG = 0{\cdot}043\,MCI - 0077N + 0{\cdot}00002\,HE \qquad (3)$$

with an R^2 of 0·92. However, if this equation is compared to the OLS equation (eqn (1)) there appears to be very little difference except that the R^2 is 0·25 greater. This is unexpected since there are outliers present which have been shown to have dramatically altered the OLS regression results and the robust regression is supposed to be insensitive to their presence. Due to the similarity of the equations it might seem that it was wrong to reject the OLS regression.

The residual plot (Fig. 8) indicated four potential outliers. The regression coefficients, after the three outliers were removed from the analysis, were all totally insignificant but the equation still had a high adjusted R^2 of 0.83. This implies that it was not the majority of the points that showed a relationship with change-proneness, but only the three outliers. Thus the robust regression is not, in fact, resilient to

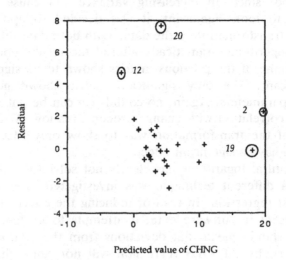

Fig. 8. Robust–residual plot (dataset 1).

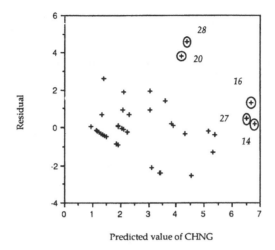

Predicted value of CHNG

Fig. 9. Robust–residual plot (dataset 2).

outliers and does not produce a more trustworthy predictive equation. In fact, the robust regression, far from reducing the problems that were occurring with the use of OLS regression, appears to increase them. The robust regression, including the outliers, has shown 25% more confidence in the predictive power of the equation. Therefore, the technique appears to produce more optimistic results than OLS, without any identified (at present) underlying cause.

Using robust regression with data set 2, the equation was similar to that obtained for data set 1; only the machine code instructions coefficient was significant (although only at 80% level), with an adjusted R^2 of 0·65. The residual plot (Fig. 9) highlighted five potential outliers. After they were removed and the regression repeated, all the coefficients were insignificant.

Both data sets have shown that the robust regression was sensitive to outliers and has not provided reliable information about the nature of the relationship of the metrics to the number of changes in the presence of these outliers.

The results so far from the robust and OLS regressions indicate that the explanatory metrics are related to each other and therefore their independent effects cannot be distinguished. It was therefore decided to investigate whether regression results could be improved by splitting the explanatory variables into design-based and code-based metrics.

This is also of interest in its own right since early indicators of change-prone modules would be of more use to a project manager than indicators which are only detected later in the development process. A natural logarithmic transformation was used on the data. Since there are six code-based metrics, it was decided to use the first principal component of them when investigating the relationship between the design metrics and size. This removed the need to decide, without justification, which was the most appropriate code metric to describe size.

When the regressions were run, it was found that problems still arose. The problems were not so much to do with statistical analysis as with characteristics and relationships which exist in the data. For both data sets, the most significant parameter was the constant in the regression of the design-based metrics against change-proneness. This implies that the currently available design metrics are not influencing the code variable (the constant cannot be interpreted because of the transformations). No consistent relationship was found between the design metrics and change-proneness with the two data sets. Data set 1 showed MC and PARMS to be influencing change-proneness, but data set 2 showed no evidence of any relationship. The regression equation of code-metrics to change-proneness showed all the signs of the existence of high collinearity between the explanatory code-metrics, so the independent influence of individual metrics cannot be determined.

Therefore, in conclusion, the division of the data sets into design and code metrics has not helped to identify any relationships.

5.3 Outlier detection

In order to investigate outlier detection, the untransformed data was used. The consequences of abnormalities in multivariate data are intrinsically more complex than in the univariate case. One reason for this is that a multivariate abnormality can distort not only measures of location and scale, but also measures of correlation. Two techniques were used to identify outliers—a plot of the first two principal components and a residual analysis from a regression.

5.3.1 Principal components

The type of outlier that may be detected by the plot is one which is inappropriately inflating the variances and correlations upon which the principal components analysis is based. The principal component plots

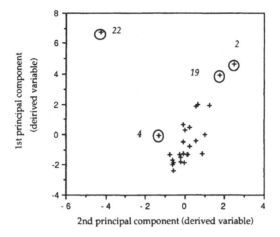

Fig. 10. Principal component plot—dataset 1. First two components.

(Figs 10 and 11) appear to identify modules that are abnormal only when a number of different metrics values are considered together, as well as the modules which are extreme for all metrics. This is likely to be of far more use to the project manager than an analysis technique which only identifies very large or very small modules.

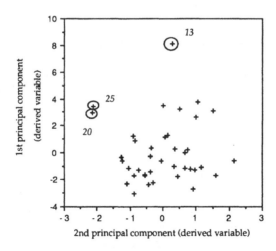

Fig. 11. Principal component plot—dataset 2. First two components.

5.3.2 Regression/residual plots

The outliers were detected by visual inspection of the residual plot. The ordinary least squares (OLS) regression for data set 1 (Fig. 6) highlighted the modules which were relatively change-prone due to their large size. It is useful to have a technique which identifies these modules, but it is likely that a project manager would already be aware of potential problems of large modules which exhibit large values for all metrics. More usefully, however, the technique identified one module that only appeared abnormal when all the metrics were considered. This module had a relatively high number of modules called, data items and numbers of operators and operands for its size and number of changes. The residual plot for the robust regression (Fig. 8) showed all the modules that the OLS plot showed as potential outliers except for the one mentioned above. The residual plots did not highlight any modules which had a relatively low number of changes with respect to all the other metrics.

The residual plots for data set 2 from the OLS regression (Fig. 7) and the robust regression (Fig. 9) were not consistent. The robust residual plot shows five potential outliers which could split into two categories—large modules (i.e. modules for which all the metrics had large values) and unusually change-prone modules (i.e. modules which were more change-prone than would have been expected for their 'size'). The OLS residual plot did not highlight any anomalous modules.

Therefore, of the two techniques used, the principal components appeared to highlight the most interesting and useful potential outliers. It is unclear whether this is because the regression technique has not established the relationships for the residual analysis to correctly highlight those modules which deviate, or whether the residual analysis technique will not highlight the multivariate outliers.

6. SUMMARY

It is clear that the underlying nature of software data causes a number of problems when using classical statistical techniques. These techniques generally assume a Gaussian distribution which is symmetrical, has constant variance and a low expected number of outliers. In contrast, software data appears to be heavily skewed, have an increasing variance and a relatively high number of outliers.

This does not, however, imply that classical techniques are inappropriate for software data but only that care must be taken to check the effect of the violation of their assumptions on the results the technique produces. If the effect of the violation is causing results that are misleading, or infeasible, then either the data must be transformed so that the assumptions are met, or robust techniques or non-parametric techniques are required.

Statistics does have a place in software engineering but it must be used with care. A clear idea of the problem which statistics is being used to help solve is essential, along with a hypothesis of what is expected. If no expectations exist, statistics cannot be used effectively.

The practical analysis of software data has shown that, in general, robust summary statistics provide a more accurate representation of the data. In addition, the results confirm the importance of scatter plots as a means of identifying modules that are anomalous with respect to a relationship, rather than anomalous with respect to being particularly large or small.

No conclusions can be drawn from this analysis about the nature of general relationships in software data due to the large differences that exist between the data sets. This makes it unlikely that relationships between metrics can be summarised in a single predictive model suitable for all data sets.

One major problem is that the metrics are all interrelated, as well as being related to size; therefore their individual effects on change-proneness cannot be distinguished if all the metrics are used in one predictive equation.

The technique of principal component analysis appears to be valuable in detecting outliers. With the available data sets, it has highlighted potentially anomalous modules that are only anomalous in multi-dimensional space, as well as modules which have extreme values for all metrics. The violation of its underlying assumptions does not appear to have had a significant effect on the results.

So far, the regression technique has not proved very useful for either determining the nature of relationships or as an outlier technique. All the regressions tended to be unstable or to produce results which were not sensible from a software engineering viewpoint.

It is important to note that relationships between program features such as size, and quality assessment criteria such as change-proneness, may differ depending on whether a module is extremely change-prone or only moderately change-prone. This suggests that a process of classification (i.e. identifying a module belonging to the group of modules which is, or is not, change-prone) might be more useful than a regression-based prediction function which would predict how many changes a module would be subject to.

Unfortunately there are differences between the relationships observed in each of the two data sets. It is essential for an algorithmic quality model to identify general relationships. The results of this analysis suggest that some relationships will be environment-specific. This implies that software metrics will need to be evaluated in many different environments before any general relationships can be confirmed.

ACKNOWLEDGEMENTS

The author wishes to acknowledge the help and discussions of colleagues in the preparation of this paper, especially that of Dr B. A. Kitchenham of the City University. The author is grateful to ICL Mainframe Systems Division for permission to use data from its VME project. The author's work was part-funded by the Alvey Directorate (Software Data Library) and the ESPRIT programme (REQUEST). The concept of COQUAMO originated with Poul Grav Petersen of ElektronikCentralen, Denmark.

REFERENCES

1. Boehm B. W., *Software Engineering Economics,* Prentice Hall, 1981, p. 5.
2. Doerflinger, C. W. and Basili, V. R., Monitoring software development through dynamic variables, *Proc. IEEE Int. Conf. on Computer Software and Applications (COMPSA),* 1983, p. 8.
3. Halstead, M. H., *Elements of software science,* Elsevier North Holland, 1977, p. 11.
4. Kafura, D. and Canning, J., A validation of software metrics using many metrics and two resources, *Proc. 8th Conf. on Software Engineering,* London, 1985, p. 8.
5. McCabe, T. J., A complexity measure, *IEEE Trans. on Software Engineering,* **SE-2**(4), 1976, p. 11.
6. Mosteller, F. and Tukey, J. W., *Data analysis and regression,* Addison–Wesley, 1977, p. 9.
7. Mosteller, F., Hoaglin, D. C. and Tukey, J. W., *Understanding robust and exploratory data analysis,* John Wiley & Sons Inc., 1983, p. 8.
8. Petersen, P. G., Software quality: the constructive quality modelling system, *ESPRIT 86: Results and Achievements,* Directorate General XIII (Editors), Elsevier Science Publishers BV (North Holland), 1987, p. 5.

8

Using Quantitative Activity Models in Project Management: a Case Study

JOAN V. SROKA

and

CHRISTINE A. GOSLING

Intermetrics Inc., Cambridge, Massachusetts, USA

ABSTRACT

Using quantitative models addresses the project manager's need to make reasoned and timely decisions. This paper presents a case study illustrating the role of the model during the implementation phase of an actual project. Following a brief overview of the technique, construction of the implementation model is described. The paper gives examples of how the model supports the project management functions of estimating, tracking and decision making. Finally, we note that data capture and analysis form the basis of a project history that includes recommendations for future projects.

1. INTRODUCTION

Reasoned and timely decision making is the cornerstone of effective project management. To make good decisions, the project manager must be able to understand why actual progress differs from expectations. The approach described in this paper provides a vehicle for obtaining such understanding. Here, project plans are based on models of the individual subprocesses that comprise the software development process. Such models not only help the project manager discover deviations from planned progress while there is still time to take corrective action, but enable him to *manage* a project effectively rather than merely to *preside* over its inevitable course.

181

This paper presents a case study illustrating the modeling technique in action. The technique was used by a software development team working on a large product development project. Our case study concentrates on the implementation phase of the project, investigating in detail how the model was constructed and used during this phase, and identifying the benefits and difficulties of its use.

The following subsections review the process model technique, describing what process models are and how they are typically used in project management. Section 2 introduces the case study project and sketches the initial planning and requirements analysis for the project. Section 3 describes the model construction and estimation for the implementation phase. The role of the model in project tracking and decision making is discussed in Section 4. Section 5 summarizes the data captured using the framework provided by the model. Section 6 presents some concluding observations.

1.1 Software engineering models

The term 'model' refers to a variety of descriptive and quantitative representations of software development. The various types of model differ in purpose, in scope, and in form. In particular, two frequently used types of model—process models and cost estimation models—are similar in scope but very different in purpose and form. Quantitative activity models are complementary to both of these, providing a detailed perspective and feedback mechanism which elaborates on the global perspective provided by process models and cost estimation models.

A panel discussion at the International Workshop on the Software Process and Software Environments put forward specific terminology to be used in describing software development.[8] Two especially relevant terms and their definitions are given below:

Software process   The collection of related activities, seen as a coherent process subject to reasoning, involved in the production of a software system.

Software process model   A purely descriptive representation of the software process. A software process model should represent attributes of a range of particular software processes and be sufficiently specific to allow reasoning about them.

Hence, a *process model* pertains to the entire software process from problem statement to post-delivery maintenance and modification. It is a descriptive model whose purpose is to facilitate understanding of the software development process. Well known process models include the waterfall model[2] and the spiral model.[5]

A *cost estimation model* is an algorithmic model for estimating resource usage throughout a project's lifetime. These models provide estimates of overall effort and time, and may also include auxiliary equations for apportioning effort among project phases. The COCOMO model[3] is a well known example of a cost estimation model. An overview of other models, and comparison among them, is given in Ref. 4.

A *quantitative activity model* is a set of equations whose variables describe a particular step of the software development process. The input variables represent observable aspects of the activity, and the output variables represent resource consumption. The concept of quantitative activity models for project management was introduced in Ref. 11.†

Activity models present precise numerical descriptions of individual activities, viewing an activity as a local subprocess in the overall software development process. These models differ from process models in form, scope and, to some extent, purpose. A process model is descriptive while an activity model is quantitative. An activity model provides the detailed view of an individual activity of the process, whereas a process model provides the top-level view of the software process in its entirety. While both types of models facilitate understanding and reasoning about the underlying process, the primary goal of activity modeling is to provide in-progress feedback during a particular software development activity.

Both cost estimation models and activity models are quantitative. They differ, however, in scope and in purpose. A cost estimation model addresses the full software lifecycle, and is not generally meant to provide the manager with in-progress feedback. Since the main objective of an activity model is to provide feedback regarding a single activity's progress, it complements a cost estimation model, which addresses the full set of activities and the feedback loops between them.

---

† These models were called quantitative process models in Ref. 11. We have chosen to call them quantitative activity models for consistency with the terminology established in Ref. 8.

By using all three types of model, the project manager obtains both an overview of the entire process and detailed feedback during each activity.

1.2 Overview of the technique

A project management approach using activity models requires the manager to analyze the underlying process continuously, explaining deviations from expectations, evaluating alternatives, and altering the process as necessary. Activity models support all phases of project management—planning, estimating, tracking, and especially decision making. Models are constructed as part of the detailed planning for an activity, and estimates established for their input variables. Tracking entails measuring the model variables and comparing the actual values to the original estimates. When progress does not meet expectations, the model helps to evaluate alternative actions. Having definitive expectations is a key element of this approach.

Our recent experience indicates that for large projects the activity modeling technique works best when applied at the team level. With this project structure, teams of three to fifteen people are established and managed by team managers who report to the project manager. The team managers construct and track individual activity models and the project manager coordinates the interfaces and dependencies between teams. Throughout the course of the project, the activity models support both the needs of the team manager and those of the project manager, providing the in-progress feedback needed on both levels.

1.2.1 Planning and estimating

The process model for the project identifies the activities that comprise the overall software process. Using this framework, the individual teams view each activity as a subprocess and activity models are constructed and reviewed by project management. Model construction involves determining the dynamics of each activity, choosing measurable variables describing the activity, and building model equations. Ideally, each team constructs a model for every activity in the entire software process.

For each activity model, the team manager makes initial estimates for the input variables. Data from previous projects provides valuable input for these estimates. This model estimation is an iterative process. Some values are assigned to the input parameters, and the output parameters are calculated. These answers are then examined to see if they seem reasonable. If not, then both the model and the estimates, along with the qualitative assessments of the team manager, should be re-examined. The model, with its inputs and outputs, should be discussed with the team staff and project management for additional opinions.

Model construction, estimation and sanity checking provide insights into the sensitivities of the model, the expectations about the activity, and where the potential risk areas lie. One can at this point consider alternatives for potential problems that may arise.

1.2.2 Tracking and decision making

Once a particular activity is underway, the activity model helps the team manager to assess and understand the current status. This is done by measuring actual values for model variables, re-computing output values, and comparing them to estimated values.

In addition to its value in the early identification of situations in which progress does not match expectations, an activity model also helps to evaluate alternatives. These can range from altering some aspects of the process (changing the values of the model's parameters) to changing the process altogether (establishing a new model).

Use of the model for tracking and decision making requires the measurement of model parameters on a continuing basis. In addition, model validation, that is, deciding whether the implicit and explicit assumptions of the model are being confirmed by project experience, occurs to some extent throughout each activity.

1.2.3 Data capture

Upon completion of a project, a comprehensive data capture and analysis can form the basis of a project history which can be shared with new projects. The project summary should include a description of the models used by each team for various activities, estimated and actual values for model variables, an analysis of the causes of discrepancies between these values, an evaluation of the utility of the model in managing the project, and specific recommendations for future projects.

A case study of management decision making is created each time a team finds that its planned progress is not being achieved. If the presumed causes of deviations and attempted corrective actions are described in the project history, then managers of later projects can learn from the experience of this project. A collection of such case studies will show managers a wide range of interpretation situations and responses.

2. THE CASE STUDY—FIZVOS

The context of our case study is the product development effort for an advanced telecommunications device. It is an embedded system containing numerous hardware components, ranging from commercial microprocessors to customized special purpose devices.

The operation of the telecommunications device is software controlled, and distributed among three primary processors—two Intel 8051s and an Intel 8088. Logically, the operational software is partitioned into three subsystems, corresponding to the three primary processors. Each subsystem contains an operating system and application software. Since the 8051 microprocessor was used for two of the processors, those subsystems contain the same operating system. The software development effort for the project was thus structured into four teams with the following responsibilities:

—application software for Intel 8051A;
—application software for Intel 8051 B;
—real-time operating system and application software for Intel 8088;
—real-time operating system for Intel 8051 (A and B).

The real-time operating system for the 8051 was dubbed FIZVOS. Implementation of FIZVOS, and the role of activity modeling in managing the implementation activity, is the subject of our case study.

2.1 FIZVOS specification

Initially, the FIZVOS team had three members: a team manager, a lead designer, and one implementor. This team worked with the other teams to determine the overall software requirements, including the functional requirements for FIZVOS. Generally, the specification for a real-time OS is driven by the design of the application software, but application design was as yet unknown. Furthermore, FIZVOS was required early in the schedule because implementation of the application software required operating system facilities. This dilemma was resolved by specifying more extensive functionality than was actually

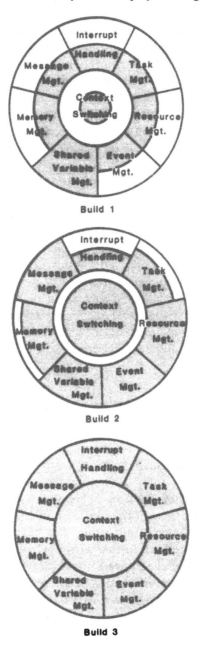

Fig. 1. FIZVOS functionality by build. ▨ Functionality implemented in this build

anticipated. Then any features or services that were not actually needed for the eventual application design could be easily eliminated.

Given this general set of requirements, the FIZVOS team performed a comparative analysis of commercially available operating systems for the 8051 and identified a product that contained many of the required features. Since modifying and extending an existing operating system would significantly reduce design time, this product was acquired to serve as a basis for FIZVOS implementation.

FIZVOS implementation was planned as three incremental builds: (1) an initial testbed version; (2) an interim version; and (3) a final version. The first build was intended to provide a test environment for application software development. The plan was to make minimal changes to the base OS, modifying only its user interface and leaving its internals unchanged. The second build provided most of the required FIZVOS functionality, although with some restrictions. The third build added the remaining functions and removed restrictions. Figure 1 illustrates the planned progression of FIZVOS from build 1 through build 3. The shaded area in Fig. 1 correspond to the amount of the feature that is implemented. The shaded areas include both fully implemented and partially implemented features.

3. FIZVOS MODEL CONSTRUCTION

An important part of the initial planning period was the construction of activity models for various project activities. For FIZVOS, an implementation model and a test-and-fix model were built. The implementation model is given in Table 1 and is intended to provide an estimate of the elapsed time that the implementation should take. This model was based on analyzing the planned implementation process and comparing it with other projects.

Constructing the model required identifying separate tasks, analyzing the dynamics of the implementation process and choosing the model's input variables. There are two types of input variable: those related to the tasks and those related to the process dynamics. Task-related variables are measures of task size, while process-related variables are measures of the resources involved in performing the tasks.

FIZVOS implementation tasks included: (1) learning the base OS;

Table 1
The Implementation Model

Input parameters	Description
$S = 4$	Staff size (excluding mgmt/QA/tools people)
$L = 2000$	Lines of code to be written
$P = 20$	Baseline productivity (LOC per day)
$O = 49$	Other work $(15 + 24 + 10)$ in person-days (PDs) (documentation, reviews, Base OS installation)
$R = 80$	Management reserves $(10 + 10 + 20 + 40)$ in PDs (Staff turnover, new work, black holes, slack)
$E = 1·66$	Environment factor $(1·0 + 0·11 + 0·11 + 0·33 + 0·11)$ (staff avail., uptime, turnaround, tool reliability)
$B = 10$	Build overhead
Output parameters	
$V = 100$	Volume of coding work $(V = L/P)$
$T = 105$	Calendar time to complete the implementation $T = ((V + R + O)/S)^{*}E + B$

(2) performing the detailed design, coding and unit testing of changes and additions to this OS; (3) reviewing proposed designs; (4) reading code; (5) integrating incremental releases; and (6) writing a user guide. In the FIZVOS implementation model, input variable **L** relates to task 2; input variable **O** relates to tasks 1, 3, 4 and 6; and input variable **B** relates to task 5. Input variable **R** is also a task-related variable, albeit the tasks are initially unknown. The process-related variables in the model are **S**, **P** and **E**.

The model's environment factor, **E**, reflects how the development environment affects progress. There are many aspects of the development environment that affect productivity:[7,12,14] **E** is, therefore, a composite of various subfactors, $e_1, e_2, \ldots, e_n$, corresponding to the components of the development environment which are less than ideal and are expected to cause loss of time. For a given component, j, one determines e_j by estimating the proportion p_j of time that is lost; that is,

$$e_j = p_j/(1 - p_j) \qquad (1)$$

The initial estimates for the model's input variables are given in Table 1. These estimates were derived as follows:

S *Staff size*: based on experiences on similar projects. Note that **S** is the number of people actually implementing code. It does not include managers, toolsmiths or testers. The model does, however, assume that the implementors are supported adequately in terms of management, tool maintenance and quality assurance.

L *Lines-of-code*: based on the size of the base OS and the size of an in-house-developed real-time operating system. The size of FIZVOS was estimated to be 3000 LOC, with 1000 of those being unchanged base OS, 500 changes to the base OS, and 1500 extensions to the base OS. This implied a total of 2000 LOC to be written.

P *Baseline productivity*: based on experience on other projects.

O *Other work*: documentation and reviews. Documentation effort was based on the initial team's assessment of the user guide effort. Review effort was based on lines-of-code to review: a design review and a code reading for every 500 lines-of-code, with three participants spending a day on each review.

R *Reserves*: based on possible scenarios requiring extra time or effort, such as necessity to train a new implementor (turnover), unanticipated tasks (new work), underestimated difficulty of some implementation task (black holes), with 20% of the total effort considered to be a lower bound.

E *Environment factor*: based on four components: uptime, turnaround, staff availability and tool reliability. Determine the percentage loss of time, p_j, and apply eqn (1).

  —*Uptime* was estimated at 95%, implying a 10% loss of time (5% for the actual downtime and 5% to regain lost files etc.).

  —*Turnaround* was defined in terms of both the number and speed of compile–link–load–download cycles. It was estimated by noting that the baseline productivity estimate of 20 LOC per day assumed 21 turnarounds per day (a 45 min turnaround cycle with two available emulators). The expected case was 16 turnarounds per day (one hour turnaround cycle with two emulators available). This implies a 25% loss of time.

  —*Staff availability* was estimated at 90%, allowing for vacations, holidays, sickness and other absences.

  —*Tool reliability*: the software development tools were newly developed and likely to contain bugs. The effect of such bugs was estimated to cause a 10% loss of time.

B *Build overhead*: the effort required to integrate, document and deliver the three builds was estimated to be 10 working days.

The schedule for the delivery of these builds was based upon the implementation model. Build 1 was estimated as approximately 20% of the effort. The remaining effort was evenly divided between builds 2 and 3. The three builds were scheduled accordingly.

4. MANAGING FIZVOS IMPLEMENTATION

During FIZVOS implementation, the activity model played an important role in project tracking. Using actual values for model input variables and computed output values, the model provided a quantitative comparison of actual progress versus expectations, giving early indication of potential problem areas.

4.1 Tracking

To make effective use of a model, it is important to have accurate and up-to-date measurements of the model's variables. For FIZVOS, this data was acquired in several ways. Where possible, measurement was automatic; lines-of-code, uptime and turnaround were measured via software. Monthly timesheet data provided the values for staff availability. The remaining variables were obtained through weekly team meetings. At these meetings each implementor reviewed the past week's accomplishments and difficulties, and outlined the next week's plans. This information was recorded in an online status report. A goal of the weekly data gathering was to expose potential problems. The team manager could then measure the variables in question to determine the extent of the problem and its impact on the schedule.

Interpretation of the observed data in light of the model and the expected values is not necessarily an easy process. Frequently there are a number of possible explanations for a discrepancy. The FIZVOS weekly meeting provided the familiarity with the day-to-day events that is essential in finding possible explanations and alternative actions, and provided a real-world backdrop on which to interpret the model's results.

4.2 Decision making

Using activity models in FIZVOS tracking helped to identify potential problems and also provided a way to compare alternative solutions to such problems. During implementation of the three FIZVOS builds, the model was instrumental in several decisions, two of which are described below.

4.2.1 Turnaround problem

Early in the development of build 1, the team complained that turnaround was inadequate. Investigation revealed that this was caused by a lack of available emulator systems rather than poor response time, which at 20 min was much better than expected. The problem was that only one emulator was available and several teams were using it. This allowed only 10 to 12 turnarounds a day, while at least 16 were needed to stay on schedule. Since turnaround is the dominant component of E, and the model is very sensitive to changes in E, it was critical to resolve this problem quickly. With so few turnarounds, time lost due to the turnaround component is around 50% and E increases to 2·33. Meeting the build 1 delivery date required keeping E at the estimated value of 1·66 or lower.

Three alternatives were considered: (A) acquiring another emulator system; (B) using a simulator to supplement the existing facilities; and (C) giving the FIZVOS team priority on the emulator in question. In terms of turnaround per day, alternatives A and C were considered equivalent; both alternatives yielded 24 turnaround per day. Lead time was required, however, to acquire another emulator. The simulator was available immediately but response time was estimated to be extremely poor—at least two hours. At best, alternative B would yield 14 turnarounds per day.

For each alternative, the predicted number of turnarounds resulted in a new value for E, 1·33, 1·83 and 1·33, respectively. Noting that alternative A was not immediately available, alternative C was chosen. The FIZVOS team was given priority on the required emulator and delivered build 1 on schedule.

In this situation the model provided a way to validate and explain the complaints of the team. The team manager used the model to compute the severity of the problem and to quantify the alternative solutions. This analysis then formed the basis of the team manager's recommendation to project management.

4.2.2 Potential black hole problem

Another situation arose during the development of build 2. One of the application teams who were experimenting with the initial FIZVOS build became concerned about overall system performance in periods of extreme real time demands. The question was: would the final version of FIZVOS meet the timing requirements in the worst case?

The FIZVOS team was asked to perform a timing analysis to answer this question.

The decision to take on this additional task appeared to be easy given the fact that there were 30 person-days of reserve available during the build 2 development period and none of this had been required so far. It was estimated that the timing study would require about 15 person-days of effort, and two FIZVOS team members (one of whom was the lead designer) were assigned to the task.

At the next weekly meeting, it became apparent that there were problems with this task. The study task was making very little progress although several additional team members were assisting in the analysis. This task was absorbing too much of the team's efforts and energy—a potential *black hole*.

Finding the solution to this problem came from investigating its cause. Why was the study task taking more effort than expected? A major part of the problem was that one needed a better understanding of the application to identify and analyze the worst case scenario. Two alternatives presented themselves. The first was that some build 2 functionality could be postponed until build 3 and the build 3 reserves could be allocated to the study task. The second was to get help from an application team.

The only model parameter affected by this problem was reserves, **R**, and analysis using the model was straightforward. From the team perspective, the second alternative was preferable for a number of reasons: (a) it did not affect the build delivery schedule; (b) it did not diminish the reserves budgeted for build 3; and (c) it better addressed the underlying cause of the problem.

However, comparing these two alternatives required a broader perspective than that of the single team. The second alternative affected the reserves of another team. The FIZVOS team manager presented the analysis of the problem and alternative solutions to the project manager who coordinated the activities of all the teams. The project manager decided that the second alternative was the best overall choice for the project.

5.   EVALUATING FIZVOS IMPLEMENTATION

A comprehensive data capture and analysis is an important part of the activity model approach. The FIZVOS implementation report summarized the three FIZVOS builds. The report described the model, the initial estimates of input variables, the actual values of those variables, and an analysis of the differences.

5.1 Data capture

During FIZVOS implementation, model data was captured following each build. The data collection was automated for lines of code and turnaround. For other variables, such as time spent for reviews, documentation and other specific tasks, the weekly status reports provided the data. Additional information was solicited from the team members by means of an informal survey. Timesheets and system logs also provided some of the data. With the exception of tool reliability, the data capture was relatively straightforward. Tool reliability, on the other hand, was difficult to measure. Information in the weekly status reports gave only an approximation of its value.

Table 2 summarizes the three builds, giving estimated and actual values for the model's variables. Note that whereas during estimation **T** was the output variable, it is a measurable variable during data capture and **P** becomes the computed output variable.

Table 2
Actual Values for Model Parameters by Build

Parameter	Build 1		Build 2		Build 3		All builds	
	Est.	Act.	Est.	Act.	Est.	Act.	Est.	Act.
S Staff size	4	4	4	4	4	3·5	4	3·8
L Lines of code	400	1145	800	2730	800	1992	2000	5867
P Productivity	20	39	20	50	20	23	20	33
O Other work	19	16	15	19	15	31	49	66
R Reserves	14	17	33	30	33	31	80	78
E Environment	1·66	1·41	1·66	1·43	1·66	1·09	1·66	1·23
B Build overhead	0	0	5	5	5	5	10	10
T Calendar days	22	22	42	42	42	50	105	114

5.2 Analysis

Although each FIZVOS build was delivered on schedule, few of the estimates on which the schedule was based were accurate. A fortuitous balance of optimism and pessimism in estimating, together with careful project monitoring, account for this success.

The mostly badly estimated variable was lines-of-code. Analysis reveals several causes for the discrepancy between estimate and actual value:

1. *Two sets of requirements were implemented.* The originally specified requirements (with some additions) were implemented in the build 2 release. A revised set of requirements evolved as a result of the application teams' experience using build 1 combined with a better understanding of their needs. Build 3 implemented these requirements.

2. *The product grew.* Additional requirements were specified after implementation began; most of these were implemented in build 2.

3. *Less reusable code.* The base OS required substantially more change than anticipated. The original estimate of 33% grew to 85%.

The baseline productivity factor varies considerably in the three build periods. Build 1 productivity was affected by startup learning. By build 2, the team had developed tools and procedures which led to efficient use of the development facilities. The explanation for the lower productivity during build 3 is twofold. On the one hand, implementors encountered more contention for source files. This resulted in occasional bottlenecks. Secondly, two weeks had been added to the schedule for this build, resulting in unneeded schedule slack. The consensus of the team is that the original deadline could have been met; this would have yielded a baseline productivity of 40 LOC per day.

Table 3 gives a breakdown of other work by build. Actual review effort was very close to the estimated 24 person-days, in spite of the fact that this estimate was based on lines-of-code. The documentation effort was greatly underestimated; only 15 person-days had been estimated. Our analysis yielded two possible explanations: (1) additional documentation required because of the incremental builds; and (2) changes to the documentation because of the revised requirements.

Table 4 gives a breakdown of reserves by build. Although the total management reserve was almost the same as the estimate of 80 person-days, this is not a result of accurate estimation. Several of the predicted contingencies (staff turnover, underestimated difficulty) did not occur. Most of the reserves were spent on completely unanticipated work.

Table 3
Actual Values for Other Work by Build

Activity	Build 1	Build 2	Build 3	All builds
Documentation	10	12	18	40
Reviews	6	7	13	26
Total	16	19	31	66

The environment factor experienced was substantially lower than estimated, due primarily to the turnaround component of **E**. Because there was no historical data relating to the software development facilities, a conservative estimate was used. Rather than the estimated hour, the team experienced 15 min turnaround and, following build 1, two emulator systems were available. The breakdown of the environment factor into its components is given in Table 5.

Table 4
Actual Values for Reserves by Build

Activity	Build 1	Build 2	Build 3
Tools	7	—	14
Test support	10	—	10
Timing study	—	23	—
HP64000 H/W problem	—	7	—
Standards retrofit	—	—	7
Total	17	30	31

Table 5
Breakdown of the Environment Factors by Build

	Build 1		Build 2		Build 3	
	p_j	e_j	p_j	e_j	p_j	e_j
Downtime	11	0·12	18	0·22	1	0·01
Tool unreliability	7	0·08	5	0·05	0	0
Staff unavailability	9	0·10	12	0·16	7	0·08
Turnaround	10	0·11	0	0	0	0

5.3 Model validation

Model validation is an assessment of the model's implicit and explicit assumptions, determining whether these assumptions were confirmed by project experience. The FIZVOS implementation model makes three principal assumptions, two of which were valid. First, it was assumed that the implementors were adequately supported in terms of management, tool maintenance and quality assurance. This was the case for the four FIZVOS implementors since the team includes a team manager, a toolsmith and a part-time QA person. Secondly, the model assumes that the technical assignments are interchangeable between implementors. For FIZVOS, this was accomplished through full team participation in reviews and the weekly team meetings.

The third assumption pertains to the software process model for FIZVOS development. The waterfall model was assumed; that is, software developed in successive stages (requirements, design, coding etc.) with feedback loops between stages. This was not the case for FIZVOS; a spiral model or evolutionary development model[9,10,13] would have been more appropriate. Note, however, that this does not so much appear to invalidate the model as to lead to poor estimation.

5.4 Recommendations

The FIZVOS experience provided useful information on the manager's role in establishing and evaluating the activity model. Based on this, the following recommendations are made:

5.4.1 *Planning and estimating*

—Evaluate the stability of the requirements specification when estimating lines-of-code, and increase the estimate accordingly. With hindsight, it is clear that the needs of the application were not really known at the outset.

—Recognize that incremental builds have an impact on the documentation effort.

—Include reserves of at least 20% of the total effort.

—Recognize that productivity is not constant; it is lower at the outset and may also decrease towards the end of implementation.

—Base the estimates relating to the development environment, such as turnaround or downtime, on projects with similar facilities. When no such projects can be found, use conservative estimates.

—Estimate review effort based on the number of implementors and the number of builds rather than on lines-of-code.

5.4.2 Tracking and decision making
—Automate the measurement of model variables wherever possible.

—Avoid selecting model variables that are difficult to measure. If such variables cannot be avoided, figure out in advance how they will be measured.

—Establish weekly meetings and create online weekly status reports for evaluating current status, identifying factors affecting progress, and facilitating post-build data capture and analysis.

6. CONCLUSION

The quantitative activity model of the FIZVOS implementation activity provided useful and timely feedback for project management. The case study experience underscores the importance of choosing measurable variables, staying in close contact with the project staff and continually analyzing the underlying process. For FIZVOS, the model enabled quantified assessments of current status, helped explain deviations from planned progress, provided a framework in which to evaluate potential remedial actions, and forms the basis of a project history to be shared with other projects.

REFERENCES

1. Bailey, J. W. and Basili, V. R., A Meta-Model for Software Development Resource Expenditure, *Proc. Fifth IEEE/ACM/NBS Int. Conf. on Software Engineering*, Mar. 1981, 107–16.
2. Benington, H. D., Production of Large Computer Programs, *Proc. ONR Symposium on Advanced Programming Methods for Digital Computers*, June 1956, 15–27.
3. Boehm, B. W., *Software engineering economics*, Prentice-Hall, 1981.
4. Boehm, B. W., Software engineering economics, *IEEE Trans. Software Engineering*, SE-**10**(1), 1984, 4–21.
5. Boehm, B. W., A spiral model of software development and enhancement, *ACM SIGSOFT Software Engineering Notes*, **11**(4), Aug. 1986, 14–24.
6. Boydston, R. E., Programming Cost Estimate: Is it Reasonable?, *Proc. of Seventh IEEE/ACM/NBS Int. Conf. on Software Engineering*, Mar. 1984, 153–9.
7. DeMarco, T. and Lister, T., Programmer Performance and the Effects of the Workplace, *Proceedings Eighth IEEE/ACM/NBS Int. Conf. on Software Engineering*, Aug. 1985, 268–72.

8. Dowson, M. and Wileden, J. C., Panel Discussion on the Software Process and Software Environments, *Proc. Eighth IEEE/ACM/NBS Int. Conf. on Software Engineering,* Aug. 1985, 302–4; also in: *ACM SIGSOFT Software Engineering Notes,* **11**(4), Aug. 1986, 4–5.
9. Giddings, R. V., Accommodating uncertainty in software design, *Comm. ACM,* **27**(5), May 1984, 428–34.
10. Gilb, T., Evolutionary delivery versus the 'Waterfall model', *ACM SIGSOFT Software Engineering Notes,* **10**(3), July 1985, 49–61.
11. Huff, K. E., Sroka, J. V. and Struble, D. D., Quantitative models for managing software development processes, *Software Eng. J.,* Jan. 1986, 17–23.
12. Lawrence, J. L., Why is software always late? *ACM SIGSOFT Software Engineering Notes,* **10**(1), Jan. 1985, 19–30.
13. McCracken, D. D. and Jackson, M. A., Life cycle concept considered harmful, *ACM SIGSOFT Software Engineering Notes,* **7**(2), Apr. 1982, 29–32.
14. Vosburgh, J. *et al.,* Productivity factors and programming environments, *Proc. Seventh IEEE/ACM/NBS Int. Conf. on Software Engineering,* Mar. 1984, 143–52.

9

*Generic Modelling of Software Quality**

H.-L. HAUSEN

GMD, St Augustin, FRG

ABSTRACT

Software engineering comprises construction, validation, measurement and assessment of software products and software projects. Software systems are often subdivided into the levels application concept, data processing concept and implementation. Evaluation, measurement and assessment have to take these three levels into consideration. Quality models have to consider active and passive elements of the software as well as dynamic characteristics on all three levels. Since software systems and software projects are unique, quality models have to be flexible. A scheme for quality modelling uses weight functions to define quality factors in terms of evaluation factors. The scheme may also be extended to cover productivity.

A selected set of quality and evaluation factors is used to demonstrate the quality modelling procedure. With respect to three levels of software description, a number of ratios are defined in order to describe software quantitatively. Using functions which reflect past experience, it becomes possible to generate estimates over the product extent and the production effort.

Both the modelling scheme and the assessment scheme are effectively implementable. An abstract program defines the computation of the quality and productivity on a common scheme.

---

* This paper comprises selected, revised sections of Ref. 13.

1. INTRODUCTION

'Nobody tells the truth
about his product's quality.
Engineers need real figures.
Management requires (other) real figures.
Everyone needs to have his own quality model.
The quality model must be specific or global or generic.
(Anonymous)

Software development is frequently subdivided into an application concept, a data processing concept and an implementation, i.e. into the three levels. At every stage, a software system may be defined completely in terms of that level. Measurement and assessment have to take this three-level division into account. They also have to take into consideration active and passive elements of the software as well as dynamic characteristics on all three levels. A number of ratios are defined in order to characterize attributes quantitatively. By using data gained from experience, it becomes possible to generate estimates of the product size and the production effort.

In the assessment of software, one might take an application-oriented or a product-centred point of view. According to the first, one has to consider the usefulness of a quality measure. The question of what could be measured is product-oriented, and considers the material of the objects in the first place. This is the approach usually taken by the engineers whereas the first approach is necessary in the management process.

Over the years, measurement of software quality and productivity has become increasingly important. As stated in Ref. 17, there is an increasing need for effective and objective means and tools for measurement, that can be applied by software engineers and software managers. Therefore, in the past few years, a quantitative approach to software engineering has emerged, whose purpose is to establish operational procedures for the development of quality software and the productivity of software projects. It includes the use of models and measures based on historical data and experience (in Ref. 5). Sometimes it is said that if you cannot measure, you do not understand. This is certainly true for the assessment of software quality and productivity. Therefore, various models and measures have been developed, tested, refined, and some of them have been established as instruments for project or product planning or controlling. Specific quality and productivity models and associated measurement methods are necessary for making comparisons of products or projects. In cost estimation, for example, it is important to know how much an extra level of reliability (Musa, Littlewood in Ref. 5), will cost or whether a modification of an existing system will be cost-effective. It should be noted, however, that the quantitative approach should augment, but not replace, good engineering practice; models and measures can only serve as aids for the qualified engineer or manager.

2. LEVELS AND VIEWS IN SOFTWARE ENGINEERING

Software development begins with problem analysis and ends with the delivery of a configured system. A pragmatic method for the development of software should take into consideration three layers: application concept, data processing concept and implementation. The functions and data types in the second layer are assigned to the activities and objects from the first layer. These functions and data types are transferred to the programs (into control and data structures) of the third layer. In the third layer a modularization method is used to put together such structured elements into executable programs. Software is constructed within every layer under the specific layer aspects; it is structured and (re-)tested. The configuration needs to consider elements on all three layers, since a software system may vary in the representation of every layer.

2.1 The view: software construction

The software development process comprises application concept (*ap-concept*) development and data processing concept (*dp-concept*) development. The latter is often again subdivided into software design, module design and operationalization or coding. Therefore, a method should provide instruments for the construction and analysis of software descriptions of every level as well as means for transformation between levels.

The activities to be performed outside the dp department must be identified, as well as the objects processed. In the descriptions of the activities, it has to be established which are to be automated by data processing. Simultaneously, the objects which must be represented in the dp-concept are identified. One receives the activity and the object model of the software system to be developed. In parallel to the definition of the activities and objects, the required states and the forbidden one(s) are identified for the application system. After this, the objects, activities and application states are determined. The data processing system has to implement the application concept specification by means of functions and data.

The functions and data are adapted in the data processing concept. It is necessary to determine which activities, objects and states of the application system must be represented by the dp-concept. States of the data processing system must ensure that the application states are entered. The states in the application concept are the basis for the definition of the states in the data processing concept. All three, functions, data and data processing states, define a system completely in the sense of supporting the application task.

The programs are developed with this specification. First, the program design and the modularization are elaborated. Then, the control and data structures are established depending on the programming language, the operating system and the hardware configuration. Finally, the executable code might be developed.

Application concept, data processing concept and programs are documented in parallel with their development. The informal explanation of tasks, requirements, conditions and the design approach should be included in the documentation as well as in the formal description. Thus, the approaches taken and the solutions selected become verifiable.

The accompanying control of the intermediate or the final products serves to avoid bad consequences or late results. Depending on the permitted effort and the stringency of required tests, formal verifications or inspection techniques have to be applied. Simulation or prototyping may also be used for the analysis of the intermediate or final products, where appropriate.

The following aspects are therefore treated in the three-layer model software development shown in Table 1. A complete system description is produced in every layer. The conversions (i.e. translations), which are particularly critical for system development, take place between the layers. The layer-specific objects and activities are defined in a layer as well as their coordination. Both within the layers and between them, the system is developed by a process of gradual and mutual construction and test.

Table 1
Software Development Aspects in the Layer Model

Layer	Representation elements	System aspects
Application concept	Activities and objects	WHY and WHAT FOR
Data processing concept	Functions and data	WHAT and WHERE BY
Data processing realization	Procedures and variables	HOW and BY WHAT

2.2. The view: software validation and assessment

In this section the tasks and problems of quality assurance are described briefly. Since the individual terms of this area have not been generally defined as yet, some terms used in the following are briefly explained. In the following software quality assurance is divided into (a) software validation and (b) administration of quality assurance and control.

Planning, control and supervision of the work required for the examination of intermediate and final products of a software development process are the central tasks of the organization of software assurance.

The term 'software validation' subsumes all the technical tasks of the analysis of intermediate and final products of a software production process. Validation may be divided into inspection, testing and verification of software. The subjects of these examinations are requirement specifications, system specifications, programs and informal system descriptions (system manuals, user manuals etc.).

Inspection of software includes examination by reading, explaining, obtaining explanations and understanding system descriptions, software specifications and programs. In organisational terms, both individual work and teamwork is suitable. For inspection the individuals involved must normally have a thorough knowledge of the problems of the applicational field and the different formal languages used to describe software systems (e.g. specification languages, programming languages). The persons who perform the examination must also be familiar with communication and representation techniques. The main problem of software inspection is the combined processing of formal descriptions (specifications and programs) and representations in natural language (manuals).

In testing, software systems are analysed by simulating or testing their dynamic behaviour in an environment corresponding to the real environment. Testing also includes consistency checks of various representations and descriptions. Consistency of descriptions is usually examined by formal methods and procedures (e.g. syntax analysis, analysis of static semantics).

An important basis for the examination of the dynamic behaviour of a software system is its structure, as described by its computation paths. To test a software system, therefore, the paths to be tested, the test data and the relations between test data and test paths have to be defined precisely. In a test only the actual paths in the present system may be examined, and not the missing, but necessary, ones. In general, the lack of necessary paths cannot be discovered by dynamic analysis.

The main problem of testing is therefore the definition of required and adequate test paths and the determination of the appropriate combination of test paths and test data so that the dynamic behaviour of the system may be observed at particularly critical points. This increases the confidence which may be placed in the system. A test shows whether or not the examined system is correct in the system states tested. Information as to the correctness of a system which has been acquired by testing therefore refers only to the system states, or classes of system states, which were explicitly tested.

Verification of a software system means proving that the programs of the system are correct with respect to the specification. For verification, formal specifications and formal definitions of specification and programming languages applied are required as well as a proof method tailored to those methods or description.

The principle of verification is to show step by step, i.e. for each operation, that the axiomatized description of the final state of a computation process may be derived from the equally axiomatically described initial state. The main problem of verification is the determination of adequate descriptions, since these descriptions are often dependent on individual proof steps.

For effective quality assurance, a combination of methods and tools from the above mentioned areas of validation is required, since it is not possible to fulfil any request for analysis (detection of an error of a specific error type) by means of methods and tools from only one or two of these areas. While inspection is particularly suitable for the detection of functional and logic errors and while testing is especially effective for the detection of implementation errors, verification constitutes the most appropriate method for detecting errors in the transformation of specifications into algorithms.

Quality control was once restricted mainly to one phase of the software life cycle, namely the validation phase after implementation; today it is assumed that quality assurance should be performed in parallel to the construction and use of software, i.e. that each intermediate and final result of the production process should be examined immediately after its completion. This is to ensure that errors are found as early as possible. Protocols of the utilization phase should also be used for examining quality criteria, since costs for fault correction increase heavily with increasing time difference between the production and the detection of an error.

The corresponding product analyses are assigned to the constructing actions. The value of accompanying validation (e.g. tests, measurements, and assessment) is often not recognized.[12] During the individual steps of the construction, or in it, several syntactic and semantic controls take place. Thus, the consistency and completeness of the individual descriptions in the respective level are tested and/or corrected. It remains to check the accuracy of the transformations between the application concept and the data processing concept. These transformations are unreliable since, within the individual transformation steps, objects not contained in the starting description have to be introduced, and decisions must be made. The translations undertaken by validated compilers constitute an exception.

The application concept may be validated by a suitable simulation (e.g. by mask simulation). For the data processing concept, an assessment might be performed by the defined prototypes. Programs are validated by tests or verification, or by other validation techniques. Which techniques have to be applied is determined by the required 'quality' of the correctness statement. Because all these techniques are not fully automatable, they have to be supplemented by the technique of the personal inspection. This technique has to be supported by a suitable information system.

2.3 The view: software assessment

As concluded in Ref. 17, quality of software is currently one of the main concerns in software development and application. For software quality assurance there exist a number of methods and procedures, which comprise the areas of software inspection, testing, formal verification and quality management. The current state of the art indicates that each of these techniques is oriented to only a small number of evaluation factors. The techniques check whether a piece of software, or the complete system, fulfils a certain evaluation condition, or indicate to what extent it does so. It is well known that each of these techniques has its own advantages and shortcomings. From the viewpoint of determining a software system's quality, there is at least one serious problem, namely the question of how quality is defined. This leads to the question of how to compute the quality of a software system, or at least factors of software quality howsoever they are defined.

There already exist a large number of so-called software metrics, but what is called a metric is in the strict sense often only an evaluation procedure. Such evaluation procedures may produce indicators of a software system's quality. As an example, ref. 8 gives a complexity measure based on nestings of *if-then-else-fi* constructs, that improves cyclomatic-number measurement.[20] But it does not say much on how this complexity influences a program's quality. A quality metric needs to be more than just a count of the statements, operators, levels of nesting, etc. As is frequently stated, it is necessary to compare the object under evaluation against a standard. Therefore a method and a computing procedure are proposed in subsequent sections, which allow the comparison of actual, i.e. measurable, factors of software quality against required ones.

An effective assessment procedure comprises at least three components:

—mapping of the object world onto a model world;
—measurement of the (mapped) object in the model world;
—assessment of the object on the basis of the measurement.

In the software development model described below, quality determination is performed for activities, objects, states, functions, data, procedures, variables and programs. For each of them

—the factors to be measured have to be established;
—for the factors to be measured, a method of measuring has to be selected;
—the nominal or target values have to be defined for all quantities to be measured;
—for all measured quantities the actual values must be determined; and

—the relation between actual value and required values has to be computed.

The nominal or target values must be identified as required values before the corresponding object is developed. Quality may only be accomplished by goal-oriented construction; but it cannot be checked into a product afterwards. The actual values may deviate from the target values. Such deviations may be used for the control of the development process.

Measures and measuring processes have to be harmonized with the method of representation. If functional, relational or other declarative languages are used, the measures must be selected in such a way that they are able to measure the characteristic attributes of the constructs of these languages (e.g. FP, ER or PROLOG type languages). Existing measures (e.g. in ref. 10) might be redefined in order to cope with innovative constructs. It might also become necessary to define new measures and measuring processes in accordance with the chosen version of a language.

In any case, operands and operators will be looked at, both for the active elements (activities, functions and procedures) and for the passive elements (objects, data and variables). Measures such as the one defined by Halstead[10] may be applied to these. He specifies measures that take into account the number of different operators and operands, the total number of operators and the total number of operands. Other more complex and more appropriate measures may be defined on the basis of these (elementary) measures (see below). Petri nets may be used as a special form of the representation of relations between passive elements, active elements and states (Table 2). Measures for special characteristics of a network may be used in this case.

Table 2
Active and Passive Elements at the Different Layers

Layer	Active elements	Passive elements	Dynamics	Texts
ap-concept	activities	objects	ap-states	application handbook
dp-concept	functions	data	dp-states	design documentation
implementation	procedures	variables	control and data flow	program documentation

3. QUALITY MODEL SCHEME

At first sight, the quality of software seems to be represented in very different ways. But a closer examination shows common characteristics. In this section common aspects are employed to develop a general quality model, or quality scheme, which is flexible and generic. First, we will briefly review some structural aspects of classic models (c.f. McCall's model), as described in Ref. 5. In the quality model of McCall[20] (Fig. 1), for example, the relations between the individual factors are defined as being existing or not existing. However, such a fixed, dichotomous assignment is not always sensible. If one does not consider software as the result of mass production, one will require a product, task or project specific quality definition. Such a definition cannot be accomplished with the classical models. Once the evaluation factors are assigned to the quality factors the influence or the meaning

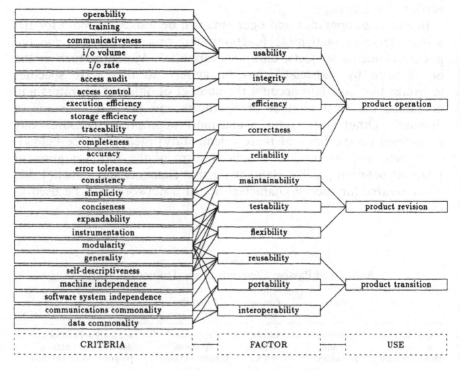

Fig. 1. The quality model of McCall.

of every measured quantity is determined for every quality factor. A second shortcoming of classical models is their fixed structure, used in decomposing high-level quality factors into quality factors of lower levels or into evaluation factors.

3.1 Decomposition of quality

In order to measure and evaluate software quality and project productivity, those quality and productivity characteristics considered as relevant have to be operationalized. This means that software quality and project productivity have to be decomposed into observable items. Therefore, it is necessary to break down the characteristics into so-called product or project features that are physical attributes (of a product or project) which can be measured. One difficulty of measuring and evaluating software quality and project productivity is the frequent occurrence of incorrect use and application of basic terms, especially for measure and metric. Therefore, it is necessary to pay attention to the formal definitions of these terms which exist in measurement theory.

Measurement requires quantification of object attributes and operations on those quantification statements. A measure is the homomorph mapping of a quantification expression onto a nominal, ordinal, interval or rational scale. It is a mapping of expressions, formulated in terms of the language of the observed world, into a quantitative expression formulated in terms of the language of the model world. The latter expression can be formalized much more easily than a qualitative one. For formalized quantitative expressions operators have to be defined which define relations between quantitative expressions, i.e. distances or correlations. Relations between objects of the observed world must be reflected by relations on the non-formalized, verbal, qualitative expression. Some formal definitions can be obtained from the Appendix.

The quality of a software system may be represented as an acyclic graph (Fig. 2, p. 225). Each leaf (end node) of the acyclic graph represents an evaluation factor. Evaluation factors are those which cannot or should not be subdivided. This leads to a two-level quality graph. The values for the evaluation factors may be obtained by application of measurement procedures, such as those for static complexity measures. Others may be defined by the user or owner of a software system. A set of evaluation factors constitutes a system quality at level zero.

In a two-level graph quality factors may be defined on the basis of these evaluation factors. For each evaluation factor a weighting factor or function determines to what degree it contributes to a quality factor. By this procedure a system value on level one is defined. Often a quality graph represents more than one level of quality factors (Fig. 3, p. 226). For such graphs, the relation between the factors of a level n and a level $n + 1$ have to be defined in a way similar to relations between the evaluation factors and quality factors a two-level model.

For the description of the system values it is necessary to define a basis for the estimation of the difference between the quality characteristics of the actual software system and those of the required software system. For the actual software system the evaluation factors can be obtained by measurement procedures. Many such procedures are given by so-called complexity measures, e.g. cyclomatic number computation.[20] Others may be defined according to a project's needs.

The factors for the ideal or required system could be obtained by definition of this system, i.e. an effort has to be made to define the system requirements in terms of required evaluation factors and in terms of required quality factors. This definition of requirements then constitutes a so-called set of required evaluation factors and required quality factors.

Both kinds of factors, actual and required ones, may be represented by n-ary vectors in order to make use of correlation functions defined for vectorial descriptions of systems. These correlation functions serve here as means for computing the relationship between an actual software system and the required system.

The quality graph comprises in principle two disjoint subgraphs, one of which is the graph of the required quality (Fig. 4, p. 227). The second subgraph shows the values of the actual evaluation factors and of the quality factors. Both subgraphs are identical with regard to the structuring of quality factors by evaluation factors. The difference between the two lies in the values at the nodes. Intermediate nodes represent quality factors and end-nodes define evaluation factors.

A formalized definition of actual and required factors is given by the following scheme:

The **evaluation factor vector** or **tuple** efv is to be defined by the evaluation factors ef_i:

$$efv = \langle ef_1, ef_2, ef_3, \ldots, ef_{n_2} \rangle$$

A **quality factor vector** or **tuple** qfv is to be defined as vector of quality factors qf_i, which are to be defined by a vector of weighted evaluation factors $f_{i,j}(a_{i,j}, ef_j)$:

$$qfv = \langle qf_1, qf_2, qf_3, \ldots, qf_{n_1} \rangle$$

where a qf_i denotes quality factor i

$$qf_i = \langle f_{i,1}(a_{i,1}, ef_1), f_{i,2}(a_{i,2}, ef_2), \ldots, f_{i,n_2}(a_{i,n_2}, ef_{i,n_2}) \rangle$$

As an example, all $f_{i,j}$ might be defined by the operation $\otimes$. Thus we obtain:

$$qf_i = \langle a_{i,1} \otimes ef_1, a_{i,2} \otimes ef_2, \ldots, a_{i,n_2} \otimes ef_{i,n_2} \rangle; a_i = \langle a_{i,1}, a_{i,2}, \ldots, a_{i,n_2} \rangle$$

$$qf_i = a_i \otimes efv$$

where $a_{i,j}$ = weighting constant, $f_{i,j}$ = weighting function, $a_{i,j}$ indicates the contribution of ef_i to qf_j, $0 \cdot 0 \leqslant a_{i,j} \leqslant 1 \cdot 0$ for reals or $a_{i,j} \in \{0, 1\}$ for boolean expressions.

Thirdly, a **quality vector** or **tuple** sqv is to be defined by weighted quality factors $g_i(b_i, qf_i)$:

$$sqv = \langle qc_1, qc_2, qc_3, \ldots, qc_{n_1} \rangle;$$

$$qc_i - g_i(b_i, qf_i);$$

$$g = \langle g_1, g_2, \ldots, g_{n_1} \rangle$$

$$g_i(b_i, qf_i) = \langle g_i(b_i, f_{i,1}(a_{i,1}, ef_1)), \ldots, g_i(b_i, f_{i,n_2}(a_{i,n_2}, ef_2)) \rangle$$

$$sqv = f_{quality} \langle g, qfv \rangle$$

where qf_i denotes quality factor i, qc_i quality content of quality factor i, g_i is a weighting function, b_i is a weighting constant, g_i: defines the contribution of qf_i to qc_i, $0 \cdot 0 \leqslant b_i \leqslant 1 \cdot 0$ for reals or $b_i \in \{0, 1\}$ for boolean expressions.

This leads to the following:

A. quality factor matrix (qf-matrix):

$$
\begin{aligned}
qf_1 &= \langle \quad f_{1,1}(a_{1,1}, ef_1), \quad \ldots, \quad f_{1,n_2}(a_{1,n_2}, ef_{n_2}) \quad \rangle \\
qf_2 &= \langle \quad f_{2,1}(a_{2,1}, ef_1), \quad \ldots, \quad f_{2,n_2}(a_{2,n_2}, ef_{n_2}) \quad \rangle \\
&\quad \ldots, \quad\quad\quad\quad \ldots, \quad \ldots, \\
qf_{n_1} &= \langle \quad f_{n_1,1}(a_{n_1,1}, ef_1), \quad \ldots, \quad f_{n_1,n_2}(a_{n_1,n_2}, ef_{n_2}) \quad \rangle
\end{aligned}
$$

B. quality matrix (q-matrix):

$$
\begin{aligned}
qc_1 &= \langle \quad g_1(b_1, f_{1,1}(a_{1,1}, ef_1)), \quad \ldots, \quad g_1(b_1, f_{1,n_2}(a_{1,n_2}, ef_{n_2})) \quad \rangle \\
qc_2 &= \langle \quad g_2(b_2, f_{2,1}(a_{2,1}, ef_1)), \quad \ldots, \quad g_2(b_2, f_{2,n_2}(a_{2,n_2}, ef_{n_2})) \quad \rangle \\
&\quad \ldots, \quad\quad\quad\quad\quad\quad \ldots, \quad \ldots, \\
qc_{n_1} &= \langle \quad g_{n_1}(b_{n_1}, f_{n_1,1}(a_{n_1,1}, ef_1)), \quad \ldots, \quad g_{n_1}(b_{n_1}, f_{n_1,n_2}(a_{n_1,n_2}, ef_{n_2})) \quad \rangle
\end{aligned}
$$

As an example one might use $\odot$ for all g_i and $\otimes$ for all f_i. This defines the following two matrices:

E.A. example quality factor matrix:

$$qf_1 = \langle \quad a_{1,1} \otimes ef_1, \quad \ldots, \quad a_{1,n_2} \otimes ef_{n_2} \quad \rangle$$
$$qf_2 = \langle \quad a_{2,1} \otimes ef_1, \quad \ldots, \quad a_{2,n_2} \otimes ef_{n_2} \quad \rangle$$
$$\ldots, \quad\quad\quad \ldots, \quad \ldots,$$
$$qf_{n_1} = \langle \quad a_{n_1,1} \otimes ef_1, \quad \ldots, \quad a_{n_1,n_2} \otimes ef_{n_2} \quad \rangle$$

E.B. example quality matrix:

$$qc_1 = \langle \quad b_1 \odot a_{1,1} \otimes ef_1, \quad \ldots, \quad b_1 \odot a_{1,n_2} \otimes ef_{n_2} \quad \rangle$$
$$qc_2 = \langle \quad b_2 \odot a_{2,1} \otimes ef_1, \quad \ldots, \quad b_2 \odot a_{2,n_2} \otimes ef_{n_2} \quad \rangle$$
$$\ldots, \quad\quad\quad \ldots, \quad \ldots,$$
$$qc_{n_1} = \langle \quad b_{n_1} \odot a_{n_1,1} \otimes ef_1, \quad \ldots, \quad b_{n_1} \odot a_{n_1,n_2} \otimes ef_{n_2} \quad \rangle$$

Both the operators $\odot$ and $\otimes$ might be either specific for each pair < weight factor, evaluation factor > (or < weight factor, quality factor >) or common to all such pairs.

3.2 Discussion of current quality models

Since most quality models proposed today define quality by a number of decomposition levels it should be possible to describe these models by the generic model. The differences between all these models lie mainly in the structure of the quality graph. Each proposed model decomposes a quality factor into different evaluation factors. Most often the quality factors are first decomposed into quality subfactors, which are defined in terms of evaluation factors. Sometimes quality factors are decomposed into more than two or three decomposition layers. In these cases one might ask how effective those decompositions could be. It might be particularly difficult to determine how effective a quantitative and checkable definition or computation of software quality is, if more than two decomposition layers are proposed.

A detailed discussion of meanings of the items used in the models is not required for the description of the scheme by which quality models might be compared. The interested reader can obtain this information from comparative studies, such as Ref. 5. A precise description of each quality factor and the related subfactors should be provided by the author of the respective quality model. Very often the syntax and the semantics of such models have been changed during application of the respective model. A difficult problem one might have to solve for these models is how to define the decomposed quality factors (i.e. a sub-subfactor) in terms of measurable, testable, provable or checkable items. The available literature gives very few indications of effectively applicable, quantitative measures in the context of these models.

Using the general scheme for the representation of quality models, we are able to correlate and rank the distinct models on a common basis. First we have to define an ideal quality model, which is composed from the set of models to be considered. The decomposition structure of the largest model, i.e. the model bearing the largest number of decomposition levels, defines the decomposition depth. At each decomposition level the union of all factors belonging to that level defines a decomposition width for that level. The nodes have to be assigned to a decomposition level depending on their distance from the evaluation factors. These factors are assigned to the bottom-most level.

3.3. Comparison and ranking of quality models

The comparison of the distinct quality models might be performed by several approaches. In principle one might want to compare the models, both at each decomposition level, and in general. The comparison regarding each decomposition level is possible by computing the distance of each model from the ideal, succeeded by a ranking of them in terms of those distances. For this procedure the evaluation model discussed in the section on formalized assessment is to be applied (see below).

$$qmatrix_{ideal} = \langle \quad qc_{ideal,1}, \quad qc_{ideal,2}, \quad \ldots, \quad qc_{ideal,n_{max}} \quad \rangle \qquad 1.0$$

$$qmatrix_a = \langle \quad qc_{a,1}, \quad qc_{a,2} \quad \ldots, \quad qc_{a,n_{max}} \quad \rangle \quad corr_{ideal,a} \leqslant 1{\cdot}0$$

$$qmatrix_b = \langle \quad qc_{b,1}, \quad qc_{b,2}, \quad \ldots, \quad qc_{b,n_{max}} \quad \rangle \quad corr_{ideal,b} \leqslant 1{\cdot}0$$

$$qmatrix_m = \langle \quad qc_{m,1}, \quad qc_{m,2}, \quad \ldots, qc_{m,n_{max}} \rangle \quad corr_{ideal,m} \qquad \leqslant 1{\cdot}0$$

where $qmatrix_i$ = quality matrix of the model i, $qc_{i,j}$ = quality matrix columns as defined above for model i, and $corr_{ideal,i}$ = correlation between the qmatrix of the ideal model and the model i.

A second approach is to compute a characteristic value for each quality model. Since the cyclomatic number[5,20] is very popular in softwaremetry, it seems to be appropriate to apply that to the proposed quality graph in order to be able to rank distinct quality models according to the structure of the graph. Table 3 shows the

Table 3
Cyclomatic Number of Quality Graphs

Model	Decomposition layer	No. of items	Cyclomatic number (graph as given by the author of the distinct model) No. of edges – No. of nodes + 2 times No. of parts
Boehm	1	2	$29 - 22 + 2 = 9$
	2	7	
	3	12	
Cho	1	2	$17 - 18 + 2 = 1$
	2	15	
Cicu	1	7	$7 - 8 + 2 = 1$
McCall	1	3	$53 - 38 + 2 = 17$
	2	11	
	3	23	
Schmitz	1	9	$9 - 10 + 2 = 1$
Schweiggert	1	4	$42 - 43 + 2 = 1$
	2	7	
	3	31	
Willmer	1	2	$20 - 21 + 2 = 1$
	2	3	
	3	15	
Hausen	1	5	$.65 - 18 + 2 = 49$
	2	12	(hypothetical)

number of decomposition layers, the number of items on each layer and the cyclomatic number of each quality graph. The numbers obtained show the limitations of the application of the cyclomatic number for the structure of graphs used to describe quality models. A graph of a quality model in general has one root and a number of leaves. Such structures frequently occur also in programs. And often a program has more than one entry, which means the control flow graph, for example, has a number of entries (i.e. roots) and a number of exits (i.e. leaves). On the other hand the cyclomatic number, as proposed by McCabe,[20] does not consider especially multiple roots or leaves.

4. YET ANOTHER QUALITY MODEL

In the following section we would like to show how the quality model might be defined according to the schema given above. For this example a set of five quality factors and twelve evaluation factors have been selected. The quality factors considered are those which are (in our view) the most frequently used. For the evaluation factors we provide a list of definitions in a succeeding subsection. With respect to our view of software development and validation the proposed evaluation (sub)factors seem to be the most interesting factors.

4.1 Quality and evaluation factors

In our quality model the following quality factors should be regarded:

Correctness = $qf_1 = \langle f_{1,1}(a_{1,1}, ef_1), \ldots, f_{1,12}(a_{1,12}, ef_{12}) \rangle$

A software system is correct if it has been proved strictly that the system accomplishes the required tasks completely, not more and not less.

Efficiency = $qf_2 = \langle f_{2,1}(a_{2,1}, ef_1), \ldots, f_{2,12}(a_{2,12}, ef_{12}) \rangle$

The evaluation of system performance comprises mainly the consideration of the measurable indicators for throughput, response time, availability and utilization of resources.

Reliability = $qf_3 = \langle f_{2,1}(a_{2,1}, ef_1), \ldots, f_{3,12}(a_{3,12}, ef_{12}) \rangle$

A system which is able to handle unexpected events in execution under allowable conditions without assuming undefined states is considered to be reliable.

Robustness = $qf_4 = \langle f_{4,1}(a_{4,1}, ef_1), \ldots, f_{4,12}(a_{4,12}, ef_{12}) \rangle$

If a system is able to process expected or unexpected events in execution under unallowable conditions without assuming undefined states, it is considered to be robust.

User benefit = $qf_5 = \langle f_{5,1}(a_{5,1}, ef_1), \ldots, f_{5,12}(a_{5,12}, ef_{12}) \rangle$

The extent to which the requirements are met indicates the benefit to the user.

Even this incomplete list of criteria clearly shows that a strict separation is not actually possible. For emphasizing individual aspects of examination and evaluation of software, however, such a division is required. At least for a quantitative definition of targets a separation of objectives is necessary. The definitions given above should not be viewed as defining new standards or redefining existing ones. The definitions are only made for a first understanding of a quality factor. Most national or international standards define those factors in different ways (e.g. reliability, robustness).

On the next level of decomposition the evaluation factors:

—modularity = ef_1 = $\langle M_1, \ldots, M_{n_M} \rangle$
—generality = ef_2 = $\langle G_1, \ldots, G_{n_G} \rangle$
—portability = ef_3 = $\langle P_1, \ldots, P_{n_P} \rangle$
—redundancy = ef_4 = $\langle R_1, \ldots, R_{n_R} \rangle$
—integrity = ef_5 = $\langle I_1, \ldots, I_{n_1} \rangle$
—complexity = ef_6 = $\langle C_1, \ldots, C_{n_C} \rangle$
—execution efficiency = ef_7 = $\langle T_1, \ldots, T_{n_T} \rangle$
—storage efficiency = ef_8 = $\langle S_1, \ldots, S_{n_S} \rangle$
—test coverage = ef_9 = $\langle TC_1, \ldots, TC_{n_{TC}} \rangle$
—verification coverage = ef_{10} = $\langle VC_1, \ldots, VC_{n_{VC}} \rangle$
—symbolic execution coverage = ef_{11} = $\langle SC_1, \ldots, SC_{n_{SC}} \rangle$
—inspection coverage = ef_{12} = $\langle IC_1, \ldots, IC_{n_{IC}} \rangle$

should be used to define the quality criteria. Each evaluation factor is defined by the formulae given in the following subsection.

4.2 Formulae for the Evaluation Factors

A number of evaluation factors are defined in the following, which can be used in the quality model represented above.

Note: In the following formulae, the number of the appropriate elements is assumed, if not otherwise specified.

Modularity can be defined by means of the tuple: $M = \langle M_1, M_2, M_3, M_4, M_5, M_6, M_7, M_8 \rangle$

—M_1 = modules/procedures
—M_2 = modules/variables
—M_3 = modules/functions
—M_4 = modules/objects
—M_5 = modules/activities
—M_6 = modules/objects
—M_7 = modules/module calls
—M_8 = modules/module interfaces

Modularity: $M = f_{modularity}(M_1, M_2, M_3, M_4, M_5, M_6, M_7, M_8)$

Example: $M = (M_1 + M_2 + M_3 + M_4 + M_5 + M_6 + M_7 + M_8)/8$

Generality is to be defined by the tuple: $G = \langle G_1, G_2, G_3, G_4, G_5, G_6, G_7 \rangle$

—G_1 = application independent modules/modules
—G_2 = application independent procedures/procedures
—G_3 = application independent variables/variables
—G_4 = application independent functions/functions
—G_5 = application independent data/data
—G_6 = application independent activities/activities
—G_7 = application independent objects/objects

Generality: $G = f_{generality}(G_1, G_2, G_3, G_4, G_5, G_6, G_7)$

Example: $G = (G_1 + G_2 + G_3 + G_4 + G_5 + G_6 + G_7)/7$

Portability might be defined by the following tuple: $P = \langle P_1, P_2, P_3, P_4, P_5, P_6, P_7 \rangle$

—P_1 = environment independent modules/modules
—P_2 = environment independent procedures/procedures
—P_3 = environment independent variables/variables
—P_4 = environment independent functions/functions
—P_5 = environment independent data/data
—P_6 = environment independent activities/activities
—P_7 = environment independent objects/objects

Portability: $P = f_{portability}(P_1, P_2, P_3, P_4, P_5, P_6, P_7)$

Example: $P = (P_1 + P_2 + P_3 + P_4 + P_5 + P_6 + P_7)/7$

Redundancy is defined by the following tuple: $R = \langle R_1, R_2, R_3 \rangle$

—R_1 = repeatable modules/modules
—R_2 = reproducible data capsules/modules
—R_3 = logged transactions/transactions

Redundancy: $R = f_{redundancy}(R_1, R_2, R_3)$

Example: $R = (R_1 + R_2 + R_3)/3$

Integrity is defined by the following tuple: $I = \langle I_1, I_2 \rangle$

—I_1 = edited system input data items/system input data items
—I_2 = edited system output data items/system output data items

Integrity: $I = f_{integrity}(I_1, I_2)$

Example: $I = (I_1 + I_2)/2$

Complexity is defined by the following tuple: $C = \langle C_1, C_2, \ldots, C_{24} \rangle$

—C_1 = code predicates/code predicate variables
—C_2 = procedures/code predicates

—C_3 = (code variables—code predicate variables)/code variables
—C_4 = procedures/variables
—C_5 = functions/data
—C_6 = activities/objects
—C_7 = activities/functions
—C_8 = objects/data
—C_9 = functions/procedures
—C_{10} = data/variables
—C_{11} = control flow complexity of the programs
—C_{12} = data flow complexity of the programs
—C_{13} = control flow complexity of the dp-concept
—C_{14} = data flow complexity of the dp-concept
—C_{15} = control flow complexity of the ap-concept
—C_{16} = data flow complexity of the ap-concept
—C_{17} = min(data-to-variable-links)/max(data-to-variable-links)
—C_{18} = min(function-to-procedure-links)/max(function-to-procedure-links)
—C_{19} = min(object-to-data-links)/max(object-to-data-links)
—C_{20} = min(activity-to-function-links)/max(activity-to-function-links)
—C_{21} = test predicates/test predicate variables
—C_{22} = procedures/test predicates
—C_{23} = (variables–predicate variables)/variables
—C_{24} = procedures/test predicate variables

Complexity: $C = f_{complexity}(C_1, C_2, \ldots, C_{24})$

Example: $C = (C_1 + C_2 + \ldots + C_{24})/24$

Execution efficiency is defined by the following tuple: $T = \langle T_1, T_2 \rangle$
—T_1 = transactions/(data processes per transaction × transactions)
—T_2 = transactions/(module calls per transaction × transactions)
Execution efficiency: $T = f_{executionefficiency}(T_1, T_2)$

Example: $T = (T_1 + T_2)/2$

Storage efficiency is defined by the following tuple: $S = \langle S_1, S_2 \rangle$
—S_1 = data items/(average capsule length × number of data capsules)
—S_2 = activities/(average activity length × number of data capsules)
Storage efficiency: $S = f_{storageefficiency}(S_1, S_2)$

Example: $S = (S_1 + S_2)/2$

Test coverage might be defined by the following tuple: $TC = \langle TC_1, TC_2, \ldots, TC_{TC_N} \rangle$

—TC_{j_i} = programs C_i tested/programs
—$TC.\ldots$ = programs $C.\ldots$ tested/programs
—TC_{k_i} = modules S_i tested/modules
—$TC.\ldots$ = modules $S.\ldots$ tested/modules
Test coverage: $TC = f_{testcoverage}(TC_1, TC_2, \ldots, TC_{TC_N})$

Example: $TC = (TC_1 + TC_2 + \ldots + TC_{TC_N})/TC_N$

Verification coverage is to be defined by the following tuple: $VC = \langle VC_1, VC_2, VC_3, VC_4 \rangle$

—VC_1 = programs for which termination is verified/programs
—VC_2 = programs for which specification fulfilment is verified/ programs
—VC_3 = functions for which activity fulfilment is verified/functions
—VC_4 = data for which object fulfilment is verified/data
Verification coverage: $VC = f_{verificationcoverage}(VC_1, VC_2, VC_3, VC_4)$

Example: $VC = (VC_1 + VC_2 + VC_3 + VC_4)/4$

Symbolic execution coverage might be defined by the following tuple: $SC = \langle SC_1 \rangle$

—SC_1 = programs symbolic executed correctly/programs
Symbolic execution coverage: $SC = f_{symbolicexecutioncoverage}(SC_1)$

Example: $SC = (SC_1)/1$

Inspection coverage might be defined by the following tuple: $IC = \langle IC_1, IC_2, IC_3, IC_4, IC_5, IC_6 \rangle$

—IC_1 = programs accepted after inspection/programs
—IC_2 = modules accepted after inspection/modules
—IC_3 = data accepted after inspection/data
—IC_4 = functions accepted after inspection/functions
—IC_5 = activities accepted after inspection/activities
—IC_6 = objects accepted after inspection/objects
Inspection coverage: $IC = f_{inspectioncoverage}(IC_1, IC_2, \ldots, IC_6)$

Example: $IC = (IC_1 + IC_2 + \ldots + IC_6)/6$

4.3 Scheme of an evaluation factor definition

The general scheme to define (ratio) measures used in this example is as follows:

—$QC_i = N_{objects\ to\ be\ counted}/N_{maximum\ of\ these\ objects}$

or

$$-QC_j = N_{objects\ to\ be\ counted} / M_{some\ average}$$
$$-QC = f_{quality\ criteria}(QC_1, \ldots, QC_n)$$

Examples:

1. $QC = (QC_1 + \ldots + QC_n)/n = \dfrac{\Sigma_i^{1,n} QC_i}{n}$

2. $QC = (QC_1 \times \ldots \times QC_n) = \Pi_i^{1,n} QC_i$

3. $QC =$ if $QC_i >$ cut value then 1 else 0 for all QC_i

4. $QC =$ if $QC_i \leqslant$ cut value then $f(QC_j)$ for all i and j,

$f \in \{f_{max}, \ldots, \}$

5. $QC = (QC_{max} + QC_{min})/2$

This formalized definition of quality criteria paves the way to the following assessment procedure.

5. FORMALIZED ASSESSMENT

A quality model with weighting is very flexible. It provides the basis for an algorithmic process that may be used by a project to determine a concrete quality model. The assessment procedure in general comprises the tasks:

1. Define the 'ideal' object in terms of assessment factors to be achieved.
2. Check whether those factors are achieved by the object under test, or obtain the grade of achievement.
3. Compute the distance between the two lists of assessment criteria and rank the systems.

The assessment method proposed is based on the following two principles:

—A quality statement should consist of a comparison of current and required values.

—Quality is proportional to the distance from the actual value to the target value.

5.1 A method for a formalized assessment

Using definitions of the attributes of a software object, its value or quality can be defined as the distance between its actual attributes and its required attributes. For the computation of this distance, statements about the attributes have to be transformed into numbers. The quality of a software object is represented as an acyclic graph. Each leaf of the acyclic graph represents an evaluation factor. Evaluation factors are defined as the quantified attributes of an object. Some of these have been discussed in a previous section. On the basis of these evaluation factors quality factors may be defined. For each evaluation factor, a weighting factor is used to determine to what extent it contributes to a quality factor. For the calculation of the system values, it is necessary to define a basis for the computation of the difference between the quality characteristics of the required software engineering system. For the actual software engineering system, all the evaluation factors can be computed by transforming the attributes into numbers.

The factors for the ideal or required object could be obtained by an abstract definition of this system, i.e. an effort has to be made to define the required system in terms of the required assessment factors and in terms of the required quality factors. This definition then constitutes a so-called set of required assessment factors and required quality factors.

Both kinds of factors, actual and required ones, may be represented by n-ary vectors in order to make use of correlation functions defined for vector descriptions of software engineering systems. These correlation functions serve here as means of computing the relationship between an actual software system and the required system.

5.2   Actual and required factors and values

5.2.1   Actual evaluation factors

$$aefv = \langle aef_1, aef_2, aef_3, \ldots, aef_{n_2} \rangle$$

where aef_i denotes the value of a measurement (e.g. number of nodes of a control flow graph).

5.2.2   Actual quality factors

$$aqfv = \langle aqf_1, aqf_2, aqf_3, \ldots, aqf_{n_2} \rangle$$

where aqf_i denotes quality factor i.

$$aqf_i = (a_{i,1} \otimes aef_1, a_{i,2} \otimes aef_2, \ldots, a_{i,n_2} \otimes aef_{n_2})$$

where $a_{i,j}$ = weighting factor, $a_{i,j}$ denotes the contribution of aef_i to aqf_j, and $0 \cdot 0 \leq a_{i,j} \leq 1 \cdot 0$ or $a_{i,j} \in \{0, 1\}$ for boolean expressions.

5.2.3   Required evaluation factors

$$refv = \langle ref_1, ref_2, ref_3, \ldots, ref_{n_2} \rangle$$

where ref_i denotes the value of the ideal or required value for ef_i.

5.2.4   Required quality factors

$$rqfv = \langle rqf_1, rqf_2, rqf_3, \ldots, rqf_{n_1} \rangle$$

where rqf_i denotes the value of the ideal or required value for qf_i, or alternatively the computed set of required quality factors.

$$rqfv = \langle rqf_1, rqf_2, rqf_3, \ldots, rqf_{n_1} \rangle$$

where rqf_i denotes quality factor i:

$$rqf_i := (a_{i,1} \otimes ref_1, a_{i,2} \otimes ref_2, \ldots, a_{i,n_2} \otimes ref_{n_2})$$

where $a_{i,i}$ = weighting factor, $a_{i,j}$ denotes the contribution of ref_i to rqf_j, and $0 \cdot 0 \leq a_{i,j} \leq 1 \cdot 0$ or $a_{i,j} \in \{0, 1\}$ for boolean expressions.

5.3   Level-specific computation of system quality

This approach to software assessment depends on a user's subjective viewpoint. A first step occurs when the user defines his beliefs in certain measures by identifying the ideals for the evaluation factors. The second step occurs since the user must define the degree of contribution of a measure to a quality factor. Therefore, this kind of procedure for software evaluation defines some 'sort of a software metric' which rests on user decision as to the value of certain measurable evaluation factors and on a user-determined definition of the relationship between evaluation values and quality factors.

After these decisions have been made, a system value might be computed for each level of the quality graph. Since every multi-level quality graph might be transformed into a two-level quality graph, at least two distinct system values could be computed (Figs 2 and 3). An extension of the two-level approach to an n-level approach is discussed below. The following formulae specify the computation procedure, an abstract implementation of which is given in the Appendix.

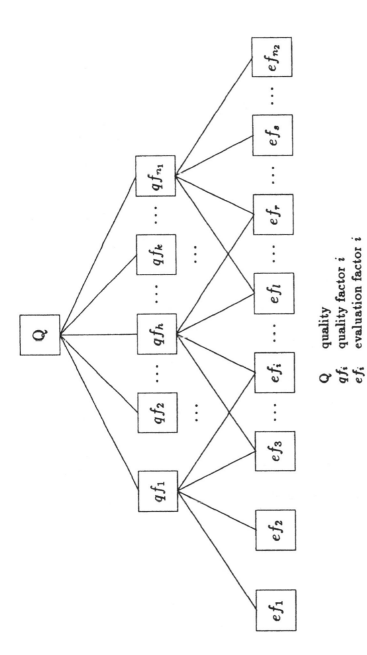

Q   quality
qf_i quality factor i
ef_i evaluation factor i

Fig. 2. Two level decomposition of quality.

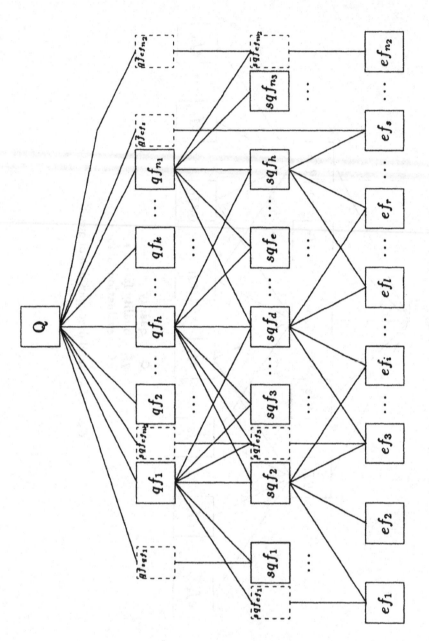

Fig. 3. Three (or more) level decomposition of quality.

5.3.1 *The computation of the level-0 system value (sv0)*

By a direct comparison of actual and required evaluation factors (Fig. 4) we propose:

Approach 0·1

$$sv0 = c(aefv, rev)$$

where $c_{0,1}$ is a correlation function (distance function).

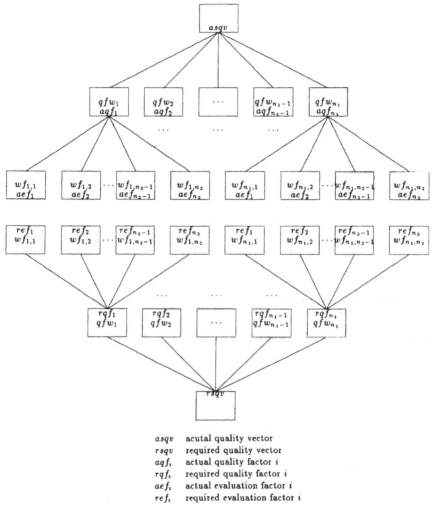

$asqv$	actual quality vector
$rsqv$	required quality vector
aqf_i	actual quality factor i
rqf_i	required quality factor i
aef_i	actual evaluation factor i
ref_i	required evaluation factor i

Fig. 4. Actual versus required quality.

This approach might not always be effective, because sometimes it is impossible to define a metric on factors each expressed in values of different scales. In those situations we compute the system value as the distance of two distances. An actual distance is defined by the distances of the pairs $\langle aef_i, ref_i \rangle$ of pairs of evaluation factors. This distance then is compared with a required distance vector for that level. In this vector each component defines the maximal value allowed for a distance between the actual and the required values. This leads to

Approach 0·2

This approach comprises two steps. At first an **actual system value vector** is computed by the formula:

$$asvv0 = \langle asv0_1, asv0_2, \ldots, asv0_{n_2} \rangle$$

where $asv0_i = c_i(aef_i, ref_i)$ and c_i is a correlation (distance) function obtained from the quality matrix. In a second step a **required system value vector** is to be defined by the user as:

$$rsvv0 = \langle rsv0_1, rsv0_2, \ldots, rsv0_{n_2} \rangle$$

where $rsv0_i$ denotes the ideal or required value for $sv0_i$

Finally we obtain the **level-0 system value** as:

approach 0·1	$sv0 = c_{0,1}(aefv, refv)$
approach 0·2	$sv0 = c_{0,2}(asvv0, rsvv0)$

where $c_{0,1}, c_{0,2}$ are correlation functions (i.e. distance functions) obtained from the quality matrix.

5.3.2 The computation of the level-1 system value (sv1)
Here we have two approaches, too. The direct comparison of actual and required quality factors is given by:

Approach 1·1

$$sv1 = c_{1,1}(aqfv, rqfv)$$

where $c_{1,1}$ is correlation function (distance function).

But this approach may often be impossible, because frequently the evaluation factors used lead to a scale of too low degree due to the chosen aggregation. Following the second approach taken on level zero we compute the system value on this level again as the distance of two other distances—a set of distances will be obtained as a result of a pairwise comparison of all tuples $\langle aqf_j, rqf_j \rangle$. An actual distance vector on level one is defined this way. The required distance vector for level one is defined by the user, as on level zero. Thus we have:

Approach 1·2
comprising the following two steps:

Actual system value vector

$$asvv1 = \langle asv1_1, asv1_2, \ldots, asv1_{n_1} \rangle$$

where $asv1_i = c_i(aqf_i, rqf_i)$ and c_i is a correlation (distance) function obtained from the quality matrix.

The user has to define a

Required system value vector
in terms of allowed distances between the actual and the required quality factors. We obtain:

$$rsvv1 = \langle rsv1_1, rsv1_2, \ldots, rsv1_{n_1} \rangle$$

where $rsv1_i$ denotes the ideal or required value for $sv1_i$

The level-1 system value is defined as:

approach 1·1	$sv1 = c_{1,1}(aqfv, rqfv)$
approach 1·2	$sv1 = c_{1,2}(asvv1, rsvv1)$

where $c_{1,1}, c_{1,2}$ are correlation functions (i.e. distance functions) obtained from the quality matrix.

5.3.3 *The computation of the system quality value*

System quality value: $sqv = c((sv0, sv1), (rsv0, rsv1))$

where c = correlation function (distance function). sv0, svv1: as defined above, and rsv0, rsvv1: the respective ideal or required values.

5.4 Extension to *N*-level factor quality

The proposed assessment procedure works for representations of system values on two levels. It is obvious that it is possible to extend the current procedure to make it possible to work with an arbitrary number of values. But it is still questionable whether a evaluation on more than two levels makes any sense. The general scheme for an extension is that factors on level N have to be expressed in terms of factors on level $N - 1$ in such a way as has been demonstrated for the definition of quality factors in terms of evaluation values. In other words, for each pair of a factor on level $N - 1$ and a factor on level N a weighting factor must be given indicating the contribution of the level $N - 1$ factor to the level N factor.

5.4.1 System quality value for N levels of factors

System quality value

$$sqv = c_N((sv0, sv1, sv2, \ldots, svN), (rsv0, rsv1, rsv2, \ldots, rsvN))$$

where c_N is a correlation function (or distance function), svi is an actual system value on level i and $rsvj$ is a required system value on level j.

One might assume problems in selecting the appropriate correlation functions. Experiences with correlation functions in the assessment of the quality of system responses of information systems[11] has given a number of indicators for effective correlation functions.

6. GENERATION OF MODELS

Both quality models and productivity models are defined within a common framework, which comprises evaluation factors, factors of quality or productivity, weight functions and weight constants. A generation procedure defined for quality models will also be applicable for generating productivity models if the procedure is parameterizable. We therefore concentrate the discussion of the generation of models on the construction of one type of model, i.e. quality models. The approach developed is directly applicable for generating productivity models.

6.1 Rule-based representation of quality models

Often quality factors are too complex to be mapped directly onto evaluation factors. Complex factors have to be decomposed into subfactors. If subfactors are too complex a further level of decomposition is necessary. In the final step quality factors and sub. . .-factors are mapped onto evaluation factors. This has been discussed above and leads to acyclic graphs as a representation of the static structure of decomposition. In the following the problem of constructing quality models with a number of decomposition levels is discussed. Rules seem to be appropriate to solve this problem. The general form of the rules is:

IF   predicate over items on decomposition level $n + 1$
or   predicate over items on decomposition level $n + 2$

          . . .

or   predicate over items on decomposition level $n + k$
THEN   predicate over an item on decomposition level n

Complex factors are constructed from subfactors, subfactors are constructed from subsubfactors or from evaluation factors. But some quality factors might be constructed in straightforward manner from a set of evaluation factors. Others might be constructed from subfactors and evaluation factors. Therefore, the general construction rule is of the form:

IF   evaluation factor predicate or subquality factor predicate
THEN   quality factor predicate
IF $\langle f_{h,1}(a_{h,1}, ef_1), \ldots, f_{h,n_1}(a_{h,n_1}, ef_{h,n_2}) \rangle$
or $\langle f_{i,1}(a_{i,1}, qf_i), \ldots, f_{i,n_2}(a_{i,n_2}, qf_{n_2}) \rangle$
THEN qf_k

For the definition of the formulae see Section 3.

One rule of this type, called the quality rule, is used to define one quality factor. The set of all quality rules defines the quality factor matrix. This rule scheme is used for quality graphs decomposed to n levels, where $n > 2$. For a two-level quality graph the rule scheme is reduced to:

IF $\langle f_{h,1}(a_{h,1}, ef_1), f_{h,2}(a_{h,2}, ef_2), \ldots, f_{h,n_1}(a_{h,n_1}, ef_{h,n_2}) \rangle$
THEN qf_k

In order to define quality completely, we also have to define the rule for the overall quality. Therefore a rule of the following type is used:

IF   evaluation factor predicate
or   subquality factor predicate
or   quality factor predicate
THEN   quality factor predicate

IF $\langle f_{h,1}(a_{h,1}, ef_1), f_{h,2}(a_{h,2}, ef_2), \ldots, f_{h,n_1}(a_{h,n_1}, ef_{h,n_2}) \rangle$
or $\langle f_{i,1}(a_{i,1}, qf_i), \ldots, f_{i,n_2}(a_{i,n_2}, qf_{n_2}) \rangle$
or $\langle g_1(b_1, f_{1,1}(a_{1,1}, ef_1)), \ldots, g_1(b_1, f_{1,n_2}(a_{1,n_2}, ef_{n_2})) \rangle$
THEN Q

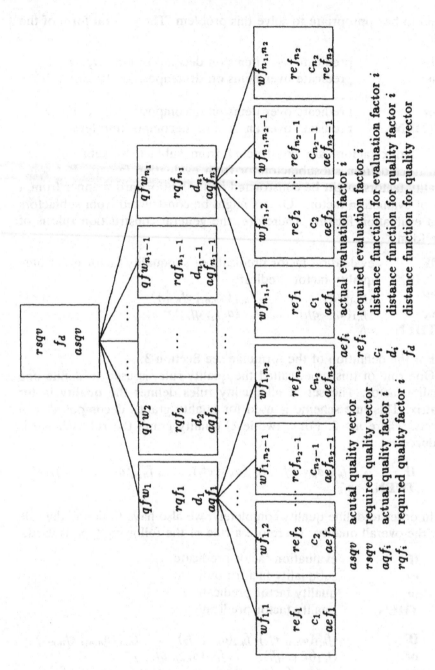

Fig. 5. The quality graph QG.

$asqv$	acutal quality vector
$rsqv$	required quality vector
aqf_i	actual quality factor i
rqf_i	required quality factor i
aef_i	actual evaluation factor i
ref_i	required evaluation factor i
c_i	distance function for evaluation factor i
d_i	distance function for quality factor i
f_d	distance function for quality vector

This is the scheme for the general case; for the two-level quality graph we get the reduced rule scheme:

IF $\langle g_1(b_1, f_{1,1}(a_{1,1}, ef_1)), \ldots, g_1(b_1, f_{1,n_2}(a_{1,n_2}, ef_{n_2}))\rangle$

THEN Q

Both types of rule are similar in structure. The quality rule is a special case of a quality factor rule; it is not used to define other quality factors. In terms of a graph, a quality rule is the root of a quality graph. Quality factor rules are the intermediate nodes of that graph (Fig. 5).

6.2 Parameterizing and weighting quality factors

Quality models may be used in a number of environments or for special purposes (type of product, type of project, etc.). On the other hand, a number of models have been proposed and more might be developed in future. In order to define the models by rules, a set of quality factor rules and a quality rule are required for each model. But certain quality factors are frequently common to certain quality models. In this case one might want to represent the models by one rule system in order to keep the overall set of rules small. On the other hand, more than one model often has to be applied in one project or in a company. Defining and maintaining a number of quality models in parallel might be very cost-effective and space-consuming. A solution to these problems is to parameterize the quality rules, the quality factor rules and the evaluation factors. But evaluation factors must not be parameterizable, since numbering keeps them distinct. The following gives a scheme of a parameterized rule:

IF   condition part

THEN   action part   **ENVIRONMENT**   parameter part

The environment component is used to define different models. The string environment is therefore replaced by a model. Two examples might illustrate how this extension is to be used:

IF   verification coverage   **MODEL**

or   inspection coverage

or   test coverage

THEN   correctness   **MODEL**   quality model$_{NN.1}$

IF   verification coverage

or   test coverage

THEN   correctness   *MODEL*   quality model$_{NN.2}$

The model of *NN.*1 requires coverage for verification, testing and inspection, whereas the model of *NN.*2 considers only the first and the last quality factor of the first model. But the parameter part is not only to be used to differentiate between complete models. It is applicable also to defining rules specific to product types or project classes or both. In this case the string environment is replaced by project type or product type. We obtain the rule schema:

IF	condition part		
THEN	action part	**PRODUCT TYPE**	parameter part
		PROJECT TYPE	parameter part

Both products and projects are to be characterized by a number of attributes (e.g. application area, programming language used). These attributes are applicable as parameters for the product or project-specific construction rules. The assignment of attributes of a product or a project to the construction rules has to be done by experts.

The general form of a rule is as follows:

IF	if conjunction 1		
or	if conjunction 2		
. . .	. . .		
or	if conjunction n		
THEN	then conjunction 1	**ENVIRONMENT**	parameter
or	then conjunction 2	**ENVIRONMENT**	parameter
. . .	. . .	**. . .**	. . .
or	then conjunction m	**ENVIRONMENT**	parameter

This rule scheme allows a compact definition of the rules. Disjunctions in the *then* part of the rules permit the definition of meta-rules, each covering a complete set of rules. The disjunction in the *if* part provides freedom to express a number of possible decompositions of quality, or of a quality factor.

6.3 Generation of a Specific Quality Model

Quality models might be defined according to the type of product. If quality has to be defined in parallel with the development, the type of the project might also be considered. Given a rule scheme as defined above, a quality model is to be generated by the evaluation of the parameter parts. The evaluation procedure selects all rules whose parameter part matches the selected attributes for the projects, products or other parameters. The set of rules selected defines the quality scheme. Next, the quality rule is evaluated. This defines the set of quality factors. Evaluating the rules defining quality factors in terms of (sub . . .-factors or) evaluation factors leads to the quality model. The last step generates the quality matrix as defined above.

6.4 Rules for Experiment Scenarios

As shown, construction rules contain correlation functions, weighting functions and weighting constants. These provide the basis for an experimental evaluation of quality models (and also productivity models). Using a fixed set of evaluation factors, experiments are to be defined for research into the semantics of the weighting functions and into the weighting constants.

A scenario for an experiment is to be defined by a set of scenario rules (SR). The SR describes the set of weighting functions and the assigned set of weighting function. The scenario rules are of the form:

Weight functions:
IF	weight function 1
or	weight function 2
. . .	. . .
or	weight function n
THEN	weight function vector **SCENARIO** experiment indicator

Weight constants:
IF	weight constant 1
or	weight constant 2
. . .	. . .
or	weight constant n
THEN	weight constant vector **SCENARIO** experiment indicator

Both rules sets define the actual weighting procedure for an experiment. This kind of scenario definition seems also to be appropriate to be used for evaluating past projects or existing products. But it might also be applied in projects investigating the best way of defining quality models from a user's point of view (cf. Ref. 25).

7. SUMMARY

The evaluation scheme presented here is based on a hierarchy, i.e. an acyclic graph, of the factors of software quality. The n-level ($n \geqslant 2$) hierarchy shown allows each quality factor to be represented by its relationship to evaluation factors, obtainable by means of commonly used software measuring procedures. A method of evaluating software based on this hierarchy is given, which computes quality values of two levels. The first-level quality value is computed on the basis of the measured evaluation factors. Quality factors, described in terms of evaluation factors, are used for the computation of system values of level two. An overall system quality is then computed by comparing quality values of both levels with user-defined target values for quality. A quality computation procedure is outlined which shows how the proposed method can be applied.

A very simple procedure is given which computes a system quality value on the basis of measurable evaluation values. It is assumed that different users have different views of what is relevant to a certain quality factor and how a measurable value relates to such a quality factor. Therefore the proposed procedure gives freedom to each user to define his or her own quality factors in terms of measurable evaluation factors. The computation procedure outlined above shows that the determination of a system's quality is as complex as a program with a number of for-loops, nested up to level one. For business applications, the proposed procedure has to be transformed into a small DB application which allows all the standardizable factors to be handled.

The quality model presented here and the associated assessment method enable us to combine the results of examination and measurement into a quality statement following an identical scheme. In contrast to other, fixed quality models, we present a generic model that allows the introduction of the assessor's intuition into the assessment process. It does not only allow it, but even requires it. In this way, the model ensures that quality statements are given in relation to a given target. The precise definition of these targets is forced, making the whole assessment process reconstructable and traceable.

The distinction between the three development phases is still one that is helpful for clarifying the acceptance questions as well as for the estimation of effort and size. An elementary, pragmatic measurement and assessment become possible by the organization of the representation of software in terms of active and passive elements. This is particularly suitable for the *relative rating* of products, since the elements which are compared occur in most modern specification and programming languages.

ACKNOWLEDGEMENT

The author wishes to thank his colleagues Jared L. Darlington, Norbert Killmeier, Monika Müllerburg, Frank Weber and Monika Sehr for a number of productive critical remarks on earlier versions of the paper. Barbara Kitchenham and Jared L. Darlington must be acknowledged for their careful editorial reading of the present text.

REFERENCES

1. Adrion, W. R., Branstad, M. A. and Cherninavsky, J. C., Validation, verification, and testing of computer software, In: *ACM Computing Surveys*, **14**, (2), June 1982, 159–92.
2. Albrecht, A., Software function, source lines of code and development effort prediction, in: *Trans. on S.E.*, **9**(6) Nov. 1983.
3. Atzmüller, H., and Hausen, H. L., Die atha-Methode der Software-Entwicklung—Vom Fachproblem zur DV-Implementierung: ein pragmatischer Ansatz. *GI-Fachgespräch Tutzing '85, Entwurf von Informationssystemen—Methoden und Modelle Tutzing*, 24–25 June 1985, 52–77.
4. Boehm B., Software Engineering Economics, Prentice Hall, New York, 1984.
5. Christ, M.-L., Itzfeldt, W. D., Schmidt, M., Timm, R. and Watts, R. (Ed.), Measuring software quality, Final Report of Project MQ, Vol. II: Software quality measurement and evaluation, Sankt Augustin, Manchester, GMD, NCC, 1984.
6. DIN 55350; Begriffe der Qualitätssicherung und Statistik, Beuth–Verlag, Berlin, Köln, 1980.
7. European Organisation for Quality Control (EOQC), Glossary of terms used in the management of quality, Bern, 1981.
8. Gong, H. and Schmidt, M. A complexity measure based on selection and nesting, in: *ACM SIGMETRICS*, **83**(4).
9. Halmos, P. R., Measure theory, Princeton, New Jersey, Van Nostrand, 1950.
10. Halstead, M. H., Elements of Software Science, Elsevier, New York, 1977.
11. Hausen, H. L., A dynamic self-tuning and adaptive information retrieval system, in: Herr, J., Theoretical issues in information retrieval, *Proc. Fourth Annual Int. SIGIR Conf.* ACM, New York, 1981, p. 15.
12. Hausen, H. L., Comments on practical constraints of software validation techniques, in: Hausen, H. L. (Ed), *Software validation, Proc. Symposium on Software Validation*, North-Holland, Oct. 1984, 12 pp.
13. Hausen, H. L., Yet another modelling of software quality and productivity—YAMOSQUAP, Technical Report, Project IVE, Gesellschaft für Mathematik und Datenverarbeitung mbH, Sankt Augustin, July 1987, 72 pp.

14. Hausen, H. L. and Neusser, H. J., Code instrumentation, GMD, Project IVE, WP HLH-HJN, Sept. 1987.
15. Hausen, H. L., Müllerburg, M. and Schmidt, M., Über das Prüfen, Messen und Bewerten von Software—Methoden und Techniken der analytischen Software-Qualitätssicherung in: *Informatik Spektrum*, **10**(3), 1987, 123–44.
16. Hausen, H. L., Software-Messung und Bewertung in einem dreistufigen Entwicklungsprozess in: *Tagungsbaad GI Arbeitsgespräch Software-Metriken*, Arbeitsgespräch der Fachgruppe Software-Engineering, IBM Bildungszentrum, Herrenberg, 12–13 Mar. 1987.
17. Hausen, H. L., Concepts, components and assessment of modern software engineering environments, in: ADV, Tagungsband 8, *International Kongreß "Datenverarbeitung im europäischen Raum, "Quo vadis EDV?- Realität und Vision 1987"*, Arbeitsgemeinschaft für Datenverarbeitung, Wien, 30.3–2.4.1987, 46–63.
18. Hausen, H. L., Müllerburg, M. and Schmidt, M., Examination, measurement and assessment of software products and projects, in: *Proc. EOQC'87*, Munich, 3–5 June 1987.
19. Levy, L. S., Taming the tiger—Software engineering and software economics, Springer, New York, 1987,.
20. McCabe, T., A complexity measure, in: *IEEE Trans. Software Engineering*, **SE-2**(4), Dec. 1976, 308–20.
21. McCall, J. A., Richards, P. K. and Walters, G. F., Concepts and definitions of software quality, in: *Factors in software quality, Vol. 1*, NTIS, Springfield, VA, Nov. 1977.
22. NASA, Measures and metrics for software development, Nasa-TM-85605, N84-26323 (microfiche).
23. Noth, T., Verfahren zur Aufwandsschätzung für die Entwicklung von Anwendungssystemen, Springer-Verlag, Berlin, 1984.
24. Putnam, L. and Fitzsimmons, A., Estimation software costs, in: *DATAMATION*, Sept. 1979.
25. Rombach, G. D. and Basili, V. R., Quantitative software-qualitätssicherung, in: *Informatik Spektrum*, **10**(3), 1987, 145–58.
26. Schmidt, M., Über das Messen und Bewerten von Software-Qualität mit Maßund Metrik, in: *Tagungsband GI Arbeitsgespräch Software-Metriken*, Arbeitsgespräch der Fachgruppe Software-Engineering, IBM Bildungszentrum, Herrenberg, 12–13 Mar. 1987.
27. Zuse, H., Meßtheoretische Analyse von statischen Softwarekomplexitätsmaßen, Dissertation, TU Berlin, 1985.

APPENDIX 1: QUALITY PROCEDURE

PROCEDURE eval-sys-value;
number-of-evaluation-factors:= READ;
FOR i FROM 1 TO number-of-evaluation-factors DO
maximum-for-evaluation-factor.vector(i)):= READ;

```
evaluation-factor.vector(i):= READ;
evaluation-factor.vector(i):=
  evaluation-factor.vector(i) DIVIDED-BY
  maximum-for-evaluation-factor.vector(i);
required-evaluation-factor.vector(i):= READ
required-evaluation-factor.vector(i):=
  required-evaluation-factor.vector(i) DIVIDED-BY
  maximum-for-evaluation-factor.vector(i)
ENDFOR;

number-of-quality-factors:= READ;
FOR i FROM 1 TO number-of-quality-factors DO
  quality-factor.name(i):= READ
  FOR j FROM 1 TO number-of-evaluation-factors DO
    contribution-weight-of-evaluation-factor(i, j):= READ
    quality-factor.vector(i):=
      contribution-weight-of-evaluation-factor (i, j) TIMES
        evaluation-factor.vector(j)
    required-quality-factor.vector(i):=
      contribution-weight-of-evaluation-factor(i, j) TIMES
      required-evaluation-factor.vector(j)
  ENDFOR;
ENDFOR;


FOR i FROM 1 TO number-of-evaluation-factors DO
level-0-required-system-value.vector(i):= READ
level-0-actual-system-value.vector(i):=
  distance-of
  (evaluation-factor.vector(i), required-evaluation-factor.vector(i))
ENDFOR;

level-0-system-value:=
  correlation-of-vector
    (level-0-required-system-value.vector,
    level-0-actual-system-value.vector);

FOR i FROM TO number-of-quality-factors DO
level-1-required-system-value.vector(i):= READ
```

```
level-1-actual-system-value.vector(i):=
  distance-of
    (quality-factor.vector(i), required-quality-factor.vector(i))
ENDFOR;

level-1-system-value:=
  correlation-of-vector
    (level-1-required-system-value.vector,
    level-1-actual-system-value.vector);

required-level-0-system-value:= READ;
required-level-1-system-value:= READ;
system-value:=
  correlation-of-vector
    ((level-0-system-value, level-1-system-value),
    (required-level-0-system-value, required-level-1-system-value));
ENDPROCEDURE
```

APPENDIX 2: DEFINITIONS OF MEASURE, METRIC AND SCALE

Definition 1:

Let A be a set, $P(A)$ the powerset of A and $\Re$ the set of real numbers.

A mapping $m : P(A) \to \Re$ is a *measure* on $P(A)$, if:

1. $m(A_i)$ exists for all $A_i \subset A$
2. $m(A_i) > 0$ for all $A_i \subset A$, $A_i \neq \emptyset$
3.a $m(A_i) = 0$, if $A_i = \emptyset$
3.b $m(A_i) = 0$, if A_i is a 'null set'
A set B is a null set if $m(B) = 0$
4. $m(A_1 \cup A_2 \cup \cdots \cup A_n \cdots) = m(A_1) + m(A_2) + \cdots + m(A_n) + \cdots$
for the set of pairwise disjoint sets A_i, $A_j \subset A$.

Definition 2:

Let A be a set and $\Re$ the set of real numbers.

A function $d : A \times A \to \Re$,

is a metric if for all $a_i \neq a_j \neq a_k$; a_i, a_j, $a_k \in A$ the following holds:

1. $d(a_i, a_i) = 0 \wedge d(a_i, a_j) > 0$ for $i \neq j$

2. $d(a_i, a_j) = d(a_j, a_i)$
3. $d(a_i, a_j) \leqslant d(a_i, a_k) + d(a_k, a_j)$

Definition 3:

A scale is a homomorphic mapping h of a set A, with relations $R_1, \ldots, R_r$ defined for it, onto a set B, with relations $S_1, \ldots, S_r$ defined for it. B is the set of real numbers. A together with its relations is called an empirical relative; B together with its relations is called a numerical relative. Scales might be differentiated by the transformation permitted on them. A transformation of a scale is a mapping of a scale into itself.

Definition 4:

A nominal scale is a scale whose permitted transformations are only the one-to-one transformations.

Definition 5:

A scale whose permitted transformations are monotonic increasing is an ordinal scale. A monotonic increasing transformation of a scale h is of the form $h \rightarrow f(h)$, where f is a strict monotonic increasing, real-valued function.

Definition 6:

A scale whose permitted transformations are positive linear is an interval scale. Positive linear transformations of a scale h are of the form $h \rightarrow \alpha h + \beta, \ \alpha > 0; \ \alpha, \beta \in \Re$.

Definition 7:

A scale whose permitted transformations are only the similarity transformations is called a ratio scale. Thereby the similarity transformations of a scale h are of the form $h \rightarrow \alpha h, \ \alpha > 0$.

Definition X:

Ordinal scales, interval scales, log-interval scales and ratio scales are also nominal scales. If ratio scales possess a *natural* unit in addition to the fixed zero point, they are designated as absolute scales. (Here, the only permitted transformations are the identity transformations under which everything remains invariant. Examples are absolute frequencies and probabilities.)

10

Aspects of the Licensing and Assessment of Highly Dependable Computer Systems

R. E. BLOOMFIELD and P. K. D. FROOME

Adelard, London, UK

ABSTRACT

The potential benefits of using computers in applications requiring high dependability are considerable. These benefits can include improved dependability and reduced equipment and operational costs. However, they will only be realised if the computer system itself is adequately dependable and can be shown to be so to the licensing bodies or organisations responsible for endorsing its operation. Over the last eighteen months, the European Workshop on Industrial Computer Systems (EWICS) Technical Committee 7 (TC7) on reliability, safety and security has been developing 'Guidelines for the reliability and safety assessment of high integrity industrial computer systems'. In the course of developing these guidelines, the authors have become concerned with the need to relate judgements about the quality of the software to some external criteria which may be expressed in a quantified, probabilistic manner. This chapter examines two aspects of this concern: the role of software reliability growth models, including the usefulness of metrics; and the broader issue of 'engineering judgement'. The role of software reliability is concluded to be one of providing additional, qualitative, evidence of a system's acceptability which will be based on some 'engineering judgement' of the development process and the product itself. A method for structuring this decision-making process is outlined. It does not, however, solve the assessment problem by reducing it to a list of simple questions. Judgement will still be essential in the assessment: it is required in answering the detailed questions and assessing the significance of any unsatisfactory features which are identified.

1. INTRODUCTION

The potential benefits of using computers in applications requiring high dependability are considerable. These benefits can include improved dependability as well as reduced equipment and operational costs. However, they will only be realized if the computer system itself is adequately dependable and can be shown to be so to the licensing bodies or organisations responsible for endorsing its operation. An overview of the software assessment process is given in Ref. 1.

Over the last two years, the European Workshop on Industrial Computer Systems (EWICS) Technical Committee 7 (TC7) on reliability, safety and security has been developing 'Guidelines for the reliability and safety assessment of high integrity industrial computer systems'. These are one of a number of guidelines produced by TC7[2] which have been part-funded by the European Commission and are being published in 1988 and 1989. In the course of developing these guidelines, the authors have become concerned with the need to relate judgements about the quality of the software to some external criteria: these criteria may be expressed either in a quantified, probabilistic manner,[3] or qualitatively in terms such as 'as low as readily achievable' (ALARA). This paper examines two aspects of this concern: Section 2 considers the role of software reliability growth models, including the usefulness of metrics; and Section 3 considers the broader issue of 'engineering judgement'.

2. SOFTWARE RELIABILITY MODELS

2.1 Introduction

In many applications there is a requirement to demonstrate that a system meets numerical reliability targets. Probabilistic risk assessment (PRA) may be an important part of the safety case and will have to include consideration of design errors and software errors. One appealing technique for dealing with such errors is to use one of the many software reliability models which have been developed over the past decade or so. The use of a model as part of the saftey case must, of course, be justified. In general one must show that the underlying assumptions of the model are valid and that the inference procedures used to calibrate the model parameters are adequate. For high reliability applications the situation is exacerbated by the absence of any failure data.

Because of the problem in collecting statistically significant amounts of data, the modelling of the reliability of safety systems will have to be based on specific experiments to justify the statistical process, data from earlier phases of the development and data from larger or more error-prone systems. The extrapolation to operation of the safety system will have to be carefully justified. The reliability models can be classified into the two categories used in the IEEE Guidelines:[4] process and product. The 'process' category is dominated by software reliability growth models, and these are discussed first. The second category, 'product', looks at attributes of the software itself. 'Metrics' are part of this and these will be discussed later.

2.2 Software reliability growth models

A comprehensive review of software reliability models is given by Ramamoorthy.[5] The models can be described by the common perception of software in terms of a functional mapping or in terms of an idealised machine such as a finite state automaton (see Fig. 1[6]). The development of the software and its subsequent statistical increase in reliability is seen either in terms of a succession of different mappings or as a series of mutations of an idealised machine. The reliability growth predicted by these models is shown schematically in Fig. 2. The reliability (probably) improves by a discrete amount at each debugging, and in the Bayesian models improves between failures as testing increases. A common feature of the most widely reported models, such as the Littlewood–Verral, Musa, Jelinski–Moranda and Shooman ones, is the assumption that the failure process is Poisson. They differ in the plausibility and sophistication of their interpretation of the rate parameter and in the inference procedures used in its evaluation. A justification for the choice of a Poisson process, apart from its analytical convenience, can be found in work done by Boeing for NASA which investigated this assumption by specific experiments in n-version software development and testing.[7] Further justification can be found in Littlewood,[8] where the predictive ability of several models is compared.

However, the past predictive performance of a model is not the only

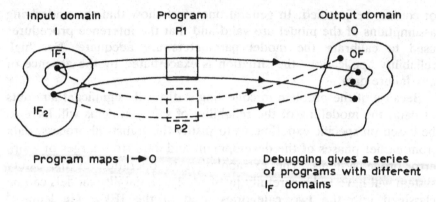

Program maps I→O

Debugging gives a series
of programs with different
I_F domains

Fig. 1(a). Input program output model of software.

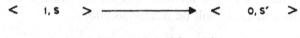

Input I causes transition of internal
state s to s' and produces output O

Fig. 1(b). Finite state automaton model of software.

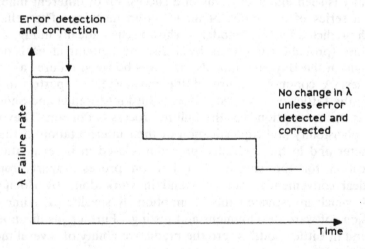

Fig. 2(a). Deterministic model. $\lambda \propto$ number of errors in system (e.g. Jelinski–Moranda).

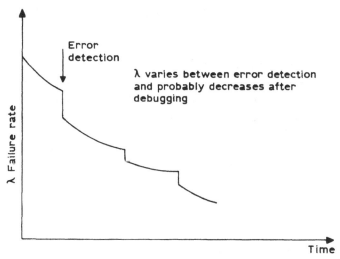

Fig. 2(b). Stochastic Bayesian model of Littlewood–Verrall.

criterion for deciding between competing models. The quality of future prediction depends on the underlying assumptions, and if these are inadequate then extrapolation outside the test domain for which there is data may not be justified. Assessing the adequacy of these 'underlying assumptions' quickly develops into a discussion of the philosophy of scientific laws: the problem of the confirmation of universal statements, the role of induction and the difference between the validity of a law and its ability as a predictor. What is required for software reliability prediction is a way of characterising the uncertainty of the prediction. This is often achieved for scientific laws when a new theory replaces an old, e.g. the predictive limits of Newtonian mechanics can be derived from quantum mechanics. However, this is not a straightforward subject, and hopefully the relevance of earlier work on confirming scientific theories and in particular the role of background information will be examined in a later paper. In the present paper the authors will assert that in safety-related applications confidence is required in making predictions much further ahead than for past predictions (the failure interval is growing perhaps exponentially) and therefore belief in the hypotheses of these software reliability models is important to the belief in their quality. The approach adopted in assessing these models is to take a radically

different view of the software development process and to view it as a
human activity.

2.3 Software development as a human activity
In order to examine further the philosophy of software reliability
prediction it is interesting to consider the development of software
from a different perspective. Instead of treating the software as some
mutating machine, the development can be considered as a human
intellectual activity and hence intrinsically error-prone. Software
development can be thought of as an interaction between software
engineers, with their own understanding and perception of the
program, and the program and test procedures. This process can then
be analysed in terms of human performance models.

A commonly used classification of human performance is that of
Rasmussen.[9] Rasmussen has identified three distinct levels of human
performance, skill-based, rule-based and knowledge-based (see Fig.
3). Skill-based behaviour generally comprises highly automated
sensor-motor actions with little conscious control and can be described
by control theoretic models, queuing theory etc. The next level of
performance, rule-based, is the recognition of situations with the
subsequent actions based on a simple procedural rule. The third level,

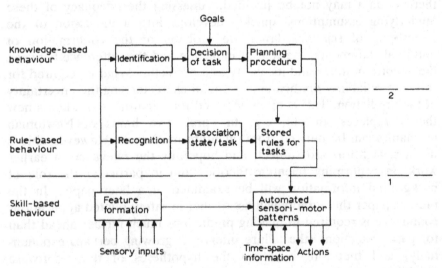

Fig. 3. Rasmussen's skill-based, rule-based and knowledge-based model of
human performance.

so called knowledge-based behaviour, consists of high-level cognitive actions based on some symbolic mental model of the situation which has a one-to-one correspondence with the system state. In other words, the third level of performance is solving difficult problems by thinking about them a lot, the second level involves recognition but little thought, and the first level does not require thinking about the problem at all.

If we apply these ideas to software development we could associate certain classes of error with different levels of performance; for example, the debugging of syntax errors can be treated as skill-based, whereas the correction of specification errors is probably knowledge-based. It is plausible to suggest that the balance between skill-, rule- and knowledge-based behaviour will vary during the different phases of the development process. It is therefore reasonable to assume that the method of describing and predicting this performance will change over the lifecycle so that models validated for early stages in the program development may well break down when used to predict final reliability.

It is interesting to speculate that the current reliability models may be improved by adopting a different underlying process. In an interim report on work sponsored by the Commission of the European Community on applications of artificial intelligence to the control and safety problems of nuclear power plants,[10] it was observed that the statistics of a simple 'attention structuring device' matched the distribution of 'times to correct response'. This device contained a checklist of hypotheses that related the occurrence of a particular signal with an appropriate action. The experiment involved randomly choosing a signal and then sequentially accessing the checklist until a correct hypothesis was encountered. When a correct hypothesis was found this was moved to the top of the list. The list did not converge but apparently stable configurations appeared over quite a long sequence. Perhaps an analysis of the statistics of this process would produce an alternative to the Poisson model for this level 1–level 2 behaviour.

Another important complication with reliability prediction occurs because there are different test requirements and strategies for the different phases of the lifecycle. This will have the effect of perturbing the number of residual errors in the Jelinski–Moranda type models, and will affect the failure rate as illustrated in Fig. 4. Indeed, in an extension to the PODS project[11] it was found that the failure rate can

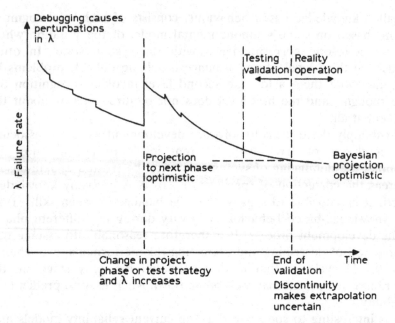

Fig. 4. Effect of different phases in software project on failure rate.

vary by an order of magnitude between different test strategies. Consequently reliability prediction based on data from one phase will not be accurate when extrapolated to the next phase, and in particular to its performance in its real environment. Even if a model is valid within a phase, it can only give a conditional result insofar as the predictions are based on a certain testing strategy which may or may not differ significantly from reality (the approach of IBM FSD reported in these proceedings recognises the importance of accurately simulating the actual operational environment). The extrapolation of reliability, therefore, is likely to be extremely uncertain even if the models are valid. There is plenty of anecdotal evidence to support this: many engineers have unpublished accounts of how high integrity software, which has been thoroughly tested for 10^5–10^6 cycles, fails when a new test is designed. However, the modelling problem is more severe than just the lack of data to correlate between different phases. There is increasing evidence that the persistent errors in high integrity software, and probably other software as well, are specification-based, emanating from an incomplete, ambiguous or incorrectly interpreted specification. For real-time systems this can be seen from specific experiments on the development of high reliability software such as the EPRI project[12] in the USA or the European collaboration between UKAEA, CEGB, VTT and Halden.[11] The abstraction of the specification is certainly a knowledge-based, level 3, process in Rasmussen's categorisation and so are elements of the verification (unless at some future date this becomes totally mechanised). It is quite clear from the human factors literature that, even if skill- and rule-based processes can be adequately modelled, the knowledge-based behaviour associated with discovering residual software errors cannot be predicted. There is no model of the cognition process which can be used to justify the use of a Poisson process, or any other process, as the underlying statistical framework for reliability prediction. Although there is some evidence that simple models may be useful in predicting human decision-making processes,[13] they are not adequate for licensing purposes. It may be that workers in artificial intelligence and psychologists will eventually provide such a description. Until then it is not appropriate to use statistical software reliability models for predicting the performance of high-integrity systems.

2.4 Metrics

A rather superficial analogy will be used to look at the role of metrics. In continuing the emphasis on the human element, an analogy is drawn between an examiner and an engineer using 'software metrics'.

Consider an examiner who decides to avoid the mental effort of the mathematics of engineering and mark the papers on the basis of metrics. He (she) uses a number of different approaches. First of all he counts the lines of text and the lines of algebra. He then applies several complexity measures he has read about in the literature such as McCabe and Halstead (see Ref. 4). He has also read Djkstra and Jackson so he assesses the design of the answer by looking at its control and data structures. He even uses mathematically formal techniques such as VDM to analyse the question he has set to see if it is consistent and unambiguous.[14] Having thoroughly measured the exam papers, he assigns grades. He even decides on the correctness in the same way. However, he is aggrieved to find that his colleagues dispute his methods.

This caricature underlines the problems of using metrics, particularly in safety-related applications. Clearly there may be some historically useful data which relate the correctness of the answer to, for example, its length or algebra content. However, for any particular paper this is only a probabilistic measure and probably of no great accuracy. The main conclusions to be drawn from this analogy is that mathematics cannot be replaced by metrics and that metrics may indicate quality but not correctness.

2.5 The future of software reliability models

If one cannot predict the future of software reliability with models, what about the future of software reliability models? If they are limited to skill-based or just rule-based behaviour then the continuing improvement in software engineering may make their use harder to justify. Already the adoption of good practice (structured programming, reviews, formalised lifecycles etc.) can produce reliable software, albeit at high cost and with large bureaucratic overheads. This trend will continue as formal methods (in the mathematical sense) become more widespread and the need for software reliability models will be for those which can predict the higher level errors.

2.6 Conclusions

The main conclusion is that the current software reliability models are inadequate for quantifying the software reliability of safety-related systems. The conclusion is based on a comparison between human performance modelling and the software development process. Although reliability models are judged inapplicable to the prediction of a quantified level of safety, they do have a role in highly dependable systems for achieving a balanced design and for project management, as well as for providing evidence for a qualitative assessment.

The problem of reliability prediction is not unique to software. Indeed, there are other aspects of risk assessment where statistical techniques are not well enough developed for adequate prediction: operator performance, design errors in general and the common mode failure of redundant systems are all hard to quantify. The assessment of safety will therefore have to depend on 'engineering judgement'.†
The issues of how to apply engineering judgement and how the decision-making process should be structured are discussed in the next section.

---

† If quantification is considered essential then limits would have to be placed on software reliability consistent with the uncertainties in the modelling process.

3.   ENGINEERING JUDGEMENT

There is unfortunately no simple method for assuring the dependability of a complex system. The assessment of safety will be based on the mass of information collected and analysed during the assessment process. This section discusses the issues of how to apply 'engineering judgement' and how the decision-making process should be structured.

3.1   Expert overconfidence

The application of judgement to new technologies and to processes characterised by infrequent events requires considerable caution and an awareness of the common judgemental biases if a sound judgement is to be made.[15] There is ample evidence from psychologists[16] that experts are prone to overconfidence; this is illustrated in Fig. 5, taken

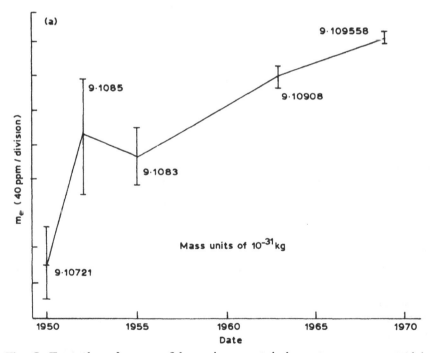

Fig. 5. Examples of overconfidence in expert judgment, as represented by failure of error bars to contain the true value. (a) Estimate of electron rest mass.

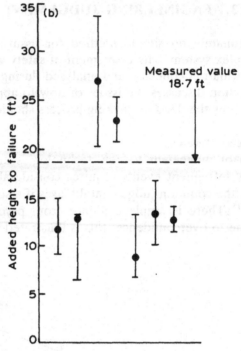

Fig. 5.—*contd.* (b) estimates of the height at which embankment would fail.

from Ref. 16, which shows how experts are inaccurate at predicting
the limits of their knowledge. Further evidence is presented in Ref. 17
which evaluates historical measurements and recommended values for
several fundamental physical constants (e.g. the speed of light,
Planck's constant). Some data specific to computer systems has been
collected and published[18] and this is reproduced in Table 1. This
emphasises the need for caution in using expert 'engineering judgement', particularly when new technologies are concerned, and confirms the need for diverse assessments and explicit analysis of the
decision process. Several techniques are suggested for making best use
of the insights gained from psychological research.[17] The first of these
calls for a broader search for relevant information by, for example,
focusing attention on extreme possibilities or examining 'horror
stories' or case histories. The second technique decomposes the
judgement into components which can then be aided by checklists.

Table 1
Computer–related disasters and egregious horrors

System
[a] Microwave arthritis therapy reprogrammed pacemaker, killed patient (SEN 5 1)
[b] Three Mile Island (SEN 4 2)
[b] SAC: 50 false alerts in 1979 (SEN 5 3);
simulated attack triggered a live scramble [9 Nov 79] (SEN 5 3);
WWMCCS false alarms triggered scrambles [3–6 Jun 80] (SEN 5 3)
[b] F14 off aircraft carrier into North Sea (SEN 8 3)
[b] NORAD alert based on BMEWS report of the moon as incoming missiles (SEN 8 3)
[b] Mercury astronauts forced into manual reentry (SEN 8 3)
[b] Frigate George Philip fired missile in opposite direction (SEN 8 5)
Credit/debit card copying easy despite encryption (DC Metro, SF BART, etc.)
Remote (portable) phones (free calls)

Software
[b] First Space Shuttle backup launch computer synchronisation (SEN 6 5 [Garman])
[b] Second Space Shuttle operational simulation: tight loop upon cancellation of an attempted abort; required manual override (SEN 7 1)
[b] Second Shuttle simulation: bug found in jettisoning an SRB (SEN 8 3)
[h] F16 simulation: plane flipped over whenever it crossed equator (SEN 5 2)
[b] Mariner 18: abort due to missing NOT (SEN 5 2)
[b] F18: plane crashed due to missing exception condition (SEN 6 2)
[b] Gemini V 100 mi landing error, program ignored orbital motion around sun (SEN 9 1)
[b] El Dorado: brake computer bug caused recall of all El Dorados (SEN 4 4)
[b] Nuclear reactor design: but in Shock II model/program (SEN 4 2)
[b] Reactor overheating, low-oil indicator; two-fault coincidence (SEN 8 5)
[b] Mariner I Atlas booster launch failure DO 100 I = 1.10 (not 1, 10) (SEN 8 5)
[b] SF BART train doors sometimes open on long legs between stations (SEN 8 5)
[b] Various system intrusions; implanted Trojan horses
Cyber command identified users with the same password (SEN 8 3)
VMS tape backup SW trashed directories on disc dumped in image mode (SEN 8 5)
Vancouver Stock Index lost 574 points over 22 months—roundoff! (SEN 9 1)
Gobbling of legitimate automatic teller cards (SEN 9 2)
Chernenko at MOSKVAX: network mail hoax, 1 April 1984 (SEN 9 4)

Hardware/Software
[b] FAA Air Traffic Control: many computer system outages (e.g. SEN 5 3)
[b] F18 missile thrust while clamped, plane lost 20,000 feet (SEN 8 5)
[b] ARPAnet: total collapse [27 Oct 1980] (SEN 6 1 [Rosen])

Table 1—*contd.*

Hardware/Software (*continued*)
SF Mini Metro: Ghost Train (SEN 8 3) (Problem STILL occurs now and then.) Harrah's $1.7 Million payoff scam—Trojan horse chip (SEN 8 5)
1984 Rose Bowl scoreboard takeover (Cal Tech versus MIT) (SEN 9 2)

Computer as catalyst; *human frailties*
[a] Air New Zealand crash 28 Nov 1979; computer flight data error detected, but pilots not informed; plane flew into Antarctic Mt Erebus (SEN 6 3 & 6 5)
[b] Exocet missile not on expected missile list, detected as friend (SEN 8 3)
[b] Wizards altering software or critical data (various cases)
   Embezzlements, e.g. Muhammed Ali swindle [$23.2 Million],
   Security Pacific [$10.2 Million], City National, Beverly Hills CA [$1.1 Million]

Compiled by Peter G. Neumann (Sept 1984) mostly from back issues of ACM SIGSOFT Software Engineering Notes (SEN vol no); vol 9 = 1984
[a] Loss of life resulted. [b] Potentially life-critical.

The third involves a learning process (see also Ref. 19) based on as wide a class of measurements as possible, and the fourth is education and possibly training in the problems of judgement.

3.2 A practical approach
A computer-based safety system will have many attributes which need to be taken into account when it is being assessed. In order to make the assessment as objective, reliable and economic as possible, it is necessary to structure both the relevant knowledge of the system and the arguments used to accept or reject it. These arguments and the corresponding safety criteria are known as the 'safety case' for the system.

3.2.1 The safety case
It is necessary to structure the safety case for the system if rational, reliable, and documented judgements are to be made of such complex problems. The structure chosen in the Guidelines[2] has three components at the top level: quality and experience; analysis; and risk management.

(1) Quality and experience
The first component of the safety case relies on the quality and experience of similar systems to give confidence that this particular system will be adequate. The system must be considered in its

broadest sense and includes the equipment, the software, the organisations and the personnel involved. This component is likely to dominate when an example of a standard system is being assessed for which there is extensive experience, e.g. a conventional railway signal.

There are several aspects which must be considered in assessing the 'Experience' component. The maturity of the design, whether it is well established and uses stable technology, is one factor. There should be positive experience with a similar system for several lifecycles and there must be experience of the functions and the environment envisaged for the system. The quality aspects should consider the complete lifecycle and these should be as good or better than previous systems. A conventional quality assurance audit will enable the procedure to be assessed. This should confirm the excellence of the project structure and the execution of the design, development, verification and validation processes. It will involve judgements of good practice embracing the nature and extent of documentation provided, the independence of the verification team, the adequacy of the configuration control, the anomaly resolution and reporting procedures etc.

(2) *Analysis*

The second component contributes to the demonstration of acceptability by an analysis of the design, production, verification and validation of the system under consideration. Analysis is necessary because a conventional audit, based on question and answer format and an evaluation of historical data, is not sufficient to establish confidence that each phase in the development of the system is an accurate translation of the previous phase; nor does it confirm that the system, particularly the software, is structured so as to facilitate comprehension, thus minimising the risk of errors of construction and easing future maintenance and modification.

The extent of the required analysis does of course depend on the criticality of the system and the extent of the evidence from the other two components of the assessment ('Quality and experience' and 'Risk management'). Extensive analysis is most likely to be necessary for systems with high levels of safety and where operational experience is of little benefit in establishing the very small failure rates required. Even where there is extensive experience of a system and the QA audit gives confidence that the system is likely to be adequate, it will be necessary to analyse the verification and validation process.

The type of analysis undertaken does, of course, depend on the specific application and phase in the lifecycle. At the project proposal phase mathematical models may be constructed and properties derived. When a formal language is used (e.g. during coding) the syntax can be checked and the software control and dataflow investigated. If rigorous software development methods are used, such as VDM (the Vienna development method), then the arguments for the correctness of the refinement can be analysed.

The analysis component can be further subdivided into techniques to demonstrate completeness, correctness and robustness of the system and a 'Safety Assessment and Design Techniques Directory' has been compiled.[2]

(3) *Risk Management*

The third component of the assessment, risk management, relies on the avoidance and management of risk by careful monitoring and control of the system. This component may dominate the safety case when a complex system, such as a plant control room display system, is being assessed and safety is assured by a simple back-up system, or during a critical phase such as commissioning.

3.2.2 *Knowledge of the system*

It is often convenient to structure the knowledge about a system in terms of a notional project lifecycle. This is the approach taken in the development of the 'Questionnaire for system safety and reliability assessment' which is a substantial Appendix to the EWICS TC7 Guidelines.

The questionnaire has been designed to help an assessor make a qualitative judgement of the system by providing a structured set of questions. The questionnaire is also intended to help focus the assessment by identifying areas requiring further investigation.

The questionnaire is structured around a simplified project lifecycle based on the classic 'waterfall' model of software development. It has eight parts corresponding to the project planning and management; specification; design; coding and construction; integration; verification and validation; qualification; operation and maintenance.

Apart from defining the questions which need to be asked, the questionnaire indicates the type of response which is expected and what constitutes a good reply. It also includes comments, observations and explanations relating to the questions.

The application of the questionnaire generates detailed information about the system being assessed. This knowledge is structured according to the project lifecycle. In order to assist in the decision-making process it is necessary to relate the answers to the components in the 'safety case', and an illustration is given in an appendix of how to cross-reference the main, numbered questions to the safety case components.

A simple marking scheme has been developed to evaluate the answers and can be used in several ways. The most straightforward, and the approach which should be used for systems in the highest safety categories, is to use it to identify those attributes which are of concern and the ways in which they affect the assessment. Either each concern can then be resolved individually or the system can be rejected with clear reasons why the decision was taken. This mode of use does not require elaboration of any of the factors.

A second use of this decision-making process is in comparing different systems, for example during the evaluation of alternative designs. In this case the factors are needed to weight the importance of different attributes and to relate the answers to a common scale. The decision process would then evaluate the competing systems and indicate their relative disadvantages.

A third mode of use is to assign threshold values to the different categories, above which any system is rejected.

Although the questionnaire and its associated evaluation system is intended to be an important tool for the assessor, its limitations should be recognised. It is recommended as a useful contribution to rational judgements, but it should not be seen as 'solving' the assessment problem by reducing it to a list of simple questions. Engineering judgement will still dominate the assessment: it is required in answering the detailed questions; deriving values for the three factors; and assessing the significance of any unsatisfactory features which are identified.

4. CONCLUSIONS

This chapter has discussed two issues pertinent to the assessment of software that is required to be highly dependable. The role of software reliability is concluded to be one of providing additional, qualitative, evidence of a system's acceptability which will be based on some 'engineering judgement' of the development process and the product itself. A method for structuring this decision-making process is outlined. It does not, however, solve the assessment problem by reducing it to a list of simple questions. Engineering judgement will still be essential in the assessment: it is required in answering the detailed questions and assessing the significance of any unsatisfactory features which are identified. Indeed, it is perhaps worth emphasising that there is no technological solution to the problem of judgement. For example, even when completely mathematically proven software becomes feasible for safety systems, there will be a need to assess the possibility of errors in the proofs, problems with the underlying mathematics, assumptions made about the boundaries of the problem and residual errors in the specification itself.

Although the proposals and the issues discussed above provide a framework for assessment, one important point has yet to be resolved. That is, in the light of the problems with a statistical approach and the overconfidence of experts, what levels of dependability can actually be achieved and assured.

REFERENCES

1. Bloomfield, R. E. and Froome, P. K. D., The production and assessment of high integrity software, *Electrotechnology*, Oct. 1986, 125–7.
2. EWICS (European Workshop on Industrial Computer Systems) Technical Committee 7 (TC7) on System Reliability, Safety and Security:

   Safety related computers: software development and systems documentation, ed. F. Redmill, Verlag TUV Rheinland, 1985.
   EWICS TC7, *Techniques for verification and validation of safety related software*, Position Paper No. 5, Jan. 1985.
   EWICS TC7, *System requirements specification for safety related systems*, Position Paper No. 6, Jan. 1985.

   The following are being published by Elsevier Science Publishers in 1988 and 1989, ed. F. Redmill:

   Guidelines for the assessment of the safety and reliability of high integrity industrial computer systems.
   Safety assessment and design of industrial computer systems techniques directory.
3. CEGB Health and Safety Dept, *Design safety criteria for CEGB nuclear power stations*, RS/R167/81, 1982.
4. IEEE, Draft IEEE Standard P982, *Software reliability measurement*, 1983.
5. Ramamoorthy, C. V. and Bastani, F. B., Software reliability—status and perspectives, *IEEE Trans. Software Engineering* **SE8**(4), 1982.

6. Littlewood, B., How to measure software reliability and how not to, *IEEE TR*, **R-28**(2), 1979, 103–10.
7. Nagel, P. and Skrivan, J., *Software reliability: repetitive run experimentation and modelling*, NASA CR-165836, 1982.
8. Abdel-Ghaly *et al.*, Evaluation of competing software reliability predictions, *IEEE Trans. Software Engineering*, **SE-12**(9), Sept. 1986.
9. Rasmussen, J., *On the structure of knowledge—a morphology of mental models in a man–machine system context*, RISO National Laboratories, RISO-M-2192, 1979.
10. Abbot, M. B., de Nordwall, H. J. and Swets, B., On applications of artificial intelligence to the control and safety problems of nuclear power plants, *Civ. Eng. Syst.*, **1**, 1983, 69–82.
11. Barnes, M., Bishop, P., Dahl, G., Esp, D., Humphries, P., Lahti, J. and Yashimara, S., Project on diverse software—an experiment in software reliability, *Proc. SAFECOMP85*, Pergamon Press, 1985.
12. Electrical Power Research Institute (EPRI), *Validation of real-time software for nuclear plant safety applications*, EPR INP-2646, 1982.
13. Fischoff, B. and Johnson, S., The possibility of distributed decision making, *Proc. Workshop on Political–Military Decision Making*, Hoover Institute, Stanford University, March 1985.
14. Bloomfield, R. E. and Froome, P. K. D., The application of formal methods to the assessment of high integrity software, *IEEE Trans. Software Engineering*, Sept. 1986.
15. Tversky, A. and Kahneman, D., Judgement under uncertainty: heuristics and biases, *Science*, (185), 1974, 1124–31.
16. Fischoff, B. and Whipple, C., Assessing health risks associated with ambient air quality standards, *Environmental Professional*, 1983.
17. Henrion, M. Assessing uncertainty in physical constants. *Amer. J. Physics* (in press).
18. Neumann, P. G., Computer-related disasters and other egregious horrors, *Minutes of Software System Working Group*, 1984; also in: *ACM Software Engineering Notes*.
19. Genser, R., *Learning in decision making*, International Institute of Applied Systems Analysis, Vienna, 1985.

11

Adaptive Software Reliability Modelling

S. Brocklehurst, P. Y. Chan, B. Littlewood and J. Snell

Centre for Software Reliability, London, UK

ABSTRACT

In this chapter two methods of adapting raw predictions by learning from past mistakes are outlined. Techniques for assessing the quality of these adapted predictions are discussed with particular reference to the prequential likelihood ratio (PLR) as a means of comparing the raw predictions with the new adapted predictions. Certain problems arise with this measure for one of the adaptive procedures and these are discussed in detail. An example is shown of these procedures in use on some real software data.

Finally, we propose criteria for the use of these methods according to the specific requirements of the user.

1. INTRODUCTION

In the problem of predicting future software reliability growth on the basis of past data much effort has been put into developing and evaluating various models (see for example, Refs 2 and 3). Here models which operate in continuous time, which is assumed to be execution time, are used. As in Refs 4, 5 and 7, the data will be a sequence, $t_1, t_2, \ldots, t_{j-1}$, of times between successive failures, which are realisations of random variables $T_1, T_2, \ldots, T_{j-1}$. The objective is to apply the models to the data in order to make predictions about future behaviour (i.e. about $T_j, T_{j+1}, \ldots$) on the assumption that the reliability growth mechanism will behave in the future in a similar way as it behaved in the past. For simplicity, only predictions about the current time to failure, T_j, based on data $t_1, t_2, \ldots, t_{j-1}$, are considered here.

It is felt[4,5] that there is no reason why, when a user is analysing a single set of data, there should be one particular model that is the 'correct' one. In fact, in reality, it is more likely that all models are 'wrong', but some may be performing better than others when applied to a particular data set. (The model which is performing the best could even vary with time within a single set of data.) It is suggested[4,5] that the choice as to which model the user might implement should be based on comparison of the closeness of agreement between predictions and the actual failure behaviour, when it is later observed (i.e. by comparing predictions about the behaviour of T_j, based on $t_1, t_2, \ldots t_{j-1}$, with the realisation, t_j, of T_j, when it is later observed). Three of these techniques are the u-plot, the y-plot and the prequential likelihood (PL) of the model under consideration.

The u-plot is constructed by first obtaining the us via

$$u_j = \hat{F}_j(t_j), \qquad j = s, \ldots, i-1, \qquad (1)$$

where the $\hat{F}_j(t)$ are the estimated c.d.f.s obtained when a model is applied to a data set over $j = s, \ldots, i-1$, and then ordering these us to obtain $u_{(s)}, \ldots, u_{(i-1)}$. We then draw a step function with step size $1/(i-s+1)$, as shown in Fig. 1. Any continual bias in our predictions may be reflected in the u-plot by the step function's departure from the 45° line.

If we evaluate

$$x_j = \ln(1 - u_j) \qquad j = s, \ldots, i-1 \qquad (2)$$

and

$$y_j = \sum_{r=s}^{j} x_r \bigg/ \sum_{r=s}^{i-1} x_r \qquad j = s, \ldots, i-2 \qquad (3)$$

then we may use the y_j to form a y-plot in the same way as the u-plot was constructed except for step size $1/(i-s)$ (there is one less y_j than the u_j). The y-plot (unlike the u-plot) preserves the order in which the u_js occurred and will indicate when the sequence of predictors, $\hat{F}_j(t)$, is not capturing the trend in the failure data. (See Ref. 6 for more detail on the y-plot.) Judgement of whether plots such as these are good or

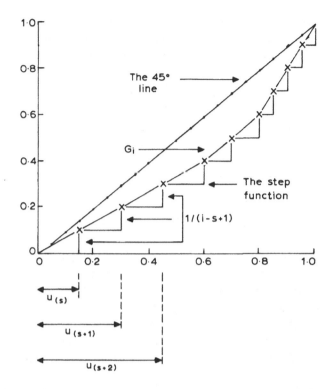

Fig. 1. The u-plot for nine ordered us and stepsize $0·1$.

bad is usually based on the Kolmogorov distance (the maximum vertical distance) from the 45° line.

In general, the u_j can be interpreted as representing the departure of our predictive system from the truth and if our predictive system is performing well, then we would expect the u_j to be i.i.d. $U(0, 1)$ random variables.

The prequential likelihood (PL) is a measure of both noise and bias over j, and if a predicted p.d.f., $\hat{f}_j(t)$, is 'close' to the true p.d.f., $f_j(t)$, for $j = s, \ldots, i - 1$, then we would expect the

$$\text{PL} = \prod_{j=s}^{i-1} \hat{f}_j(t_j) \tag{4}$$

to be 'large'. If our predicted p.d.f., $\hat{f}_j(t)$, is noisy or biased, or both, then we would expect the PL to be 'small' (this is discussed in greater detail in Ref. 7). The PL is really only meaningful when used as a comparison between two models. Suppose we have two models, model α and model β. We can then use the prequential likelihood ratio

$$\text{PLR} = \prod_{j=s}^{i-1} \hat{f}_j^{\alpha}(t_j)/\hat{f}_j^{\beta}(t_j) \tag{5}$$

to compare the relative merits of the two models. If the PLR increases without limit as i increases, then we would reject model β in favour of model α and, conversely, if it decreases to zero as i increases model β would be preferable to model α.

2. ADAPTIVE MODELLING

It can be seen that, due to the normalisation of the y_js, if we had a biased predictor (over j) then this would not be reflected in the y-plot but would be reflected in the u-plot (i.e., we should get a good y-plot and a bad u-plot). There seems to be evidence that, in some practical contexts, such (approximately) 'merely biased' predictions occur. It is just such a situation, where there is stationarity (over j) in the departure of the predictors from reality, for which adapting is intended.

So, if we have u_js which are trend-free but non-uniform, this indicates that the departure of our predictor, $\hat{F}_j(t)$, from the true c.d.f., $F_j(t)$, is also trend-free and biased and this consistent bias will be represented by the departure of the u-plot from the 45° line. The method of adapting uses this, together with the assumption that the departure of $\hat{F}_i(t)$ from $F_i(t)$ will be similar to the departures of $\hat{F}_j(t)$ from $F_j(t)$, for $j = s, \ldots, i - 1$, to form a new c.d.f.

$$\hat{F}_i^*(t) = G_i(\hat{F}_i(t)) \tag{6}$$

where G_i is the joined-up step function of the u-plot (see Fig. 1). This procedure of obtaining an adaptive predictor at stage i can be repeated for $i = p, \ldots, q$ to obtain an adaptive prediction system (see Ref. 8 for more details on adaptive modelling).

In Ref. 9 this simple approach to adapting is applied to a set of data, published by Musa,[1] called SS3. Two models are applied to this data: JM[2] and LV.[3] Figure 2 plots the median predictions for T_{105} to T_{278}, and it can be seen that there is huge disagreement between the predictions for the two models. On observation of the u-plots in Fig. 3

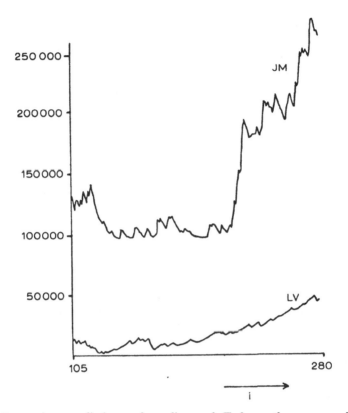

Fig. 2. Successive predictions of medians of T_i from the raw models for $i = 105, \ldots, 278$.

we can see that the JM model is being far too optimistic (since optimistic predictions are likely to give us more small us than would be expected if the u_j came from $U(0, 1)$) while the LV model is being pessimistic. Hence the medians obtained for the JM model will be too large and those for the LV too small.

Figure 4 shows the corresponding y-plots and these suggest approximate stationarity of the departure of our predictions for the LV model from the truth while the JM model may not be adequately capturing the trend in the failure data. (This suggests that the LV predictions are more appropriate for the adapting procedure.)

Figure 5 shows the median plots for the adaptive predictors $\{\hat{F}_i^*(t)\}$. Clearly these are in much closer agreement than the raw predictions.

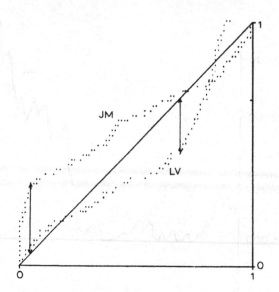

Fig. 3. u-plots for predictions of $T_{105}-T_{278}$. The Kolmogorov distances are 0·2350(LV) and 0·2755(JM). These plots are reproduced from line-printer plots so dots do not correspond exactly to steps in the sample c.d.f.

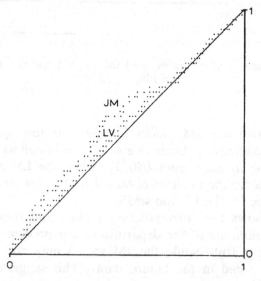

Fig. 4. y-plots for predictions $T_{105}-T_{278}$. Kolmogorov distances are 0·0357 (LV) and 0·1298 (JM). Again, plots are reproduced from line-printer plots.

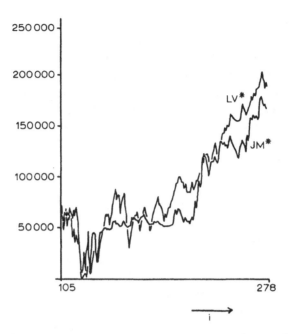

Fig. 5. Successive median predictions using the joined-up c.d.f. adaptive procedure. Notice great improvement over Fig 2: the two adaptive models are in close agreement.

The justification for this method is as follows. Suppose that we are given $t_1, \ldots, t_{i-1}$ and $\hat{F}_i(T_i)$ and $F_i(T_i)$. Let $\mathbf{t}_{i-1}$ represent the vector $\{t_1, \ldots, t_{i-1}\}$ and let the p.d.f. and c.d.f. of $U_i = \hat{F}_i(T_i)$ be $f_i^u(U_i)$ and $F_i^u(U_i)$ respectively. Then, from eqn (1) and using

$$\int_0^{U_i} f_i^u(x \mid \mathbf{t}_{i-1}) \, dx = \int_0^{T_i} f_i(y \mid \mathbf{t}_{i-1}) \, dy$$

where $f_i(t)$ is the p.d.f. associated with $F_i(t)$, we get

$$F_i^u(U_i \mid \mathbf{t}_{i-1}) = F_i(T_i \mid \mathbf{t}_{i-1}) = F_i(\hat{F}_i^{-1}(U_i \mid \mathbf{t}_{i-1})) \qquad (7)$$

Hence, using eqns (1) and (7), we have

$$\hat{F}_i^*(T_i \mid \mathbf{t}_{i-1}) = G_i(\hat{F}_i(T_i \mid \mathbf{t}_{i-1})) \simeq F_i^u(\hat{F}_i(T_i \mid \mathbf{t}_{i-1}))$$
$$= F_i(\hat{F}_i^{-1}(\hat{F}_i(T_i \mid \mathbf{t}_{i-1}))) = F_i(T_i \mid \mathbf{t}_{i-1})$$

as required.

To summarise, the adaptive procedure can be used on a real data set as follows. Fit the chosen model to obtain $\hat{F}_j(t)$, based on $t_1, \ldots, t_{j-1}$ for $j = s, \ldots, i - 1$. Then use $t_s, \ldots, t_{i-1}$ to obtain $u_j = \hat{F}_j(t_j)$, $j = s, \ldots, i - 1$, and hence draw the appropriate u-plot and y-plot. Fit the model at stage i, based on $t_1, \ldots, t_{i-1}$, to obtain $\hat{F}_i(t)$ and, if there is evidence to suggest that there is stationarity in the departure of the fitted model from reality, but bias (i.e. the y-plot is good but the u-plot is bad), use the joined-up step function of the u-plot to obtain G_i; hence our adapter

$$\hat{F}_i^*(t) = G_i(\hat{F}_i(t))$$

may be obtained. Then this whole procedure can be repeated for $i = p, \ldots, q$ in order to obtain our adaptive prediction system (i.e. $\hat{F}_p^*(t), \ldots, \hat{F}_q^*(t)$).

It should be noted that the adaptive procedure is truly predictive since our adapter at stage i only depends on data obtained before T_i is observed. Our raw predictor at stage i, $\hat{F}_i(t)$, is based on t_1, $t_2, \ldots, t_{i-1}$, and the 'learning' via G_i involves analysis of previous predictions (i.e. predictions of $T_s, \ldots, T_{i-2}, T_{i-1}$).

3. ASSESSMENT OF THE QUALITY OF OUR ADAPTED PREDICTIONS

Having formed our adaptive prediction system, i.e. $\hat{F}_i^*(t)$ for $i = p, \ldots, q$, we wish to assess its performance. Using

$$u_i^* = \hat{F}_i^*(t_i), \qquad i = p, \ldots, q \tag{8}$$

we can form u^*- and y^*-plots in the same way as before (see Section 1).

Figure 6 shows the u^*-plots for the SS3 data when the JM and LV models are adapted. These confirm that our adapted models are giving us approximately unbiased predictions.

At this stage all seems well, and we appear to have a procedure which allows a model to learn from its past mistakes and produce remarkably improved predictions. At this point we wish to examine the

$$\text{PLR} = \prod_{i=p}^{q} \hat{f}_i^*(t_i)/\hat{f}_i(t_i) \tag{9}$$

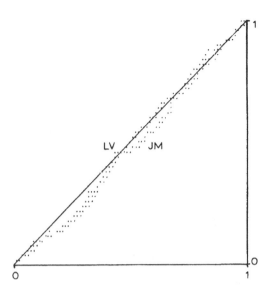

Fig. 6. u^*-plots using the joined-up c.d.f. adaptor for predictions $T_{105}-T_{278}$. The Kolmogorov distances are 0·0872 (LV) and 0·0992 (JM). Reproduced from line-printer plots.

in order to assess the relative merits of the adapted versus raw predictions with respect to noise and bias. The PLR plots for the adapted versus fitted predictions (Fig. 7), however, suggest otherwise: in neither case is there strong evidence that the adaptive model is superior to the raw. Indeed, for the LV model the plot seems to be going down, indicating that the adapted model is performing worse than the original! Since the u^*-plots suggest that the adapted predictions have less bias than the raw predictions, it seems likely that in adapting we have gained some form of noise.

In Ref. 10, replications from various popular models are generated and these same models are fitted to the data and then adapted as outlined above. Comparisons of the c.d.f.s of the fitted and adapted predictors with the (known) truth are made and it is found that, under certain conditions (a good y-plot and a bad u-plot) the adapted predictions are almost always better than the raw predictions. It is also the case that the u^*-plots tend to be better than the u-plots. Yet, again, the PLR for the adapted versus fitted predictions nearly always goes down, suggesting that the adapted prediction system is worse

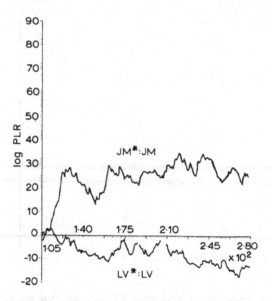

Fig. 7. Log PLR plots for $q = 105$ to $q = 278$ (see eqn (9)).

than the original prediction system. The simulation suggests that the poor PLR performance of our adapted predictions is due to the fact that the adapted p.d.f. tends to be very discontinuous (see Ref. 10 for a plot of such a p.d.f.) as distinct from having noise over i. It can be seen that, by the way the adapter is constructed, it is not likely to be much more noisy over i than the raw predictor. This is because the u-plot changes very little from one stage to the next.

It is trivial to prove (see Ref. 9 or 10) from eqns (6) and (9) that

$$\text{PLR} = \prod_{i=p}^{q} g_i(u_i) \qquad (10)$$

where $g_i = G_i'$. Figure 8 shows such a function for the LV model at $i = 278$; a similar plot for the JM model shows similar irregularity. It is again important to note that the 'noise' occurring is noise over t, at a stage i, due to the extreme lack of smoothness in the g_i and hence of each predictive density f_i^*, as distinct from noise over i. Also, Ref. 10 shows that this noise does not affect predictive results but it will cause the PLR to report badly about our adapter.

This creates a dilemma for the user since, although the work of Ref.

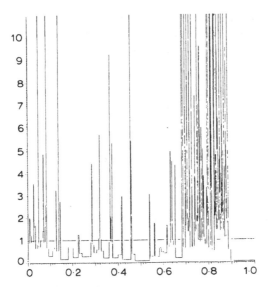

Fig. 8. g_{278} for the LV model. Notice the many excursions beyond the range of this plot.

10 suggests that if we adapt under the right conditions we can be reasonably sure that we are getting improved results, he/she may wish to check for noisiness of the adapted predictions using the PLR for a particular case (i.e. for the data set in question).

4. PARAMETRIC SPLINE APPROACH TO ADAPTIVE RELIABILITY MODELLING

The obvious way to overcome this problem is to smooth the density of our adapter in some way. After experimenting with various ways of achieving this, it was found that the method which gave the best results in a wide class of problems was to smooth the G_i function using a parametric spline as follows.

Consider the joined-up c.d.f. u-plot, which we have called G_i (see Fig. 1). Let the ith vertex of the polygon have coordinates (x_i, y_i). Let p_i represent the distance, along the polygon, of this point from the origin. Consider now the plots of x_i against p_i and of y_i against p_i. We fit the spline to each of these points: in each case 5-knot least squares cubic splines constrained to be increasing and to pass through $(0, 0)$ and $(\Sigma p_i, 1)$. Call these functions $\text{LSS}_x(p)$ and $\text{LSS}_y(p)$ respectively. The solution of the parametric equations

$$x = \text{LSS}_x(p)$$

and

$$y = \text{LSS}_y(p)$$

is the least squares parametric spline

$$y = G_i^s(x)$$

Our adaptive procedure is then exactly the same as described in the previous section, except that instead of using the joined-up c.d.f., G_i, we use the spline G_i^s. Thus, the parametric spline adaptive (PSA) predictive distribution is

$$\hat{F}_i^{*s}(t) = G_i^s(\hat{F}_i(t)) \tag{11}$$

The PSA density, $\hat{f}_i^{*s}(t)$, can be obtained easily, and is smooth (differentiable).

The computational requirements of the procedure are generally not as onerous as might be expected. In fact, for most models, the successive re-estimation of the model parameters presents more of a problem.

Figures 9–11 show the performance of the new adaptive procedure on the SS3 data considered previously. In Fig. 9 we can see how the PLR now favours the PSA over the raw model for both the JM and LV models. The similarity of Figs 10 and 5 confirms our belief that, for predictive purposes, the unsmoothed adapter is approximately as good as the smoothed adapter. Figure 11 shows the predictive densities for the raw predictors and for the PSA predictors of T_{278}. The closeness of the PSA densities imply that we are getting closer to the 'truth'.

Table 1 shows the Kolmogorov distances for the u-plots and y-plots from all the predictive methods under consideration. According to these, there is little to choose between the two adaptive procedures. Note that as well as improvement in the u-plot after adapting there is also improvement in the y-plot for the JM model. In Ref. 10, it is suggested that there are many cases of non-stationarity of the departure of our original predictions from the truth, for which adapting will give us better predictions and more stationarity. Thus, although adapting was only intended to improve bias, and hence the u-plot, we may often get improvement in the y-plot.

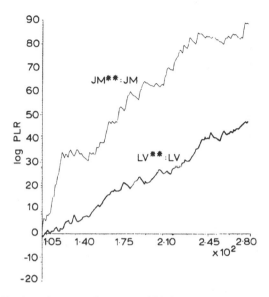

Fig. 9. Log PLR plots for $q = 105$ to $q = 278$ for the parametric spline adapted predictions versus the raw predictions.

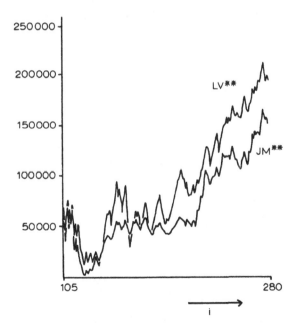

Fig. 10. Successive median predictions from PSA models. Note the great improvement over Fig. 2 and the similarity to Fig. 5.

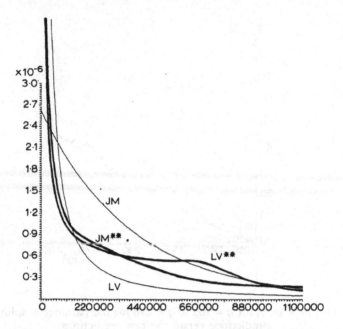

Fig. 11. Predictive densities of T_{278} for SS3 data. Note the closeness of the PSA densities for the JM and LV models.

Table 1
Kolmogorov Distances for the u-plots and y-plots of the SS3 Data

	u-plot	y-plot
JM	0·2755 (<1%)	0·1298 (<1%)
JM*	0·0992 (NS)	0·0593 (NS)
JM*ˢ	0·0773 (NS)	0·0612 (NS)
LV	0·2350 (<1%)	0·0357 (NS)
LV*	0·0872 (NS)	0·0404 (NS)
LV*ˢ	0·0874 (NS)	0·0344 (NS)

There are 174 predictions involved here, from T_{105}. All adaptive results are statistically non-significant, whereas both raw u-plot distances are highly significant (significant at the 1% level).

5. CONCLUSIONS

For a user wishing to use the adaptive method to get better predictions it is recommended that, if the joined-up c.d.f. adaptive procedure is used, as outlined in Section 2, this will generally give better results, particularly when the u-plot is bad and the y-plot is good. In this case results can be checked using the u^*- and y^*-plots as in Section 4, but the PLR results cannot be used as they will usually reject the adapter, whether it is better for predictive purposes or not. (The work of Ref. 10 also suggested that, for cases where the y-plot is bad, adapting will often still improve results but a careful eye must be kept on the u^*- and y^*-plots.)

If, in a particular case, the user wishes to check for noise, then the PLR can be used only if the PSA procedure is applied as outlined in Section 4. It should be noted, though, that whichever adaptive procedure is applied, predictive results are likely to be the same.

REFERENCES

1. Musa, J. D., *Software reliability data*, Report available from Data and Analysis Center for Software, Rome Air Development Center, Rome, NY.
2. Jelinski, Z. and Moranda, P. B., Software reliability research, in: *Statistical computer performance evaluation*, W. Freiberger. (Ed.), Academic Press, New York, 1972, 465–84.
3. Littlewood, B. and Verrall, J. L., A Bayesian reliability growth model for computer software, *J. Royal Statist. Soc.*, C (Applied Statistics) (22), 1973, 332–46.
4. Keiller, P. A., Littlewood, B., Miller, D. R. and Sofer, A., On the quality of software reliability predictions, *Proc. NATO ASI on Electronic systems effectiveness and life cycle costing*, (Norwich, UK, 1982), Springer, 1983, 441–60.
5. Keiller, P. A., Littlewood, B., Miller, D. R. and Sofer, A., *Comparison of software reliability predictions*, IEEE FTCS-13, 1983, 128–34.
6. Cox, D. R. and Lewis, P. A. W., *Statistical analysis of series of events*, Methuen, London, 1966.
7. Abdel Ghaly, A. A., Chan, P. Y. and Littlewood, B., Evaluation of competing software reliability predictions, *IEEE*, **SE–12**(9), Sept. 1986, 950–67.
8. Keiller, P. A. and Littlewood, B., *Adaptive software reliability modelling*, IEEE FTCS–14, 1984, 108–13.
9. Chan, P. Y. and Littlewood, B., *Parametric spline approach to adaptive reliability modelling*, CSR Technical Report, 1986.
10. Brocklehurst, S., *On the effectiveness of adaptive software reliability modelling*, CSR Technical Report, 1987.

12

Modelling the Support Process

PETER MELLOR

Centre for Software Reliability, London, UK

ABSTRACT

Methods of software reliability assessment have been aimed mainly at reliability 'now'. For some purposes, particularly the prediction of support cost for commercial software, a longer term prediction is required, ideally one which covers the whole service life of the product. Also, other factors must be taken into account in addition to reliability growth, most notably market behaviour, maintenance policy, and the effect of 'stress' on user-perceived reliability. This chapter examines the problems of this type of estimation, and concludes that a 'rough-and-ready' approach is required, employing models that treat the occurrence of failures in the field as a non-homogeneous Poisson process (NHPP) and that deal with the interaction of market forces, support and basic reliability by 'time-slicing' and the application of queuing theory. The chapter proposes directions for future development of large-scale models, based on previous results and possible outcomes from current research projects.

1. INTRODUCTION

A software system is a single product, even though many copies or 'instances' of it are run simultaneously on many different installations. Its reliability must therefore be assessed from a trial of the delivered system prior to shipment to the field. The application of a software reliability growth model to analyse the records of failure against execution time during trial, possibly taking account of other information such as system size, can yield estimates both of reliability at the end of the trial and of future growth of reliability under continued use, with removal of faults according to some maintenance policy as those faults become manifest.

Armed with such an estimate, a producer of software can then make objective forecasts of quantities which vitally affect the commercial success of his enterprise, in particular:

—life-cycle support cost;
—size of support teams, distributed over system life-cycle;
—expected user-perceived reliability of system in service under various levels of 'stress';
—optimum release point, taking account of the above;
—further debugging time required to achieve given reliability at release;
—product price to cover expected support cost.

A few pertinent remarks need to be made here. It is assumed that 'software reliability' is a meaningful term, i.e. that software failure is a random process and can be predicted stochastically. This fundamental point has been argued at length elsewhere.[9] For the purposes of this chapter, the opposing view—that software, being a logical entity, is either correct or incorrect and cannot be said to 'fail'—is dismissed out of hand. Anyone who has ever used software *knows* that it fails! Large software systems are never perfect and always require maintenance. In the real world, decisions about 'optimum release points' are usually overridden by other commercial pressures, such as the need to aim release to hit a 'window of opportunity' in the market. In the academic world (and in certain parts of the industrial world, where safety-critical systems are employed) techniques for producing 'perfect' software are relevant. In the commercial world, the vendor usually needs to make the best of a bad job, and should do so with his eyes open to the consequences, rather than relying on blind faith.

Given these circumstances, how is the vendor to arrive at a decision? To start with, three mutually interacting factors determine support costs:

—inherent software quality;
—market behaviour;
—maintenance practices and policy.

The interaction of these can be represented by Fig. 1. Arrows denote that one quantity drives another, and a solid line indicates a positive effect while a dotted line indicates a negative effect. For example, user-perceived failure rate and number of installations both drive maintenance workload up, while maintenance workload drives support

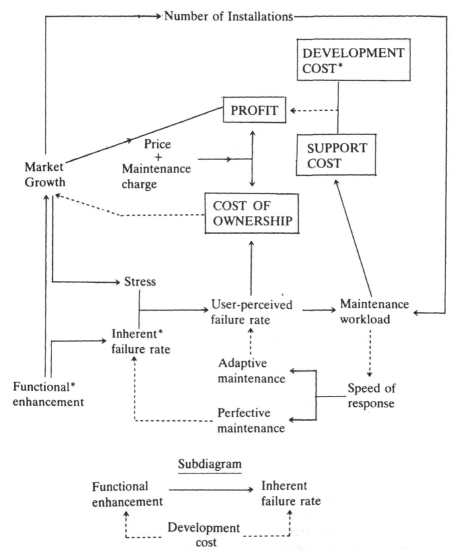

Fig. 1. Interactions of support cost factors.

cost up, and speed of response (by the support organisation to failure reports) down.

The basic quantities are, from the vendor's point of view:

—profit, which is:
the accumulation of sales × unit price
+ maintenance charge rate × total installed time
—development and support costs,

and, from the customer's point of view:

—cost of ownership, which is:
purchase price + accumulated maintenance charge
+ accumulated cost of failures.

These are life-cycle costs. In practice, both vendor and customer are also interested in cash flow: the difference between the *rates* at which revenues accrue and costs are incurred. It will be seen that the nature of 'driving' varies over Fig. 1. In some cases, it represents the accumulation of a rate into a life-cycle total quantity. In other cases, it represents the immediate effect of one rate upon another. The nature of the functional relationship also varies. In particular, it may be linear or non-linear, depending on the circumstances. The following sections take each of the vendor's three main factors in turn and consider how their interaction may be modelled. The treatment is deliberately general; practical considerations are glossed over and specific functional forms avoided wherever possible.

2. MODELLING SOFTWARE RELIABILITY FOR SUPPORT PURPOSES

Certain empirical facts about large commercial software systems dictate the type of reliability model which is most applicable. These are:

—Such software contains very many faults, each of which makes a tiny contribution to the total rate of occurrence of failures (ROCOF).[1]
—There is a difference of several orders of magnitude between the manifestation rates of the largest and smallest faults.[1]
—The first manifestation of a new fault costs around 100 times as much to the vendor as a repeated failure due to the same fault.[7]

The family of model most applicable is therefore that of exponential order statistic (EOS) models, which have been treated as a whole by Gray[4] and Miller.[10] Every model of this family is uniquely defined by a fault-generating function, which describes the distribution of manifestation rates over the faults in the product. Given this function, and estimated values of the model parameters, quantities of interest such as the inherent failure rate can be derived as a function of total product running time.

Furthermore, in the case of commercial software, the data from which the model parameters are estimated tends to be of the discrete variety.[7] Fortunately, all EOS models possess a discrete variant of the objective function.

EOS models are of two varieties: binomial and NHPP.[11] For large-scale estimation there is no distinction between these two types, and since (i) each binomial model possess an NHPP equivalent obtained by treating the 'n' parameter ('fixed but unknown number of faults in the product') as an 'N' parameter ('random variable representing the number of faults') and (ii) the NHPP variant is more mathematically tractable, the NHPP EOS models with a non-uniform fault manifestation rate would appear to be the most promising candidates for research.

The object of this part of the research must be to develop:

—means of obtaining parameter estimates which will allow reliability growth to be realistically forecast for a complete life-cycle based on a relatively short trial or early life observation;

—means of making such forecasts within defined confidence intervals, rather than as point estimates;

—means of coping with imperfect and delayed fault repair, which does not come 'naturally' to EOS models.

All of these threaten to pose serious problems.[7] The last point was tackled in a simple way in Ref. 6, but is in urgent need of sounder treatment.

'Stress' was also dealt with by Mellor[6] in an over-simplified way. It was assumed that 'stress factors' could be determined which would affect the manifestation rates of all faults linearly. Investigations by Iyer[5] into such objective measures of 'stress' as CPU used time and page-swapping rate show that they affect failure rate non-linearly. If one extends the meaning of 'stress' to cover variations in input selection (the probability distribution of selection over the input space is referred to as the 'operational profile'), the effect is likely to be even more complex, changing the ordering of fault manifestation rates.

The object of this part of the model is to derive ROCOF as a function of total execution time on all installations, for a given mix of stresses, taking account of market growth and of feedback effects from the maintenance process.

3. MODELLING MARKET BEHAVIOUR

Again, in Ref. 6, this was treated simply, assuming a given level of sales in a given period of calendar time, and assuming that growth was linear in each period. This reflects quite well the way in which sales targets are normally expressed (100 in year 1, 200 in year 2, etc.) and is probably good enough to allow rough 'what if' estimates to be made for various future market scenarios. Mellor[6] also allowed for withdrawals to occur from the field with a normal distribution around a given average life from delivery.

Both these assumptions should be revised. Oliver,[12] for example, has used modelling techniques remarkably similar to those used for software reliability growth. The growth of accumulated sales up to market saturation corresponds exactly to the growth of accumulated faults found up to the total present at delivery, and the mathematics of the two processes are almost identical. The support cost estimate should therefore include a market growth estimate, based on parameters estimated from early sales performance.

A further effect that could be modelled is illustrated in Fig. 1. Cost of ownership, which partly depends on user-perceived reliability, may be expected to retard market growth. To model this is to attempt to represent the effect of the bad reputation acquired by an unreliable product, and this is obviously affected by a number of imponderable factors. Even so, it may be worth investigation.

4. MODELLING MAINTENANCE PRACTICE AND POLICY

'Maintenance' is used loosely to cover three separate activities:

—*Perfective maintenance*: modification of the product to remove faults already manifest, for example, by the selective or total replacement of an early release of the product by a 'bug clearance' release.

—*Adaptive maintenance*: modification of the product to enable it to be used in circumstances not originally envisaged in the requirements.

—*Functional enhancement*: modification of the product to provide additional functions, either as part of an 'incremental release' or to meet new market demands.

The three activities present completely different modelling problems. Mellor[6] dealt solely with perfective and adaptive maintenance, but adopted a classification which cut across the two. This was:

—*Fix-on-fail*: repair of a fault on manifestation on a single installation.

—*Known faults database*: publication of symptoms to aid recognition and details of repair action for faults already manifest, to suppress reports of repeated failures due to those faults.

—*Bug-clearance release*: see 'Perfective maintenance' above.

Perfective and adaptive maintenance are driven by failure reports from the field. The essential distinction is between practices which affect individual installations and those which affect the whole field. Mellor[6] showed that a well-timed bug-clearance release was (in theory at least) devastingly more effective than fix-on-fail. Certain practical complications should be addressed by the model, particularly delay in taking up new releases, resulting in a staggering of the effect on the field.

Functional enhancement has two effects:

—introduction of new code and facilities to all installations;
—introduction of new faults ditto.

(It may also be expected to improve saleability and so boost market growth.)

An approach to modelling incremental release is described by Dyer,[2] representing the inherent failure rate of the updated system as a linear function of the rates of the code introduced at each increment. The picture is complicated by the fact that each increment may have a different distribution of fault manifestation rates. The ROCOF from a single instance of the product is, on the previous modelling assumptions, the superposition of several NHPPs. Theoretical work on such combinations has been published.[3]

The total maintenance workload is driven by the flow of failure reports from the field. The activities of diagnosis and devising repairs within the support organisation (which may be multi-level) can be modelled as a queuing process. Distributions of effort per failure will need to be established. The queuing discipline will depend on maintenance policy. A priority system is often found in practice. Excessive workload (workload is driven up by rapid market growth, low inherent product reliability and frequent functional enhancement) will result in a fall in percentage turn-round of failure reports in a given time, hence in reduced effectiveness of maintenance in reducing the flow of reports. In a priority system, low priority reports will suffer disproportionately. (True story: a low priority report once received a birthday card from its originator!)

Queueing theory should be employed to describe the relationship of the incoming flow of reports to the outgoing flow of responses. The lack of a steady-state solution would be of interest, since it would indicate inadequate availability of support effort.

5. INTERACTION OF PARTS OF MODEL

Most of these have already been described. The main loop of drivers which will interest the vendor is that relating market growth to flow of reports into support, and back via responses out to improvement in reliability. This feedback loop will be negative or positive depending on whether the queuing equation representing maintenance activity has a steady-state solution or not, at any given phase of product life. Ascertaining this will answer the practical question: 'Can a given size of support team cope with a given rate of sales of a product of a given quality?'.

Market growth can affect the flow of reports via stress. It will generally result in increased variance of stress. The precise effect will depend on the functional relationship between inherent reliability, stress and user-perceived reliability.

One last interaction is shown in the subdiagram in Fig. 1. Development cost may reduce inherent failure rate and the need for functional enhancement. Practically speaking, this represents the beneficial effect of extra money 'up front' in defining requirements more precisely, developing a more complete product before first release, and achieving better quality by longer testing. Incorporating a development cost model will then enable total life-cycle profit and cash flow to be estimated for a given product.

Accounting policy will affect many of the relationships; for example: 'Does functional enhancement come out of the development or support budget?'.

6. MATHEMATICAL TREATMENT AND APPROXIMATIONS

It is shown by Mellor[6] that, if each fault is a Poisson source of failure (as assumed in all EOS models), the flow of reports from the field (the basic driver for a support cost model) is NHPP. Even taking account of discontinuities representing such maintenance activities as bug-clearance release and arbitrary market behaviour, the accumulated number of reports received at any time is Poisson distributed. Life-cycle cost up to any point is then obtained by mixing the distribution of cost per failure over this Poisson distribution. The large means and variances involved justify certain simplifying assumptions, such as approximating the Poisson by a normal distribution.

The problem lies in defining total field ROCOF as a function of time. This was done in Ref. 6 by using a time-slice technique and computer simulation. The approach was found in practice to have certain drawbacks, particularly if length of slice exceeded product MTBF. Research should address alternative, possibly simpler, approaches.

A further problem concerns the accuracy of long-term reliability growth forecasts. Initial investigations[8] indicate that this may not be good. Taking account of additional information derived from development process metrics and software properties may improve them.

7. CONCLUSIONS AND FUTURE WORK

This paper has highlighted a number of problem areas to be addressed by future research into the modelling of software support cost estimation. Some of the questions may be answered by work now being undertaken within the Alvey Software Reliability Modelling Project ALV/PRJ/SE/072, and the ESPRIT TRUST (Testing and Reliability Using Systematic Techniques) project. Others will require separate and specifically aimed research. The Alvey Software Data

Library Project ALV/PRJ/SE/042 may yield information for the estimation of the relevant cost distributions.

ACKNOWLEDGEMENTS

The author would like to thank his colleagues in CSR and in the above-mentioned research projects for suggestions and helpful discussions too numerous to recall in detail.

This paper was produced as part of the Alvey Software Reliability Modelling Study ALV/PRJ/SE/045.

REFERENCES

1. Adams, E. N., Optimizing preventive service of software products, *IBM Research J.*, **28**(1), 1984, 2–14.
2. Dyer, M., An approach to software reliability measurement. *Information and Software Technology*, **29**(8), 1987, 415–20.
3. Gray, C. T., *Superposition models for reliability growth*, PhD Thesis, University of Birmingham, 1985.
4. Gray, C. T., A framework for modelling software reliability, in: Ref. 13, 81–94 and 249–50.
5. Iyer, R. K. and Rosetti, D. J., Effect of system workload on operating system reliability: a study on IBM 3081, in: Ref. 14, 1438–48.
6. Mellor, P., Modelling software support, *ICL Tech. J.*, **3**(4), Nov. 1983, 407–38.
7. Mellor, P., Analysis of software failure data (1): adaptation of the Littlewood stochastic reliability growth model for coarse data, *ICL Tech. J.*, **4**(2), Nov. 1984, 313–20.
8. Mellor, P., Experiments in software reliability estimation, *Reliability Engineering*, **18**(2), Elsevier Applied Science, 1987, 117–29.
9. Mellor, P., Software reliability modelling: the state of the art, *Information and Software Technology*, **29**(2), Butterworth Scientific Press, Mar. 1987, 81–98.
10. Miller, D. R., *Exponential order statistics models of software reliability growth*, NASA Contractor Report CR–3909, National Aeronautics and Space Administration, Scientific and Technical Information Branch, 1985; a shortened version of this report appears in Ref. 15, 12–24.
11. Musa, J. D., Iannino, A. and Okumoto, K., *Software reliability: measurement, prediction, application*, McGraw-Hill, New York, 1986.
12. Oliver, R. M., A bayesian model to predict saturation and logistic growth, *J. Operation. Research Soc.*, **38**(1), 1987, 49–56.
13. Bendell, A. and Mellor, P. (joint editors), State of the Art Report R2/86 on *Software reliability*, publ. *Pergamon Infotech Ltd*, Apr. 1986.
14. Goel, A. (Ed.), Special issue on software reliability—Part 1, *IEEE Trans. Software Engineering*, **SE–11**(12), Dec. 1985.
15. Goel, A. (Ed.), Special issue on software reliability—Part 2, *IEEE Trans Software Engineering*, **SE–12**(1), Jan. 1986.

13

An Engineering Theory of Structure and Measurement

N. E. Fenton and A. A. Kaposi

Centre for Software and Systems Engineering, London, UK

ABSTRACT

*Classical measurement theory requires that metrics should describe numerically some well-understood attribute or characteristic manifested by the class of objects on which they are defined. We argue that many important characteristics of a system relate to its **structural** properties, and therefore that it is these which should be measured if we can find suitable formal models for the many different types of structural property exhibited. We describe a 'meta-theory' for studying structural properties of systems which has potential use in many areas of engineering systems-in-the-large. We provide examples of how this theory may form the basis for objective measurement of several types of structural property, and show that many of the so-called software 'complexity' metrics are just simple examples of these.*

1. INTRODUCTION

A mature engineering discipline is characterised by three closely linked features:

—well defined, theoretically verified and empirically validated mathematical *models*;*

---

* In this paper a model will be considered to be a purposefully abstracted representation of an object system.

—formal *theories*; and
—a comprehensive *system of measurement.*

The paper argues that *structural properties* are essential features of modern systems for which few adequate engineering models, theories and measures are available. Research into system structure is necessary for solution of engineering problems in-the-large which are beyond the scope of the classical engineering discipline. The purpose of structural research is to promote the development of such young disciplines as software and systems engineering, where the properties of artefacts are critically dependent on the structure of their specifications and internal construction. Thus, structural research is committed to finding suitable mathematical models, formal theories and measurements of system structure.

The paper goes on to describe a 'meta-theory' for studying structural properties. We argue that this is an appropriate basis for defining all metrics which capture structural attributes. We offer examples of the use of this theory in two contexts: imperative programming and logic programming, and also outline how it could be applied to formal design and specification languages as well as parallel computation.

2. SCIENTIFIC FOUNDATION OF ENGINEERING

2.1 Measurement

Measurement is a notion which arises naturally from the need to keep a reliable, objective record of observations. Kyburg[24] writes:

> 'Measurement is so fundamental to the physical sciences and engineering that it is difficult to know where we would be without it.'

Measurement may evolve in the following manner:[13]

—An *attribute* is intuitively recognised in terms of which items of a certain class may be described, categorised or ordered. For example, solid objects have *height, temperature,* etc., processes have *duration,* moving bodies have *velocity.*
—A *relationship* is identified which the attribute imposes on the items of the class (taller than, hotter than, longer than, faster than).

—A *mapping* is defined from the item to the set of real numbers (or some other number system, such as the complex numbers in the case of measuring impedance in an electrical circuit). The mapping must preserve the intuitive relationship (the largest number is to denote the height of the tallest, hottest, longest, fastest of the entities). The mapping is to be described in a *procedure* which ensures the objectivity and repeatability of the measurement.

Given appropriate standards, units and measurement procedures, almost any observable property can be quantified, provided that it admits to objective comparison. Such measures yield information which can characterise a given situation and *describe* individual properties of specific entities. However, if we need to understand the *relationships* between the measured properties of a given object, explore the effect of the change of some property on the others, or *predict* the properties of any object yet to be constructed, then we need a framework of formal models (theoretical structures).

2.2 Models, theories and the role of science
It is widely (although not universally) accepted that the function of science is to propose and validate *models* which articulate the underlying patterns in data obtained by measurement. Science assigns a variable to each attribute of the entity under study and seeks to explain the relationships between the variables of the model. Once the self-consistency and stability of the relationship is verified and the model is empirically validated, the relationships are accepted as the *laws* and *theories* of science.

The theories of science provide formal systems for reasoning about the object under investigation by means of mathematics, and reliably deducing its important properties from its measurable ones. For example, the laws of thermal expansion allow us to calculate temperature by means of measuring distance; the theory of geometry tells us how to derive the volume of a solid object from its linear dimensions; the theory of electromagnetism lets us work out the energy of radio waves at known distances from the transmitter, etc.

Scientific theory also serves as the foundation of our universal system of measurement. The SI system defines a frugal set of 'base' measures, tied to internationally agreed standards and units. Using the theories of the natural sciences, the base measures combine to form a comprehensive system of 'derived' measures. The base and derived measures of the SI system together can quantify all attributes of any entity within the disciplines of the natural sciences and the classical engineering disciplines they support.

2.3 Engineering

The classical disciplines of engineering exploit the natural sciences for a constructive purpose. Engineers use the models and theories of science for *describing* (specifying) the future object and those elementary parts from which it is to be constructed. They apply scientific theories for *predicting* that the design, when implemented according to the engineer's instructions, will meet the specification. It is the engineer's obligation to validate design predictions by measurement and comparison against the specification. It is the expert use of the predictive power of theory which distinguishes a mature engineering discipline from craft practice.

However, current-day engineering poses problems which lie beyond the scope of models, theories and measurement systems of the classical disciplines. Part of the difficulty stems from the 'reductionist' philosophy of classical science, and the traditional engineering disciplines which grew out from it.[31] In engineering, reductionism is akin to bottom-up design; break down the whole problem into its small parts, study the parts independently and combine the knowledge of the parts to comprehend the whole.

The method works well enough so long as the behaviour is easy to capture, the parts are few and are combined in simple ways. The method breaks down when the behaviour is elaborate and the construction is complex in the sense that the parts are many, varied and intricately combined. Structural complexity of specification and interconnection is the central problem in such modern engineering domains as VLSI design and software engineering. To cope with such problems, we need to extend classical engineering science, providing appropriate structural models, formal theories and a comprehensive metrication system.

2.4 The models, theories and measures of software engineering

A software model is a simplified representation of a software system. Depending on the purpose, and given well-defined modelling procedures, many different (but equally valid) models, preserving different features of the system, can always be constructed. Thus, for example, a data-flow graph and a statistical distribution of errors would be two different models highlighting different features of the same piece of code. One would not use the latter model to resolve questions or derive measures about data-flow any more than one would use the IQ ratings model to measure the height of a human being.

There is a need for valid models, formal theories and associated measures in software engineering as in other engineering domains. Without these, engineering design is impossible, and we are reduced to creating software by craft practice.

Maurice Halstead[16] must be credited with the initiative to create a comprehensive science of software engineering, comprising models, theoretical relationships over the models and a system of associated measures of model properties. Although he was aware of the obligation to validate models through practical application, Halstead did not discharge this obligation adequately and by now few people accept that Halstead's measures offer useful insight into the properties of code. Even if it had been proven valid, Halstead's 'software science' would be dated by now because of the changing emphasis from *product* to *process*. Historically, software engineering was concerned with the product rather than the process. Traditionally formal models were only associated with the code itself. With improved software engineering education, and with the advent of better tools, in many environments software is no longer designed by writing code. Indeed, the final stages of the software and all the processes associated with it need not have a monopoly of the formal models even if that has been the case in the past.

The current drive is toward a more formal approach to the *specification* and *development* of software. This is embodied, for example, in the principles of the Alvey and ESPRIT software engineering programs, and is practised now by many enlightened software houses. Thus for example, an initial specification written in a formal notation such as Z^{29} or VDM^{20} may be viewed as a model of the problem requirements (or more specifically the *functional* requirements).

Unfortunately, there is little or no collaboration at present between the developers of such formal methods and groups working on software metrication. In the absence of a suitable measurement system, there is no chance of validating the claims of the formal methods community that their models and theories enhance the quality of software products and improve the cost-effectiveness of software processes. Conversely, in the absence of a supporting theory, it is not clear what the relevant attributes are and so any empiricism may be based on the wrong observables. Consequently, the metrics community cannot produce results of lasting value, and the use of metrics in software development is restricted at best to informal heuristic approaches such as that proposed by Gilb,[14] who offers a pragmatic basis for **design** based on measurable quality objectives.

However, quoting Kyburg[24] once again,

'... however cleverly we measure something, however reliable the test or reproducible the measurement, without a theoretical framework into which that quantity enters, it is useless'.

It should be noted that a perfectly acceptable theoretical framework is that of probability (including sampling and statistics). Hence we believe that software **reliability** measurement and prediction based on sample measurements of behavioural aspects of the product (once a number of invariants like target machine etc. have been identified) is valuable measurement even in the strict sense of Kyburg.

The modern view of software engineering is to recognise that all the phases of software development may create valuable products in their own right. Formal models exist, or can be found, for describing different aspects (structure, efficiency, reliability etc.) of these. The modeller should be free to choose the mathematical medium which can best capture key features and which yields the most elegant and tractable model. The use of formal methods which provide such models is an exciting breakthrough. It offers opportunities for implementing formal models and theories by a measurement system, thus laying the foundations of a mature discipline of software engineering.

Research into the modern scientific foundations of software engineering promises an extra bonus. There is reason to believe that the models, theories and methods may be helpful in solving some of the difficult structural problems of complex systems in other engineering domains.

3. MODELLING STRUCTURES AS DIGRAPHS

One of the principal aims of our research is to provide a rigorous theoretical foundation for the study and measurement of structural properties of systems in general and software in particular. Our ultimate objective is the formal characterisation of various structural attributes by means of metrics which preserve the relationships imposed by the attributes and have the potential to capture the relationship between different attributes. The latter is the pre-requisite of any predictive theory of software.

We are interested here in developing models of structure at all stages of the software process from specification to post-design phases, and we are not restricting ourselves to any one notion of structure. The types of relational structure which may be amenable to our approach could be control, data, semantics, hierarchical or goal-based. The plan is to extend our attention to non-functional aspects such as performance and quality constraints at a later stage of this research.

We observe that the initial specification is itself a model of the final product. In the course of design this product model is gradually transformed to other product models which are increasingly more detailed until finally the implementation (in the case of software the source code) is produced. This series of product models forms a major part of the design documentation. The product models undergo further transformation in the course of post-production processes such as maintenance. Our research is concerned with structural properties of all these product models.

When selecting the most suitable mathematical medium, and without prejudicing subsequent research decisions, we observe that graph theory has proven to be particularly suitable for abstracting structural properties of such diverse systems as electrical circuits, process control, product management and software itself. Graphs also have a particular significance in expositions on category theory which provides a theoretical foundation for many of the mathematical formalisms used so far in computer science. The reader may refer to Ref. 41 for a suitable introduction to graph theory, which is consistent with the notation and definitions used here.

3.1 Meta-theory for structure

A structure G of property X is simply a digraph satisfying a set of rules encapsulated by property X. The set of all such digraphs will be denoted $\mathcal{G}_X$. The rules will generally be determined by the kind of structural property to be captured. In general we shall be considering a structural property exhibited by a class of systems S, so that there will be a mapping (*modelling process*)

$$M : S \rightarrow \mathcal{G}_X$$

which associates a unique digraph in $\mathcal{G}_X$ with each object in S. The mapping M (the formal procedure linking the system in the application domain with the model in the domain of mathematics) will in general be the most difficult thing to define, but this is true of any formal modelling process. In order for the model to be meaningful, we need some means of identifying those objects in S which themselves do not exhibit any manifestation of the particular structural property concerned. We shall call these the *units* of S's members. The units will be mapped by M onto nodes of the digraph G, say, and the arcs of G will then correspond to the structural relationship between various corresponding units.

As a concrete example, let S be the class of programs in a particular high-level language. Two obvious structural properties pertinent to S are control flow and data flow. We would need two classes $\mathcal{G}_X$, $\mathcal{G}'_{X'}$, of graphs to represent the kind of structures which model these properties respectively. The reader may have in mind suitable notions, viz. control- and data-flowgraphs (some authors have used the same class of graphs for both properties[4]). In the case of control flow, the units of programs which will be mapped onto nodes should be those statements which contain no explicit control flow. For example, simple input, output and assignment statements might be considered as units. The value of the modelling process (the descriptive power of the model and the formal deductions which can be drawn from it) depends on these decisions.

The key to the effective engineering design of any system is the structural notion of compositionality. In the example of sequential imperative languages there are two composition operations, namely sequence and nesting (procedure calling);[11] in functional languages we have function application; in graphical design languages (e.g. Refs 18, 19) we have component expansion, and in a formal specification language like Z we have the various schema operations.

Once a system has been constructed compositionally, we would also like to be able to determine retrospectively the system's structure by inspection and analysis.

In our meta-theory there will be a set of operations O defined formally on the class of graphs $\mathcal{G}_X$ which effectively model the relevant operations in the real world system. We shall also require a suitable definition of *substructures* in $\mathcal{G}_X$ to allow us to identify those structures which are indecomposable in the sense that they could not have been constructed from smaller structures using the operations. We also need to find inverse operations to each member of O for the purpose of decomposing the substructures. In general a substructure of a member G of $\mathcal{G}_X$ will be a digraph G' which is properly contained in G and which is itself a member of $\mathcal{G}_X$, i.e. satisfies all the rules encapsulated by property X. There may also be some limiting conditions attached.

Given a well-defined notion of substructure, we are able to define a very important subset of $\mathcal{G}_X$, namely the set of *primes*. We shall say that G is *prime* if it contains no substructure. Thus the primes are the indecomposable structures of the theory and are thus the building blocks for the structural design. We will be especially interested in those classes $\mathcal{G}_X$ whose substructures and operations are so defined that at every possible stage of decomposition of a structure there is a uniquely defined set of **maximal** substructures (called **components**) whose decomposition results in a member of $\mathcal{G}_X$. (Note that uniqueness will follow when the maximal substructures are *mutually disjoint*.) In such cases it may be possible (and in fact is the case in each of the examples we consider) that every member of $\mathcal{G}_X$ will be expressible as a unique hierarchy of prime structures. To explain this suppose that we have a member G of $\mathcal{G}_X$. The *decomposition tree* of G, denoted Tree(G), is the tree defined by the recursive procedure:

Procedure Tree(G)
{returns a tree T for a given structure $G \in \mathcal{G}_X$.
The nodes of T themselves correspond to members of $\mathcal{G}_X \times O$}
    Begin
    if G is prime
        then T is a single node, G
        else
        Begin
        Let $G_1, \ldots, G_n$ be the 'component' substructures of G
        (with respect to an operation OP);
        Simultaneously decompose these in G (with respect to OP);
        store the resulting structure as G';
        root(T) := (G', OP);
        subtrees of root(T) are Tree(G_1), $\ldots$, Tree(G_n)
    end {else}
end.

The procedure is guaranteed to terminate since decomposition of the components at each stage leads to a smaller structure. Moreover, the tree is uniquely defined (in the Finite Church–Rosser sense[37]) by virtue of the uniqueness of the components at each stage. If, in addition, a prime structure results from each stage of the decomposition, then each structure G in $\mathcal{G}_X$ will give rise to a **unique** tree whose nodes are labelled by a pair consisting of a prime in $\mathcal{G}_X$ together with an associated operation. We shall call this the *uniqueness property*. The question remains however: under what circumstances do we have the uniqueness property? (or, more succinctly, when can we prove it?) The answer will generally depend on the way the operations and their inverses are defined; in the examples considered in this paper, the result of decomposing all the components guarantees a prime by virtue of the **maximality** (which would otherwise be contradicted) of the components as substructures.

In summary the uniqueness property will follow when:

—the set of maximal substructures is always uniquely defined, and
—their decomposition always results in a prime structure.

This property is of paramount importance for our work, since it means there is a one-to-one correspondence between the structures in $\mathcal{G}_X$ and a certain class of labelled trees. Thus any studies of the structural property X can be restricted to this class of trees, which is in general inherently more tractable than the class $\mathcal{G}_X$.

Let us consider a very simple example of a structure class in order to test our theory.

Example
Suppose we wish to model pure hierarchical structure. In this case our real world systems in S consist of a hierarchy of modules over a set $\mathcal{A}$, say, and there is only one type of relation of any interest, namely that of hierarchical inclusion. In a certain sense this is the simplest structural notion which we can model because, as we shall see, there is only one operation associated with it.

The appropriate structure class here is the set of digraphs $\mathcal{T}$ consisting of all rooted, directed trees labelled over $\mathcal{A}$. The mapping

$$M : S \to \mathcal{T}$$

is defined in the obvious way. Figure 1, for example, models a system A with subsystems A_1, A_2 which respectively have subsystems A_{11}, A_{12} and A_{21}, A_{22}.

For objects in S there is just one composition operation, namely that

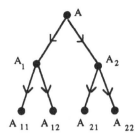

Fig. 1. Hierarchical system.

of 'expansion', by which a 'leaf' module is replaced by some hierarchy. In terms of the digraph model this corresponds to an operation

$$OP : \mathcal{T} \times \mathcal{T} \times \mathcal{A} \to \mathcal{T}$$

in which a tree T_1 with leaf node labelled A, say, (the *pivot*) has this leaf node replaced by a tree T_2 whose root node is A.

Thus the tree in Fig. 1 is the result of applying OP to the trees T_1, T_2 of Fig. 2 with the node A_2 acting as the pivot.

What are the substructures of a given structure T in this case? They are not simply any subtrees of T but are those 'terminal' subtrees which consist of all the descendants (in T) of a node if that node is in the subtree.

The inverse to the expansion operation is the operation in which, for a given node A of a tree T, the whole substructure of T rooted at A is replaced by a single node A.

What are the primes in this case? They are simply those trivial trees consisting of a single node and no arcs, since any other tree has a

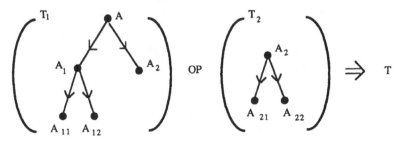

Fig. 2. Expansion operation.

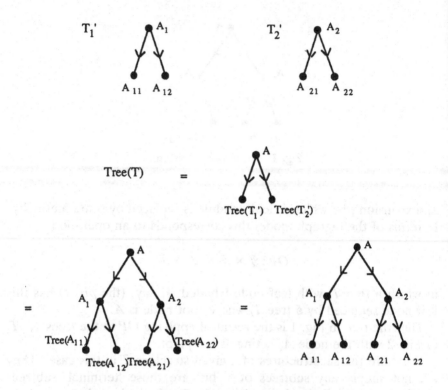

Fig. 3. Applying the algorithm to the tree of Fig. 1.

substructure. Thus the primes are the image under M of the members of $\mathscr{A}$. The test of our theory in this case should be that for a given tree T the decomposition algorithm should yield $Tree(T)$ as equal to (or more accurately *isomorphic to*) T. The reader might attempt to supply a proof of the general case; it is clearly demonstrated by the example in Fig. 3, which describes the process of applying the algorithm to the tree of Fig. 1. Since there is always only one possible operation, there is no ambiguity in not adding this to the node labels. Note that at the first stage there are two maximal substructures T_1', T_2' with respect to the expansion operation, namely the subtrees rooted at A_1, A_2 respectively.

Finally, the uniqueness property of the decomposition trees in this example should now be clear.

3.2 Metrication schemes

All structural properties of a member of $\mathcal{G}_X$ are clearly characterised in its decomposition tree. If we have the uniqueness property, then we may just as well study the latter—which provides a clearer picture of the relevant structural hierarchy. The case of the previous example, where the decomposition tree of a structure turned out to be the same as the original graph, was of course exceptional. In particular, if there are any structural properties which could be *measured* then such measures should be derivable directly from the decomposition tree.

Suppose that s is some structural feature which we hope to measure using a metric m_s. Then, for any structure G, we expect $m_s(G)$ to be the measure of s in G. We now know that it is enough to measure (or define):

M.1: The value $m_s(P)$ for each prime $P \in \mathcal{G}_X$
M.2: The value of m_s with respect to each operation $OP \in O$. This means we need a function f_{OP} such that if

$$G = OP(G_1, \ldots, G_n)$$

  then

$$m_s(G) = f_{OP}(m_s(G_1), \ldots, m_s(G_n))$$

Once we know M.1 and M.2 it follows from our definition of the decomposition tree that the metric m_s will be (uniquely) defined recursively for *all* structures G. Such a metric we shall call a *structural metric*. But what is to be gained by this approach? The answer is that not only do the minimal defining equations M.1 and M.2 constitute a complete metric definition but that with respect to the property s these are the *only subjective* parts. If we have a true intuitive understanding of s then we ought to have no difficulty in determining the most appropriate values for M.1 and M.2. If we do not have this intuitive understanding, then the structural metric which results from assigning necessarily arbitrary or subjective values will be meaningless (although this approach still offers a good framework for fine-tuning by empirical validation).

We need to consider some concrete applications of structural models, theories and metrics to solidify the abstract notions introduced so far.

4 SOME APPLICATIONS OF STRUCTURAL SCHEMAS AND METRICS

4.1 Sequential programs

Structural features of sequential programs (or detailed designs) written in imperative languages have been extensively investigated. In particular the control and information structures have been modelled and these models have formed the basis for numerous structural metrics.[17] Most of the models are based on directed graphs, but there have been certain problems with some of these approaches. In the context of the notation of the previous section these may be summarised as:

(1) The class $\mathcal{G}_X$ is generally informally defined (e.g. 'Flow diagrams'). This makes it difficult to define the relevant operations and the relevant substructures, and hence the very notion of decomposition.

(2) The mapping

$$M : \{Programs\} \rightarrow \mathcal{G}_X$$

is never formally defined. There is generally an assumption (without justification) that a unique control (data) flow diagram can be associated with a program in an obvious way.

(3) Metrics which are directly derived from the model are claimed to be descriptive of notions of 'complexity', although these notions are clearly beyond the descriptive power of the model. An example is McCabe's metric[27] which is claimed as a measure of cognitive complexity as well as being an indicator of bugs and maintenance costs. In truth, it simply measures the number of decision branches in a program.

Our approach[8,9,11,12] and related work[34,35] has avoided the first of these problems by the construction of a formal *flowgraph* model and its associated theory. The second problem—like any modelling process in an applied theory—is difficult to resolve to everybody's satisfaction and involves an inevitable compromise between conciseness and detail. Subjective judgements may often dictate the level of detail which we wish to preserve with the mapping. Examples which should dispel the myth that there is always a unique and obvious graphical representation include *recursion, external procedures, exception handling, compound booleans* and *function calls within booleans*. A detailed account of the difficulty of modelling these, together with language-specific approaches to dealing with them, appears in Ref. 39. The way we have avoided the third problem will be shown after a summary of the flowgraph theory work of Refs 11 and 12 in the context of our meta-theory.

The class S of systems to be modelled will generally be the set of programs in some imperative language, and the structural property X is that of *control flow*. The class $\mathcal{G}_X$ is the class of *Flowgraphs* $\mathcal{F}$ which consists of directed labelled graphs having designated start and stop nodes and satisfying certain path properties. The modelling function M will generally be dependent on the language of the class S. We have already noted that there are two pertinent operations effecting control flow for sequential programming, namely *sequence* and *nesting*. There are analogous operations OP_1, OP_2 defined on $\mathcal{F}$ and generally denoted

$$OP_1(F_1, \ldots, F_n) = F_1; \ldots; F_n$$

(sequence of n flowgraphs)

$$OP_2(F, F_1, \ldots, F_n) = F(F_1, \ldots, F_n)$$

(nesting of n flowgraphs $F_1, \ldots, F_n$ onto n procedure nodes of F)

To be precise, there are in fact two *schemas* of operations. Instead of the sequence operation OP_1 we really have a set of operations OP_1^n (sequence of n for each $n \geq 1$) and instead of the nesting operation OP_2 we really have a schema of operations OP_2^F (nesting with respect to the prime F for each prime).

The substructures within the class $\mathcal{F}$ correspond precisely to the *proper subflowgraphs*—single entry, single exit proper subgraphs which are themselves flowgraphs. The additional limiting conditions for the definition of substructure is that the flowgraphs of type P_0, P_1 (see Fig. 4) are never considered to be proper subflowgraphs, and those of type P_n in general are not considered to have subflowgraphs (i.e. of type P_m for $m < n$). Each occurrence of a subflowgraph may be viewed as a result of either a sequence or a nesting and so the inverse (decomposition) operations of the latter are easily defined with respect to subflowgraphs. Not surprisingly, the prime structures of $\mathcal{F}$ are just the prime· flowgraphs—those flowgraphs having no proper sub-flowgraphs. The primes may be considered to be the building blocks of structured programming inasmuch as they correspond to specific control structures. Of course, most languages allow only a small set of these, including, for example, some of those in Fig. 4, but arbitrary

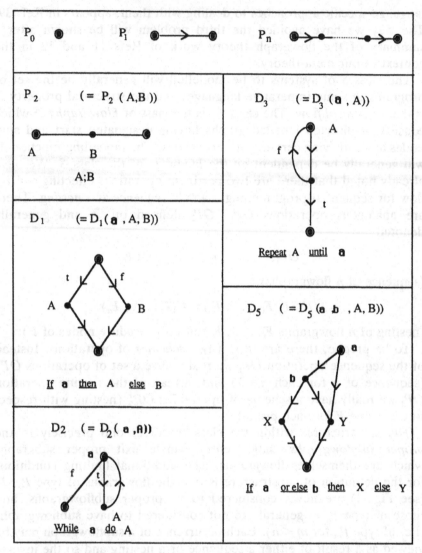

Fig. 4. Some well-used primes and associated control structures.

primes may be constructed if one wishes to use the dreaded **goto** statement or if the language allows user-defined structure names.

The uniqueness property for the decomposition tree of members of $\mathscr{F}$ is proved in Ref. 12. It is based on the observation that if a flowgraph is sequential then its maximal non-sequential subflowgraphs form a uniquely defined set; if it is non-sequential then its maximal subflowgraphs are edge-disjoint and hence again form a uniquely defined set.[12] Thus the notion of components is well-defined.

An example of applying the decomposition algorithm is given in Fig. 5. Note that in this case the 'program' is a pseudo-code algorithm of Knuth[23] to calculate an approximation to $y = log_b x$ for a number x, $1 \leqslant x < 2$. The algorithm is actually written in an unstructured manner, but the decomposition tree clearly shows that its prime components are those which are generally considered as 'structured' and the tree provides an automatic mechanism for rewriting the algorithm in structured form.

While the above example indicates a general practical use of the decomposition tree as a tool for automatic code restructuring, we are especially interested in its use for structural metrics. In Refs 9, 12 we observed that (in the case of $\mathscr{F}$) it was sufficient for a structural metric m to define

(1) the value of m for each prime,
(2) the value of m with respect to sequence, and
(3) the value of m with respect to nesting.

Note that in the context of our meta-theory both (2) and (3) above are merged into eqn M.2 (of Section 3.3) which defines the value of m with respect to the two (schemas of) operations.

Thus, as a simple example, the intuitive notion of *depth of nesting* is precisely characterised by the metric α defined as:

M.1: $\alpha(P_n) = 0$ for each n
$\alpha(F) = 1$ for each prime $F \neq P_n$
M.2: $\alpha(F_1; \ldots ; F_n) = \max(\alpha(F_1), \ldots, \alpha(F_n))$ for each n
(OP_1^n definition)
$\alpha(F(F_1, \ldots, F_n)) = 1 + \max(\alpha(F_1), \ldots, \alpha(F_n))$ for each prime F
(OP_2^F definition)

Note also that our metrics are confined to structural features only, and do not claim to be descriptive or predictive of any other software property. In this way we have avoided the third problem mentioned at the start of this section. Structural 'base' measures similar to nesting depth above, like 'volume', 'breadth' and a whole range of metrics describing the 'prime distribution', are easily characterised by this method. What is especially illuminating is that we have been able to show[9,12] that a wide range of the well-known metrics of the literature,

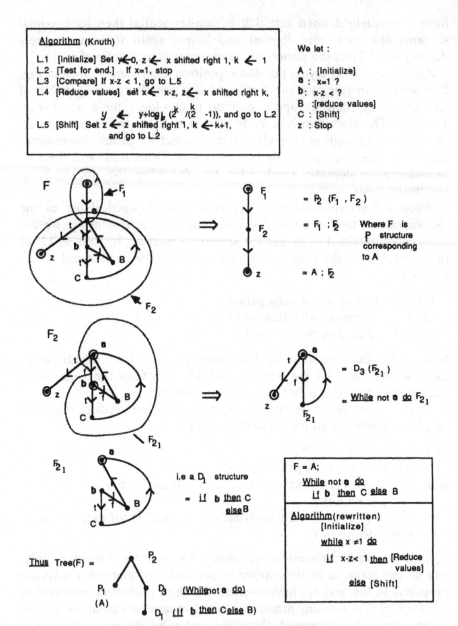

Fig. 5. Decomposition of Knuth's algorithm.

which are claimed by their authors to be 'complexity measures', may be easily characterised in this way (that is by defining M.1 and M.2 alone). Of particular interest are those like the classes defined by Basili and Hutchens[2] and Prather.[34] These metrics were specifically intended to return a value for a program which reflected its overall structure, taking account of such notions as nesting levels and use of structured programming (thereby providing a considerable improvement on the gross over-simplicity of McCabe[27]). Bearing in mind our earlier comments about where subjectivity is inevitable within structural metrics' definitions, we observe, for example in the case of Basili–Hutchens' *SynC,* that the part of equation M.2 which defines nesting is given by

$$SynC(F(F_1, \ldots, F_n)) = SynC(F) + 1.1 \sum_{i=1}^{n} SynC(F_i)$$

for each prime $F \neq P_n$.

This amounts to an assertion about the value of nesting with respect to the property being measured, which in this case appears to be the degree of structuredness (in the structured programming sense). Providing meaningful values to the subjective parts of the metrics' definitions is a task which ultimately may only really be tackled effectively in collaboration with cognitive psychologists. We could, for example, learn from the work of the Yale group,[38] which has attempted to assess the relative cognitive complexity of certain primes (in this case corresponding to looping structures), and input this knowledge into our M.1 and M.2 definitions. In the absence of the necessary resources to take this experimental work further, we may on the other hand agree to certain restrictive axioms for certain classes of metrics. For example, Prather has argued that one should only consider metrics for which the sequence operations OP_1^n are *additive*. Bache[3] has taken this further by defining seven other axioms which appear to be reasonable for measures of levels of structuredness; as a result this has led to the construction of a family of metrics which are to be used for quality assurance purposes on design structures.

We believe that motivation to define an overall structuredness rating such as those mentioned above, as well as our work in Ref. 12, stems from the classical measurement theory principles described in Section 2, but these have never been articulated in this way. We feel we have a sufficiently intuitive understanding of structuredness (in the above sense) to be able to agree generally which of two programs is more structured, provided we know the structuring conventions used. Thus, in due course, we should be able to quantify this knowledge with an appropriate metric in the classical sense, i.e. one which preserves the intuitive relationship; however, at present this may all be slightly premature. The particular structuredness property in question is more likely to be a derived measure of a number of those base measures (and others) described above.

The important task of investigating the possible correlation of some of the proposed metrics with some *process* and *performance* metrics forms part of industrially collaborative projects.[1,6]

Note that a similar model to the one described above may be used for data-flow in sequential programs.[3]

4.2 Design structures

We have already indicated that the special case of the meta-theory applied to sequential programs may also be used to model control in **algorithmic design languages** or **pseudo code.** The appeal of this approach is that metrics derived from these are available at an earlier stage in the product development than code, allowing early corrective action to be taken as a result of the values (if these can be meaningfully interpreted).

A number of studies on metrics have already been carried out for certain graphical design languages.[32] In particular, the meta-theory for sequential subsets of languages such as **SDL** (the CCITT standard 'System Design Language') and British Telecom's **KINDRA** is almost identical to that for sequential programs—only the nature of the allowable primes is generally different and there may be extra operations. A study of KINDRA in the context of our theory (with associated metrics) is contained in Ref. 3. A study of metrics applied to SDL is contained in Ref. 25, and it is planned that this work will be reviewed within the context of the meta-theory.

In the case of the structured **JSP** *design charts* of Jackson,[18] the structures of the meta-theory are quite different but result in an isomorphism with the decomposition trees of a subsequent implementation. In this case the class of systems S to be modelled is the class of *design decisions*. The units are the identifiable procedure blocks. A unit is mapped by M onto a node labelled by the procedure. The class $\mathcal{G}_X$ in this case is not dissimilar to the class of pure hierarchical structures given in the example (Section 3.1). Once again these are rooted, labelled trees. We prefer to give a precise definition of the members of $\mathscr{G}_X$ recursively in terms of the allowable operations. There are three operations: sequence, selection and iteration.

Sequence is defined with respect to a single 'procedure' node structure, P say, and a number of arbitrary structures. In particular if we have n structures whose root nodes are labelled $P_1, \ldots, P_n$ respectively then the operation of sequence (interpreted as P being the sequences of $P_1, \ldots, P_n$) in $\mathscr{G}_X$ results in a structure represented in Fig. 6.

Similarly the operations of selection and iteration are given in Fig. 7.

Note that these are rather special cases of the expansion operation for the hierarchical structures of the example in Section 3. The inverses of these are straightforward to define, and the notion of substructure here is the same as in the Example (Section 3.1). Similarly, the primes are precisely the single procedure nodes. The decomposition tree (which again has the uniqueness property) of a structure T in $\mathscr{G}_X$ is easily derived from the algorithm and is isomorphic to T. An example is given in Fig. 8.

Note that in this case the nodes of Tree(T) are labelled not just with a prime but also with the named operation describing the relationship with the subtrees.

We have already noted in Ref. 12 that the decomposition tree of a program implementation of a JSP chart is isomorphic to the chart, and we have shown that structural metrics for programs may all be defined from the decomposition trees. It follows that any such metrics which are useful for programs are directly applicable and immediately derivable from the JSP charts.

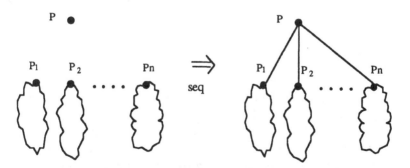

Fig. 6. Sequence.

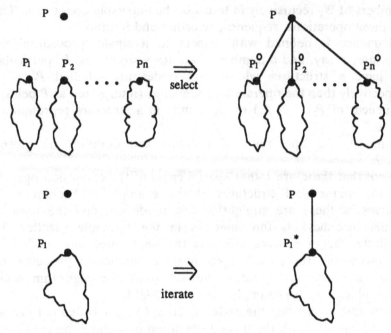

Fig. 7. Selection and iteration.

The primes in JSP turn out to be particularly simple, mainly because the allowable structures are already trees. In the case of some design structure chart languages such as those described in Ref. 42 this is not the case, and it will be a useful exercise to describe the example of the meta-theory in such a case. This is especially pertinent as this reference surveys a number of metrics derived from the charts. The charts arising in JSD[19] may also prove an interesting example of our theory.

4.3 Parallel programming

Analysing and measuring structural properties of programs (or systems) which contain parallel computation (or operations) will inevitably attract growing interest with the development of parallel architectures. As far as our meta-theory is concerned we have to determine if there are appropriate digraph models for describing these systems. A naive approach would be to use something like the simple flowgraph model, using special labels for the parallel operations. The problem with such

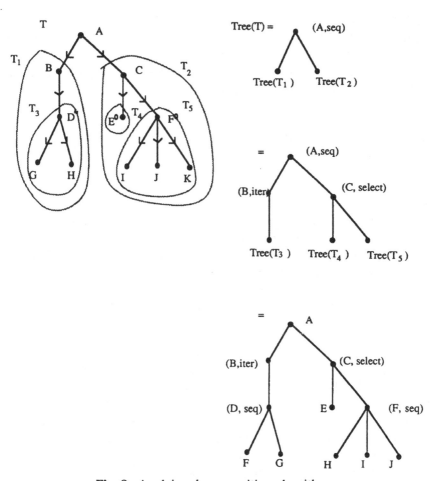

Fig. 8. Applying decomposition algorithm.

an approach is the limited descriptive power of the model; it is clear that key structural information is hidden within labels rather than being captured by the graph itself. More promising are the various types of Petri Net models (which are special types of digraphs with well-defined transition operations). It would be of great interest to define the various meta-theory concepts in these examples. An indirect study of this nature appears in Ref. 15, where a theory of decomposition and primes (irreducibles) is applied to a class of Petri Nets modelling a limited class of parallel computation systems. It is intended that the important link with this work will be further exploited in the Alvey project.[1] The use of the meta-theory for parallel and concurrent structures will also now be explored in the British Telecom project.[6] It will first be applied to the complete language KINDRA and then to CCITT SDL.

4.4 PROLOG programs

In this example we wish to model a fundamentally different structural property to those of the previous examples. An informal approach to the modelling and measurement of all static properties of PROLOG programs has been presented in Ref. 26. Instead, here we confine attention to the goal–subgoal calling structure problem. For a detailed description of the modelling process see Ref. 30, and for a fully formal account of the associated theory of structure (which is still being developed in this case) see Ref. 33.

Briefly, the class S consists of the set of PROLOG programs, a member of whose units contain the named goals appearing. The class $\mathcal{G}_X$ consists of the set of *P-graphs*, where a P-graph G is a labelled digraph having a distinguished node a (*start* node) such that every node of G lies on a directed path from a. In the modelling process a goal is mapped onto an appropriately labelled node of G, and an arc (A, B) of G indicates that B is a subgoal of A. For a full definition of the operations in $\mathcal{G}_X$, which correspond to the PROLOG operations of conjunction and disjunction, see Ref. 30. A rough idea of how the modelling process works may be seen by the P-graph representation (shown in Fig. 10) of the program given in Fig. 9.

What makes P-graphs interesting, however, is the extra family of recursion 'operations'. Recursion is generally defined as a schema of equations with $\leqslant n$ rules involving n goals (for $n \geqslant 1$) for which the removal of any rule means no unique solution. Two very simple, but common recursion schemas, together with their parameterised P-graphs (named R_1, R_2), are shown in Fig. 11.

For a P-graph G, *a sub-P-graph* G' is a subgraph of G which is itself a P-graph whose start node is an entry node from G. In addition G' has no nodes which arcs to nodes in $G \backslash G'$. In a recursion schema P-graph the labelled nodes are also considered to be (trivial) sub-P-graphs. This describes the relevant notion of substructures in $\mathcal{G}_X$. With respect to this definition the prime structures in $\mathcal{G}_X$ are those P-graphs corresponding to the recursion schemas with the labels removed

```
/* Given 2 lists, where the second one is
   the concatenation of a third one with the
   first one, find this third list and build
   up a palindrome with it. */

palindrome(L1,L2):-
     list(L1,Y),list(L2,Y),
     concatenate(X,Y,Z),
     write('Third list: '),write(X),nl,
     reverse(X,W),
     concatenate(X,W,K),
     write('Palindrome: '),write(K),

concatenate([],L,L).
concatenate([E|R],L2,[E|L]):-
concatenate(R,L2,L).

reverse([],[]).
reverse([E|R],L):-
     reverse(R1,R,R1),
     concatenate(R1,[E],L).

list(a,[1,3,5,7]).
list(b,[a,b,c,d,e,1,3,5,7,9]).
```

Fig. 9. PROLOG program.

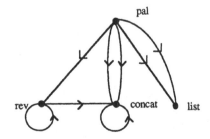

Fig. 10. *P*-graph for program in Fig. 9.

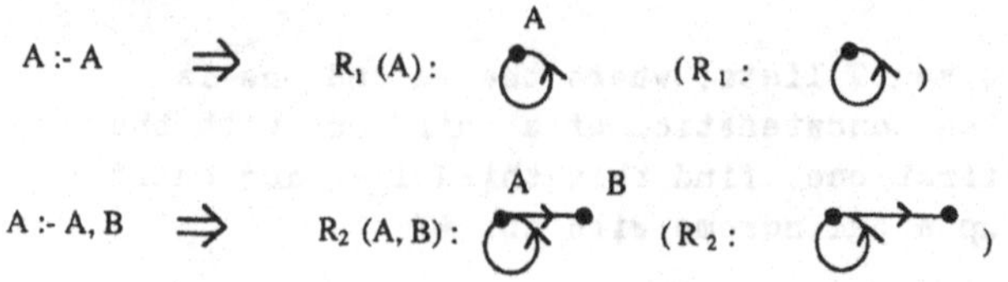

Fig. 11. Two simple recursion schemas.

(e.g. R_1, R_2 above), together with the trivial single-node graphs with a label. (A graphical characterisation is contained in Ref. 33.)

Figure 12 indicates the sub-P-graphs of the graph G of Fig. 10.

Notwithstanding the fact that we have not described here the formal definition of the operations and their inverses, the reader should have little difficulty in understanding how the decomposition algorithm may be applied to the P-graph G of our example to produce the unique prime tree as indicated in Fig. 12. At the first stage of the algorithm we find that, *with respect to the operation of conjunction* for node *pal*, there are five maximal sub-P-graphs. Each of the graphs G_2, G_3 were conjuncted twice since they each have two entries. Note that without considering the operation of conjunction, G_2 is *not* a maximal sub-P-graph in G.

4.5 Formal specifications and other work

The need to control the complexity of the product at the **specification** stage is well recognised. Structural decomposition of the specification is the only effective means of achieving this. The drive toward formal approaches to software and system specification is unified by two fundamental assumptions:

—the necessity for (mathematical) formality to reason about the intended system behaviour and the correctness of any implementation;

—the necessity for a compositional approach.

There are, of course, a multitude of different specification methods and notations, ranging from broadly based ones to others applicable only to particular types of systems, from methods of data abstraction to process algebras and modal logics. The tendency to make use of some of these in functional specification documents is very helpful for our arguments; once a formal representation of the specification exists, our minimum requirement of a formal model on which to apply

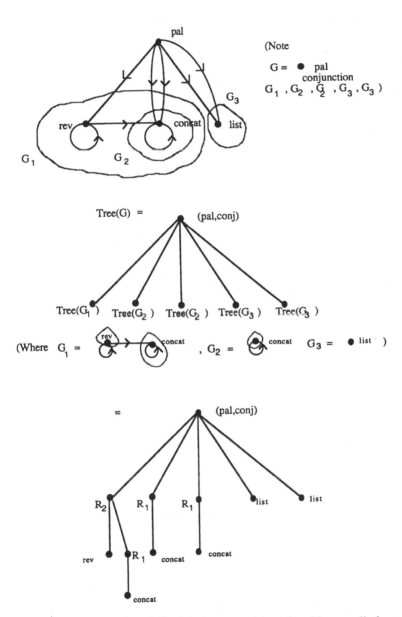

Fig. 12. Subflowgraphs of *G* with decomposition algorithm applied.

metrics is satisfied. The fact that *structural* features are of such importance to these models adds to the practical significance of our work on structural methods.

Consider as an example the popular specification language Z.[29] One of the key features of Z is the use of *schemas* for representing identifiable components of the specification. Schemas may incorporate previously defined components (or parts thereof), so that there is a well-defined relationship on schemas which may be represented as a digraph in the usual way.

Some specification notations have explicit control structure and hence may be subjected to the kind of control flow metrics described in Sections 4.1 and 4.2, provided that a suitable graphical model can be found for their representation. Once again it is argued that if control flow metrics are 'predictors' of certain complexity notions at the code level, then the earlier in the life cycle that these can be determined the more useful they will be. By way of example, we cite a recent Alvey project[36] which has investigated the correlation between control-flow metrics of OBJ specifications and the resulting implementations.

4.6 Beyond software

It is worth noting that, although our examples were chosen from the domain of software engineering, the meta-theory of structures is equally applicable to hardware, provided that the criteria of mathematical formality and compositionality are satisfied. The most obvious hardware application is in the design of complex systems or VLSI components. Other applications, already explored in an informal way, include process control systems specified in ladder diagram logic[7] and reliability models of complex systems.

ACKNOWLEDGEMENTS

We are indebted to our colleagues on the Alvey and BT projects whose comments have led to a slightly revised version of this paper. In particular, written comments were received from Bev Littlewood, Geoff Markham, Gabor Nyerges, Sinclair Stockman and Robin Whitty. We also note the original contributions of Margaret Myers, Gabor Nyerges, Ronald Prather and Robin Whitty. We would also like to thank the CSR for their invitation to write this paper, with special thanks to Bev Littlewood who has not only been supportive of our work but has often provided us with valuable insights. Finally, we are indebted to the Alvey Directorate, British Telecom Research Laboratories and South Bank Polytechnic for their part in supporting this research.

REFERENCES

1. Alvey Project SE/69, *Structured based software metrication,* Project Proposal Document, South Bank Polytechnic, 1985.
2. Basili, V. R. and Hutchens, D. H., An empirical study of a syntactic complexity family, *IEEE Trans. Software Eng.,* SE–9(6), 1983, 652–63.
3. Bache, R., *Metricating A-KINDRA,* BT Project 610287, Document W021, South Bank, 1987.
4. Bieman, J. M. and Debnath, N. C., An analysis of software structure using a generalised program graph, *Proc. COMPSAC 85,* 254–59.
5. Bieman, J. M. and Edwards, W. R., Experimental evaluation of the data dependency graph for use in measuring software clarity, *Proc. 18th Hawaii Intl. Conf. on Systems Science,* 1985, 271–6.
6. British Telecom, Project 610287: System Design Automation Facility, South Bank–BT, 1986.
7. Chandra, R. C., Low complexity functional approach to logic controller design, *IEE Proc.,* Vol. 132, Pt. E(1), 1985, 8–24.
8. Fenton, N. E., The structural complexity of flowgraphs, in: *Graph theory and its applications to Algorithms and Computer Science,* J. Wiley & Sons, 1985, 273–82.
9. Fenton, N. E. and Kaposi, A. A., Metrics and software structure, *J. Information & Software Tech.,* 29(6) 1987, 301–20.
10. Fenton, N. E., Minoughan, M., and Mole D., *Review of Program Complexity Metrics* Alvey Project Report SE/69/SPB/046.
11. Fenton, N. E., Whitty, R. W. and Kaposi, A. A., A generalised mathematical theory of structured programming, *Theor. Comp. Sci.,* 36, 1985, 145–71.
12. Fenton, N. E. and Whitty, R. W., Axiomatic approach to software metrication through program decomposition, *Computer J.* 29(4), 1986, 329–39.
13. Finkelstein, L., A review of the fundamental concepts of measurement, *Measurement* 2(1), 1984, 25–34.
14. Gilb, T., *Principles of software engineering management,* Addison Wesley, 1987.
15. Ginsburg, A. and Yoeli, M., Reducibility of synchronisation structures, *Theor. Comp. Sci.,* 40, 1985, 301–14.
16. Halstead, M. H., *Elements of software science,* Elsevier North Holland, 1977.

318 N. E. Fenton and A. A. Kaposi

17. Harrison, W. A., Software complexity metrics: a bibliography and category index, *SIGPLAN Notices*, **19**(2), 1984, 17–27.
18. Jackson, M. A., *Principles of program design*, Academic Press, 1975.
19. Jackson, M. A., *System development*, Prentice Hall, 1983.
20. Jones, C. B., *Systematic software development using VDM*, Prentice Hall, 1986.
21. Kaposi, A. A. and Jackson, L. A., A system approach to complexity management in designing information systems, *Brit. Telecom Technol. J.*, **4**(3), 1986.
22. Kearney, J. K., Sedlmeyer, R. L., Thompson, W. B., Gray, M. A. and Adler, M. A., Software complexity measurement, *CACM*, **29**(11), 1986, 1044–50.
23. Knuth, D. E., *The art of computer programming, Vol. 1: Fundamental algorithms*, Addison Wesley, 1969.
24. Kyburg, H. E., *Theory and measurement*, Cambridge University Press, 1984.
25. Lennselius, B., Wohlin, C. and Vrana, C., Software metrics: motivation and fault content estimations, *Microprocessors & Microsystems*, 1987 (in press).
26. Markusz, Z. and Kaposi, A. A., Complexity control in logic-based programming, *Comp. J.*, **28**(5), 1985, 487–96.
27. McCabe, T. J., A complexity measure, *IEEE Trans. Software Eng.* **SE2**, 1976, 308–20.
28. Mole, P. D. A., *The use of Z for the specification of the structural decomposition of control flow*, Alvey Project SE/69, Report PSB/006, 1986.
29. Morgan, C., *Schemas in Z—a preliminary reference manual*, Oxford University PRG, 1984.
30. Myers, M., *The extension of the axiomatic theory of structure to PROLOG*, Interim Report 2.4, CSSE, South Bank, June 1987.
31. Nadler, G., System methodology and design, *IEEE Trans. on Systems, Man and Cybernetics*, Vol. SMC-**15**(6), 1985, 685–97.
32. Navlakha, J. K., A survey of system complexity metrics, *Comp. J.* **30**(3), 1987, 233–8.
33. Nyerges, G., *Structural modelling and decomposition of PROLOG programs*, Interim Report W063, South Bank, 1987.
34. Prather, R. E., An axiomatic theory of software complexity measure, *Computer J.*, **27**, 340–7, 1984.
35. Prather, R. E. and Giulieri, S. G., Decomposition of flowchart schemata, *Computer J.*, **24**(3), 258–62, 1981.
36. Samson, W. B., Nevill, D. G. and Dugard, P. I., *Predictive software metrics based on a formal specification*, Alvey Project SE/75, Dundee College of Technology.
37. Sethi, R., Testing for the Church-Rosser property, *J. ACM*, **21**(4), 671–9, 1975.
38. Soloway, E., Bonar, J. and Ehrlich, K., Cognitive strategies and looping constructs: an empirical survey, *Commun. ACM*, **26**(11), 853–60, 1983.

39. Whitty, R. W., *The flowgraph model of sequential processes,* Alvey Project SE/69, Report GCL/004/01, 1987.
40. Whitty, R. W., Fenton, N. E. and Kaposi, A. A., A rigorous approach to structural analysis and metrication of software, *IEEE Software and Microsystems,* **4.1,** 2–16, 1985.
41. Wilson, R. I., *Introduction to graph theory,* Academic Press, 1972.
42. Yin, B. H. and Winchester, J. W., The establishment and use of measures to evaluate the quality of system designs, *Proc. Software Quality and Assurance Workshop,* 45–52, 1978.

14

A Conceptual Model of the Effect of Diverse Methodologies on Coincident Failures in Multi-version Software*

B. LITTLEWOOD

Centre for Software Reliability, London, UK

and

D. R. MILLER

Washington DC, USA

ABSTRACT

Eckhardt and Lee have shown that, in a precisely defined sense, the independent development of multi-version software cannot result in independence of failure behaviour. We have shown in earlier work that the use of diverse methodologies (forced diversity) for the development of the several versions may overcome this problem. Indeed, it is theoretically possible to obtain versions which exhibit better than independent behaviour. In this paper we try to formalise the notion of methodological diversity by considering the sequence of decision outcomes which comprises a methodology. We show that diversity of decisions implies likely diversity of behaviour for the different versions developed under such forced diversity. We define a measure of diversity of methodologies and show that there are simple orderings in the behavioural diversity resulting from the particular choices in design decisions. In particular it is possible to make design decisions in such a way as to optimise diversity and so minimise the chance of coincident version failure.

* Reproduced from F. Belli and W. Görke (eds), *Fault-Tolerant Computing Systems* (3rd International GI/ITG/GMA Conference, Bremerhaven, 9–11 September, 1987), Springer-Verlag, Berlin, 1987.

1. INTRODUCTION

Design fault tolerance is now established, with other software engineering practices, as a method of achieving reliability of software. However, there has only recently been available the beginnings of a theoretical framework for understanding some of the fundamental issues.

For example, in all actualisations of the fault-tolerant approach there is a tacit assumption that the benefits will arise from the *diversity* implicit in the use of several versions. One might expect that the 'more different' these versions were, the greater the toleration of faults, but until recently there did not exist any precise definition of diversity, much less measures of 'degree of diversity'.

Similarly, notions of *independence* have been crucial in the early literature. Indeed, there has been general agreement that independent failure behaviour of the versions was the ideal goal, although it has been widely acknowledged that this would be difficult to achieve. Unfortunately, little attention was paid to the relationship between the independence of the software processes involved in the creation of several versions, and the independence (or dependence) in the behaviour of the versions.

The work of Eckhardt and Lee[1,2] (EL hereafter) began to formalise some of these concepts and define their interrelationships. EL dealt with the case of several versions using a single common development methodology. Their most important achievement was to demonstrate that *truly independently* developed versions (and they give a precise definition of independence in this context) will necessarily fail *dependently*. The implications of this seem serious: it means that attempts to develop different versions independently using different programming teams (and such independence is acknowledged to be difficult to achieve) are doomed never to achieve the goal of independent failure behaviour. Indeed, such multi-version software will exhibit worse behaviour than would be the case if independence could be achieved: the probability of simultaneous failure is increased.

Our own recent work[3,4] (LM hereafter) generalises EL by introducing the idea of *diverse methodologies*. In a certain theoretical sense this rescues multi-version programming from the EL impasse, since we show that EL is a worst case which is almost never attained.

This result indicates the importance of distinguishing between *diversity of process* (the LM case) and mere *diversity of product* within a single process (the EL case). However, there is a sense in which every case of *product* diversity is a result of *process* diversity inasmuch as there will always be differences between the development processes of different versions if we look closely enough. Even the (necessary) use of different personnel, for example, can be seen as a difference in process.

This suggests that, instead of the issue of methodological diversity versus non-diversity for multi-version software, we should acknowledge the presence of *some* diversity and instead be concerned with *degrees* of diversity. It is to this question that our recent work, reported here, is addressed. First though, we shall recapitulate the EL and LM results in order to set the scene.

2. EL AND LM: THE BASIC MODELS

We shall not concern ourselves in this paper with actual fault-tolerant architectures involving adjudication. Our intention is to elucidate the more fundamental issues surrounding the execution of multi-version software on common input cases, in particular simultaneous failures. We shall, in addition, restrict ourselves for simplicity to the case of two versions.

The EL model, augmented slightly for clarity, is as follows. For a particular set of requirements there is, conceptually at least, a population of all programs which might be written: $\mathcal{P} \equiv \{\pi_1, \pi_2, \ldots\}$. The development of an actual product is then the random selection of a program π from $\mathcal{P}$, i.e. the product is a random variable Π with $P(\Pi = \pi) = S(\pi)$ for some measure $S(\cdot)$ over $\mathcal{P}$.

Execution of a program version involves the random selection of an input case x from the input space $\mathcal{X} = \{x_1, x_2, \ldots\}$. Here $P(X = x) = Q(x)$ for some measure $Q(\cdot)$ over $\mathcal{X}$, which can be thought of as the usage distribution over the inputs.

The failure behaviour of a program is described by the score function $v(\pi, x)$ which takes the value 1 if π fails on x, and 0 otherwise. Thus the random variable $v(\Pi, X)$ represents the behaviour of a randomly chosen program on a randomly chosen input.

A key average measure is then

$$\theta(x) = E_S[c(\Pi, x)] = \sum_{\mathcal{P}} v(\pi, x)S(\pi) \tag{1}$$

which is the probability that a randomly chosen program fails for the particular input case x. It can be thought of as the proportion of all programs which would fail on x.

The key to EL's model[1,2] lies in their observation that $\theta(x)$ will usually take different values for different x. This represents the fact that some inputs are intrinsically more difficult to process correctly than others, corresponding, in some sense, to harder parts of the problem being solved.

For a randomly chosen input, X, $\theta(X)$ is a random variable, Θ. The variability in the magnitudes of the θs over the inputs can be represented by

$$G(\theta) = P(\Theta < \theta) \tag{2}$$

By a similar argument

$$\phi(\pi) = E_Q[v(\pi, X)] = \sum_{\mathscr{X}} v(\pi, x)Q(x) \tag{3}$$

is the probability that a given program π fails on a randomly chosen input. Thus $1 - \phi(\pi)$ is the reliability of the program π, and is a realisation of a random variable $1 - \Phi$ since different programs will have different reliabilities. Clearly $E(\Phi) = E(\Theta)$ and represents the probability that a randomly chosen program fails on a randomly chosen input.

Consider now the independent creation of two program versions. This is the selection of Π_1, Π_2 independently from $\mathscr{P}$, i.e. $P(\Pi_1 = \pi_1, \Pi_2 = \pi_2) = P(\Pi_1 = \pi_1) \cdot P(\Pi_2 = \pi_2)$. It follows[3] that

$$P(\Pi_2 \text{ fails on } x \mid \Pi_1 \text{ failed on } x) = P(\Pi_2 \text{ fails on } x) \tag{4}$$

However, for a *randomly chosen input*[4]

$$P(\Pi_2 \text{ fails} \mid \Pi_1 \text{ failed}) \geqslant P(\Pi_2 \text{ fails}) \tag{5}$$

with equality if and only if $\theta(x) \equiv \theta$ for all x.

This is the crux of EL: it shows that 'independent programs' do not in general 'fail independently'; indeed, they exhibit *worse* behaviour than the naive assumption would suggest. The reason is unexpected and concerns the variability of the θs. Intuitively, the fact of Π_1's failure makes us believe that the input selected 'probably had a large θ', and so makes us believe more strongly that Π_2 will also fail on that input. This argument can be formalised[2,4] in a stochastic ordering:

$$\Theta \mid \Pi_1 \text{ has failed} \overset{st}{>} \Theta \tag{6}$$

Since the problem lies in the variability of the θs over the input space, we might expect that the degree of this variability determines the seriousness of the problem. In fact, for the randomly chosen input

$$P(\Pi_1, \Pi_2 \text{ both fail}) = [E(\Theta)]^2 + \text{Var}(\Theta) \qquad (7)$$

The first term here is the answer we would get if, incorrectly and naively, we assumed independent failure behaviour. The variance of the $G(\cdot)$ distribution, then, indicates the degree of departure from this naive answer. Only when all $\theta(x)$ are identical, and hence the variance zero, do we get independent failure behaviour.

LM[3,4] generalise this set-up so as to admit more than one development methodology. We assume that each methodology induces a measure on $\mathcal{P}$, the set of all possible program versions. Thus for method M_1 we have $P(\Pi_{M_1} = \pi) = S_{M_1}(\pi)$. In practice it seems likely that a particular program would have a non-zero probability of selection under only one methodology, i.e. methodologies will form a *partition* of the program space $\mathcal{P}$.

Within a particular methodology the situation is as for EL, with $\theta_{M_1}(x)$ representing the probability of a randomly chosen M_1 failing on input x, etc. The key idea here is that the θs will not vary not only from one x to another, but also from one methodology to another. This last will happen because different methodologies will not be identical in the ways they find input cases 'difficult'.

It turns out that this new source of diversity, between methodologies, removes the impasse in the EL scenario (represented by eqns (5), (6) and (7) where the only diversity available is that of *versions within a single methodology*. In fact, using an obvious notation for the two version case, for a program Π_{M_1} chosen randomly from M_1 and Π_{M_2} chosen independently and randomly from M_2

$$P(\Pi_{M_1}, \Pi_{M_2} \text{ both fail}) = E(\Theta_{M_1})E(\Theta_{M_2}) + \text{Cov}(\Theta_{M_1}, \Theta_{M_2}) \qquad (8)$$

for a randomly selected input.[3,4] Once again, the second term represents the modification to the naive assumption of independent behaviour represented by the first term. However, in this case it can be either positive or negative; in the event that it were negative we would have a two-version system with failure behaviour *better than independence*. Although this may be an unattainable practical goal, the EL result can be seen to be the most pessimistic version of eqn (8) and will occur only when Θ_{M_1} and Θ_{M_2} are identical (i.e. $\theta_{M_1}(x) = \theta_{M_2}(x) \; \forall x$), i.e. when the methodologies are the same. We believe that the development of two versions will always, in practice, involve some methodological differences (if only cultural differences of the personnel involved) and so this worst-case scenario will never happen.

This being so, we need to consider the degree to which methodological diversity can help. This is determined by factors such as $\text{Cov}(\Theta_{M_1}, \Theta_{M_2})$ in eqn (8) and it seems implausible to us that it will be possible to measure or estimate these in practice. The problem is that they are averages over populations of programs which *could* be written to satisfy a particular set of requirements. However, even though quantification of diversity may not be possible, there are orderings of diversity (with corresponding orderings on probabilities of coincident failure) which could be useful in the design of multi-version software. We consider these next.

3. DESIGN DECISIONS AND DEGREES OF DIVERSITY

Another way of looking at the EL scenario is as an *aggregation* of the multi-methodology LM case. This can be shown formally if we assume that there are very many methodologies and none of them dominate; then the Θ random variable for EL is a mixture of the Θ_M random variables corresponding to the different constituent methodologies.

This ideas throws some light on how we might model the process of *design for diversity*. Consider a single design decision (an example might be to use, or not to use, a particular programming language). This will create two methodologies and it seems reasonable, as we have argued earlier, that these form a *partition* of the program space $\mathcal{P}$ into A and $\bar{A}$ (Fig. 1). There will be more than one design decision possible, and a second decision could now be taken (e.g. to use, or not to use, a particular testing strategy). This will partition $\mathcal{P}$ into B and $\bar{B}$ (Fig. 2), giving now four different methodologies.

This design process would continue to partition $\mathcal{P}$ more finely. At any stage we can think of there being an aggregation over possible later decision outcomes. Thus a blind choice of a pair of versions from $\mathcal{P}$ is an aggregation over the $(A, \bar{A})$ decision: it gives the EL case, in contrast to the LM case of one version from A and one from $\bar{A}$. Similarly, A and $\bar{A}$ are each aggregations over $(B, \bar{B})$, and so on.

The important questions are whether it is possible to quantify, or at least order, the amount of diversity in such cases, and whether greater diversity necessarily implies better failure behaviour. Is there a sense,

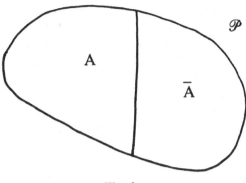

Fig. 1.

for example, in which a two-version $(AB, \bar{A}\bar{B})$ system is better than a two-version $(AB, A\bar{B})$?

Theorem 1 (see Ref. 8 for proof). If (1) $P(A \cap B) = P(A)P(B)$ and (2) we are indifferent between certain methodological choices related by permutations of labelling then

$$E(\Theta_{AB}\Theta_{\bar{A}\bar{B}}) = E(\Theta_{A\bar{B}}\Theta_{\bar{A}B}) < E(\Theta_{AB}\Theta_{A\bar{B}}) = E(\Theta_{AB}\Theta_{\bar{A}B}) = \cdots$$

The first condition here asserts that the decisions about A and B are logically unrelated in the sense that a developer left to his or her own devices would not allow the B or $\bar{B}$ decision to be influenced by the A or $\bar{A}$ decision. It may often be the case, for example, that a decision on testing regime is unrelated to a decision on language.

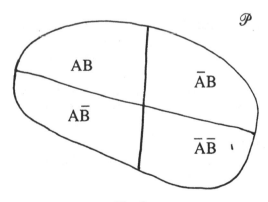

Fig. 2.

The second condition first of all states that we are indifferent between the four methodologies AB, $\bar{A}B$, $A\bar{B}$, $\bar{A}\bar{B}$ in the following sense. If we were to build a two-version program by randomly selecting two versions independently from a single methodology, we would not prefer any methodology over any other, in the sense that the probability of both versions failing on a randomly selected input is the same in all cases. Secondly, if we were to build a two-version program by randomly selecting the versions from *two* methodologies, we would be similarly indifferent between the $(AB, A\bar{B})$, $(AB, \bar{A}B)$, $(\bar{A}B, \bar{A}\bar{B})$ and $(A\bar{B}, \bar{A}\bar{B})$ choices.

Under these conditions, the theorem tells us that greater diversity of design decisions results in a greater chance of freedom from coincident failures. It can thus be seen as a means of relating the development process of a two-version system to the likely behaviour of the resulting product. The $(AB, \bar{A}\bar{B})$ methodologies exhibit more 'decision diversity' than the $(AB, A\bar{B})$ methodologies, and a randomly chosen two-version system from the former has less chance of coincident failure on a randomly chosen input than one chosen from the latter.

The theorem has been stated in its simplest form, but it extends obviously in two ways. Firstly, we can have non-binary decisions: instead of A, $\bar{A}$ we could have an $A_1, A_2, \ldots, A_n$ partition. Secondly we can have more than two levels of decision: A, B, $C \ldots$. Then, as an example, $(A_1 B_1 C_1, A_2 B_2 C_2)$ are more diverse methodologies than $(A_1 B_1 C_1, A_2 B_1 C_2)$ and consequently would be preferred when building a two-version system. In turn, $(A_1 B_1 C_1, A_2 B_1 C_2)$ are more diverse than $(A_1 B_1 C_1, A_2 B_1 C_1)$, and so on. Of course, similar independence and indifference conditions to those of Theorem 1 are needed.

These results relate to *ordering* of levels of diversity in this special situation of independent design factors. We think it is unlikely that quantification of diversity will be possible in general, but it should be possible to work with subjective or qualitative feelings about diversity and derive additional preferences or even show inconsistencies.

Consider the case of three methodologies M_1, M_2, M_3, where we feel that (M_1, M_3) are more diverse than (M_1, M_2) or (M_2, M_3). This can be represented schematically as in Fig. 3.

Now remember that a methodology is completely characterised by its $\theta(\cdot)$ function. The geometric representation of Fig. 3 can be formalised if we define a distance in this function space:

$$\|\theta_{M_i} - \theta_{M_j}\|^2 = \int (\theta_{M_i}(x) - \theta_{M_j}(x))^2 \, \mathrm{d}Q(x) \tag{9}$$

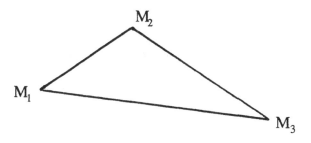

Fig. 3.

Clearly, $\|\theta_{M_i} - \theta_{M_j}\|^2 > 0$ unless $\theta_{M_i} \equiv \theta_{M_j}$. It follows trivially that

$$\int \theta_{M_i}(x)\theta_{M_j}(x)\,dQ(x) < \int \theta_{M_i}^2(x)\,dQ(x) = \int \theta_M^2(x)\,dQ(x)$$

if we assume indifference between methodologies for constructing two-version systems from a single methodology. This is precisely the LM result which says that the forced diversity (M_i, M_j) two-version choice is better than either an M_i two-version choice or an M_j two-version choice.

Using eqn. (9) as a measure of degree of diversity, we can now show that greater diversity gives less chance of coincident failures:

Theorem 2 (see Ref. 8 for proof). If (1) (M_1, M_3) are more diverse than (M_1, M_2), i.e.

$$\|\theta_{M_1} - \theta_{M_3}\| > \|\theta_{M_1} - \theta_{M_2}\|$$

and (2) we are indifferent between non-diverse two-version systems, i.e.

$$E(\Theta_{M_1}^2) = E(\Theta_{M_2}^2) = E(\Theta_{M_3}^2)$$

then

$$E(\Theta_{M_1}\Theta_{M_3}) < E(\Theta_{M_1}\Theta_{M_2})$$

It is unlikely that we could obtain the distance measure, eqn (9), in practice (although it might be interesting to investigate this experimentally in a suitably simple case). An assertion that one pair of methodologies is more diverse than another will therefore necessarily be an essentially subjective judgement. However, Theorem 1 shows that such a judgement can be based on the number of complementary decisions in the possible pairs of methodologies.

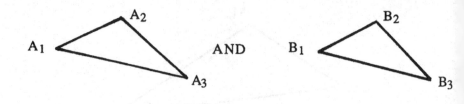

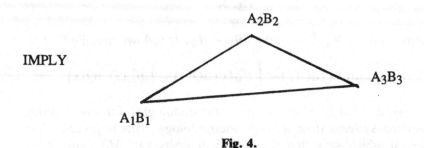

Fig. 4.

We are now in a position to try to combine the ideas of Theorems 1 and 2. Consider the case of two decisions (i.e. two partitions of $\mathcal{P}$), each of three cases: A_1, A_2, A_3 and B_1, B_2, B_3. Assume the same independence and indifference conditions exist as before.

Conjecture. If (1) (A_1, A_3) is more diverse than (A_1, A_2) or (A_2, A_3) and (2) (B_1, B_3) is more diverse than (B_1, B_2) or (B_2, B_3) then (A_1B_1, A_3B_3) is more diverse than (A_1B_1, A_2B_2), etc.

Figure 4 shows a schematic representation of this.

4. CONCLUSIONS

The results of Eckhardt and Lee can be viewed as concerning multi-version software *within a single methodology*. They show that the apparently desirable goal of independent failure behaviour of the different versions is essentially unattainable. Actual behaviour will be worse than would be the case if the versions exhibited independent behaviour. The reason for this result is unexpected: it lies in the varying 'difficulty', or 'failure-proneness', of the possible inputs. The greater this variation, the worse the problem.

Our own work has been motivated by the realisation that, in a sense, different versions *never come from a single methodology.* If we look sufficiently closely there will always be some methodological differences: for example, even the necessary use of different personnel can be seen in this way.

Starting from this viewpoint, we have formalised the notion of forced diversity: multi-version software with *diversity of methodologies.* We show that EL is a worst case in this scenario and will, in general, never be attained. Quite surprisingly, it is possible to do better than the case of independent failure behaviour. This happens when the error-proneness of the inputs are negatively correlated, i.e. there is a tendency for an input which is highly error-prone for versions from one methodology to be much less so for versions from other methodologies. Whether this can be exploited in practice is a matter which needs experimental investigation.

Whatever results from such studies, it seems clear that it will never be the case that methodologies can be specially created to have these desirable properties. The most we can hope for is that in a particular context it will be possible to take advantage of 'natural' methodological diversity. It seems clear, though, that there will be different ways of doing this and some will be better than others.

It is to this question that our later (and current) work is addressed. It relates the software development *process* (here choice of methodologies) to the failure behaviour of *products* (versions). In particular, we are interested in whether it is possible to understand the way in which the 'diversity of version behaviour' (specifically, low probability of simultaneous version failure) depends on 'diversity of methodologies'.

In Section 3 we present some results which, in a simple and restricted context, formalise this relationship. We begin with a notion of methodology based on design decisions: here a methodology is specified completely by the decisions which have been taken, represented formally by partitions of the program space $\mathcal{P}$. We show that the diversity of the design decisions involved in these methodologies determines the diversity of the likely behaviour of the versions (Theorem 1).

Observing that the vector of θs specifies a methodology completely for our purposes, we next define a 'distance' measure for two methodologies: this can be understood as a measure of their diversity. We show that the greater the diversity of methodology (according to this measure), the greater the diversity of behaviour (chance of no coincident failure) (Theorem 2).

An elementary design decision can be thought of as giving rise to diverse methodologies since it induces a partition of $\mathcal{P}$. Therefore the above distance measure also represents the extent of diversity between alternative decision outcomes. We finally conjecture how multiple decisions should be combined so as to maximise the likely behavioural diversity of the resulting versions.

It seems certain that we shall never know the exact 'distance' between two methodologies (although it might be interesting to estimate this using the replicated-run, multi-version approach).[5,6,7] However, developers might build up considerable experience, over many projects, of the diversity in the available decisions at the many stages of the design process. These results indicate how such knowledge may be used optimally in the creation of multi-version software.

ACKNOWLEDGEMENT

D. R. Miller was supported by National Aeronautics and Space Administration, USA, under Grant NAG-1-179. B. Littlewood was partially supported under the same grant, and partially by the Alvey Directorate/Science and Engineering Research Council, UK.

REFERENCES

1. Eckhardt, D. E. and Lee, L. D., A theoretical basis for the analysis of redundant software subject to coincident errors, *NASA Tech. Memorandum*, No. 86369, Jan. 1985.
2. Eckhardt, D. E. and Lee, L. D., A theoretical basis for the analysis of multi-version software subject to coincident errors, *IEEE Trans. on Software Engineering*, **SE-11**(12), 1511–17, 1985.
3. Littlewood, B. and Miller, D. R., A conceptual model of multi-version software, *Digest of 17th Annual Symposium on Fault-tolerant Computing* FTCS-17, Pittsburgh, July 1987, IEEE Computer Society Press, 150–5.
4. Littlewood, B. and Miller, D. R., A conceptual model of multi-version software, *CSR Tech. Report*, December 1986 (available from first author.)
5. Knight, J. C. and Leveson, N. G., An empirical study of failure probabilities in multi-version software, *Digest of 16th Annual Symposium on Fault-tolerant Computing* (FTCS–16), Vienna, 165–90, 1986.
6. Nagel, P. M., *et al.*, Software reliability: additional investigations into modelling with replicated experiments, *NASA Contractor Rep.*, 172378, June 1984.

7. Kelly, J. P. J. and Avizienis, A., A specification-oriented multi-version software experiment, *Digest of 13th Annual Symposium on Fault-tolerant Computing* (FCTS–13), Milan, 120–6, 1983.
8. Littlewood, B. and Miller, D. R., A conceptual model of the effect of diverse methodologies on coincident failures in multi-version software, *CSR Tech. Report,* June 1986 (available from first author).

15

The Relationship between Specification and Implementation Metrics

W. B. Samson, P. I. Dugard, D. G. Nevill, P. E. Oldfield,
A. W. Smith

Dundee College of Technology, Dundee, UK

and

G. Titterington
STC Technology Ltd, Newcastle-under-Lyme, UK

ABSTRACT

A set of metrics is proposed for algebraic specification languages and for implementation languages. These metrics are determined for data comprising five algebraic specifications and matching implementations. A statistical analysis highlights a number of correlations between specification and implementation metrics, and indicates that prediction of code size in terms of lines of code is possible. The prediction formulae are found to vary from data set to data set, indicating the importance of a consistent implementation style.

1. INTRODUCTION AND BACKGROUND

One perennial problem facing computing professionals is that of estimating development effort early in the life-cycle of a software product. Any estimation, in any field of engineering, must be based on some kind of specification. For example, the cost of developing a hardware product will normally be estimated on the basis of drawings and/or a bill of materials, coupled with knowledge gained from previous experience of developing similar products. In some cases, a prototype or model will be built in order to assess alternative options in the final product.

A parallel may be drawn with the development of a software product. Unfortunately, cost estimation is, in practice, based almost entirely on informal guesswork by an experienced software engineer, who has available a functional requirements document for the product. The functional requirements document is usually written in natural language, and contains little or no explicit reference to design alternatives. In effect, then, software engineers have been trying to estimate costs at an earlier stage in the development process than their hardware colleagues, whose estimates are based on a detailed design specification.

There is clearly a need to formalise the estimation process, but a number of difficulties remain to be overcome. The most immediate difficulty facing workers in this area is a lack of data. A Software Data Library[10] is currently being built up, but little data is yet available in terms of development effort, standardised requirements and design documentation. Until such data is available in large enough quantities to enable reliable statistical analyses to be done, it is only possible to look at some specific cases.

The authors have been able to collect a number of data sets which comprise an algebraic specification and a matching implementation. While executable algebraic specifications are often criticised as requirements specifications for their lack of abstraction, when compared with model-based specification languages such as VDM or Z, they have been successfully adopted for design specifications and rapid prototyping. The most widely used languages in this area are OBJ,[6] HOPE[2] and ML.[8]

Engineers using algebraic specification in the software development process take varying approaches to the transformation of specification into implementation. Probably the least formal approach involves coding the top level implementations independently and using the specification to identify test cases against which the implementation is to be verified.

At the other extreme,[3] the software engineer would start off by writing a requirements specification for top-level operators in terms of predicates. The second step is to identify constructor operators for the data types involved, and to specify all operators algebraically in terms of their values when applied to an exhaustive set of combinations of constructors for their arguments. These algebraic specifications are then verified against the requirements specification.

The engineer has, by this stage, effectively taken some design decisions. For example, if a sorting routine is specified algebraically, it will be easily identifiable as a tree-sort, quick-sort or whatever, by inspection of its specification. The engineer must now decide on the concrete representation of his/her, until now, 'abstract' data types. For example, a list may be represented by, say, an array, or by a linked list using pointers. Having chosen the representation, an abstract model of the representation is specified, and then an abstraction function is defined, which maps the abstract representation onto the abstract data type, allowing operators on the abstract representation to be verified.

The software engineer now has an abstract representation which is close to the chosen implementation. A set of selector operators must be defined which operate in such a way as to decompose the constructors with parameters into these parameters. For example, a list may use constructors

$$\text{empty:} \ \rightarrow \ \text{list}$$
$$\text{cons} \ : \ \text{item} \times \text{list} \ \rightarrow \ \text{list}$$

The operator 'cons' has two parameters, which may be decomposed using the selector operators

$$\text{head} \ : \ \text{list} \ \rightarrow \ \text{item}$$
$$\text{tail} \ \ \ : \ \text{list} \ \rightarrow \ \text{list}$$

to return the head and tail of a list in the usual way.

Using these selectors, the left-hand side pattern matching which is common to all executable algebraic specification languages may be replaced by explicit conditions on the right hand side; e.g.

$$\text{right\_append} \ : \ \text{list} \times \text{item} \ \rightarrow \ \text{list}$$

may be defined using pattern matching as:

$$(\text{right\_append(empty, x)} = \text{cons(x, empty)} \ )$$
$$(\text{right\_append(cons(h, t), x)} =$$
$$\text{cons(h, right\_append(t, x))} \ )$$

The equivalent equations *without* left-hand side pattern matching are then (in OBJ syntax)

$$(\text{right\_append(l, x)} = \text{cons(x, empty) if l} = \text{empty})$$
$$(\text{right\_append(l, x)} = \text{cons(head(l), right\_append(}$$
$$\text{tail(l), x)) if l} \neq \text{empty})$$

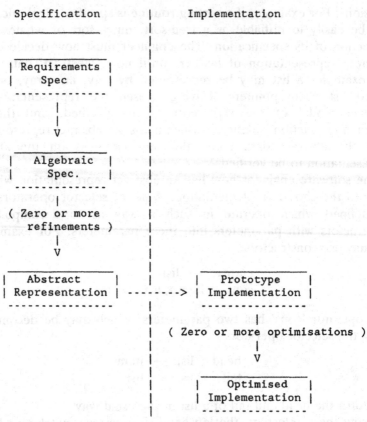

Fig. 1. Transition between specification and implementation.

or (ML syntax)

```
fun right_append (l: list, x: item): list =
    if l = empty then cons(x, empty)
        else cons(head(l), right_append(tail(l), x))
```

This is very easily transformed into the implementation function
(Pascal syntax)

```
function right_append(l: list, x: item): list;
begin
    if l = empty then
        right_append := cons(x, empty)
```

```
        else right_append := cons(head (l),
                        right_append (tail(l), x))
    end
```

assuming, of course, that a suitable data type 'list' has been declared, as have operators cons, empty, head and tail.

Having written a prototype implementation in this way, the engineer may then wish to optimise it by, for example, replacing recursion by iteration; by 'sharing' data areas to avoid duplication of data structure, by modifying data structures to make commonly used operators more efficient, and so on.

The work described in this paper deals with specification and corresponding implementation at the point of transformation. Optimisation is therefore ignored, as is requirements specification.

The sets of specifications and matching implementations discussed below have all been developed in the spirit of the methodology outlined in Fig. 1, although some differences at a detailed level were discovered during the analysis. These differences will be discussed further below; see Appendix A for full details.

2. DATA SOURCES

This report contains five data sets consisting of specifications written in either HOPE or OBJ, and the matching implementations developed from them, written in C or Modula 2. These matched pairs are analysed to determine whether any predictive equation can be found to apply to the specifications, which will return an accurate estimate of implementation metrics. Three of the data sets, SE1, SE2 and SE3, were collected from the Postgraduate Diploma Class in Software Engineering, one, ANDY, from A. Wakelin (Research Assistant), all of whom are presently working at Dundee College of Technology, and one data set, EVA, from E. Wong,[11] also formerly of the college.

The EVA data set specifies an Abstract Data Base, with specification written in HOPE and implemented in MODULA-2. A. Wakelin's data set performs database operations and is specified in HOPE and implemented in C. The three Software Engineering data sets are different versions of a Kwic Index, all of which are specified in OBJ and implemented in C.

3. DEFINITIONS OF METRICS FOR SPECIFICATION LANGUAGES

3.1. Method of determining OBJ metrics

The following metrics were determined for the OBJ specifications which constituted part of the 'SE' data:

1. Cyclomatic 1, equation count + and/or count. This is referred to in short as 'm1'. This is intended as a predictor for a McCabe-like metric. To obtain the value for this metric, for each operator specified start with a count of zero; add one for each occurrence of the boolean operators 'AND' or 'OR'; add one for each equation, within the specification of the given operator.

2. Cyclomatic 2; count of equations with distinct RHS. Also referred to as 'm2' for short. This is intended to predict the value for a McCabe-like metric that gives for an operator a count of the number of pieces of sequential code in the implementation of the operator being specified. Add 1 for each equation for a given operator that has a unique rewrite term. Duplicated rewrite terms are only counted once. Note that 'AND' and 'OR' operators are ignored in this case.

3. Number of calls to user-defined routines, ignoring selectors. Also referred to as 's1' in short. This is an attempt at a degree of structure predictor. Add 1 for each call in the RHS of an equation for a given operator to a different user-defined operator, implied selectors from pattern matching against data constructors excepted. Implied selectors are discussed later in the section on predicting vocabulary metrics. These could be implemented as either in-built or user-defined operators, affecting the implementation metric that we are attempting to predict here.

4. Calls on user-defined routines, ignoring recursion and selectors. Also referred to as 's2' in short. This is an attempt to define a degree of structure predictor. Add 1 for each call in the RHS of an equation for a given operator to a different user-defined operator, implied selectors from pattern matching against data constructors, and recursive calls, excepted.

   Note: this presupposes that selectors are user-defined if explicitly specified, in-built in the target language if implied.

6. Halstead-like n1, including implied selectors from pattern

matched terms on LHS of equations. The number of distinct operators occurring within the equations defining an operator. Add one for each new identifier that identifies an OBJ operator that takes some parameters or arguments. Also for each variable used in the equations describing an operator; if that variable occurs on the RHS of an equation, and that variable does not occur at the lowest possible level of nesting on the LHS of the same equation, add 1 for a predicted selector for that argument.

Note: If an implied condition test occurs on the LHS of an equation, i.e. test by pattern matching, this is counted as if the test reads 'IF $a = b$' where a and b will be non-unique operands.

Note also: If an LHS constructor-based term is rewritten unchanged on the RHS of the equation, it is considered to be a single, distinct operand rather than several selectors, constructors and operands.

7. Halstead-like N1; this is an attempt to predict the number of operators occurring in the implementation of the specified operator. Predicted selectors (see n1 above) are counted once for each mention of the relevant variable on the RHS of the equation. Also add one for each occurrence in the equations defining an operator of an operator as defined in n1 above.

   Note: see note for metric 6; add 2 for each constructor to be pattern matched on the LHS of the equation provided: (i) that the constructor has not already occurred in that position in a previous equation for the same operator; and (ii) that there is at least one more constructor which may occur in that position but which has not yet appeared there. The reasoning behind this last proviso is that if a term is known to be one of a finite set, but also known not to be all but one of that same set, then its identity can be deduced without testing.

8. Halstead-like n2; the number of distinct *operands* occurring within the equations defining an operator. Add one for each new identifier on the LHS of the equations that identifies an OBJ operator that takes no parameters or arguments; add one for each new variable or numeral.

   Note: see note for metric 6.

9. Halstead-like N2; operands on LHS not counted. Add one for each occurrence in the RHS of equations defining an operator of an operand as defined in n2 above.

Note: see note for metric 7. Add 2 on each occasion that 2 would be added to the value of N1 because of pattern matching on the LHS of the equation.

10. Vocabulary; n1 + n2 (see 6 and 8 above). This metric, referred to in short as voc, is intended to predict the number of distinct operators and operands in the implemented code. Add the value of metrics 6 + 8, giving the value of voc.
11. Length; N1 + N2 (see 7 and 9 above). This metric, referred to in short as 'len', is an attempt to predict the total number of independent tokens in the implemented code generated from the specification. Add the value of metrics 7 + 9 to give the value of len.
12. Volume; Halstead-like Vol. This metric, referred to in short as 'vol', is an attempt to predict the volume (after Halstead) of the implemented code. It is obtained by applying the formula.

$$\text{length} * \log_2(\text{voc})$$

where length = N1 + N2; voc = n1 + n2.

Example (from SE1)

```
VARS t1 : title
     ts1 : titlesequence
EQNS
     (cat(^ts, ts1) = ts1)
     (cat(^ts(t1, ts1), ts2) = ^ts(t1, cat(ts1, ts2)))
```

There are two distinct rewrite terms, ts1 and ^ts(t1, cat(ts1, ts2)), two equations, no 'and' or 'or', no duplicate rewrite terms. Thus m1 and m2 are both equal to 2. Two user-defined operators, ^ts and cat, are called on the RHS of the equations, once each. Thus s1 equals 2. However, the call to the function cat is recursive, and does not add to s2. Thus s2 equals 1. There is a constructor-based term on the LHS of the second equation; ^ts(t1, ts1), so there must be selectors, for t1 and ts1 where mentioned on the RHS (unless the whole constructor-based term occurs). The constructor-based term, ^ts, in the same position in the first equation, has no arguments. The two constructors ^ts and ^ts are the only ones that may occur in that position on the LHS of the equations for cat, thus a single condition test is implied; any term not constructed from ^ts must be constructed from ^ts. Thus implied operators are IF, = = (from implied condition test), t1, ts1 (implied selectors). The two explicitly mentioned operators are ^ts and cat, as for s1. Operands are t1, ts1 and ts2, with ts1 occurring twice, but make no statement as to their identity; i.e., they do not count as distinct operands. Thus the values for n1 and N1 are both 6, n2 equals 4, N2 equals 6. The values for voc, len and vol are derived from these four. The values of the metrics are summarised below:

name	m1	m2	s1	s2	n1	N1	n2	N2	voc	len	vol
cat	2	2	2	1	6	6	4	6	10	12	40

3.2 Method of obtaining Hope metrics
Where the specifications are written in HOPE, the metrics are the same as for OBJ with the following exceptions (all due to the availability of if_then_else in HOPE)

1. As 'm1' in OBJ, but add one for each if_then_else occurrence in the equations for a given operator.
2. As 'm2' for OBJ but instead of counting distinct RHS terms, consider only that part after 'then' or 'else' where there is an occurrence of the 'if_then_else' operator.
6. As 'n1' for OBJ, but where there is an implied condition test assume an occurrence of the operators 'if_then_else' and ' = ' instead of 'IF' and ' = = '.
7. As 'N1' for OBJ, but see 'n1' above.

4. DEFINITIONS OF METRICS FOR IMPLEMENTATION LANGUAGES

4.1 Method of determining 'C' metrics
All of the metrics below are obtained from the function bodies only; the declarations part is excluded. This method compares closely with the other implementation methods, with slight differences being noted in cyclomatic complexity.[9] This is simply due to the use of different keywords for similar actions.

1. Cyclomatic complexity—obtained by counting the keywords 'if', 'while', 'for', 'case', along with the symbols '$\delta\delta$', and '11' (logical 'and', and 'or'). One is added for the basic control path.

2. Cyclomatic complexity as above, without counting the 'and's and 'or's.
3. Degree of structure 1—count calls to functions, excluding calls to 'return' values. Includes the number of recursive calls.
4. Degree of structure 2—as 3, but without recursive calls.
5. Number of executable statements, obtained by counting the number of semicolons. Initially, this count included local declarations. However, these have nothing to do with the specification equations, and so are now excluded from the count.
6. n1 count—the number of different operators, excluding the number of control structures
   Note: From the expression 'X = Y * 3;', the operators are '=' and '*'. The operands are 'X', 'Y' and '3'.
   Control structures are those keywords found in 2,—cyclomatic complexity without and/ors, along with the keyword 'else', which does not add to the program's complexity but is nevertheless a control structure. Another control structure is 'braces' which are equivalent to 'BEGIN – END' control structures. Also excluded are round brackets and commas, which are control structures for function calls.
7. N1 count—the total number of operators in the function; i.e., the amounts of each operator, from 6, added together.
8. n2 count—the number of different operands. See *Note* in 6, and worked example below.
9. N2 count—the total number of operands.
10. Voc—vocabulary of the function. Add up the number of different operators and operands used, i.e. n1 + n2.
11. Length of the function. Add up the total number of operators and operands, i.e. N1 + N2.
12. Volume of the function—length * $\log_2$(Vocabulary).

Notes 6–12 above are metrics first formulated by M. H. Halstead.[7] Elshoff[5] showed that the exact method of metrics collection was not the important factor; instead, the method must remain consistent over all collections of data.

Example
Given below is an example of C code, and the metrics derived

```
pointtitle dotitle()
{
```

```
              char * tpoint;
              if ((fcount = 0) || (fcount = 10))
                {
                return (snoct(dotitle(), mktitle() ));
                }
              else
                {return(tpoint);
                }
            }
```

This gives for Halstead (metrics 6–9):

Metric 6 (n1) will have a total of five, being the operators:

$$= =, \text{return, snoct, dotitle, mktitle.}$$

Metric 7 (N1) will have a total of seven, this being the sum of all the operators shown above; i.e., there are two ' = ' and 'return' operators, and one of each of the others.
Metric 8 (n2) has a total of four, being the operands:

$$\text{fcount, 0, 10, and tpoint}$$

Metric 9 (N2) has a total of five as there are two 'fcount' operands.

The full list of metrics is as follows:

	Metrics											
	1	2	3	4	5	6	7	8	9	10	11	12
FNAME												
dotitle	3	2	3	2	2	5	7	4	5	9	12	38

4.2. Method of determining 'Modula-2' Metrics

All of the metrics are obtained from the procedure or function bodies within *implementation modules* only; i.e., between the BEGIN and END of the procedure/function body. This keeps the method consistent with the metrics collected from the bodies of C functions only.
Modula-2 key (metric number)

1. Cyclomatic complexity—obtained by counting the keywords 'IF', 'WHILE', 'FOR', 'AND', 'OR', 'REPEAT' and 'ELSIF'. The symbol ';' has been included here as it compares with the keyword 'WHEN' in ADA CASE statements, and cannot be used in IF statements. One is added for the basic control path.
2. Count of McCabes as above, without the 'AND's and 'OR's. McCabe's complexity metric is explained more fully in Ref. 9.

3. Degree of structure—count of calls to procedures/functions. This includes the number of recursive calls.
4. Degree of structure without recursive calls.
5. Number of executable statements, obtained by counting the number of semicolons.
6. n1 count—the number of different operators, excluding the number of control structures. Brackets and commas were also excluded.
7. N1 count—the total number of operators in the function.
8. n2 count—the number of different operands.
9. N2 count—the total number of operands.
10. Vocabulary of the function: n1 + n2.
11. Length of the function: N1 + N2.
12. Volume of the function: length $* \log_2$(vocabulary).

5. STATISTICAL ANALYSIS OF RESULTS

The five data sets SE1, SE2, SE3, ANDY and EVA were analysed separately as they were the work of three programming teams and two individuals. Tables of the results of determining the above metrics for the data sets are provided in Appendix B. It seems likely that successful prediction can be developed for a particular programmer or team, but that some predictors will not be transferrable from one team to another. We consider three aspects of the results: (1) correlations among implementation metrics; (2) relationships between specifications and implementations for the same metric; and (3) relationships between implemented lines of code and specification metrics.

5.1 Correlations between implementation metrics

Table 1 shows the correlations between the two cyclomatic complexity metrics for the target code implementations of the five data sets. Clearly these two metrics are very similar. A correlation of plus or minus one between two metrics would imply that they were linearly related, so that once one were known, no further information would be obtainable from the other. Only SE2 has a correlation less than 0.9. This group used a rather eccentric method of implementing one of the operators in the target language, using several 'or' operators. Also shown are the correlations between the two structure metrics. Again, SE2 is the only group with a correlation less than 0·9. This group used

Table 1
Correlations between McCabes with and/or and without and/or from the implementations.
SE1 1·000 SE2 0·422 SE3 0·925 ANDY 0·955 EVA 0·913

Correlations between two structure metrics from the implementations
SE1 0·947 SE2 0·842 SE3 0·989 ANDY 0·948 EVA 0·981

recursive techniques more than the others. The two metrics were chosen since it is largely a matter of programming style whether recursive specifications are implemented recursively or as loops. Thus, for a particular programmer or group, one metric should be consistently better than the other where recursive specifications occur.

Correlations among the four basic Halstead's metrics are shown in Table 2. Only the correlations between N1 and N2 exceed 0·9 for all

Table 2
Correlations Among the Basic Halstead Metrics from the Implementations

		n1	*N1*	*n2*	*N2*
SE1	n1	1·000			
	N1	0·752	1·000		
	n2	0·452	0·678	1·000	
	N2	0·605	0·907	0·865	1·000
SE2	n1	1·000			
	N1	0·433	1·000		
	n2	0·113	0·801	1·000	
	N2	0·203	0·964	0·877	1·000
SE3	n1	1·000			
	N1	0·916	1·000		
	n2	0·332	0·357	1·000	
	N2	0·843	0·913	0·490	1·000
ANDY	n1	1·000			
	N1	0·856	1·000		
	n2	0·780	0·900	1·000	
	N2	0·808	0·989	0·912	1·000
EVA	n1	1·000			
	N1	0·948	1·000		
	n2	0·686	0·793	1·000	
	N2	0·907	0·975	0·847	1·000

data sets. This latter is not unexpected since the number of operands per operator will remain fairly constant.

5.2 Relationships between specification and implementation metrics

It is of interest to identify those metrics whose values are well predicted in the implementation by values obtained for corresponding metrics from the specification. Table 3(a) summarises the values for our data sets of the correlations between the specification and implementation values of each metric. Only the cyclomatic complexity without and/or (m2), Halstead's n1 and N2, length and vol (the latter two are simple functions of n1, N1, n2 and N2) produced high correlations for all five data sets (taking 'high' as 0·7).

In general, we expect to be able to predict an implementation metric from the corresponding specification value if the two are highly correlated: in fact the percentage variance in the implementation values accounted for by the specifications is just the square of their correlation. Hence it is no surprise to observe, from Table 3(b), that

Table 3(a)

Correlations between Specification and Implementation Values of the Metrics

	$m1$	$m2$	$s1$	$s2$	$n1$	$N1$	$n2$	$N2$	voc	len	vol
SE1	1·00	0·77	0·92	0·85	0·80	0·98	0·68	0·93	0·85	0·97	0·97
SE2	0·84	0·87	0·57	0·31	0·89	0·75	0·84	0·79	0·63	0·76	0·70
SE3	0·58	0·81	0·67	0·65	0·83	0·81	0·54	0·72	0·75	0·80	0·79
ANDY	0·87	0·89	0·58	0·61	0·87	0·67	0·70	0·75	0·79	0·72	0·73
EVA	0·78	0·79	0·75	0·72	0·79	0·67	0·73	0·76	0·81	0·72	0·71

Table 3(b)

Percentage Variance Accounted for by Regression of Implementation Values on Specification Values

	$m1$	$m2$	$s1$	$s2$	$n1$	$N1$	$n2$	$N2$	voc	len	vol
SE1	100	59	84	73	64	96	46	86	73	94	95
SE2	70	70	32	9	79	56	70	63	40	58	49
SE3	34	65	44	43	70	66	29	51	57	63	63
ANDY	76	79	34	37	74	45	49	55	63	51	52
EVA	61	62	56	51	62	45	53	57	65	52	50

Table 4

Examples of Optimal Regressions for the 5 Data Sets
Regressions of implementation on specification for m2

SE1	imp = 0·333 + 0·889 * spec
SE2	imp = 0·587 + 0·783 * spec
SE3	imp = 0·270 + 0·966 * spec
ANDY	imp = − 0·022 + 1·12 * spec
EVA	imp = 0·049 + 0·957 * spec

Regressions of implementation on specification
for Halstead's N2

SE1	imp = 0·720 + 0·985 * spec
SE2	imp = − 0·395 + 1·40 * spec
SE3	imp = 2·80 + 0·492 * spec
ANDY	imp = 0·632 + 1·48 * spec
EVA	imp = 0·529 + 1·626 * spec

m2, n1, N2, length and vol are the metrics for which the specification value best predicts the implementation value. New data sets produced by the same programmer(s) will have their own optimal regressions. However, we would hope to find that the regression obtained from one data set produced by one programmer or team would would be reasonably successful at predicting the implementation metrics from the next set of specifications produced by the same team.

We may be less successful if we try to predict for one programmer or team using the regression obtained for another. Taking as examples m2 and N2, the optimal regressions for the five data sets are given in Table 4. Figure 2 shows the actual against the predicted value for the SE1 data on N2, using the optimal regression for that data set. Figure 3 shows the actual SE1 values for N2 against the values predicted by the regression which is optimal for the SE2 data set. It is clear that the SE2 predictor applied to the SE1 data is giving values which are too high; this graph is included only to illustrate the point that we expect successful predictors to be programmer or team specific.

As described above, each implementation metric was regressed on its own specification metric. Table 4 gives examples of these regressions. Scanning each regression (11 for each data set) we listed those operators which were far from the regression line. It was observed that for each data set, one or more operators appeared repeatedly. These operators were considered individually and in some cases the specification had not been followed in the implementation (see Appendix A). Such operators are denoted 'outliers' and we omitted them and

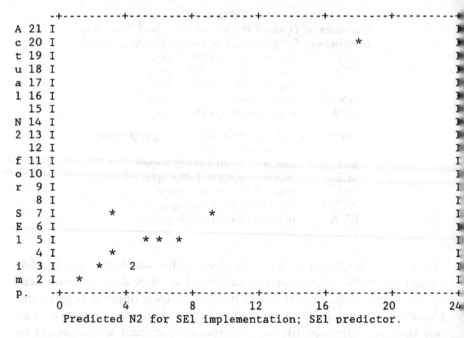

```
  -+---------+---------+---------+---------+---------+---------+
A 21 I                                                         )
c 20 I                                        *                )
t 19 I                                                         )
u 18 I                                                         )
a 17 I                                                         )
l 16 I                                                         )
  15 I                                                         )
N 14 I                                                         )
2 13 I                                                         )
  12 I                                                         )
f 11 I                                                        I
o 10 I                                                        I
r  9 I                                                        I
   8 I                                                        I
S  7 I          *                 *                           )
E  6 I                                                        )
1  5 I                   * *  *                               I
   4 I          *                                             I
i  3 I          *    2                                        I
m  2 I    *                                                   I
p. -+---------+---------+---------+---------+---------+---------+
    0         4         8        12        16        20        24
       Predicted N2 for SE1 implementation; SE1 predictor.
```

Fig. 2. SE1 dataset, Implementation N2 metric; Actual versus predicted values using optimal N2 predictor for SE1.

tried the analyses again. The outliers so omitted are:

Set	Number
SE1	4
SE2	1
SE3	1,4,5,10
ANDY	30,32
EVA	11,25,26

Table 5 summarises the results for the reduced data sets in exactly the same way as Table 3 gave the results for the full data sets. The correlations are a little higher but the improvement is not dramatic.

Within the three 'SE' data sources, the outliers were a good indicator of either specification errors, programming errors or unspecified additions in the implementation. The three outliers within the EVA data set were noted before the statistical analysis as being poor matches; features were occurring in the implementation that

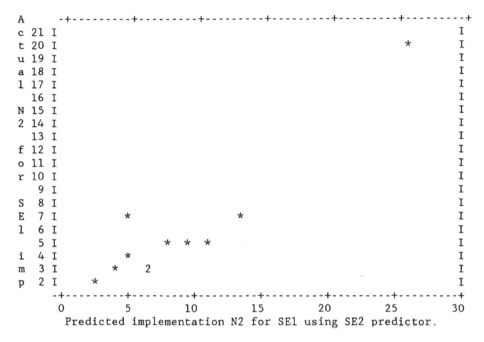

Fig. 3. SE1 dataset, implementation N2 metric; Actual versus predicted values
using optimal N2 predictor for SE2.

were not specified. Within the ANDY dataset, however, there are
many minor mismatches between specification and implementation;
these are all cases of the specification and the program performing the
same function in a slightly different way. There appears to be some
limited promise, therefore, in detecting outliers to identify problem

Table 5(a)

Outliers Excluded: Correlations between Specification and Implementation
Values of the Metrics

	m1	m2	s1	s2	n1	N1	n2	N2	voc	len	vol
SE1	1·00	1·00	0·92	0·86	0·91	0·98	0·66	0·94	0·91	0·97	0·97
SE2	0·81	0·90	0·87	0·74	0·91	0·90	0·87	0·93	0·93	0·93	0·96
SE3	0·78	0·87	0·67	0·65	0·94	0·98	0·59	0·91	0·94	0·96	0·96
ANDY	0·89	0·89	0·74	0·75	0·82	0·66	0·72	0·79	0·77	0·75	0·76
EVA	0·89	0·87	0·86	0·83	0·87	0·91	0·92	0·92	0·95	0·92	0·94

Table 5(b)
Percentage Variance Accounted for by Regression of Implementation Values
on Specification Values

	m1	m2	s1	s2	n1	N1	n2	N2	voc	len	vol
SE1	100	100	84	73	83	96	44	88	83	95	95
SE2	65	81	75	55	82	80	76	87	86	86	91
SE3	61	76	44	42	89	95	35	82	88	92	92
ANDY	79	79	54	56	67	44	52	63	59	56	57
EVA	79	76	74	70	75	82	84	86	90	85	88

areas in the implementation, either through poor specification or poor
programming. This method, however, can never be completely
foolproof, since an implementation that faithfully follows an erroneous
specification will not show as an outlier.

5.3 Relationships between implemented lines of code and specification metrics

It is highly desirable to predict lines of code (LoC) from one or more
of the specification metrics; Boehm[1] has used 'delivered source
instructions' as the major cost-estimation factor in his COCOMO
model. Table 6(a) shows the percentage of variance in LoC accounted

Table 6
Percentage Variance in Lines of Code Accounted for by Regression on Each
of the Specification Metrics

	m1	m2	s1	s2	n1	N1	n2	N2	voc	len	vol
(a) With outliers											
SE1	66	39	42	32	60	50	41	37	66	47	44
SE2	79	1	1	1	4	17	59	32	5	25	18
SE3	41	68	24	24	50	51	12	48	45	51	50
ANDY	18	25	30	19	33	30	39	41	46	37	41
EVA	22	27	28	14	43	29	31	40	41	36	35
(b) Outliers removed											
SE1	58	58	55	42	73	62	39	34	73	50	51
SE2	87	76	30	22	34	67	63	66	45	70	65
SE3	72	77	24	25	57	74	33	74	64	75	74
ANDY	44	51	46	26	33	34	23	46	41	41	42
EVA	37	65	55	40	69	68	62	74	71	75	75

Table 7
Best Regressions of LoC on Specification Metrics

SE1	all data	LoC = − 1·94 + 0·39 * voc − 0·02 * vol + 0·45 * m1	91%
	outliers excl.	LoC = − 1·30 + 0·44 * voc − 0·08 * length	94%
SE2	all data	LoC = 0·77 + 1·21 * m1 − 0·62 * m2	87%
	outliers excl.	LoC = 0·5 * m1 + 0·5 * m2	93%
SE3	all data	LoC = 0·34 + 0·90 * m2	68%
	outliers excl.	LoC = − 0·13 + 0·80 * m2 + 0·26 * n2	88%
ANDY	all data	LoC = − 0·80 + 0·31 * voc	46%
	outliers excl.	LoC = 0·10 + 0·92 * m2 + 0·32 * s1	64%
EVA	all data	LoC = 1·073 + 0·65 * n1	43%
	outliers excl.	LoC = 1·518 + 0·185 * length	75%

for by regressions on each of the specification metrics for each data set. Table 6(b) gives the same results omitting the outliers. It is clear that, even if the outliers are omitted, none of the specification metrics gives good results for all data sets. If we attempt to predict LoC from more than one specification metric we can do much better. Table 7 summarises the results of these attempts. Stepwise regression was used to obtain a near-optimal predictor for each data set, with and without the outliers. It can be seen that SE1 and SE2 produced excellent, but different, predictors. SE3, ANDY and EVA produced good predictors only if the outliers were omitted.

We can obtain some idea of the likely effectiveness of attempts to predict LoC from specification metrics produced by a given team as follows: for a particular data set, remove the first operator, calculate the best predictor from the others; then, using this, obtain the predicted value for the first operator. Compare this with the actual value. This tells us something about our ability to predict a new result for the given team. Repeat this for all the operators. The results for each data set appear in Table 8. This process is adapted from the 'jackknife'.[4] Ideally we would test out our regressions by predicting LoC from appropriate specification metrics for a new project for each programmer or team, and then await completion to count the actual LoC. It appears unlikely that such a programme of work can be completed in the near future; what we have done is attempt to validate the regressions using data already available. The results are encouraging. The mean squared errors quoted in Table 8 are just the average

Table 8

	LoC	Predicted value
SE1		
1	2	1·92
2	2	2·31
3	2	1·89
4	3	2·96
5	2	2·10
6	2	2·12
7	3	3·01
8	2	1·90
9	3	2·90
10	2	1·91
Mean squared error		0·02
SE2		
1	2	2·00
2	2	2·00
3	2	2·00
4	3	2·37
5	1	1·00
6	2	2·63
7	3	3·00
8	2	2·00
9	2	2·00
10	4	4·00
11	3	3·00
12	3	3·00
13	2	2·00
14	2	2·00
15	2	2·00
Mean squared error		0·05
SE3		
1	1	0·90
2	4	3·12
3	2	1·98
4	2	1·98
5	2	1·98
6	2	1·32
7	4	4·17
8	2	1·97
9	2	2·26
10	2	2·26
11	3	2·72
12	2	2·26

Table 8—*contd.*

	LoC	Predicted value
13	2	1·98
14	2	1·98
15	2	2·26
16	2	1·93
17	1	0·90
18	2	1·98
19	2	2·26
20	2	2·26
21	2	2·26
Mean squared error		0·09

ANDY

	LoC	Predicted value
1	1	1·36
2	1	1·36
3	1	1·03
4	1	1·03
5	1	1·03
6	1	1·03
7	1	1·03
8	1	1·03
9	1	1·03
10	3	3·89
11	2	2·28
12	2	2·93
13	4	2·18
14	1	1·71
15	3	2·28
16	3	2·89
17	4	1·47
18	3	3·22
19	3	2·23
20	4	4·17
21	5	4·07
22	3	2·89
23	7	6·07
24	2	4·73
25	4	3·81
26	2	4·15
27	5	4·74
28	1	1·71
29	2	3·37
30	7	3·41
31	2	2·93
Mean squared error		1·41

Table 8—*contd.*

	LoC	Predicted value
EVA		
1	5	4·84
2	1	2·39
3	2	1·87
4	5	3·67
5	7	7·49
6	4	3·92
7	1	2·20
8	1	2·20
9	5	4·84
10	6	4·60
11	5	4·84
12	4	3·92
13	10	8·44
14	5	6·63
15	8	10·53
16	11	8·78
17	2	5·77
18	3	3·58
19	4	3·73
20	3	3·19
21	5	3·47
22	6	3·67
23	5	3·47
24	6	5·18

Mean squared error   1·96

Omitting the 17th, 24th, 26th and 30th items of 'ANDY' which are all badly predicted by the rest, we obtain for the others a mean squared error of 0·45

squared difference between actual and predicted LoC using the process described in this paragraph.

For each data set (omitting the 'outliers') we have listed the actual LoC for each item, together with the value predicted for it using all the other items. For each data set we chose the specification metric(s) which gave the optimal prediction of LoC on the whole data set, as they appear in Table 7. It can be seen that the results, while far from perfect, give grounds for some optimism. The large mean squared error for ANDY is caused by four items (17, 24, 26 and 30) which are badly predicted, and the large mean squared error for EVA is caused by one item (17) which is badly predicted.

As explained above, we expect successful predictors to be programmer or team specific. Figures 4 and 5 illustrate what happens when we try to predict LoC for one team using the predictor obtained from another. Figure 4 gives the actual LoC for SE3 (omitting the outliers) against the values predicted from the SE3 predictor. Figure 5 gives the actual LoC for SE3 against values predicted by the SE1 predictor. Nobody would want to claim that Fig. 5 is illustrating good prediction, and it supports our suggestion that good predictors will not generally transfer from one team to another. However, a new data set for software developed in a highly disciplined way has been obtained; and

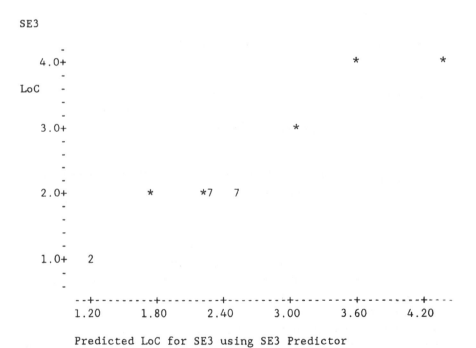

Fig. 4. SE3 dataset; Actual versus predicted lines of code using SE3 optimal predictor.

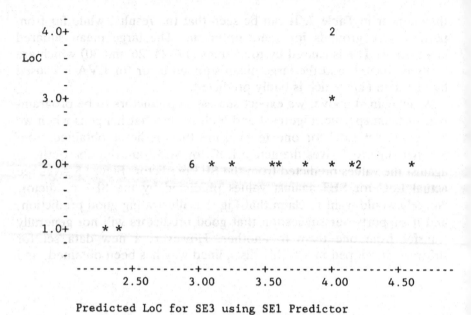

Predicted LoC for SE3 using SE1 Predictor

Fig. 5. SE3 dataset; Actual versus predicted lines of code using SE1 optimal predictor.

initial analysis indicates that, for teams which pursue a well defined methodology, the results are much less dependent on the idiosyncracies of the team. This will be the subject of a future paper.

6. CYCLOMATIC COMPLEXITY METRICS PREDICTION FROM SPECIFICATIONS

There are two main factors to be considered in the assessment of control path metrics from algebraic specifications. Firstly, the number of distinct rewrite terms on the RHS of the equations for a given operator will give the number of contiguous sections of sequential code to be written. Typically, some of these pieces will contain the minimum code, possibly none at all—where, for example, an 'else' clause may be omitted without affecting any program outputs, once written in the target implementation language. Secondly, the number of distinct tested conditions specified gives the minimum number of conditions to be tested in the final code.

Each specification language is likely to give its own set of difficulties when attempting to evaluate these two factors by machine. In OBJ it is relatively easy to identify the rewrite terms on the RHS of the equations; we also need to ascertain which operator the equation is defining, and, with more difficulty, whether any other equations for this operator rewrite to this term. In HOPE and ML, the situation is only slightly more complex in that the RHS of an equation may describe several paths for the operator; it is the terms representing individual paths that must be cross-checked for overlap, not the whole RHS of the equation. Note that in either language these terms need not be absolutely identical to describe the same path; in different equations for the same operator there may, for example, be a different identifier used for the same variable throughout the equation, including the rewrite term. Though this may be condemned as poor specification technique, its possible occurrence must be taken into account.

It is difficult to approach the question of condition tests without resorting to heuristics; for example, 'If there are N paths through the program then $N-1$ conditions (minimum) must be tested'. Useful though this is as a rule of thumb, it is not strictly accurate, since a condition may be tested more than once. More correctly, $N-1$ tests must be made) these may or may not be of single or distinct conditions.

Typically, condition tests in algebraic specifications are either explicit or implicit; included explicitly in the RHS of an equation or implied in the pattern matching on the LHS of the equation. Since a variable argument on the LHS of an equation will match any passed parameter of the required type, only constructor terms need be considered as potential condition test generators. The difficulty here is to determine just what condition or combination of condition tests is represented by the constructor term on the LHS of the equation. It is, in theory, possible to obtain a precise definition of the conditions tested by any LHS constructor term since it can be determined which of the type constructors are ruled out by the constraints imposed in matching the constructor term. However, the problems with this approach are firstly that the range of syntactically valid terms may be extended at a later stage—though this is recognised as bad practice— and secondly the more intractable problem that a syntactically valid term may be semantically invalid; the implied test may not need to be coded since the condition cannot occur. An example of this occurs in the SE1 specification of the operator 'insert', where there appears to be an implied condition test between the two constructors for sort 'title'. Further examination of the whole specification shows that the operator 'insert' is only called from 'create|tree', and then only with the 'title' constructor $\hat{}(\_,\_)$. Thus the implied condition test (against the null 'title' constructor) would be superfluous within the context of the complete specification.

There are considerable differences in the representations of explicit condition tests between HOPE and OBJ specifications. In HOPE any call matching the LHS of an equation must be dealt with on the RHS; whereas in OBJ an equation may be ruled out even when the LHS pattern matches, by the preconditions (the 'IF' clause). In OBJ, HOPE and ML it is possible to go on to the other extreme and ensure that each equation for an operator will match all instantiations of the parameters for a call on the operator. This is done by making all parameters on the LHS of the equation variables of the correct sort (i.e. type). To ensure the correct rewrite under this regime, the preconditions are written on the RHS of each equation. In a correctly written specification any term should be capable of being rewritten by at most one equation; that is to say, for each operator the set of equations is conditioned to avoid overlap. This condition leads to problems in predicting complexity metrics from OBJ specification, since the use of 'ELSE' clauses makes coding of many tests redundant.

In HOPE, the counting of explicitly specified condition tests is relatively simple since the RHS of an equation is either a simple expression or one compounded of possibly nested 'IF THEN ELSE' statements. The main problem remaining is the possibility of overlapping condition tests between different equations which may be redundant when the equations are combined in the target code. However, note that HOPE to some extent encourages overlapping RHS terms, as below:

Taken from Eva Wong's data—

   dec sequal : scheme × scheme → truval;
   – – – sequal (s, senull) ⇐ true;
   – – – sequal (senull, s) ⇐ true;
   – – – sequal (secons(s1, a1), s2) ⇐ if attof(s2, a1)
              then sequal(s1, s2)
              else false;

Conversely, in OBJ, to correctly condition against overlap it is often necessary to pair each condition tested over the whole set of equations for that operator; half (say) having a precondition 'IF A', the rest having the precondition 'IF not A'. This can normally be coded in the target language as a single test: 'IF A THEN—ELSE—'. For example, the following equations are taken from the SE3 OBJ specification:

$$(\text{sigrot}(t) = F \quad IF \ (t = \ = \ \sim))$$
$$(\text{sigrot}(t) = \text{sigword}(\text{first} \mid \text{word}(t)) \ IF \ \text{not} \ (t = \ = \ \sim))$$

Thus the number of explicit condition tests specified in OBJ often exceeds the number that will be necessary in the target code. This situation occurs more frequently as a specification is refined toward an implementation and selectors, as 'first | word' in the above example, are introduced. Probably the best approximation to the number of explicit condition tests required in the target language is obtained by assuming that each distinct condition need only be tested once.

The number obtained by the latter method may be compared with the number of distinct rewrite terms for the operator. Ideally, the number of distinct conditions to be tested should be one less than the number of distinct rewrite terms. An excess of conditions implies combinations using AND, OR etc.; a shortfall of conditions implies some are tested more than once. Unfortunately, the 'right' number of conditions does not necessarily imply that the single, distinct conditions are used throughout.

Taking all factors mentioned above into account for both rewrite terms and condition tests, we can arrive at a reasonably accurate figure for the prediction of cyclomatic complexity metrics in the code developed from the specifications. This is probably as close as we can get to the prediction of cyclomatic complexity metrics using purely syntactic analysis.

7. VOCABULARY METRICS PREDICTION FROM ALGEBRAIC SPECIFICATIONS

Within certain restrictions, good predictions may be made from algebraic specifications for both the number of distinct operators and operands, and the number of occurrences of each, in the implementation language code developed from the specification. In particular, a given operator and its associated separators (parentheses, identifiers, commas, terminating semicolons, etc.) are considered as a single unit.

This gives us a description of the generalised implementation; we will not know the details until a particular implementation language has been chosen. At this stage an approximation for the number of tokens in the implemented program may be obtained, without knowing the implementation language, by assuming, for example, the number of separators for any given operator is one more than the number of arguments taken by that operator. A more accurate estimate of the number of tokens in the implemented program may be obtained if reference can be made to a library giving the number of tokens produced in the writing of each operator in the implementation language, and giving mappings from specification language operators to implementation language operators.

Implementation of a specified call to a function may be achieved in several ways. Firstly, the body of the function may be written in full without any call. This will probably occur only when writing in low level languages. Secondly, a variable may be assigned to receive the returned value of the function before its use elsewhere. Thirdly, a call to a function may be used directly as a parameter without an intermediate assignment to a temporary store. The style chosen by the programmer will affect some of the metrics of the implemented code.

A call to a function using the second style will assign the returned value to a variable before using this value in another call. This will involve an extra occurrence of the assignment operator and two extra occurrences of a (possibly distinct) variable, over and above those needed using the third style. The use of a function call directly as a parameter in another call is often optional, and may be implemented, if the programmer so desired, in either style. Thus a general purpose predictive vocabulary metric is necessarily only an approximator, even though it may be tailored, by use of either statistically derived conversion factors or language mapping libraries, to a particular implementation language.

The counting of operators by their identifier/s is preferred to the alternative methodology whereby an identifier is considered to be an operand taken by a general purpose operator, as may occur if a language is considered to have an inbuilt, inextensible set of operators. This provides results that are more generally applicable across a wide range of language types, especially where prefix and infix usage for a given operator may differ between specification and implementation.

The number of condition tests required in an implementation has been discussed earlier in the section on cyclomatic complexity. For implied condition tests a reasonable approximation in assessment of predicted vocabulary may be obtained by assuming an occurrence in the implementation of a test of the form 'If $a = b$', where a and b are a parameter and a value respectively. Note that this assumption has been made in the accompanying data sets, but that redundant condition tests (important in OBJ) have not been eliminated.

Parentheses used to modify operator precedence remains a problem for two reasons. Firstly the operator may vary from infix to prefix between specification and implementation; prefix operators never require extra parentheses to disambiguate operator precedence, whereas superfluous parentheses may be added while using infix notation, at the discretion of the programmer. In the accompanying data set these parentheses have been ignored.

Parentheses may also be used in some algebraic specification languages as data grouping operators to form tuples whose type is a cartesian product of other types. This does not occur in OBJ but occurs in HOPE and ML. In such cases these pairs of parentheses have been counted as an operator where they occur in the data sources.

In cases where pattern matching is used as an implied condition test, the non-variable term on the LHS of the equation may contain variables. If, in such cases, the variable is referred to on the RHS of the equation, this implies the use of a selector in the implementation to retrieve the value of the variable. It is again a matter of programming style whether inbuilt selectors or user-defined selectors are employed. However, one may argue that the use of inbuilt selectors is implied unless user-defined selectors are specified. Note that in the latter case the use of pattern matching on the LHS is unneccessary since the test can be specified explicitly on the RHS of the equation. In the accompanying data set each distinct variable implying a required selector has been considered as both a distinct operator and a distinct operand, though it may be more appropriate to assume the existence of only one general purpose selection operator; e.g. the 'dot' selector of 'C' and other languages, as in:

struct.elem

where the selector selects the element 'elem' from the structure 'struct'.

8. CONCLUSIONS

Formal specifications may be used either to specify the behaviour of a system or to specify the method of achieving this behaviour. We are concerned here chiefly with the latter case, where the algorithm itself is specified in an algebraic specification language. It must be noted that the use of such a language does not in itself imply specification of the algorithm to be used; indeed it is often necessary to use models of interface behaviour when specifying an algorithm. The study of predictive metrics from behavioural or model-based specifications would be more complex than the task undertaken here. Each of the data sets studied included some portion of the specification that modelled the behaviour of the implementation language. The data sets ANDY and EVA also displayed optimisation of the implementation, where the specification described the original implementation algorithm and modelled the behaviour of the optimised algorithm. Such parts of the specification and implementation are generally excluded in the present study.

Four main factors must be considered when predicting the value of an implementation metric from algebraic specifications of the algorithm. The value of the metric may be affected by:

(1) factors inherent in the algorithm;
(2) factors inherent in the implementation language; or
(3) the programming style employed in the implementation.

We have reduced as far as possible the effect of the factors inherent in the implementation language by considering an operator and its associated 'separators' to be a single unit, and by ignoring certain sequence control constructs. Where necessary, correction factors tailored to a particular implementation language may be developed to offset this simplification.

The influence of the two remaining factors varies between metrics. The cyclomatic complexity metrics m1 and m2 were expected to show little dependence on programming style. In fact, Table 5 indicates that the algorithm alone cannot account for all the variation in implementation values for m1 and m2. If rigorous techniques were adopted throughout, it is expected that predictions of m1 and m2 would be much more accurate. Later work with the GT data set in fact shows considerable improvement for all metrics when applied to a rigorously developed data set. Of the remaining metrics, n1 and n2 were expected to be only slightly affected by programming style, though, as explained earlier, acceptable variations in programming style may add to the value of either implementation metric. The results in Table 5 show that, for n1, the variation that exists is reasonably consistent for a programmer or team. For n2, however, the results are not in general so good. It is worth noting that the metric 'voc', derived solely from n1 and n2, generally shows better results than either n1 or n2 taken individually.

The results for metrics N1 and N2 are, perhaps, surprising, given the results for n1 and n2. In four of the five data sets the correlation between the specification and implementation values for N1 and for N2 are better than 0·9. The results are in most cases better than for the corresponding values of n1 and n2. Comparisons of results for the metrics n1, n2, N1, N2, voc and len suggest that there is some scope for the programmer to interchange operators and operands, but the total numbers of each required to do a job are comparatively independent of programming style. In fact in Table 5, for all data sets except ANDY, six of the seven vocabulary-based metrics showed high correlations between their specification and implementation values.

The metric LoC is clearly dependent on programming style, as shown in Fig. 5. There appear to be good prospects for predicting the implementation value of LoC from the specification for a given programmer or team, within certain limitations. The underlying causes for the outliers found in the data sets have not yet all been studied in detail; however, they may prove to have certain factors in common, for example they may all involve output, or implement the work of specified datatype constructors.

REFERENCES

1. Boehm, B. W., *Software engineering economics,* Prentice-Hall, Englewood Cliffs, New Jersey, USA, 1981.
2. Burstall, R., MacQueen, D. and Sannella, D., *HOPE: an environmental applicative language,* Edinburgh Univ. Internal Report CSR–62–80, 1980.
3. Coleman, D. and Gallimore, R. M., *Software engineering using executable specifications,* Dept of Computation, UMIST, UK, 1985.
4. Efron, B., The jackknife, the bootstrap and other resampling plans, *SIAM, CBMS,* **38,** Philadelphia, 1982.
5. Elshoff, J. L., An investigation into the effects of the counting method used in software science measurements, *ACM SIGPLAN Notices,* **13,** 30–5, 1978.

6. Goguen, J. and Meseguer, J., Programming with parameterised objects, in: *Theory and practice of software technology,* ed. Ferrari, D., Bolognane, N. and Goguen, J., North-Holland, 1983.

7. Halstead, M. H., *Elements of software science,* North-Holland, Elsevier Computer Science Library, New York, 1977.

8. Harper, R., MacQueen, D. and Milner, R., *Standard ML,* Edinburgh Univ. Internal Report ECS–LFCS–86–2, Edinburgh, 1986.

9. McCabe, T. J., A complexity metric, *IEEE Trans. on Software Engineering,* **2,** 1976.

10. Ross, N., *Data definitions—deliverable 13,* SWDL/9WDL/COLL/DEFS/ISS1, UKAEA, 1987.

11. Wong, E. B. Y., *Specification of a relational database using abstract datatypes,* M. Phil. Dissertation, Dundee College of Technology, May 1985.

APPENDIX A: ERRONEOUS FUNCTIONS—REASONS FOR OUTLIERS

Initial analysis of the data has shown that certain functions are giving unexpected results. Therefore, they have been studied to find an explanation for the results.

SE1 data set

4. The rotmany function :

specification - in OBJ.

```
OBJ rotate|many / rotate|once words
SORTs titlesequence
OPS
      ~ts       :                          -> titlesequence
      ^ts       : title titlesequence      -> titlesequence
   rotmany      : title nat                -> titlesequence
VARS
      tl        : title
      wl        : word
      n         : nat
EQNS

  ( rotmany(~,n)  = ~ts  )
  ( rotmany(tl,0) = ~ts  )
  ( rotmany(tl,n) = ^ts(tl, rotmany( rotonce( tl), n-1))
                       IF not ( n=0 )  )
JBO
```

```
Implementation - in C.

  pointtitle  rots(p, n)
  pointword  p;
  int        n;
    {
      if (p -- empty() )
        return (tempty() );
      if (n -- 0)  return(tempty() );
      else
      return(tcons(p, rots(rot(p), (n-1))));
    }
```

This is a poor specification because of overlaps. The problem above is the dangling 'else', which refers only to the second IF statement. This is because the predicted 'or' was *not* implemented, and will account for a difference in the cyclomatic complexity metric m1.

The predicted 'NULL' operands have been implemented as operators, thus affecting Halstead's metrics. This is justified, however, and can be accounted for by different language features. The implementation avoids the overlap found in the specification.

SE2 data set

1. The nonsig function :

Specification

```
OBJ Nonsig /Words
OPS nonsig : word -> BOOL

VARS  w1 : word

EQNS
  ( nonsig(w1) - (w1--and) or (w1--the) or (w1--seven)

                  or (w1--three) or (w1--.) )
JBO
```

Implementation

```
BOOLEAN nonsig(word)
char word[];
{
  char *w1, *w2, *w3, *w4, *w5;
  w1 - "and";
```

```
w2 - "the";
w3 - "seven";
w4 - "three";
w5 - ".";
if (strcmp(word,w1) — 0 || strcmp(word,w2) — 0 ||
    strcmp(word,w3) — 0 || strcmp(word,w4) — 0 ||
    strcmp(word,w5) — 0
    ) return( FALSE );
  else return( TRUE );
}
```

The problems here lie in the lack of the data type Boolean in C, and the use of the function strcmp. The inclusion of superfluous assignments in the C affects Halstead's metric and lines of code.

SE3 data set

    1. The lessthan function :

Specification

```
(lessthan(a,b) - F IF (b—. or a—b) )
(lessthan(a,b) - T IF (a—.) and not(a—b) )
(lessthan(a,b) - lessthan( next(a),next(b) )
                 IF not(a—b or a—. or b—.) )
```

Implementation

```
BOOLEAN lessthan(w1,w2)
char * w1, * w2;
{
  if ( strcmp(w1,w2) < 0 ) return(TRUE);
    else                    return(FALSE);
}
```

Here, the specification has not been followed, and the built-in string comparison feature of C has been preferred. As a consequence, the implementation is not correct, as it omits consideration of the word '.' referred to in the specification.

    4. The catlot function :
Specification

```
( catlot(a, b) - a IF (b — nil) )
( catlot(a, b) - b IF (a - nil and not (b — nil) ) )
( catlot(a, b) - catlot( trap( a, first|title(b)),
                    end|of|l(b) ) )
```

Implementation

```
/*------------------------------------------------*/
/* Catlot - add one list of titles to another    */
/*                                                */
ptr_list catlot(list1, list2)
ptr_list list1, list2;
{
  ptr_list end_of_l(), trap();
  ptr_word_node first_title();

  if ((list1 == NIL_LOT) && (list2 == NIL_LOT))
  {
    return(NIL_LOT);
  }
  else if ( list1 == NIL_LOT )
  {
    return( list2 );
  }
  else if ( list2 == NIL_LOT )
  {
    return( list1 );
  }
  else
  {
    return( catlot( trap( list1, first_title(list2) ),
            end_of_l( list2) ) );
  }
}
```

There is serious overlap in the specification. The implementation starts with a redundant extra condition where both parameters must be nil. Overlap in the specification is accounted for by an 'else' construct in the implementation. Halstead's N1, N2, length and vol (columns 7, 9, 11 and 12) are therefore affected, along with lines of code (column 5) and complexity with ands/ors (column 2).

```
    5. The cycle function :
```

Specification

```
    ( cycle(t, n) = nil IF ( t == ~ or n == 0 ) )
    ( cycle(t, n) == cons( t, cycle( rotation(t), n-1) )
                IF not (n == 0 or t == ~) )
```

370   *W. B. Samson* et al.

Implementation

```
/*---------------------------------------------------------------*/
/* Cycle - cycles through a title until it reaches the end  */
/*                                                          */

ptr_list cycle( t, num)
ptr_word_node t;
int  num;
{
ptr_list lot_left_append();
ptr_word_node rotation();

  if ( t -- EMPTY_TITLE || num -- 0 )
  {
    return(NIL_LOT);
  }
  else if ( t !- EMPTY_TITLE && num -- 0 )
  {
    return( lot_left_append( t, cycle( rotation( t ),
           num-1 )) );
  }
}
```

The two 'if' conditions for the specification could have been covered by only one 'if ~ ~ ~ then ~ ~ ~ else ~ ~ ~' construct in the implementation. In the event, the second 'if' condition has been implemented wrongly, and the function will return a nil value if num equals zero. If num is anything else, an undefined value will be returned as no statement can be matched.

A major contribution to badly correlated lines of code within these functions is the inclusion of local declarations, which has nothing to do with the specifications. Therefore all counts of lines of code have been revised, omitting counts of declarations within function bodies.

Note: The lines of code count is actually a count of the number of statements.

   10. The first_word function :

Specification

```
(first|word( ~ ) - . )
(first|word( ^(wl,tl) ) - wl )
```

Implementation

```
char * first_word(title)
ptr_word_node title
{
  static char dot[2];
  dot[0]= '.';
  dot[1]= ' ';

  if ( title == EMPTY_TITLE )
  {
    return( dot )
  }
  else
  {
    return( title -> word )
  }
}
```

The full stop was specified separately in OBJ (as a constant of type word) while it was defined within the C function body. This will affect Halstead's metric and lines of code.

11. The insert function :

Specification

```
(insert( rootlet,t ) = t IF (rootlet==~) )
(insert( rootlet,t ) = newtree(rootlet)
        IF (t==empty) and not (rootlet==~) )
(insert( rootlet,t ) = constree(left(t),top(t),
                 insert(rootlet,right(t)))
        IF not (before(rootlet,top(t)) or t==empty ) )
(insert( rootlet,t ) = constree(insert(rootlet,left(t)),
                 top(t),right(t))
        IF ( before(rootlet,top(t)) and not t==empty ) )
```

Implementation

```
ptr_tree insert(root,tr)
ptr_word_node root;
ptr_tree tr;
{
```

```
ptr_tree constree(), newtree(), left(), right();
ptr_word_node top(), first_title();

if ( root--EMPTY_TITLE ) return(tr)
    else
if ( tr--EMPTY_TREE ) return( newtree(root) )
    else
if ( before(root,top(tr)) )
        return(constree(insert(root,left(tr)),top(tr),right(tr)));
    else
        return(constree(left(tr),top(tr),insert(root,right(tr))));
}
```

The use of 'else' in the implementation accounts for any difference in the cyclomatic complexity metric, by preventing any overlap found in the specification (by cutting out the use of 'and' and 'or' in the implementation). Also, the several extra operators and operands predicted affect Halstead's metrics. However, this follows the specification, and is thus still included in the data sets. An improvement to the methodology of gathering predictive metrics could help alleviate this problem.

A. Wakelin's data set

```
    The mmult function :
```

```
dec mm : matrix X matrix -> matrix ;
--- mm(null,m1) <- null ;
--- mm(m1,m2) <- if mult_compatible(m1,m2) then
                        matcons(mkrow(getrow(m1),m2),mm(rows(m1),m2))
                        else errormatrix ;


mmult(m1,r1,c1,m2,r2,c2,m3)
float m1[5][5],m2[5][5],m3[5][5];
int r1,r2,c1,c2 ;
{
int row,col ;
        if (c1 -- r2)
            {
            for (row=0 ; row < r1 ; row++)
            for (col=0 ; col < c1 ; col++)
        m3[row][col] - m1[row][1] * m2[1][col] + m1[row][2] * m2[2][col] + m1[r
            }
        else printf("Matrices not compatible0);
```

The problem above involves matrix multiplication, where the C data structures for matrices are totally different from the OBJ structures and have been handled in a totally different manner. Therefore, though the functions carry out the same action, this is where similarity between the two ends.

The show function :

Specification - in Hope

```
dec show : relation -> list void;
--- show(mt,s) <- nil;
--- show(~(t,r),s) < - let x::rest -- getcoord(t) in
                        let y::r1 -- rest in
                        let z::r2 -- r1 in
                        let x1 :: r3 -- r2 in
                        let y1 :: r4 -- r3 in
                        move_to(x,y) <> draw_to(x1,y1) <> show(r,s);
```

Implementation - in C

```
show(rel)
relation *rel;
{
tuple *head;
typevar fir;
llist *sec;
float firstx,firsty,firstz;
float secondx,secondy,secondz;

        if (rel->tuples -- NULL) return(0);
        else
                {
                head - rel->tuples;
                while (head !- NULL)
                {
                fir - head->item;
                firstx - fir->item.real;
                firsty - fir->next->item.real;
                firstz - fir->next->next->item.real;
                sec - fir->next->next->next;
                secondx - sec->item.real;
                secondy - sec->next->item.real;
                secondz - sec->next->next->item.real;

                moveto(firstx*100,firsty*100);
```

```
                    drawto(secondx*100,secondy*100);
                    head - head->next;
                    )
                    )
)
```

Here, recursion has been replaced by a 'while' loop, which overlaps with the 'if' statement in the implementation. This produces extra lines of code, and adds one to the cyclomatic complexity metric. The main problem, however, is a difference in data structures. Accessing list elements is done in a different way in the implementation.

In general, the implementation part of this data set has also been optimised, and does not reflect the specification to the same extent as the other data sets.

Eva Wong's data set

The tinsert function :

Specification - Hope

```
dec tinsert : ( relation X tuple ) -> relation;

--- tinsert(rnull, t)
        <= rcons(rnull, tscheme(t), t);
--- tinsert(r, tempty)
        <= r;
---tinsert(rcons(r, s, t1), t2)
        <= if not (sequal(s, tscheme(t2)))
            then undefine
            else if tuple_of(rcons(r, s, t1), t2)
                then rcons(r, s, t1)
                else rcons(rcons(r, s, t1), s, t2);
```

Implementation - In Modula-2

```
PROCEDURE tinsert (r : relation; t : tuple) : relation;
VAR rans : relation;
    rpl : rptr;
BEGIN
    IF t - NIL THEN rans := r
      ELSIF r - Nil THEN rans := t
    END;
    (* rans := NIL;
    IF NOT (sequal(r.rsch, tscheme(t))) THEN
      WriteS("undefined"); NewLine;  *)
```

```
       IF tupleof(r, t) THEN
          rans := r;
       ELSE rans := rcons(r, tscheme(t), t)
       END;
     RETURN rans
END tinsert;
```

In the above implementation, the undefined part has been commented out. There are clearly other errors in the implementation.

```
The tproj and tcat procedures :
```

Specification

```
dec tproj : (tuple X scheme) -> tuple;
dec tcat : (tuple X tuple) -> tuple;

--- tproj(tempty, s)
      <- tempty;
--- tproj(t, senull)
      <- tempty;
--- tproj(t, secons(s,a))
      <- if atoftp(t,a) then
             tcons(tproj(t, s), a, getval(t, a))
             else tproj(t, s);

--- tcat(tempty, t)
      <-  t;
--- tcat(t, tempty)
      <-  t;
--- tcat( tcons(t1, a, v), t2)
      <- tcons( tcat( t1, t2), a, v);
```

  Implementation

```
PROCEDURE tproj ( t: tuple; s : scheme) : tuple;
VAR tans : tuple;
    val : ARRAY[0..12] OF CHAR;
    tpl : tptr;
BEGIN
    tans := tempty();
    IF (T /- NIL) OR (NOT(sequal(s, senull())))) THEN
      IF attof(s, t.attrib) THEN
        CASE aRetNum(t.attrib) OF
          1: tpl := t;
             t := t.tp;
```

```
                gettxt(val, tpl.valnum);
                tans := tcons( tproj(t, s), tpl.attrib, 1, val) |

          2: tpl := t;
             t := t.tp;
             gettxt(val, tpl.valnum);
             tans := tcons( tproj(t, s),
                                 tpl.attrib, 2, tpl.valstr) ;
        END
      ELSE tpl := t;
           t := t.tp;
           tans := tproj(t, s);
      END;
   END;
RETURN tans
END tproj;


PROCEDURE tcat (t1, t2 : tuple) : tuple;
VAR tans : tuple;
    tpl : tptr;
    val : ARRAY[0..12] OF CHAR;
BEGIN
  tans := tempty();
  IF (t1 -NIL) AND (t2 /- NIL) THEN
    tans := t2
  ELSIF (t2 - NIL) AND (t1 /- NIL) THEN
    tans := t1
  ELSE Wrch(" ");
    CASE aRetNum(t1.attrb) OF
      1: tpl := t1;
         t1 := t1.tp;
         gettxt(val, tpl.valnum);
         tans := tcons(tcat(t1, t2),
                 tpl.attrib, 1, val) |
      2: tpl := t1;
         t1 := t1.tp;
         tans := tcons(tcat(t1, t2),
                 tpl.attrib, 2, tpl.valstr) ;
    END
  END;
RETURN tans
END tcat;
```

The two specifications and implementations above do not match because of overlap in the specification.

Due to the inaccuracies explained above, the functions given have been taken out of the data sets before revised analysis. However, it must be remembered that many systems will contain functions which only follow the specifications up to a point. Therefore, some note should be taken of the first analysis, to see whether functions implemented in this manner will affect the predictive equations and therefore the high level metrics (time and cost) substantially.

APPENDIX B

SE1 OBJ - Specification

name in OBJ	metrics 1	2	3	4	5	6	7	8	9	10	11	12
rap	2	2	2	1	0	6	7	4	7	10	14	47
rotonce	2	2	1	0	0	5	5	5	5	10	10	33
length	2	2	1	0	0	5	5	4	4	9	9	29
rotmany	3	2	3	2	0	7	9	5	10	12	19	68
remove	3	3	6	4	0	9	15	5	8	14	23	88
allrotat	2	2	3	2	0	7	7	3	5	10	12	40
cat	2	2	2	1	0	6	6	4	6	10	12	40
insert	3	3	13	11	0	11	25	7	19	18	44	183
create|												
tree	2	2	2	1	0	6	6	3	3	9	9	29
flatten	2	2	4	2	0	8	9	4	4	12	13	47
sort	2	2	4	4	0	7	7	2	2	9	9	29

SE2 OBJ - Specification

names OBJ	metrics 1	2	3	4	5	6	7	8	9	10	11	12
nonsig	5	1	0	0	0	2	9	6	10	8	19	57
length	2	2	1	0	0	5	5	2	4	7	9	25
rap	2	2	3	2	0	6	7	4	7	10	14	47
nrot	2	2	1	1	0	5	5	3	5	8	10	30
allrots	3	2	3	2	0	7	9	5	10	12	19	68
sigrot	1	1	1	1	0	2	2	1	2	3	4	6
prune	3	2	2	2	0	5	9	3	7	8	16	48
cat	3	3	5	3	0	8	15	3	8	11	23	80
list	2	2	2	1	0	6	6	3	6	9	12	38
lt	2	2	4	3	0	8	8	3	5	11	13	45
tlt	5	3	4	3	0	6	15	5	12	10	27	90
ins	3	3	2	1	0	9	17	5	11	14	28	107
ins	3	3	7	5	0	8	20	5	17	13	37	138
treelist	2	2	2	1	0	6	6	3	5	9	11	35
flatten	2	2	4	2	0	8	9	4	6	12	15	54
sortl	2	2	3	3	0	5	5	2	4	7	9	25

SE3 OBJ - Specification

OBJ name	Metric 1	2	3	4	5	6	7	8	9	10	11	12
lessthan	7	3	3	2	0	7	19	5	18	12	37	133
allrots	1	1	2	2	0	2	2	1	2	3	4	6
before	4	3	10	9	0	8	19	4	13	12	32	115
catlot	4	3	4	3	0	8	11	3	11	11	22	76
cycle	4	2	2	1	0	8	13	6	13	14	26	99
end|of|l	2	2	0	0	0	3	3	2	4	5	7	16
end|of|t	2	2	0	0	0	3	3	2	4	5	7	16
first| title	2	2	0	0	0	3	3	2	4	5	7	16
enlist	1	1	2	2	0	2	2	3	3	5	5	12
first| word	2	2	0	0	0	3	3	2	4	5	7	16
insert	7	4	1	1	0	12	30	4	24	16	54	216
left	2	2	0	0	0	3	3	2	4	5	7	16
length	2	2	2	1	0	6	8	3	6	9	14	44
listtree	2	2	4	3	0	6	9	3	7	9	16	51
prune	5	3	9	7	0	10	20	2	12	12	32	115
rap	2	2	3	2	0	7	10	3	9	10	19	63
right	2	2	0	0	0	3	3	2	4	5	7	16
rotation	2	2	3	3	0	6	8	2	7	8	15	45
sigrot	2	2	2	2	0	5	7	3	6	8	13	39
sigword	4	1	0	0	0	3	8	5	8	8	16	48
sortlist	1	1	2	2	0	2	2	1	1	3	3	5
top	2	2	0	0	0	3	3	2	4	5	7	16
trap	2	2	5	4	0	7	10	3	9	10	19	63
treelist	2	2	3	1	0	8	11	3	8	11	19	66
newtree	2	2	1	1	0	4	6	3	8	7	14	39

ANDY Data Set - HOPE Specification

FNAME	1	2	3	4	5	6	7	8	9	10	11	12
move_to	1	1	1	1	0	1	1	3	3	4	4	8
draw_to	1	1	1	1	0	1	1	3	3	4	4	8
pt_sch	1	1	0	0	0	3	8	6	8	9	16	51
ln_sch	1	1	0	0	0	3	10	7	10	10	20	66
surf_sch	1	1	0	0	0	3	10	7	10	10	20	66
vox_sch	1	1	0	0	0	3	12	8	12	11	24	83
ln_lnk_sch	1	1	0	0	0	3	4	3	4	6	8	21
sur_lnk_sch	1	1	0	0	0	3	4	3	4	6	8	21
vox_lnk_sch	1	1	0	0	0	3	4	3	4	6	8	21
choose	3	3	3	1	0	11	22	11	22	22	44	196
cardinality	2	2	1	0	0	5	5	4	6	9	11	35
project	2	2	3	2	0	9	16	9	17	18	33	138
tag	2	2	1	0	0	8	10	6	11	14	21	80
schjoin	1	1	2	2	0	2	3	4	4	6	7	18
schunion	2	2	1	0	0	11	14	9	14	20	28	121
union	3	2	3	2	0	6	8	4	9	10	17	56
runion	1	1	2	2	0	7	7	4	4	11	11	38
sch_isin	4	3	1	0	0	5	9	5	11	10	20	66
pinpoint	2	2	1	0	0	8	8	6	9	14	17	65
getval	4	4	1	0	0	5	9	6	7	11	15	55
sel	5	3	4	2	0	7	16	5	13	12	29	104
select	5	2	3	3	0	9	21	7	22	16	43	172
jj	5	4	8	5	0	10	25	8	29	18	54	225
join	3	2	7	7	0	12	22	7	16	19	38	161
intersect	4	3	3	1	0	7	13	3	11	10	24	80
prod	3	2	6	4	0	10	19	5	14	15	33	129
prod1	4	3	6	4	0	9	23	6	19	15	42	164
product	1	1	2	2	0	7	8	4	5	11	13	45
tail	3	3	1	0	0	5	6	4	5	9	11	35
mm	3	3	7	6	0	7	9	4	10	11	19	66
alter	2	2	7	7	0	8	15	15	24	23	39	176
show	2	2	4	3	0	11	20	14	22	25	42	195
exhibit	3	2	3	3	0	6	7	3	5	9	12	38

EVA Data Set - Hope Specification

FNAME	1	2	3	4	5	6	7	8	9	10	11	12
concat	2	2	9	9	0	7	11	4	7	11	18	62
atcompat	1	1	1	1	0	2	2	2	2	4	4	8
getd	1	1	0	0	0	1	1	1	1	2	2	2
oscom	4	3	3	2	0	5	5	5	7	10	12	40
socons	4	3	9	8	0	12	21	6	11	18	32	133
atcons	3	2	4	3	0	6	6	4	7	10	13	43
getsche	2	2	0	0	0	1	1	2	2	3	3	5
gettup	2	2	0	0	0	1	1	2	2	3	3	5
tupleof	5	3	3	2	0	7	8	6	10	13	18	67
tdelete	3	3	3	2	0	7	9	5	8	12	17	61
tinsert	5	5	9	9	0	9	23	7	19	16	42	168
runion	4	3	3	2	0	8	9	6	9	14	18	69
join	3	2	3	2	0	5	5	5	8	10	13	43
inter	5	4	7	6	0	9	17	8	22	17	39	159
project	4	4	7	4	0	8	14	5	13	13	27	100
union	5	5	8	5	0	10	20	7	25	17	45	184
differ	5	5	8	6	0	11	19	8	23	19	42	178
union_comp	6	3	4	4	0	7	11	7	11	14	22	84
attof	3	3	1	0	0	5	5	5	6	10	11	37
sequal	4	3	2	1	0	5	5	5	7	10	12	40
sjoin	3	2	2	1	0	4	4	4	5	8	9	27
tscheme	3	3	3	2	0	4	6	3	5	7	11	31
compatt	4	3	2	1	0	5	5	5	7	10	12	40
atoftp	3	3	1	0	0	5	5	5	6	10	11	37
tproj	4	3	5	3	0	7	10	4	11	11	21	73
tcat	3	2	2	1	0	5	5	5	6	10	11	37
tequal	5	3	3	2	0	9	10	6	10	15	20	78

SE1 Kwic Index

FNAME	1	2	3	4	5	6	7	8	9	10	11	12
rap	2	2	4	3	2	7	10	2	5	9	15	48
rot	2	2	5	5	2	6	7	1	3	7	10	28
length	2	2	3	2	2	6	7	3	4	9	11	35
rots	3	3	6	5	3	9	11	4	7	13	18	67
removens	3	3	8	6	3	9	14	1	5	10	19	63
allrotat	2	2	7	6	2	7	10	1	3	8	13	39
cat	2	2	5	4	2	7	7	2	5	9	12	38
insert	3	3	11	9	3	9	23	6	20	15	43	168
create_tree	2	2	6	5	2	7	9	1	3	8	12	36
flatten	2	2	6	4	3	7	12	4	7	11	19	66
sort	2	2	6	6	2	7	9	1	2	8	11	33

SE2 Kwic Index.

FNAME	1	2	3	4	5	6	7	8	9	10	11	12
nonsig	6	2	5	5	8	4	18	14	27	18	45	188
length	2	2.	1	0	2	5	6	5	6	10	12	40
rap	2	2	3	2	2	5	8	4	9	9	17	54
rot	2	2	1	1	2	4	6	4	7	8	13	39
nrot	3	3	3	2	3	7	10	6	10	13	20	74
allrots	1	1	2	2	1	3	3	1	2	4	5	10
sigrot	2	2	1	1	2	4	5	4	5	8	10	30
prune	3	3	4	2	3	6	11	4	11	10	22	73
cat	2	2	3	2	2	5	7	5	7	10	14	47
list	2	2	4	3	2	7	9	4	7	11	16	55
lessthan	3	3	2	2	5	5	9	7	11	12	20	72
title_order	3	3	3	3	3	7	14	7	15	14	29	110
insert	3	3	6	4	3	6	18	7	23	13	41	152
tree_list	2	2	2	1	2	5	7	5	7	10	14	47
flatten	2	2	4	2	2	6	10	6	9	12	19	68
sort	2	2	3	3	2	5	6	2	4	7	10	28

SE3 Kwic Index.

FNAME	1	2	3	4	5	6	7	8	9	10	11	12
lessthan	2	2	1	1	2	3	5	5	5	8	10	30
allrots	1	1	2	2	3	3	3	1	2	4	5	10
before	4	4	9	8	7	8	15	5	13	13	28	104
catlot	5	4	4	3	6	7	13	3	14	10	17	56
cycle	5	3	3	2	4	8	12	6	13	14	25	95
end_of_l	2	2	0	0	3	3	4	3	5	6	9	23
end_of_t first	2	2	0	0	3	3	4	3	5	6	9	23
_title	2	2	0	0	3	3	4	3	5	6	9	23
enlist first	1	1	2	2	2	3	3	3	3	6	6	16
_word	2	2	0	0	6	7	12	7	9	14	21	80
insert	4	4	12	10	6	10	22	3	15	13	37	137
left	2	2	0	0	3	3	4	3	5	6	9	23
length	3	3	2	1	3	6	7	4	7	10	14	47
listtree	2	2	4	3	5	6	6	3	5	9	11	35
prune	3	3	8	6	7	7	12	2	7	9	19	60
rap	2	2	5	4	4	6	7	3	7	9	14	44
right	2	2	0	0	2	3	4	3	5	6	9	23
rotation	3	3	3	3	5	6	7	2	7	8	14	42
sigrot	2	2	2	2	4	4	5	3	4	7	9	25
sigword	2	2	2	2	5	5	5	3	5	8	10	30
sortlist	1	1	2	2	3	3	3	1	1	4	4	8
top	2	2	0	0	2	3	4	4	5	7	9	25
trap	2	2	4	3	4	6	7	3	7	9	14	44
treelist	2	2	6	4	5	7	8	3	6	10	14	47
newtree	2	2	1	1	3	3	4	3	5	6	9	23

ANDY - C Implementation

FNAME	1	2	3	4	5	6	7	8	9	10	11	12
moveto	1	1	1	1	1	1	1	3	3	4	4	8
drawto	1	1	1	1	1	1	1	3	3	4	4	8
ptsch	1	1	3	3	1	2	4	5	6	7	10	28
lnsch	1	1	3	3	1	2	4	5	6	7	10	28
facetsch	1	1	3	3	1	2	4	5	6	7	10	28
tetronsch	1	1	3	3	1	2	4	5	6	7	10	28
lnlnksch	1	1	2	2	1	2	3	4	5	6	8	21
face_lnksch	1	1	2	2	1	2	3	4	5	6	8	21
tetron_lnksch	1	1	2	2	1	2	3	4	5	6	8	21
choose	3	3	4	2	3	7	17	9	22	16	39	156
cardin_ality	2	2	1	0	2	5	6	5	6	10	12	40
project	2	2	3	3	2	5	9	5	11	10	20	66
tag	3	3	3	2	4	9	17	13	23	22	40	178
schjoin	1	1	3	3	1	4	5	5	5	9	10	32
schunion	3	2	3	2	3	9	17	11	22	20	39	169
sunion	3	3	2	1	3	5	9	6	13	11	22	76
runion	1	1	4	4	5	8	17	8	18	16	35	140
schisin	4	3	2	1	3	6	12	9	16	15	28	109
schplace	3	3	2	1	3	6	14	9	15	15	29	113
getval	4	4	1	0	4	4	8	6	12	10	20	66
sel	4	4	5	3	5	9	19	9	25	18	44	183
select	3	3	5	5	3	7	13	6	17	13	30	111
jj	6	5	8	5	8	10	31	12	41	22	72	321
join	3	2	7	7	2	7	16	7	16	14	32	122
intersect	4	4	4	2	4	6	15	6	20	12	35	125
prod	3	2	4	3	2	8	12	6	13	14	25	95
prodl	3	2	4	2	6	8	19	8	24	16	42	168
product	1	1	3	3	1	5	8	4	8	9	16	51
tail	2	2	0	0	2	3	4	3	5	6	9	23
mmult	4	4	0	0	6	8	25	13	31	21	56	246
alter	2	2	14	14	8	8	24	17	34	25	56	269
show	3	3	2	2	18	9	43	17	58	26	101	475
exhibit	2	2	2	2	2	5	5	4	5	9	10	32

EVA - Modula2   Implementation

FNAME	1	2	3	4	5	6	7	8	9	10	11	12
concat	2	2	7	7	5	8	11	7	11	15	22	86
compat	1	1	3	3	1	4	5	3	4	7	9	25
getd	1	1	0	0	2	3	3	3	4	6	7	18
oscom	2	2	2	1	5	6	12	9	20	15	32	125
soccons	4	3	8	7	7	10	24	9	32	19	56	238
otcons	3	2	6	5	4	8	14	8	19	16	23	92
getsche	1	1	0	0	1	3	3	4	5	7	8	22
gettup	1	1	0	0	1	3	3	4	5	7	8	22
tupleof	4	4	3	2	5	7	15	10	25	17	40	163
tdelete	3	3	3	2	6	7	17	8	27	15	44	172
tinsert	4	4	5	5	3	10	16	6	23	16	39	156
runion	4	3	4	3	5	10	20	9	29	19	49	208
join	3	2	4	3	4	8	12	10	23	18	35	146
inter	6	5	15	13	10	14	30	11	47	25	77	358
project	4	4	9	6	5	12	21	7	29	19	50	212
union	5	5	11	8	8	13	25	11	44	24	69	316
union	5	5	12	10	11	14	31	11	51	25	82	387
unioncomp	5	3	7	7	2	8	15	10	20	18	33	146
attof	2	2	2	1	3	5	11	9	18	14	29	110
sequal	3	3	2	1	4	6	13	9	22	15	35	137
sjoin	2	2	2	1	3	6	12	8	19	14	31	118
tscheme	2	2	3	2	5	7	12	6	15	13	27	100
compatt	3	2	5	4	5	9	15	9	21	18	36	150
atoftp	2	2	2	1	5	6	13	10	23	16	36	144
tproj	5	4	12	9	12	14	33	12	47	26	80	376
tcat	6	4	8	6	9	12	30	13	47	25	77	358
tequal	4	4	5	4	6	8	19	12	34	20	53	229

Index

Acceptance tests, 15
Accountability between specifiers and
    developers, 5
Adaptive maintenance, 285
Adaptive modelling, 266–70
    quality assessment, 270–3
Algorithmic design languages, 308
Algorithms, 130
Alvey Software Data Library Project,
    288
Alvey Software Reliability Modelling
    Project, 287
AND/OR graph, 60–1
Artificial intelligence, software
    metrics, 58–61
Assumptions, 50
Attributes, 290
    improved estimation of, 72

Basili–Hutchens' SynC, 307
Bayesian models, 245
Bebugging, 34–5
Bivariate techniques, 144–5
Boxplots, 138, 143, 165, 167, 171
Bug-clearance release, 285

'C' metrics, 343–5
Change-proneness prediction, 171–6
Classification tables, 145
Cleanroom software development
    process, 1–26

Cleanroom software development
    process—*contd.*
    current models, 19
    ingredients for, 3–5
    technology transfer, 24–5
COBOL, 2, 29
COCOMO, 54, 66, 68–9, 183, 352
Complexity against size scatterplot,
    169
Composite metrics, 43–4
Compositionality, 296
Compound booleans, 302
Computer-based safety system, 256–9
Computer-related disasters, 255
Computer systems, highly
    dependable, 243–61
Control flow, 149–50, 303
Control flow metrics, 39–43
COPMO, 66, 70
COQUAMO, 120, 157–9, 165
    extrapolation/assessment mode,
        158
    monitoring/steering mode, 158
    planning mode, 157–8
Correctness proofs, 12–13
Correctness theorems, 12
Cost estimation, 28, 63–88
    analogy approach, 66, 78–85
        bottom-up estimation, 84–5
        top-down (global) view of each
            module, 78–84
    background, 64–7
    bottom-up, 65
    forecasting, 71

Cost estimation—*contd.*
  future trends, 85–6
  improved estimation of attributes, 72
  knowledge-based techniques in, 66–7
  main approaches, 66
  methods of, 65–7
  model, 183
  parametric forecasts, 66
  parametric models, 67–72
  quality monitoring, 71
  top-down, 65
  use of, 65
Cumulative fault graphs, 139
Curve fitting, 145
Cyclomatic complexity, 41–2, 55, 343, 345
Cyclomatic complexity metrics
  cyclomatic complexity, 346
  prediction from specifications, 358–61
Cyclomatic number, 164

Data abstraction, 11
Data analysis
  credibility and usability in, 134–6
  criteria for selecting, 134–47
  graphical techniques, avoiding problems with, 136–42
  initial exploratory, 165–78
  juxtapose or superpose of datasets, 138–40
  software project control, 128–33
  statistical techniques, 155–7
  support for, 152
  technique requirements, 136
Data classification, 144
Data collection
  compulsory, 150
  feedback of results, 152
  graphical, 152–3
  monitoring software projects, 125–54
  procedures for, 150–3
  stage completion monitoring, 150–1

Data collection—*contd.*
  support for, 151
Data distribution, 134–6
Data encapsulation, 11
Data observation, 129–30
Data presentation
  choosing graphical elements for, 140–2
  graphical, 156
Data sources, 339
Data typing, 10
Data use
  in-project, 147–50
  monitoring software projects, 125–54
  procedures for, 150–3
Debugging, 15
Decomposition algorithm, 300, 305, 311, 315
Decomposition tree, 297, 300, 301, 305, 309
Depth of nesting, 305
Design charts, 308–10
Design decisions, 308, 326–30
Design fault tolerance, 322
Design metrics, 31–4
Design notation, 39
Design process
  elements of structured design, 9–10
  overview, 6–7
  structured data design, 10–11
  see also System design metrics
Design structures, 308–10
Design-to-code effort ratio, 150
Design-to-cost approach, 71
Deterministic algorithm, 10
Deterministic models, 246
Development methods evaluation, 36–7
Digraphs, 294–301
Directed graph, 39–40
Disasters, computer-related, 255
Distribution plots, 143
Diversity, 322
  design for, 326
  process, 322
  product, 322–3
Diversity degrees, 326–30

Edges, 40
Effort distribution, 143
Effort expansion, 55, 142
  graph, 153
  ratios, 148–9
Effort metric, 164
Embedded mode, 54
EML-I, 73–4
  data store, with, 74–5
  help text, 76–7
  implication of changes, 77
  multiple simple calculations, 76
  potential extension to, 78
  potential uses, 75–6
  use with expert systems, 77–8
Engineering
  classical disciplines of, 292
  judgement, 253–9
  scientific foundation of, 290–4
Erroneous functions, 366–77
Error detection and removal, model
    for, 130
ESPRIT, 87, 157, 293
ESPRIT REQUEST, 120
ESPRIT TRUST, 287
Estimation Modelling Language,
    72–8
European Workshop on Industrial
    Computer Systems (EWICS)
    Technical Committee 7 (TC7),
    244
Evaluation factor vector, 212
Exception analysis, 132–3
Exception handling, 302
Expansion operation, 299, 309
Expert overconfidence, 253–6
Expert systems, 58, 59, 77–8
Exponential order statistic (EOS)
    models
  binomial, 283
  NHPP, 283
External procedures, 302

Failure behaviour, multi-version
    software, 321–33
Failure rate, 249
Feedback of results, 152

Financial modelling, 75
Finite state automation, 245
Fix-on-fail, 285
FIZVOS, 186–98
  analysis, 194–6
  data capture, 194
  decision making, 191–3, 198
  environment factor, 189
  estimating, 197
  functionality by build, 187
  implementation, 188
  evaluation, 193–8
  management, 191–3
  model, 189
  model construction, 188–91
  model validation, 197
  planning, 197
  potential black hole problem,
      192–3
  recommendations, 197
  software requirements, 186–8
  specification, 186–8
  tracking, 191, 198
  turnaround problem, 192
Flowgraphs, 302–304
Forecasting and cost estimation, 71
FORTRAN, 42, 43
Frequency histogram, 143
Function calls within booleans, 302
Function metrics, 71
Function point analysis, 28–31
Functional enhancement, 285

Graph impurity, 47
Graph structure, 47
Graph theory, 295
Graphical techniques. *See* under Data
    analysis; Data collection; Data
    presentation; Data use

Halstead metrics, 38–9, 347
Hierarchical structures, 299, 309
Highly dependable computer
    systems, 243–61
Histograms, 140, 143–5
Human performance model, 248
Hybrid metrics, 44

IMP Workbench, 73, 74, 87–8
Implementation languages, metrics
    for, 343–6
Implementation modules, 345
Incremental development, 71
Independence, 322
Information flow through program
    units, 50–1
Information flows, 149–50
Information-to-control flow ratio, 150
Inspection efficiency graph, 141
Intelligent tools, 60

Jelinski–Moranda type models, 249
JSP design charts, 308–10

KINDRA, 308, 312
Knowledge-based techniques in cost
    estimation, 66–7
Knowledge structure of system,
    258–9
Known faults database, 285
Kolmogorov distances, 265, 268, 271

Lines of code, 149–50, 164
    specification metrics, and, 352–8
Local metrics, 95
LOCOMO, 72
Logical complexity metric, 43
Lotus-123, 72

McCabe's Complexity V, 169, 173
Machine code instructions (MCI),
    160, 167
Macro estimators, 53–4
Maintenance, 31, 32, 45, 50
Maintenance practice and policy
    modelling, 284–6
Mapping, 291, 295–6
Market behaviour modelling, 284
Matrix algebra, 49
Maximality, 298
Mean and median comparison, 165–7
Mean time to failure (MTTF), 3, 4,
    17–22, 24

Measurement, 292–4
    concept of, 290–1
    evolution, 290
Measures, definitions, 240–1
Median
    mean comparison, and, 165–7
    prediction from raw models,
        267–70
Meta Model, 69–70
Metrication in procurement, 89–102
Metrics, 27–62
    artificial intelligence, 58–61
    automation, 58
    'C', 343–5
    classification of, 93–5
    definitions, 28, 100–1, 240–1
    determination of relationships
        among, 171–6
    future research and development,
        55–61
    implementation
        correlations between, 346–8
        specification, and, 335–84
    implementation languages, 343–6
    integration, 57
    'Modula-2', 345–6
    performance, 308
    process, 308
    project management, 57–8
    review criteria, 101–2
    role of, 251–2
    software procurement and
        evaluation, 92–5
    specification, and lines of code,
        352–8
    specification languages, 340–3
    structural, 301, 305
    types of, 28
    uses on software project, 36–7
    validation of, 55–7
    vocabulary, prediction from
        specifications, 361–3
    see also under specific metric types
Metrics analysis, 155–80
    data sets, 160–4
    requirements for, 158–60
    techniques for, 158–60
Model predictions, 22–4

Modelling, 130–1
Models, 292–4
Monitoring, software products, 125–54
Multivariate techniques, 145–7
Multi-version software, failure behaviour, 321–33
Mutation testing, 35–6

Nodes, 39–40
Numerical techniques, 156

Open custom-built metrics, 94, 101
Open decision support metrics, 93
Ordinary least squares (OLS) regression, 171–5, 178
Organic mode, 54
Outlier detection, 176–8
Overconfidence in expert judgment, 253

Parallel programming, 310–12
Parametric forecasts, 66
Parametric models, 67–72
Parametric spline adaptive (PSA) predictive distribution, 274
Pascal, 42
Pass/fail determination, 16
Performance maintenance, 284–5
Petri net models, 311
PL/1, 29
PODS project, 249
Poisson distribution, 287
Poisson process, 245
Predictor metrics, 28
Prequential likelihood (PL), 264–6
Prequential likelihood ratio (PLR), 266, 271–3
Primes, 297, 310
Principal component plots, 176–7
Principal components, 147
Probabilistic risk assessment (PRA), 244
Probability distributions, 17
Probability matrix, 49

Procedure, 291
Process metrics, 28, 56
Procurement, 89–102
    bought-in, bespoken, 91
    bought-in, general purpose, 91
    definition, 90
    in-house, bespoken, 91
    life-cycle, 91–2, 96–100
    metrics for, 92–5
    procedures for, 90–2
    recommendations, 95–6
Product life-cycle costs, 282
Product metrics, 28
Productivity models, 203
Profiles, 146–7
Project inspection efficiency, 147–8
Project life-cycle, 258
Project management, 181–99
Project modes, 54
Project productivity measurement, 52–3
PROLOG programs, 312–14
Pseudo code, 308

Quality assurance enforcement, 36
Quality decomposition, 211–14, 225, 226
Quality factor vector, 212
Quality Management System (QMS), 103–5
Quality models, 201–41
    actual evaluation factors, 223
    actual quality factors, 223
    comparison and ranking, 215–16
    complexity, 219
    correctness, 217
    current, 214–15
    defining according to given schema, 217–22
    efficiency, 217
    evaluation factor definition schema, 221–2
    evaluation factors, 218
    execution efficiency, 220
    experiment scenario rules, 234–5
    formalized assessment, 222–35
    generality, 219

Quality models—*contd.*
  generation of, 234
  inspection coverage, 221
  integrity, 219
  level-0 system value (sv0), 227
  level-1 system value (sv1), 228–9
  level-specific computation of
    system quality, 224–9
  modularity, 218
  N-level factor quality, 229–30
  parameterizing and weighting
    quality factors, 233–4
  portability, 219
  redundancy, 219
  reliability, 217
  required evaluation factors, 224
  required quality factors, 224
  review of, 210–16
  robustness, 217
  rule-based representation, 230–1
  rule schema, 233–4
  storage efficiency, 220
  symbolic execution coverage, 221
  system quality value, 229
  test coverage, 221
  user benefit, 217
  verification coverage, 221
Quality monitoring and cost
    estimation, 71
Quality procedure, 238–9
Quality Requirements Specification
    Subsystem (QRSS), 104–22
  assessing chance of success, 119–20
  assessing relationships among
    quality factors, 114–17
  evaluating requirements, 109–11
  implementation, 120–1
  influence matrix for quality factors,
    115
  intention of, 112
  option of reuse, 113
  percentage of techniques common
    to pairs of quality factors, 115
  problem definition, 104–5
  production version, 122
  quality factor levels, 113
  quality factor templates, 107–9
  quality profile, 111, 113

Quality Requirements Specification
    Subsystem (QRSS)—*contd.*
  safety factors, 120
  scale of task, 111–17
  specifying requirements, 105–7
  tailoring the system, 119
  technique selection, 117–19
  techniques to support usability, 118
Quality vector, 213
Quantile–Quantile plot, 22–4
Quantitative activity models, 181–99
  data capture, 185–6
  decision making, 185
  definition, 183
  estimating, 184–5
  overview of technique, 184
  planning, 184–5
  tracking, 185
Questionnaire for system safety and
    reliability assessment, 258–9

Rayleigh curve, 53
Recursion, 302, 314
Regression, 144
Regression/residual plots, 178
Relationships, 290, 291
Reliability
  experience, 24
  measurement, 19–20
    illustration of, 20–1
  overview, 17–18
  prediction, 18, 249, 294
  see also Mean time to failure
    (MTTF)
Reliability growth curves, 148
Reliability growth models, 245–8, 280
Reliability growth prediction, 263
Reliability measurement, 294
Reliability modelling
  adaptive, 263–77
    parametric spline approach,
      273–4
  support process, 282–4
Reliability models, 244–52
  future of, 252
REQUEST, 157
Residual analysis, 145
Resource requirements prediction, 36

Result metrics, 28
Risk analysis, 75
Risk management, 258

Safety assessment and design
    techniques directory, 258
Safety system, computer-based,
    256–9
Scales, definitions, 240–1
Scatterplot matrix, 145–6, 149–50
Scatterplots, 133, 142, 144, 169
Science
    laws and theories of, 291
    role of, 291–2
SDL, 308, 312
Semi-detached mode, 54
Semi-intelligent tools, 60
Sequential programs, 302–8
Single-variable models, 67–8
SLIM, 53, 66, 69, 73
Smoothing, 145
Software
    assessment, 202, 205–9
    bespoken, 90
    bought-in, 90
    construction, 203–4
    design. *See* Design process
    made in-house, 90
    maintenance. *See* Maintenance
    specification. *See* Specifications
Software Data Library (SWDL), 125,
    126, 132, 134
Software development, 202, 293
    application concept, 203
    data, 128–33
    data processing concept, 203
    human activity, 248–51
    three-layer model, 204
    tools, 37
Software engineering, 203–9, 292–4
    models, 182–4
Software metrics. *See* Metrics; Metric
    analysis; and under specific
    metric types
Software packaging, 9–10
Software process, 182
Software process model, 182–3

Software procurement. *See*
    Procurement
Software product metrics, 37–53
Software products, monitoring,
    125–54
Software reliability. *See* Reliability
Software science, 293
Software tools, 16
Software validation. *See* Validation
Software verification. *See* Verification
Specification languages, metrics for,
    340–3
Specification metrics, 51–3
Specifications, 5–6, 293, 314–16
    cyclomatic complexity metrics
        prediction from, 358–61
    implementation metrics, and,
        335–84
    vocabulary metrics prediction
        from, 361–3
Staff performance evaluation, 36
Statistical analysis, 75, 346
Statistical quality control, 2–5
Statistical techniques, 142–7
    data analysis, 155–7
Statistical testing
    approach, 15–16
    experience, 16–17
    overview, 14–15
    strategy, 15–16
    verification synergism, 17
STC Generic Toolset, 120–1
Stepwise refinement practice, 7–9
Stochastic Bayesian model, 247
Stress effects, 283
Structural properties, 301
    measurement of, 294
Structure chart, 46
Subflowgraphs, 303–5, 315
Substructures, 296–7, 303
Summary decision support metrics,
    93
Support modelling
    interactions, 286–7
    mathematical treatment and
        approximations, 287
Support process
    modelling, 279–88

Support process—*contd.*
  reliability modelling, 282–4
SWDL, 136, 138, 142, 150, 151
System analysis, 257–8
System design, need for intelligent or
  semi-intelligent tools, 59
System design metrics, 44–51
System tests, 15

Technology factor, 53
Technology transfer, 24–5
Theories, 292–4
Time-series charts, 140
Time-varying plots, 144
Token metrics, 37–9
Transformations, 137, 143, 169–70
Tree structure, 47
Trend analysis, 132–3

Uniqueness property, 298
Unit programming and testing, 45
Unit tests, 15
Univariate techniques, 143–4
UNIX operating system, 32

Validation, 205–6
  lack of, 51
  software metrics, 55–7
VDM technique, 251
Verification
  experience, 13–14
  functional procedure, 12–13
  overview, 11–12
  questions concerning, 12
  statistical testing synergism, and,
    17
Vocabulary metrics, prediction from
  specification, 361–3